# THE OXFORD HISTORY
# OF ENGLISH ART

*Edited by* T. S. R. BOASE

# THE OXFORD HISTORY OF ENGLISH ART

Edited by T. S. R. BOASE

*President of Magdalen College, Oxford*

## Plan of Volumes

SHELDON MANUFACTORY: MAP OF WORCESTERSHIRE (DETAIL)
Bodleian Library, on loan to the Victoria and Albert Museum

# ENGLISH ART

## 1553–1625

———

ERIC MERCER

OXFORD
AT THE CLARENDON PRESS
1962

*Oxford University Press, Amen House, London E.C.4*

GLASGOW  NEW YORK  TORONTO  MELBOURNE  WELLINGTON
BOMBAY  CALCUTTA  MADRAS  KARACHI  LAHORE  DACCA
CAPE TOWN  SALISBURY  NAIROBI  IBADAN  ACCRA
KUALA LUMPUR  HONG KONG

PRINTED IN GREAT BRITAIN
AT THE UNIVERSITY PRESS, OXFORD
BY VIVIAN RIDLER
PRINTER TO THE UNIVERSITY

# PREFACE

THE art of the reigns of Elizabeth and James I is of a higher standard than is generally admitted, but it has very few great names and not many outstanding works, and its history cannot be told in the form of biographies of its artists. English society was changing rapidly at this time, and the changes in English art can be adequately explained only when they are related to the forces and counter-forces that were then maturing in England at large. Despite our imperfect knowledge of the period, and the many unresolved controversies about it amongst historians, an attempt at such an explanation is overdue. I am well aware that I could not have begun without the earlier labours of other men and I trust that this may serve as an acknowledgement to all those of my predecessors that I have not elsewhere referred to. If there is any man who finds that I have borrowed his ideas without a thank you, I hope that he will not regard it as proof of wilful plagiarism, but of an influence that has gone so deep that I have become unconscious of it.

Her Majesty the Queen has graciously permitted me to reproduce works of art in her collections. I wish also to thank the following for similar permissions: the Duke of Bedford, the Duke of Portland, the Marquess of Salisbury, the Earl of Derby, Earl Fitzwilliam, the Earl of Radnor, the Earl of Verulam, Lord Tollemache, Lt.-Col. Sir Edmund Bacon, Brinsley Ford, Esq., Loel Guinness, Esq., Sir Westrow Hulse, R. H. G. Leveson-Gower, Esq., Hon. Robin Neville, Hon. Clive Pearson, Derek Sherborn, Esq., Col. V. N. Stopford Sackville, Trustees of the late A. J. C. Wall, Esq., Oliver Watney, Esq., the British Museum, the Bodleian Library, the Cleveland Museum, the Ministry of Works, the National Portrait Gallery, and the Tate Gallery. For their help so generously given in various ways I am indebted to Mr. J. W. Goodison, Sir James Mann, Mr. Robert Sherlock, Mr. Lawrence Stone, Dr. Pamela Tudor-Craig, and Professor E. K. Waterhouse, and to the staff of the National Buildings Record and of the photographic department of the Royal Commission on Historical Monuments. I am grateful to Miss Nola Hobbs for her skill and patience in dealing with unruly manuscripts, and to Mr. John Hopkins for being ever ready to help me with his unrivalled knowledge of the contents of the library of the Society of Antiquaries. The Royal Commission on Historical Monuments have kindly allowed me to use their photographs in advance of official publication and for this my thanks are due to the Commissioners. I owe very much to those who have read chapters in typescript and made many valuable comments and suggestions, to my colleagues, Mrs. Helen Bonney, Mr. Manfred Bräude, and Mr. J. T. Smith, and especially to Mr. Christopher Hill, Mr. Oliver Millar, and Mr. David Piper, who have watched over my footsteps in fields in which, more than elsewhere, I tread with confidence rather than competence. Readers of earlier volumes in this series will doubtless take my debt to the Editor for granted: I, however, who best know how great that debt is, may not do so and am happy to confess how much I owe to his wide knowledge and wise advice. My greatest debt of all is to my early teachers at Battersea Grammar School, to R. H. Geare and R. A. Clarke. What merits, if any, this volume may be found to possess will be mainly due to them; its defects, those I mean that are *vitia hominis* and not *vitia temporis*, are my own contribution. Lastly, I thank my wife for creating the conditions that made the writing of this book possible.

E. M.

# CONTENTS

# LIST OF PLATES

51.  HANS EWORTH: JOAN THORNBURY. 1566. Oliver Watney, Esq., Cornbury Park. [35×28 in.]

52 *a*.  1ST LORD WENTWORTH. 1547. National Portrait Gallery. [38½× 28¾ in.]
   *b*.  2ND LORD WENTWORTH. 1568. National Portrait Gallery. [39¼× 27¼ in.]

53 *a*.  CORNELIS KETEL: WILLIAM GRESHAM (DETAIL). 1579. R. H. G. Leveson-Gower, Esq., Titsey Park. [40½×30½ in.] *Photograph by courtesy of the City Art Gallery, Manchester.*
   *b*.  SIR EDWARD HOBY. 1578. Miss E. Paget. [20×16 in.] *Photograph by National Portrait Gallery.*

54 *a*.  SIR CHRISTOPHER HATTON AS CHANCELLOR OF THE UNIVERSITY OF OXFORD. National Portrait Gallery. [29×23 in.]
   *b*.  HENRY CARY, LORD HUNSDON. 1591. Col. V. N. Stopford Sackville, T.D., O.B.E., Drayton House, Kettering. [36×29½ in.]

55 *a*.  GEORGE GOWER: LADY KITSON. Tate Gallery. [26¾×20½ in.]
   *b*.  GEORGE GOWER: SELF-PORTRAIT. 1579. Earl Fitzwilliam, Milton, Peterborough. [23¾×19½ in.] *Photograph by National Portrait Gallery.*

56 *a*.  THE 'COBHAM' QUEEN ELIZABETH. National Portrait Gallery. [43¾× 30¼ in.]
   *b*.  THE 'RAINBOW' QUEEN ELIZABETH. The Marquess of Salisbury, Hatfield House. [50×39 in.] *Photograph by courtesy of the Courtauld Institute of Art.*

57 *a*.  LADY TANFIELD. Loel Guinness, Esq.; on loan to the Tate Gallery. [81×50 in.]
   *b*.  LADY AND CHILD. Trustees of the late A. J. C. Wall, Esq.; on loan to the Birmingham Art Gallery. [69½×43½ in.]

58.  SIR HENRY NEVILL. 1582. Lt.-Col. Sir Edmund Bacon, Bt., Raveningham. [35×29 in.] *Photograph by courtesy of the Royal Academy.*

59.  PAUL VAN SOMER: ANNE OF DENMARK BEFORE OATLANDS. 1617. Windsor Castle. *Reproduced by gracious permission of Her Majesty the Queen.* [103×81 in.]

60.  THE EARL OF ESSEX. The Duke of Bedford, Woburn Abbey. [84×50 in.] *Photograph by National Portrait Gallery.*

61.  THE 'DITCHLEY' QUEEN ELIZABETH. National Portrait Gallery. [93× 59 in.]

62 *a*.  THE EARL OF SUSSEX. *c.* 1595. Tower of London. [85½×55½ in.] *Photograph by Ministry of Works. Crown copyright.*

62 *b.* PRINCE HENRY HUNTING. Hampton Court. *Reproduced by gracious permission of Her Majesty the Queen.* [75×64 in.]

63 *a.* NICHOLAS HILLIARD: UNKNOWN MAN AGAINST A BACKGROUND OF FLAMES. Victoria and Albert Museum. *Crown copyright.*
  *b.* NICHOLAS HILLIARD: YOUNG MAN AMIDST BRIARS. Victoria and Albert Museum. *Crown copyright.*

64 *a.* GEORGE GELDORP: 2ND EARL OF SALISBURY BEFORE HATFIELD HOUSE. The Marquess of Salisbury, Hatfield House. [84×51 in.] *Photograph by National Portrait Gallery.*
  *b.* SIR NATHANIEL BACON: SELF-PORTRAIT. Earl of Verulam, Gorhambury. [81½×60½ in.]

65 *a.* LADY ANNE RICH. British Embassy, Madrid. [87×54 in.] *Photograph by Ministry of Works. Crown copyright.*
  *b.* UNKNOWN LADY 1614. National Portrait Gallery. [44×31½ in.]

66. LUDOVIC STUART, DUKE OF RICHMOND AND LENNOX. 1608. Lord Tollemache, Helmingham Hall. [84×51½ in.] *Photograph by courtesy of the Courtauld Institute of Art.*

67. MARCUS GHEERAERTS: LADY RUSSELL. 1625. The Duke of Bedford, Woburn Abbey. [77×42 in.] *Photograph by National Portrait Gallery.*

68. SIR NATHANIEL BACON: JANE BACON. Earl of Verulam, Gorhambury. [18×14 in.]

69 *a.* SIR NATHANIEL BACON: THE COOKMAID. Earl of Verulam, Gorhambury. [60×81 in.]
  *b.* SIR NATHANIEL BACON: COMPANION TO THE COOKMAID. Earl of Verulam, Gorhambury. [51×80 in.]

70. NICHOLAS HILLIARD: SIR ANTHONY MILDMAY. *c.* 1605. Cleveland Museum of Art, Ohio. [9¼×6⅞ in.] *Photograph by Victoria and Albert Museum. Crown copyright.*

71. ISAAC OLIVER: RICHARD SACKVILLE, EARL OF DORSET. 1616. [9¼×6 in.] Victoria and Albert Museum. *Crown copyright.*

72 *a.* EDWARD NORGATE: JUDITH NORGATE. 1617. Victoria and Albert Museum. *Crown copyright.*
  *b.* NICHOLAS HILLIARD: 'ELIZABETH OF BOHEMIA'. Collection of the Earl of Derby. *Photograph by Victoria and Albert Museum. Crown copyright.*
  *c.* ISAAC OLIVER: UNFINISHED PORTRAIT OF QUEEN ELIZABETH. Victoria and Albert Museum. *Crown copyright.*
  *d.* NICHOLAS HILLIARD: MRS. HOLLAND. 1593. Victoria and Albert Museum. *Crown copyright.*

# LIST OF FIGURES

# ABBREVIATIONS

| | |
|---|---|
| Add. Mss. | Additional Manuscripts |
| *Antiq. Journ.* | *Antiquaries Journal* |
| *Arch. Journ.* | *Archaeological Journal* |
| *Arch. Rev.* | *Architectural Review* |
| B.M. | British Museum |
| *Burl. Mag.* | *Burlington Magazine* |
| *C.L.* | *Country Life* |
| *Cal. S.P. Dom.* | *Calendar of State Papers, Domestic* |
| *Cal. S.P. Ven.* | *Calendar of State Papers, Venetian* |
| *Conn.* | *The Connoisseur* |
| *D.N.B.* | *Dictionary of National Biography* |
| Eg. Mss. | Egerton Manuscripts |
| H.M.C. | Historical Manuscripts Commission |
| H.S.L. | Huguenot Society of London |
| Harl. Mss. | Harleian Manuscripts |
| Harl. Soc. | Harleian Society |
| *Journ. R.I.B.A.* | *Journal of the Royal Institute of British Architects* |
| *Journ. Brit. Arch. Ass.* | *Journal of the British Archaeological Association* |
| *Journ. W.C.I.* | *Journal of the Warburg and Courtauld Institutes* |
| *J.H.I.* | *Journal of the History of Ideas* |
| *J.K.S.W.* | *Jahrbuch der Kunsthistorischen Sammlungen in Wien* |
| *L.C.C.S.L.* | *London County Council Survey of London* |
| *L.P.H. VIII* | *Letters and Papers of Henry VIII* |
| Lans. Mss. | Lansdowne Manuscripts |
| N.P.G. | National Portrait Gallery |
| *O.H.E.A.* | *Oxford History of English Art* |
| *P. and P.* | *Past and Present* |
| *Proc. Brit. Acad.* | *Proceedings of the British Academy* |
| P.R.O. | Public Record Office |
| *Proc. Soc. Ants.* | *Proceedings of the Society of Antiquaries* |
| R.A. | Royal Academy |
| R.C.A.M. | Royal Commission on Ancient Monuments (Wales and Monmouth) |

| | |
|---|---|
| R.C.H.M. | Royal Commission on Historical Monuments (England) |
| *R.K.S.* | Repertorium für Kunstwissenschaft, Stuttgart |
| *Trans. R. Hist. Soc.* | *Transactions of the Royal Historical Society* |
| V. & A. | Victoria and Albert Museum |
| V.C.H. | Victoria County History |
| Wal. Soc. | Walpole Society |

# INTRODUCTION

IN the course of the sixteenth century English art broke with
much of its past and made a belated entry into the ranks of the
Renaissance. It has been customary to explain this change as
the result of English contacts with Italy, and later with France and
Flanders, and of the import of Continental artists and publications.
Attractive as this theory is in its simplicity it does not account for
the delay of over a hundred years, years in which there were multifarious contacts with Italy, before the Renaissance had any welcome in England. Renaissance art would never have appeared here
if it had not first existed abroad, but whether and when and in what
forms it would come were determined at least as much by social
and intellectual developments in this country as by artistic changes
on the Continent. 'The history of learning', it has been said, 'is not
a free field; it is the history of society.' The same is true of art, and
the art historian must indicate to his reader, however briefly and
generally, his conception of the nature and development of the
society whose art he is discussing.

Such an indication must indeed be summary, undocumented,
and second hand; anything else would involve writing several
books instead of one. It will be clear to anyone acquainted with
the period how much I owe—to mention some recent writers
only—to the work of R. R. Bolgar, F. Caspari, Maurice Dobb,
Christopher Hill, Eleanor Rosenberg, P. N. Siegel, Lawrence
Stone, R. H. Tawney, and H. R. Trevor-Roper. At the same time
I must make it equally clear that I do not know whether any one
of these would agree with all or anything that I have written. In
mentioning their names I acknowledge a debt; I do not buttress
my credit.

By the middle of the sixteenth century there had developed in
England a centralized monarchy whose power against any one, or
any section, of its subjects was so great that, despite parliamentary
institutions and occasional armed uprisings, it could act in most
circumstances as an absolute State. Its authority was based upon

support from decisive sections of the greater landowners, whose fortunes it repaired and maintained, of the gentry, to whom it had given power in the countryside as absolute as its own within the country, and of the yeomen and prosperous urban classes whose security in their pursuits and possessions it guaranteed. It had detached the English Church from the Papacy and had dissolved the monasteries, thereby acquiring control of the most persuasive disseminator of religious and social ideas, binding to itself all who acquired church lands by whatever means, and establishing itself amongst all, or nearly all, who held Protestant views as the champion of their cause. Throughout the century it maintained itself with little difficulty by appealing to its subjects as the guardian of civil peace, the guarantor of the land settlement consequent upon the Reformation, the defender of the reformed faith, and the indispensable shield against foreign aggression.

To establish such a State it had also been necessary to develop a body of men capable of running the immensely more complicated machinery of government. Those imbued with the thought and scholarship of the Renaissance were best able to fill this role because of their wider training and their power of seeing the problems of statecraft and politics, in the fashion of their Greek and Roman mentors, from a purely secular viewpoint. Doubtless many a medieval ruler or counsellor who had never consciously learnt any lessons from Antiquity was capable of such detachment, but the Tudor State needed not one or two such men but a whole corps of them. The situation can be compared in one way with that in Britain today, where, it is widely agreed, our production of a few remarkably brilliant scientists will not, by itself, save us from the perils of not having produced a great many good ones. The Tudors were content at first to solve their problems in an *ad hoc* fashion by continuing the medieval practice of employing outstanding and quite exceptional churchmen, and the two most prominent ministers of the first fifty years of the régime were the cardinals, Morton and Wolsey. Henry VII, however, had early begun to patronize and recruit foreign scholars, mostly for the diplomatic work that the existence of other modern States was heavily increasing. In the early sixteenth century there began an expansion of the Universities, particularly of Cambridge, and a modification of their curriculum that was to provide a native source of Renaissance men, who both by inclination and opportunity would look to the State for employment and advancement.

But there was more than the 'mechanics' of the State to be considered, more than the provision of effective force to defend it against its enemies; there was the greater problem of maintaining it in the minds of men, of persuading all who could be persuaded that it was beneficent, and of convincing all others that it was irresistible. Renaissance thought with its secular assumptions, its stress on the potentialities of a few great individuals, its development of a doctrine of unalloyed 'sovereignty', its tendency to restrict its historical gaze to the early period of the absolutist Roman Empire, was a powerful intellectual aid to the attainment of these ends. The Tudor State was thus a great patron of Renaissance men and ideas and they, in their turn, were pillars of the State.

Men who surrendered themselves wholeheartedly to Renaissance thought were likely to be sympathetic to Renaissance art, particularly if the traditional art of their own country had become formalized and stereotyped. It would be false to proclaim an absolute repulsion between medieval views and Renaissance art, or between Renaissance views and Gothic art, but, if we do not make the mistake of equating 'medieval' with 'Catholic', a tendency that way is clear. For reasons to be considered in later chapters, Renaissance art largely, to quote Sir John Summerson, 'made its way in England . . . as a mode of decorative design'. We shall understand why it did this if we add that it first established itself as the indirect expression of the absolute State.

The absolute State, however, is a theoretical concept; in practice there are always limitations upon it, one of which is that it cannot avert the consequences of its own policies. The essence of Tudor policy was to preserve as much as possible of the content of the old society by giving it a new form. The new form meant the advent to position and power of new men, of a new type of man. 'England', said the Duke of Norfolk, 'was never merry since the new learning came in.' He meant, of course, that the Dukes of Norfolk could no longer merrily take their place and power for granted, but had to compete with others in a race in which mere merit had a chance of success. The famous speech by Ulysses from *Troilus and Cressida* in praise of 'Order' and 'Degree' has often been quoted as an illustration of Tudor social ideals. Another speech, however, from the same play and by the same character, recognizes how fragile those ideals were:

> Time hath, my lord, a wallet at his back
> Wherein he puts alms for oblivion,
> A great-sized monster of ingratitudes:
> Those scraps are good deeds past; which are devour'd
> As fast as they are made, forgot as soon
> As done: perseverance, dear my lord,
> Keeps honour bright: to have done, is to hang
> Quite out of fashion, like a rusty mail
> In monumental mockery. . . .
> . . . O, let not virtue seek
> Remuneration for the thing it was;
> For beauty, wit,
> High birth, vigour of bone, desert in service,
> Love, friendship, charity, are subjects all
> To envious and calumniating time.
> One touch of nature makes the whole world kin,
> That all with one consent praise new-born gawds,
> Though they are made and moulded of things past,
> And give to dust that is a little gilt
> More laud than gilt o'er-dusted.
> The present eye praises the present object:
> Then marvel not, thou great and complete man,
> That all the Greeks begin to worship Ajax;
> Since things in motion sooner catch the eye
> Than what not stirs.

All those who withdrew from this hurly-burly, whether from pride or modesty or that amalgam of the two that thwarts so many capable men, tended to look back with regret on a recent past, in which honour had been achieved by qualities that they considered themselves to possess. Those, on the other hand, who profited from their opportunities achieved thereby a new place in the old order, and were not without a certain admiration and awe for the glories of a feudal past with which they were now able to identify themselves. By two routes a romantic attitude towards the later Middle Ages was thus arrived at, and this was reflected in art in several ways; in collections of imaginary portraits of historical forerunners, in manufactured effigies of ancestors, in sham castles, in an unprecedented display of heraldry, and in a reinforcement of the conservative liking among provincial master-masons for perpetuating late-Gothic architectural forms.

The second and more important effect of State policy was upon its closest supporters and those most imbued with Renaissance ideas. The whole cloth of Renaissance thought consisted of far more than the few strands that it suited the State to pick out; it was not a bundle of disparate views, although it might have conflicting elements within it, but a consistent ideology and a way of thought. It was extremely difficult for men who genuinely held such views to separate the strands and to use some and reject others. In short, to be a Renaissance man one had to be a Renaissance man; light half-believers of their casual creeds were not of the stuff to achieve such an integration. But the State, for all its fostering of certain aspects of Renaissance thought, was a powerful obstacle to the full development of Renaissance men. It tended to turn even the greatest individual into a mere creature, into 'a sponge . . . that soaks up the king's countenance, his rewards, his authorities . . . when he needs what you have gleaned, it is but squeezing you, and, sponge, you shall be dry again'. Hamlet's words applied not only to the Rosencrantzes and Guildensterns but, more or less, to the very greatest. As a result the leading men of the time developed a public art—in architecture, in painting and in sculpture—whose character was determined not so much by Renaissance aesthetics as by the social and political needs that their position as creatures of the State imposed upon them. In compensation, as a private refuge from State-dominated art, they encouraged and brought about a flowering of miniature painting in which, for a brief period, the English had no rivals.

But the course of English history was not wholly determined by the men of the absolute State and the Renaissance. There were other men, those wider sections whose support of, or acquiescence in, the Tudor State made it possible; and there was another source of intellectual and artistic expression—the Reformation. The Reformation preached an individualism as pronounced as that of the Renaissance theorists, but of a very different order. The Renaissance thought essentially in terms of the exceptional individual, of those who by their social position or native genius were among the princes of men. Machiavelli issued a plain warning, which some of his disciples would have done well to take to heart, that none but the great were in a position to follow his precepts. What was true in politics was true in wider fields; the 'Complete Man' was not a figure that the masses could aspire to be. The individualism of the Reformation, on the other hand, was a doctrine for the common man. It placed just as much emphasis as the Renaissance on individual fulfilment, but this fulfilment was of a kind that was open to far more men; the achievement of salvation—or of the worldly success that came to be widely regarded as the outward sign of it— by a man's own activities and primarily by carrying out the tasks that lay to hand and labouring in his calling. This was a doctrine that appealed not only, as one would expect, to merchants and industrialists but to the landed classes as well, and especially the 'improving' landlords: Richard Brathwait in *The English Gentleman* made it almost the hall-mark of gentility.

Like other intellectual trends the Reformation had its own artistic reflection, and not solely, and not primarily, in the iconoclasm that is usually associated with it. Where they had so much in common it is not always possible to draw a distinction between the reflection of Renaissance and of Reformation ideas, and the stress on the portrayal of the individual that is so noticeable in painting and sculpture is a case where the two worked happily to one end. But yet they worked on a different level. The Elizabethan portrait had been developed by the courtiers; some of its attributes were taken over by wider classes, who had different reasons for wanting much the same thing. In some other matters the Reformation had a different effect from that of the Renaissance, and minor men were fonder of biblical than of classical themes, and occasionally celebrated upon their tombs their occupations and exploits rather than their social standing.

At first, however, the two worked in harmony and many of the most Renaissance-conscious men of the mid-century were the most extreme Protestants, and the stoutest supporters of the Tudor State. But that State had another, and more important, limitation upon its power; although it might hinder, divert, or even exploit the social, economic, and intellectual developments within the country it could never control them. By the early seventeenth century these developments were bringing about a divergence of interest between the State and some of its former supporters. All those landowners, merchants, and nascent industrialists, who were too far removed from the court to enioy its bounty in the form of offices, pensions, patents, were increasingly restive at its open and necessary policy of reviving feudal practices and exploiting feudal revenues in town and country; of hindering 'improving' en- closures, of taking ruinous fines for wardships, of enforcing gild restrictions and of granting irritating monopolies on innumerable articles. It would be wrong to suggest that this discontent had reached serious proportions before 1603, but the beginnings of an opposition were appearing, and in time, as the near unanimity of the early months of the Long Parliament showed, even a section of the 'courtiers' were to find themselves in opposition, not to the Crown itself but to certain aspects of its policy.

Ideology too had developed in the years since the Elizabethan Settlement and, with the dangers of a Catholic *revanche* receding, a split was appearing between the hierarchy of the Church and their more extreme fellow Protestants. Protestantism is not necessarily a revolutionary or even a reforming doctrine. Luther had early demonstrated with his distinction between the *geistliche* and *welt- liche Regiment* that it could easily be given a quietist tone, but it had elements within it that could be developed in an anti-authori- tarian direction; and it had been with their help that the State had succeeded in destroying the medieval Church. Among those who took part in the attack on that Church were many who, in the name of 'individual judgement', were ready to attack any authorit- arian Church at all, whether the 'Supreme Head' or the 'Supreme

Governor' was the Pope or the King. The bishops who translated the King James Bible were not being merely peevish when they complained of those who 'give liking to nothing but what is hammered and framed upon their anvil'. They were recognizing the source of their danger, that disagreements with the Church's discipline and doctrine tended to turn into attacks upon the Church itself, and therefore upon the State that both buttressed and leant upon it.

If attacks upon the Church were to be successfully resisted, then its old prestige and authority must be restored, and this meant ending the plunder of its revenues and the control of a vast number of its appointments by local gentry and nobility. It meant, in short, a Laudian policy, filling many men with indignation at the menace to their religion, many others with alarm for their property, and many with both. Thus the growing opposition of some sections to the social and economic policies of the State inflamed and was inflamed by the tendency of their more thorough-going co-believers to attack its religious policy. Religious and political opposition was beginning to merge into a menacing combination.

This occurred at a time when Renaissance thought and learning had taken on a new character in England and had become established not merely as the property of a small and partly professional group but, to a greater or lesser degree, as a quality of all the upper classes. By 1600 Humanism, in Bolgar's words, 'was no longer the esoteric possession of a few. It leavened the whole of England's intellectual life.' For the first time there were wide classes who had both the classical heritage—something more than a tendency to follow other men's fashions in copying classicist motifs—and the necessary leisure to indulge a deep interest in Renaissance art. Of these the men with the greatest opportunities were not those in the counting-house counting out their money, or in a far-away shire busy improving their estates, but those who because or in expectation of royal bounty were frequenting a court at the centre of cultural life. It was from this small section that most of the virtuosi were recruited, the first conscious champions of a new and different art in England since the mid-sixteenth century.

Unlike those earlier innovators the virtuosi were not professional humanists with a bias towards the learned aspects of Renaissance art, but Renaissance-educated gentlemen, amateurs with a shallower knowledge but wider interests and potentially sympathetic towards the latest productions of that art. These were mainly appearing in Roman Catholic countries, were indeed in part the artistic expression of the Counter-Reformation, and in earlier years such an origin had been sufficient in itself to keep many of them out of England. But hostility to Rome was not as strong at all levels of English society as it once had been. Menaced by the developing combination of Puritan and political opposition the State had recoiled along a reciprocal bearing, emphasizing the less Protestant and more authoritarian elements in the Elizabethan compromise, leaning towards a High Anglicanism, looking more favourably upon English Catholics and attempting to arrange marriage alliances with foreign ones. In consequence its protégés—some taking colour from their patron, some drawn towards their patron because their colours matched—were better able to appreciate the many merits of contemporary Catholic art, for they looked at it with eyes that were freer than most men's from anti-Catholic prejudice. As a result they developed a highly sophisticated art, borrowing widely and consciously from European, and mainly Catholic, sources and justifying their activities with a great amount of aesthetic theorizing.

Yet the virtuosi were not Roman Catholics but Anglicans, and their borrowing tended to limit itself to the less extreme aspects of Catholic art, and to draw mainly upon the Catholic Low Countries, upon France, and upon North Italy and especially Venice which, although Catholic, was not always a wholehearted friend of Rome. Further, they were gentlemen addressing gentlemen and not dedicated servants of Christ proselytizing amongst all men, and in consequence they eschewed those features of contemporary Catholic art that were designed to have a mass appeal. At the same time their relationship with the State that freed them from one set of prejudices rendered them liable to others. Contemporary Dutch art was in many ways the equal of that of Catholic countries, but the republicanism and militant Protestantism of the Dutch, which had made Elizabeth herself uneasy, did not recommend itself to English courtiers, and the virtuosi, while ransacking much of the rest of Europe, paid less attention than she deserved to Holland.

This new art reached its culmination under Charles I: in Jones's Palladianism, in the patronage of Rubens and Van Dyck, of Le Sueur and Fanelli. Its origins are to be found in the previous reign: in a fondness for New Testament themes, in the abandonment of Anglo-Flemish motifs and the introduction of French and 'Italian', in the application of conscious design to interior decoration, and in a tendency in sculpture, and to a lesser degree in painting, to break away from the rigidity and ostentation of the old art.

Although their potential audience was a wide one, the virtuosi were very much a leadership without a following. By 1600 Humanism had spread widely among the upper classes, but Protestantism had sunk deeply; and for all the limitations of the old art it had one surpassing value, it exactly suited the Protestant ethos. There were therefore many among the educated classes, and especially among those who were pursuing salvation by diligently attending to their affairs, for whom the new art had no over-riding appeal. Further, it was not only the Protestant ethos that was reflected in the old art but the prevailing social ideas as well. The virtuosi were very far from challenging or wishing to challenge those ideas, but by their elevation of art, as something quite distinct from costly magnificence, and of the artist, who might be any nobody endowed with nothing but genius, they were in fact offending against them.

Nevertheless, the new art might still have made its way against more impediments than these but for the manner of its introduction. It accompanied, and was propagated by those associated with, the State's swing away from the traditional religious and foreign policy of Protestant England; and while on two counts it could have reckoned on a cold reception it was thereby assured of a hostile one. In consequence it was taken up not even by all of the courtiers but by a very small section of them. The rest of the upper classes clung to and continued the old art and many of the most developed examples of 'Jacobean' work are, in fact, Carolean.

In the late sixteenth century the absolute State had been a fetter upon artistic development; in the early seventeenth century it became a liberating agent, but mainly for those few men who had no qualms about its policies. Thus there appeared in England at this time the unusual phenomenon of an old art developing side by side with a new that failed, after nearly four decades of unprecedented propaganda in its favour, to spread beyond the narrow court circle that had introduced it. Discussing Cromwell's portraits, a recent critic has remarked that 'the conservative taste in art of the revolutionaries in politics is astonishing'. We need not find it so. The split between the State and important sections of the upper classes, that was to help to bring about the Civil War, made it possible for the virtuosi to develop but at the same time limited their appeal, and was thereby being reflected in art by the end of James I's reign.

# I

# ARCHITECTURE

THE social and political changes expressed in the advent of the Tudors brought about a decisive turn in the development of English architecture. The new relationship with the State of the greater men of the time revolutionized house-planning, and the introduction by that State of Renaissance ideas transformed conceptions of architectural design and the nature of architectural ornament. These two factors, however, worked in conjunction and not merely side by side, and the new house-plans were themselves affected by Renaissance ideas of symmetry, while the disposition, and to some extent in consequence the character, of Renaissance ornament was determined by the planning of the buildings upon which it was placed.

For our purpose the most important social result of the establishment of the absolute State was the transformation of feudal magnates into courtiers and office-holders. The wealth of these men, although often very great, was not perhaps significantly greater than that of their predecessors, but there were fewer feudal calls upon it, and although they had many new expenses they could devote a greater proportion of their income than before to their personal wants, and especially to their houses.

Because of this new relationship with the Crown the houses of these men could, and had to, take on a new character. It was no longer necessary, politic, or even possible to build fortresses—as Buckingham's execution in 1521 partly showed, it was dangerous even to seem to do so—and one of the restrictions upon medieval domestic building was thus ended. Another was removed by the change that had come about in the relations between these men and those on their lands. Direct farming of the demesne was no longer an important preoccupation and a significant source of their income; instead their wealth came to them mainly in the form of rent. This had two results: the nature of their houses was no longer conditioned by a possible function as a centre of economic activity, and the siting of them was no longer determined by the location of their owners' estates. It was noticed by Bishop Goodman that one of the greatest and most famous, Theobalds, had 'neither lordship nor tenants nor so much as provision of fuel'.[1] This was an extreme case, but it was different only in degree and not in kind from others. These new men, therefore, partly as a result of their lack of political freedom, had more freedom in the planning of their houses than the Middle Ages had known.

Yet they were not wholly free, for there was one important limitation upon them; they had to build very big houses. Partly this was because their owners needed to keep up a certain 'port' and have their suites of gentlemen and pages; partly because the one essential condition for retaining their wealth and standing was to continue in royal favour, in office, in possession of patents and monopolies; and to do this it was wisdom to entertain and accommodate the court. The combination of office, 'port', and court in determining the pattern of a man's building is brought out in the well-known biography of Burghley by a contemporary:

He buylt three houses. One in London, for necessity. Another at Burghley, of computency, for the mansion of his barony. And another at Waltham [Theobalds] for his younger sonne.Which, at the first, he ment but for a little pile, as I hard him saie. But, after he came to enterteyne the quene so often there, he was inforced to enlarge it, rather for the quene and her greate traine, and to sett (the) poore on worke, then for pompe or glory.[2]

Entertainment of the court reached its height under Elizabeth and James, but it had begun earlier, and the ill-fated Buckingham himself had received Henry VIII at Penshurst in 1519. It could be an expensive business. Burghley's early biographer reckoned that it cost £2,000–£3,000 every time that Elizabeth stayed at Theobalds;[3] that may have been an exaggeration, but certainly her stay of four

---

[1] G. Goodman, *Court of James I*, ed. J. S. Brewer (1839), i. 174.
[2] F. Peck, *Desiderata Curiosa* (1779), p. 25.      [3] *Desiderata Curiosa*, p. 15.

days at Gorhambury in 1577 cost Sir Nicholas Bacon £577.[1] This, however, was an occupational risk and one that the builders of the time had to be ready to take. After her first visit to Gorhambury in 1572 Elizabeth pointedly told Bacon, the Lord Keeper, that his house was too small. His first response was to pay a courtly compliment: 'Nay, Madam, you have made me too big for my house.'[2] His next was to set about enlarging. In 1579 Burghley, referring to Theobalds and Holdenby, wrote to Hatton: 'God give us long life to enjoy her for whom we both meant to exceed our purses in these.' Hatton vowed to Heneage in the following year that he would not look on 'his other shrine' (Holdenby) until 'that holy saint [a blasphemous euphemism for Queen Elizabeth] might sit in it'.[3] As late as 1633 the Earl of Newcastle, whose entertainment of Charles I at Welbeck and Bolsover, with all the architectural improvements that it necessitated, was intended to get him court preferment, wrote that he had 'hurt [his] estate with the hope of it'.[4] Thus, however these men might wish to build, they needed, and understood that they needed, to build big.

This restriction, however, was of minor importance in comparison with those upon earlier builders, and men like Hatton and Burghley were more or less free—and it was a new freedom in England—to make their houses objects of architectural design. This opportunity, however, occurred just at the time when, for reasons of its own, the State was encouraging Renaissance thought and learning in England. With that came Renaissance art and canons of architectural composition. At first these canons made slow headway, for they were invading a land with its own tradition of domestic building and planning. That tradition, derived from the military and economic needs of the great feudalists, was to build houses for their isolated semi-independent communities that looked on to courtyards and turned their backs on the world.

[1] J. Rogers, 'The Manor and Houses of Gorhambury', *St. Albans and Herts. Archaeological Soc.* iv. (1933), 35–112. All dates are in the New Style.

[2] D. Lloyd, *State Worthies* (1766), p. 355. Bacon's reply may be apocryphal, for the authority is a late one, but his subsequent actions are not.

[3] E. St. J. Brooks, *Sir Christopher Hatton* (1946), pp. 155, 158.

[4] *Letters and Despatches of the Earl of Strafford*, ed. W. Knowler (1739), i. 101.

At Sutton Place (1521–7)[1] and at Hengrave (begun *c.* 1525) these new men, still needing large houses, followed the tradition of an introvert courtyard plan. In consequence they could recognize Renaissance art mainly by a scattered use of some of its decorative motifs, and it is this that is the basis of Sir John Summerson's remark that Classical architecture 'made its way in England . . . as a mode of decorative design'.[2]

Yet that remark does not contain the whole truth. As early as Sutton Place Renaissance canons of design were over-riding tradition. One may say 'Renaissance', for what is seen there is not a mere attempt at symmetry, which is not in itself alien from Gothic art, but a striving after it at all costs. The courtyard elevation of the Hall is made symmetrical by removing the entrance from its traditional position, at one end and opening on to the screens passage, and placing it centrally. This device, which in effect abandons the screens passage, was formidably impractical, and later builders faced with the same problem refused to pay the same price, but went instead to considerable trouble and expense to attain symmetry without forgoing the customary and convenient siting of the Hall entrance.[3]

Before long Renaissance ideas, taking advantage of social changes, began to turn the great house inside out and to give prime importance to the exterior rather than to the courtyard elevations. The process was a slow one, but its result can be seen by a comparison of Sutton Place with the final form of Longleat as it was rebuilt after the fire of 1567.[4] At Sutton Place (Fig. 1), apart from

[1] There are three monumental works on the architecture of the period: J. A. Gotch, *Architecture of the Renaissance in England* (2 vols. 1894); T. Garner and A. Stratton, *The Domestic Architecture of England during the Tudor Period* (2 vols., 2nd ed. 1929); and H. A. Tipping, *English Homes*, Period III: Late Tudor and Early Stuart (vol. i, 2nd ed. 1929, vol. ii, 1927). To these must be added the twenty-one volumes so far published by the R.C.H.M. (England). To avoid a mass of footnotes I have documented the date that I give to a building only when it is not to be found in these authorities, or when there is some reason for disagreeing with or amending their conclusions.

[2] *Architecture in Britain 1530–1830* (1953), p. 22.

[3] Even in so late a house as Danny Park, Sussex (1595), the symmetry of the fenestration, but not of the build, was sacrificed in order to accommodate a two-story hall.

[4] C. Hussey, 'Longleat, Wiltshire', *C.L.* cv (April 1949), 798, 862, 926, 990; M. Girouard, 'More Light on Longleat', *C.L.* cxx (Sept.–Oct. 1956), 594, 785, 954.

the now destroyed entrance front, all the architectural interest was concentrated on the interior elevations of the courtyard, not only in the regular disposition of the windows and the careful symmetry of the Hall block, but also by the use of terracotta panels and dressings. On the exterior elevations there was no attempt at symmetry or design, and such features as windows and chimney-breasts were

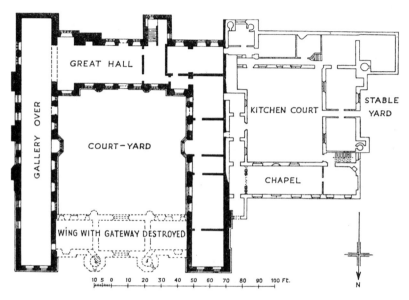

FIG. I. *Plan of Sutton Place*

put where 'use' and not 'uniformity' demanded. At Longleat (Fig. 2) each exterior elevation was the subject of careful design and was symmetrically arranged. Longleat contains all the elements necessary to a great house of the time, the Hall, the Gallery, parlours, lodgings, and offices, but because of the wealth that could be expended on it and its great size the individual units of its plan could be welded into symmetrical elevations.

Having established this extrovert and design-conscious character, the great courtyard was generally superseded by the 'H' and the 'half-H' plan type, of a main block with long wings at the ends at right-angles to its axis, projecting from both fronts in the 'H' and from one front in the 'half-H' or 'U' plan. Great courtyard houses were not within reach of the purse of any but the very wealthy,

and even they might well pause before embarking upon them.
The heirs of the first Marquis of Winchester were pulling down,
before the Civil War, parts of the vast house that he had erected
earlier at Old Basing.[1] Writing towards the end of our period,
Bacon felt it necessary to remind some of his contemporaries that

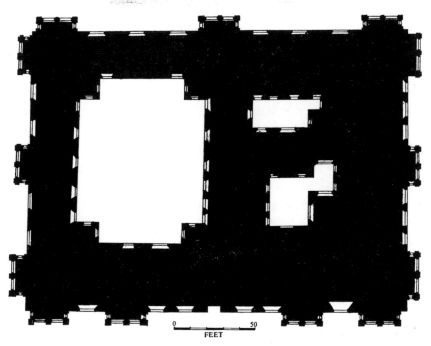

FIG. 2. *Plan of Longleat*

'Houses are built to Live in, and not to Looke on: Therefore let
Use bee preferred before Uniformitie; Except where both may be
had: Leave the Goodly Fabricks of Houses, for Beautie only, to
the enchanted Pallaces of the Poets: Who build them with small
Cost.'[2] This, however, was advice that could not be followed, for
'Uniformitie' was now the first consideration to any builder. The
importance attached to it is shown by the bold and heart-felt
declaration of Robert Lyminge, employed by Cecil at Hatfield,
when certain economies and alterations of design were proposed—

[1] Camden, *Britannia*, ed. Gough (1798), pp. 120–1.
[2] Bacon, *Essays* (1625), p. 257.

'it will be very deformed for the uniforme of the build, both within and without, which I will never agree to'.[1] The problem, therefore, was not how to dispense with the design, but how to obtain
it in another way.

There was, too, more than the design alone to be considered:
there was the need to evolve a type of plan that would allow for
most of the accommodation that the great courtyard house provided. In particular, it was necessary to incorporate a Long Gallery,
which was now *de rigueur* in a house of any pretensions. This was
the most important of the additions that Sir Nicholas Bacon made
to Gorhambury when rendering it worthy of another visit from
the Queen. It was the main feature of those that Newcastle made
to Bolsover in 1633 when he was 'hurting his estate' to get preferment from Charles I by entertaining him sumptuously. If these
men built too magnificently they risked ruin; if they built too
meanly they risked ostracism. There were doubts whether Loseley,
for example, was big enough to lodge the Queen.[2] The problem
that faced them was how to build at a smaller cost than the builders
of Basing, Longleat, Burghley, and yet have all or nearly all of the
amenities and of the opportunities for external design of the great
courtyard houses.

A solution was the more urgent as the courtiers, the favoured
and the would-be favoured, became commoner. This began in the
later years of Elizabeth but it was under James I, when the court
followed a policy of ennobling widely and extending the numbers
of those who benefited or hoped to benefit from royal favour, that
it had its greatest effect.[3] It was under James, and not Elizabeth,

[1] L. Stone, 'The Building of Hatfield House', *Arch. Journ.* cxii (1955), 114.

[2] Letter of 2 Aug. from Anthony Wingfield to William More (*Loseley Manuscripts*,
ed. A. J. Kempe (1835), pp. 265-6). This letter is undated, but refers to Dudley as
'Earl of Leicester' and cannot therefore be before 1564. It was presumably written by
Wingfield in his capacity as a Gentleman Usher, a position which he is not recorded as
holding before 1569 (A. Feuillerat, *Documents relating to the . . . Revels in the Time of
Queen Elizabeth* (Louvain 1908), p. 437), and Loseley had been finished by then.

[3] Professor Neale has shown that by the 1590's the acceptance of bribes by courtiers
for obtaining royal favours was common practice ('The Elizabethan Political Scene',
*Proc. Brit. Acad.* xxxiv (1948), 97), an early sign of future developments. The great
increase in court pickings that followed the accession of James has been pointed out
several times, and most recently by Professor Tawney (*Business and Politics under*

that the greatest number of new houses was built and of old ones refurbished; it was of James's reign that Goodman said 'No Kingdom in the world spent so much in building as we did in his time.'[1] This vast expenditure upon the 'Jacobean Prodigy Houses' and, more important, upon the prodigies of Jacobean building, was occasioned in great part by the increase in the numbers of men

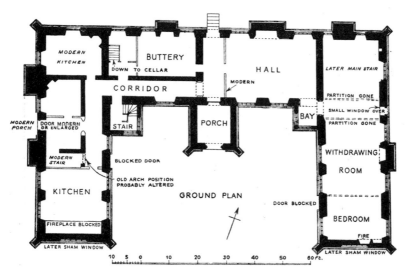

FIG. 3. *Barrington Court*

anxious to entertain the court. Though the wealth of the whole class was probably greater than before, that of the individual members, in general, was less, and there was thus a widespread need to build imposing houses more cheaply. At the same time, the possibility of doing so was there, for these later courtiers on a smaller scale would not and could not keep up expensive suites of gentlemen and pages, and needed, on that account, less room than their predecessors.

In this situation the H plan came into its own. In itself it was nothing new; it had been a common type among the lesser houses of the later Middle Ages and had had its more recent precursors in such H plan houses as Barrington Court (Fig. 3) and Poundis-

*James I* (Cambridge, 1958), pp. 134–42); and Mr. L. Stone has illustrated the prolific ennoblings and knightings of James's reign ('The Inflation of Honours 1558–1641', *P. & P.* xiv (1958), 45).        [1] Goodman, *Court of James I*, i. 199.

ford Park. It now acquired a new content and in so doing solved
the major planning problems of the time. It saved a great amount
of exterior walling and yet, by the addition, if necessary, of an
extra story, could regain much of the space lost by the abandonment of the courtyard plan. Its length in the wings was great
enough to take a Long Gallery, which, with the Great Chamber,
was becoming the most important room. The Hall, as houses

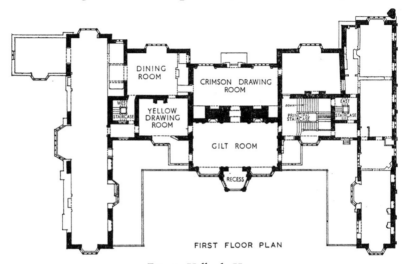

FIG. 4. *Holland House*

became less community centres and more individuals' residences,
was declining in importance, and its decline was reflected in the
growing practice of making it one story high, as it was originally
at Quenby.[1] This permitted the Great Chamber, or Saloon as it
was later called, to occupy the most important position in the
house—on the first floor of the main block—and yet be close to
the Gallery, which could be put into a wing on the first floor. At
Longleat, at Hardwick, and in an early type of H plan such as
Montacute, the Gallery is on the second floor and away from the
Great Chamber. In most of the later H houses and other houses of
the great on a non-H plan the Gallery and Great Chamber are
together, and generally on the first floor,[2] as at Holland House

[1] *Leics. Arch. Soc. Trans.* xvi (1929–31), 25.
[2] At Charlton, Kent, where there is a two-storied Hall, both Great Chamber and
Gallery are put on the second floor.

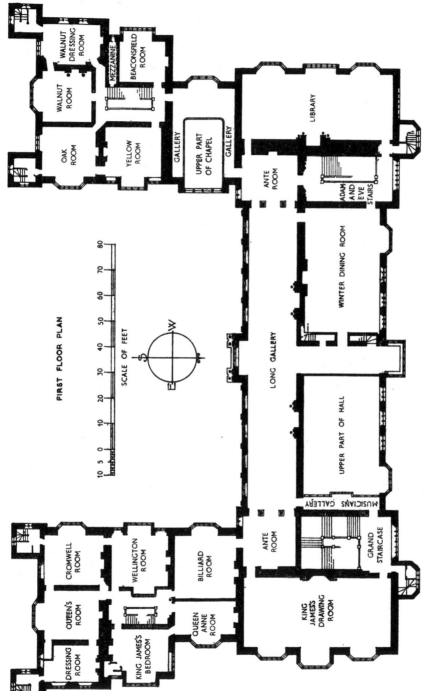

FIG. 5. *Hatfield House*

(1605–7) (Fig. 4) and Hatfield (1607–12) (Fig. 5). Further, this plan permitted the developing 'well' staircase to be sited in the main block, giving easy access to all parts of the house, and ending the need, as at Castle Ashby (Fig. 6), for inconvenient newel stairs at

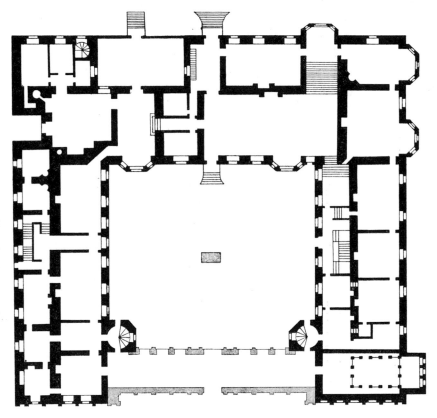

FIG. 6. *Plan of Castle Ashby*

the ends of long wings. In distributing the space on both sides of the main block, it made accommodation more flexible and did away with or considerably reduced the wasted space of long corridors or the inconvenience of inter-communicating rooms. In time, its advantages were increased by doubling the width of the main block, thus reducing the length of the wings without reducing the length available for a Long Gallery, and allowing the Hall, which at Doddington (c. 1595)[1] is still set axially in the main block (Fig. 7),

[1]   *C.L.* lxxx (1936), 356, 382, 392–8.

to be set with more convenience transversely, as at Charlton, Kent (1607–12) (Fig. 8). By the second decade of the seventeenth century a classic type-plan had been evolved, with a main block two rooms thick containing a well staircase and a one-storied transverse Hall, a Great Chamber above and a Gallery in a wing on the same floor (Fig. 9). This does not mean that all, or even any, of the later H plan houses had every one of these features in com-

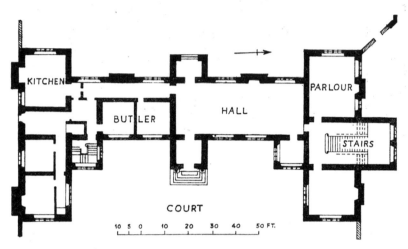

FIG. 7. *Plan of Doddington*

bination, but that most of them were to be found in all the more developed examples such as Holland House, Charlton, and Somerhill (*c.* 1613).

The H plan, however, did more than solve the planning problems of the time: it solved them within the framework of contemporary aesthetics. It allowed of an easy and obvious symmetry, it provided long expanses of exterior walling, and with these and by building high it was able to present an imposing and magnificent appearance. It achieved its great popularity because it was perfectly fitted to be the architectural expression of the new rulers of England, great subjects living in their Sovereign's world, not semi-independent sovereigns of more or less isolated communities.

The courtier house, although the most obvious, was not the only kind that was being built under the Tudors and early Stuarts.

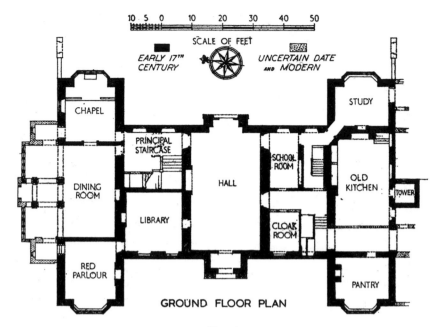

GROUND FLOOR PLAN

FIG. 8

SECOND FLOOR PLAN

FIG. 9. *Charlton House, Kent*

The courtiers, even at their most numerous, were only a section of the upper classes. There were others—the gentry, the minor lawyers, the merchants, manufacturers, and nascent industrialists—who had nothing material to hope for from the court. Many of them were throughout the period as ardent adherents of the absolute State as the courtiers themselves, but, unlike the courtiers, they were independent of it. They had little need to entertain royalty on its progresses or to keep up a 'port', although many of them went out of their way to imitate the great, and they could afford to dispense with, even when they could afford to build, the great mansions of their dependent neighbours. At the same time they were more than yeomen and their homes did not have to be centres of economic activity or more comfortable farmhouses. They could, in fact, build purely residential houses intended for nothing but their own accommodation and comforts.

Because of this, because of their heterogeneous social composition, and because of the greater attention that many of them had to pay to costs, the non-courtiers were much longer in evolving a recognizable type-plan. There was indeed in the later years of the sixteenth century a multiplicity of types: Eastbury, Essex, was built on an H plan; Berden Hall, Essex, on a half-H; Barlborough, Derbyshire, around a very small courtyard; Whitehall, Shrewsbury, as a square block; and very many as a single narrow range or two or more such ranges joined in an L or T or other form. Examples of all of these can be found throughout the period, but there was one that became increasingly common: the square or rectangular block. This plan is important partly for its wide occurrence, partly as the forerunner of the dominant plan type for all men in the latter half of the seventeenth century and for lesser men throughout the next, but mainly because it illustrates with the greatest clarity the considerations that determined the planning of the non-courtier house.[1]

These were partly stated and partly unconsciously assumed by Sir Roger Pratt in *Certain Short Notes concerning Architecture*, in 1660. He commended this 'double-pile' house, as he called it, a

[1] For a rather lengthier discussion of these points see E. Mercer, 'The Houses of the Gentry', *P. & P.* v (1954), 11–32.

block two rooms thick, for its qualities of economy and convenience, for its 'great spare' of walling and roofing compared with the single-pile ranges of courtyard and H plans, and for avoiding the inconvenience of room opening into room or the wasted space of long corridors.[1] Writing after the Restoration, Pratt assumed correctly that these advantages would recommend it to all men, for with the destruction of the Tudor and early Stuart state the class of courtiers had disappeared, and it was a combination of rank and wealth, and not a dependence upon or independence of the court, that then divided the upper class. The difference between the houses of the two sections lay then in the façades and not in the plans, and a purely residential plan met all the requirements of both. Had Pratt been writing half a century earlier he could not have made that assumption, for he would have known that only the non-courtiers could build without thinking of anything but their pockets and convenience. Long before Fuller wrote *The Holy State* they had been following his commonsense precepts: 'a house had better be too little for a day than too great for a year. And it's easier borrowing of thy neighbours a brace of chambers for a night than a bag of money for a twelve-month. It is vain therefore to proportion the receipt to an extraordinary occasion.'[2] Vain it was when Fuller was writing, but to the courtiers of a generation before such advice was useless, for it was precisely those 'extraordinary occasions' that were both the cause and effect of their position.

Lesser men, however, were in a different position: they needed neither suites of rooms nor single rooms with a particular function and form. They could dispense with the Long Gallery, which had been so important in shaping the H plan, and in most of their houses it is either omitted or else forced, as at Claverton,[3] into its old inconvenient place on the top floor. They did not want the Great Hall of the courtiers or the generalized Hall of a farmhouse,

[1] R. T. Gunther, *The Architecture of Sir Roger Pratt* (Oxford, 1928), pp. 18–33.
[2] T. Fuller, *The Holy State* (1642), pp. 167–8.
[3] For plans of the now destroyed Claverton see C. J. Richardson, *Observations on the Architecture . . . of Queen Elizabeth and James I* (1837). Claverton was built in the late 1620's on a rectangular block plan.

and in their homes the Hall is turned at first into another room and at last into a mere vestibule: a process that begins at Whitehall, Shrewsbury (1518–82) (Fig. 10), and continues through Toseland,

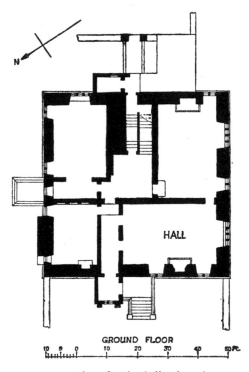

FIG. 10. *Plan of Whitehall, Shrewsbury*

Huntingdonshire (*c.* 1600), Gaythorne Hall, Westmorland (*c.* 1600–10),[1] Wharton Court, Herefordshire (Fig. 11), and Kew Palace (1631).[2] In consequence, they could house themselves within a few rooms of more or less uniform shape and size, and

[1] R.C.H.M. *Westmorland* (p. 16) and a more recent writer have both dated Gaythorne to the late sixteenth century (R. W. Brunskill in *Cumberland and Westmorland Archaeological Soc. Trans.* lvi (1957), 83–86). Both appear to have been influenced by the nature of the plasterwork in the house; but in such a remote county style and technique is more likely to be retarded than advanced, and while there may be some difficulty in putting the plasterwork into the early seventeenth century there is a greater one in putting the plan and the staircase construction into the late sixteenth. It is not a matter on which anyone can lay down the law, but for these reasons I prefer a date after rather than before 1600.

[2] J. Charlton, *Kew Palace* (M.O.W. Official Guide, 1956), p. 10.

could build on a compact plan. Cost and convenience directed
them towards the 'double-pile', and there were no counter considerations to sway them from it.

The combination of these positive and negative factors was
essential to the widespread development of this plan and explains,

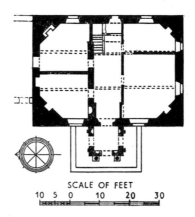

SCALE OF FEET
10  5  0      10      20      30

FIG. 11. *Plan of Wharton Court*

and is illustrated by, the buildings of some men who were socially
or economically above the ordinary gentleman or merchant or
prosperous lawyer, but yet built in their fashion. These were men
indifferent to or excluded from the court: builders of Lulworth
Castle, of Sherborne Castle, of Bolsover, of Wootton Lodge. Lulworth's history is not wholly clear, but it was probably begun by
Henry, second Viscount Bindon, a troublesome character, im-
prisoned in 1584 for his 'undutiful behaviour' towards the Queen.[1]
Sherborne was built by Raleigh, a notable courtier and one of the
greatest of 'patentees'; but it was built when he was already in

[1] H. Howard, *Memorials of the Howard Family* (Corby, 1834), pp. 17–18. Thomas
Gerard of Trent writing in the 1620's says that Lulworth was built by Thomas, 2nd
Viscount Bindon (Coker's *Survey of Dorset* (1732), p. 43). J. Hutchins (*History of
Dorset* (3rd ed. 1861, i. 374)) corroborates and adds, but without giving any source,
that the foundations were begun in 1588 and the building completed in 1609. However,
Thomas was not the second Viscount but the third; his elder brother Henry preceded
him and died in 1590 (Howard, loc. cit.). If building was begun in 1588 then it was
begun, as Gerard and Hutchins say, by the second Viscount, but by Henry and not by
Thomas. It seems likely that Gerard and Hutchins have run the two into one and that
Henry began—and planned—the building and Thomas completed it.

disgrace for his clandestine marriage to Elizabeth Throckmorton, was being accused of 'Atheism', was annoying the courtiers with his attacks on monopolies, and making himself obnoxious to the gentlemen of the House of Commons by publicly exposing their perennial sin of shifting the burden of taxation on to their poorer neighbours.[1] Bolsover was built by Sir Charles Cavendish; its limitations are shown clearly enough by the great additions that his son felt obliged to make when preparing to entertain Charles I there.[2] Wootton was begun about 1610 by Richard Fleetwood, of a very wealthy gentry family, who had sundered himself from whatever hopes he may have had of court preferment by turning Catholic about two years earlier.[3]

On the other hand, some courtiers recognized the economy of the 'double-pile' and used it as much as they could, although the very size of their houses precluded them from building a square or rectangular block. Cecil spent large sums upon Hatfield, but he would have spent larger sums and yet had no more accommodation to show for it, if he had built on an H plan with wings one room thick and not, as he did, on a U plan with 'double-pile' wings. He could, of course, do so because its great size, especially the length of the main block, made Hatfield impressive on a U plan with broad wings; smaller houses needed the apparent length of narrower wings to obtain their effect.

It is necessary to go to some trouble to establish these parallel developments and explain their causes. Firstly because these are matters of importance in themselves, and secondly because it is only when they are understood that the changes in architectural design, and to a lesser extent in architectural ornament, can be seen as a continuous process and a reflection of English history, rather than as the result of the automatic and unexplained responses

[1] It is clear, of course, that Raleigh was not an Atheist, but his views were highly suspect to the right-minded. He was singled out for attack by Parsons, and was the obvious target of a Commission of Inquiry at Cerne Abbas in 1594; see E. A. Strathmann, *Sir Walter Ralegh—A Study in Elizabethan Skepticism* (New York, 1951).

[2] Bolsover was begun in 1613; it may not have been finished at Cavendish's death in 1617 (D. Knoop and G. P. Jones, *The Bolsover Castle Building Account 1613*; R. W. Goulding, *Bolsover Castle*).

[3] M. Girouard in *C.L.* cxxv (12 Mar. 1959), 522–5.

of English patrons to foreign fashions. Because of this it is also
necessary to examine the only explicitly stated and consistently
applied interpretation of house-plans in this period, that of Dr.
Nikolaus Pevsner. As I understand his argument, Elizabethan
house-plans have their origin in the replacement of an 'aristocratic'
by a 'bourgeois' ruling-class or in the replacement, in some un-
specified way, of 'aristocratic' by 'less exacting, less disciplined'
'bourgeois' ways of life; their forms are due to a Renaissance desire
for symmetry coupled with some 'Mannerist influence'.[1]

To label such qualities as discipline or a love of comfort as in
themselves 'aristocratic' or 'bourgeois' is a question-begging pro-
cedure. There are different kinds of bourgeois; there are different
kinds of aristocrat; and if every *bourgeoisie* is unexacting and un-
disciplined, then Weber and Tawney have been deceiving us all.
One cannot help suspecting that Dr. Pevsner—who has put us all
in his debt by weaning us from some of our English insularity
—is here falling into German provincialism and seeing every
aristocracy in terms of the Prussian Junkers' conception of themselves, and every *bourgeoisie* as blood-brothers of the irresolute and
compromising German middle-classes of the Frankfurt Assembly.

As important as, and giving rise to, this looseness of formulation
is the assumption of fact. 'Bourgeois' is a very misleading description of the Tudor and Stuart nobility. It is true that nearly two-
thirds of them invested at one time and another in trading or
colonial or industrial ventures, but there were few if any who
obtained the greater part of their income from such sources, and
for most investment in these concerns was little more than a
'flutter'.[2] In any case, 'bourgeois' and 'aristocratic' are not always
mutually exclusive categories, and if the Tudor upper-classes were
ten times as 'bourgeois' as they appear to have been, they were still
undeniably 'aristocratic' and therefore, by Dr. Pevsner's definition,
still 'exacting' and 'disciplined'. Of course these plans develop

[1] N. Pevsner, 'Double Profile', *Arch. Rev.* cvii (Mar. 1950), 148. In a later and longer
account Dr. Pevsner appeared to rely wholly upon Humanism for an explanation of
these house-plans (*The Planning of the Elizabethan House*, Inaugural Lecture delivered
at Birkbeck College in 1960, printed by J. E. Ruddock and Sons, Lincoln and London).

[2] L. Stone, 'The Nobility in Business 1540–1640', *The Entrepreneur* (Research Center
in Entrepreneurial History, Harvard (1957)), pp. 14–21.

under the influence of the Renaissance desire for symmetry, but all that that desire does is to ensure that they are symmetrical; it does not determine the form that the symmetry takes, nor can it explain the progression from courtyard to 'H' to square-block plan. For this it is necessary to analyse the social needs of the builders, not by labelling them 'bourgeois' or 'aristocratic', but by investigating the actual social relations of the time.

To counter the claim of 'Mannerist influence' is less easy, mainly because of the unhistorical manner in which the term is used by its devotees. Anything that is at all odd, for example the plan of Longford Castle, can rely upon having a 'Mannerist' accusation hurled at it[1] and one can, if one wishes, call Tresham's Triangular Lodge and Liveden New Build 'Mannerist', although there is no evidence that Tresham knew or cared anything about Continental art. Again the great length of Long Galleries is called 'Mannerist', although the English Long Gallery antedates Mannerism in Italy, let alone in England. It is clear, of course, that a term which, when used within a certain art-historical context, is of great value, is being perverted by a disregard of elementary logic into a 'blanket' description of anything that has any feature in common with that art.[2] Thus it is not good enough to point out that there are resemblances between some English house-plans and selected Continental ones and to label them all as 'Mannerist'. Nor is it sufficient to attempt to save the argument by admitting the differences and seeing them as the English version of Mannerism brought about by native forces. Instead it is necessary to analyse these forces and the way in which they worked. When that is done it will be seen, I hope, that an historically determined and evolving society, applying Renaissance ideas that had themselves been introduced by one of the elements in that society, worked in several ways upon native building practice to produce the house-plans of the Elizabethans and Jacobeans. This does not, of course, mean that no Englishmen consciously or unconsciously

[1] E. Wüsten, *Die Architektur des Manierismus in England* (Leipzig, 1951), pp. 225–7.
[2] How far this habit can go is shown by Wüsten (op. cit., p. 201), who has discovered 'Mannerism' in Gothic architecture. His more historically-minded predecessors had been content to show that there are 'Gothic' elements in Mannerism.

copied Mannerist exemplars, but that if any did so their copying occurred within, and was determined by, this broader framework.

It is with these house plans in mind that the nature and history of English architecture in our period must be discussed. From about 1525 'English architecture' in a wholly new way means something over and above 'English building'. For the first time, to any significant extent, English houses were designed as nothing but residences and as an artistic whole, instead of being forced into a form dictated by other considerations, or conceived of as so many bays of building or so many buildings associated only by their functions. This, however, was a large-scale and costly business; and it coincided with the cessation of church building. In consequence, for nearly a century English architecture was essentially the architecture of the mansions and manor-houses of the countryside, and the smaller yeomen's houses, restricted by lack of wealth, and town houses, often restricted for the same reason and nearly always by a confined site, are a very minor part of it. They are sometimes examples of architectural decoration, they are important evidence for the social historian, and they must figure prominently in any history of building, and especially of timber-framing, technique; but they are not relevant to the main theme of English architecture in this period.[1]

At the same time any discussion of that architecture must at first exclude from its terms of reference the nature, but not the disposition, of its ornament. In any period such a distinction is generally useful; in this it is essential. Conscious design was then the new and decisive feature of domestic architecture, and although it is possible, it is fruitless to express the differences between Sutton Place, Longleat, and Hatfield in terms of a difference in ornament. Such an analysis, as J. A. Gotch long ago discovered,[2] reveals nothing but a disconnected succession, when not a complete confusion, of apparently arbitrary styles, and is in any case quite

[1] A critical bibliography of the published material upon these lesser buildings is being prepared by Mr. J. T. Smith for the Vernacular Architecture Group. Four parts have already been issued and typescript copies are deposited in the British Museum and in the library of the Society of Antiquaries.

[2] Gotch, *Architecture of the Renaissance in England*, i, pp. xxi–xxii.

inapplicable to a vast number of imposing houses that had almost no decoration at all. If, however, the history of that architecture is conceived of as a succession of attempts to weld houses with a specific social function into a coherent design, then a continuous progress can be seen, and it can be shown that the great Jacobean houses are less the productions of architectural publicists in Italy and of pattern-book makers in Flanders, than of the Renaissance-trained servants of the absolute State in England.

In attempting this, it is perhaps best to begin with a considera-tion of Longleat, because it was the first completely extrovert courtyard house, and therefore the first in which the problem of a symmetrical design for four long fronts had to be tackled. Com-pared with both earlier and later buildings, Longleat is noticeable for its very slight vertical emphasis. Its façades are broken up by bays, but of small, and all of equal, projection. Its entrance is emphasized now by nothing more than flanking columns to a pedimented doorway (Pl. 1a) and, unless the original design intro-duced a deliberate discordance, it could never have been highly emphasized. Sir John Summerson has called Longleat the 'Momen-tary High Renaissance of our Architecture';[1] and it was momentary indeed. Neither Longleat nor its builder, Sir John Thynne, was unknown; his Wiltshire neighbour, 'Wild Will' Darrell, made great fun of Thynne's constant preoccupation with the decorative details,[2] and there is a contemporary or nearly contemporary plan of Longleat at Hatfield.[3] The building was a famous one in the later years of the sixteenth century, and yet its design was never copied nor in essentials borrowed from. Darrell's jeers suggest why, for it was Thynne's continual alteration of details—of the order of a column, of the carving of a frieze—that he ridiculed. To contemporaries these matters, though important, were not the essential parts of a design; rather they were subordinate to such considerations as the contrast of bold masses, and the emphasizing of the ends and central features of a façade. In essence Longleat was an Italian town house greatly enlarged, and set down in the

[1] Summerson, *Architecture in Britain 1530–1830*, p. 33.
[2] For Darrell's remarks see J. A. Jackson in *Wilts. Archaeological Mag.* xxiii (1887), 29.
[3] A photostat copy is in the B.M. Mss. Dept. Facs. 372.

English countryside. In some circumstances such a translation might have been successful enough, but the taste of the time, for all its parade of classicism, was yet sufficiently close to the traditional to be unable to break with it completely. Towers and battlements and imposing entrances were still in demand, and Longleat played its part in later development, not as an influence, but as an example of what to avoid. It is for this very reason that its 'High Renaissance' features were so momentary; not because they were not known but because they were not liked.[1]

Although this preference is not easy to demonstrate from written sources, partly because they are few but mainly because their way of expressing themselves is not free from ambiguity, it is possible to adduce some evidence in favour of it. A contemporary evaluation of such an ornamental flat façade as that of Longleat is suggested in Sidney's encomium in *Arcadia* of Kalander's house:

> The house itselfe was built of faire and strong stone, not affecting so much any extraordinary kinde of finenes, as an honorable representing of a firme statelines. The lightes, doores and staires, rather directed to the use of the guest, than to the eye of the Artificer: and yet as the one cheefly heeded, so the other not neglected; each place handsome without curiositie, and homely without lothsomenes: . . . all more lasting then beautifull, but that the consideration of the exceeding lastingnesse made the eye beleeve it was exceeding beautifull.[2]

The impression left by this, with its emphasis on 'statelines' and 'exceeding lastingnesse' and its comparative neglect of 'extraordinary finenes' and 'curiositie', is also produced by Dr. Francis

[1] The contrast between contemporary comment on Longleat and the equally grand Theobalds is impressive. There is no record of anyone's admiring Longleat in the late sixteenth century; Hatton in 1579 said that he had built Holdenby in imitation of Theobalds (Brooks, *Sir Christopher Hatton*, p. 158) and Northumberland, when preparing to build in 1603, singled out Copt Hall and Theobalds as worthy of imitation (H.M.C. *Cecil*, xv. 383). Unfortunately it is difficult to know just what it was about Theobalds that was admired, for, despite Sir John Summerson's imaginative reconstruction ('The Building of Theobalds 1564–1583', *Archaeologia*, xcvii (1959), 107), less is known about its exterior than that of Nonsuch. Northumberland expressly referred to 'curiosities' and it may well be that it was the famous interior decorations that he hoped to borrow from. The point, however, still stands; Theobalds was admired, Longleat was not.

[2] *Works*, ed. A. Feuillerat (Cambridge, 1912), i. 15.

Andrewes's praise, in some doggerel verses on Bolsover, of 'Hard-wick for hugeness, Worsope for height' and the further praise of Worksop as 'Statelie'.[1] Here again it is the effect of mass, and, of course, of contrasted masses, that has most impressed the observer.

This was true not only of the great houses but of the smaller as well. The entrance front of Poundisford Park, built in the mid-century, resembles Longleat in its avoidance of bold projections, and although it has the end bays and the symmetrically balanced entry so common in later years, they are in almost the same plane as the main face. Poundisford, however, resembles Longleat in something else; its manner was not copied. On the contrary, the wholly different manner of the contemporary or slightly earlier Barrington Court, with its long wings and its dominant porch, became almost universal (Pl. 1b). At the much later and greater Hatfield (1607–12), the façade with projecting wings is made the entrance front (Pl. 4), while that in more or less one plane is the neglected 'backside' (Pl. 5).[2] Wimbledon (c. 1588) was a bold example: the entrance front, approached by several double-ramps, was set deeply between very long and narrow wings (Pl. 2a), but at the rear there were only slight projections.[3] The manner of design was a consequence of the half-H plan, but it was not an inevitable consequence; for Poundisford was built on the same plan. It was therefore not solely the half-H plan that determined the design, although that plan facilitated a particular manner, but an aesthetic preference, derived from the old society that was still present beneath the new State form, in favour of effect by mass and not by decoration.

After Longleat and Poundisford the use of large masses

[1] B.M. Harl. Mss. 4955, No. 27. From his reference to Cavendish as 'Viscount Mansfield', Andrewes must have written his verses between 1620 and 1628. He did not, of course, regard the qualities here quoted as the only, or even the most important, virtues; taste was changing by then, but even then these qualities were worthy of praise.

[2] That the south front was the original entrance front has recently been established by Mr. L. Stone; *Arch. Journ.* cxii (1955), 123.

[3] Wimbledon was pulled down early in the eighteenth century. Its date is known, apart from what can be surmised from grants of the manor to Thomas Cecil, from the inscription over the entry recorded by Aubrey (*The Natural History and Antiquities of Surrey*, i (1719), 14–15). Its appearance is preserved in engravings of the north and south fronts made by H. Winstanley in 1678.

projecting boldly from a main face became the rule, and the use of shallow bays in association only with other shallow bays ended. The great courtyard house at Burghley was given its present form from 1577 onwards, and there Longleat's uniform and shallow projections were wholly avoided. The entrance front has the greatest possible amount of broken surface and contrasting mass; the end bays project boldly forward and are further emphasized by turrets, rising above the main roof-line, that give them the aspect of towers; the entry is heavily emphasized with similar turrets that combine in the skyline with those of the end bays. Burghley was one of the last of the great courtyard houses to be built, but at Wollaton (1580–8) (Pl. 8) and Hardwick (1590–7)[1] and in the side elevations of the larger H type houses the same effect was striven for. An early example is Castle Ashby, begun in the 1570's or 1580's on a half-H plan. The ends of the wings are here raised one story above the level of the range and are further emphasized by octagonal turrets rising another story above them (Pl. 3a). At Hardwick Hall the long façade is terminated at each end by square bays which project boldly from the main face and rise a full story above the main block (Pl. 3b). At Hatfield the south wings have each three slightly projecting bays, lower in height than the wing itself, and at the end a square tower of greater projection than the bays and rising higher than the wings (Pl. 4). Perhaps the boldest use of all such terminal towers is at a house with an eccentric plan—the triangular Longford Castle (c. 1588) in Wiltshire, where the highly ornamented façade is terminated by two massive round bastions that break boldly forward from the main plane (Pl. 2b).

These contrasted masses are saved from heaviness and given, as Muthesius says, 'a spirit of vigour, of the joys of life, of good cheer',[2] by the equal contrast between the solid walling and the vast windows. While Hardwick and Howsham—'more glass than

---

[1] Gotch, nodding for once, dates Hardwick to 1576. B. Stalleybrass, 'Bess of Hardwick's Buildings and Buildings Accounts', *Archaeologia*, lxiv (1913), 347–89, has put the date beyond dispute.

[2] 'ein Geist der Frische, Lebensfreude und Gemütlichkeit'; H. Muthesius, *Das englische Haus* (Berlin, 1908), i. 41.

wall'—are out of the ordinary they are only the extreme form of a universal type. In part we may agree with Frey, without condoning his racialist nonsense about Anglo-Saxon blood, that these great windows derive from the late-Gothic mason's and the contemporary carpenter's method of building a weight-bearing skeleton;[1] in part, as we shall see later, they had a decorative function; in part, however, they are intended by their height and their never-ending expanse to emphasize the height and length of the block. In later years, as the long façades of courtyard and H plan houses gave way to the shorter ones of the square-block plan, windows were not only fewer, they were smaller; and this in houses whose character showed that their designers knew nothing of Palladianism and its dogmas about the relation of voids to solids.

Another problem of design in these great houses was that of emphasizing the entrance, both because of the tradition of making the entry imposing and because of the need to punctuate the central portion of a long front. Even in such earlier introvert houses as Sutton Place and Hengrave Hall, begun in 1525, the entrance was singled out for display. At Worksop the entrance, in the centre of the elevation, was heavily emphasized, with a projecting porch-bay that rose above the roof and above the level of the flanking end bays.[2] The most striking example of all is probably Brereton Hall in Cheshire, which was built about 1586. Here the entrance dominates the elevation even more than at Burghley. Twin towers project boldly from the main front, well beyond the plane of the end bays, and are carried, as the bays are not, above roof height, where they are joined by a pointed arch. There are bands of enriched panelling above and below the windows between these towers, and they are the only ornament in the composition (Pl. 6a). A comparison of Brereton with Layer

[1] D. Frey, *Englisches Wesen in der bildenden Kunst* (Stuttgart, 1942), pp. 177–96.
[2] Worksop, which has long since disappeared, is illustrated in a drawing by Richard Hall in R. Thoroton, *Antiquities of Nottinghamshire* (1677), p. 458, and in a drawing by S. Buck in the Bodleian. The latter has been reproduced by Summerson (*Architecture in Britain*, pl. 17 a), who dates the building to before 1590. From Hall's drawing it is reasonably clear that, unlike most of its contemporaries, Worksop was not built in one operation, but that an early-sixteenth-century house was probably altered, and certainly heightened, in later years.

Marney (*c.* 1522) reveals the two aspects of the development of design in the sixteenth century: the old tendency to emphasize the entry continues and so at Brereton it is still made as imposing as it had been at Layer Marney; on the other hand, the symmetrical balancing of masses is a new necessity, and so the entrance at Brereton, unlike Layer Marney, is not isolated but is related to the flanking masses at the ends of the elevation.

In the early years of the seventeenth century great courtyard houses were very rare, but there were institutions, the Oxford and Cambridge colleges, for example, whose role in society had changed little and who continued to build around a courtyard, for the very good reason that they had the same needs as their predecessors had had. Further, they continued, again with the same good reason, to build inward-looking courtyards. In the building at the Oxford colleges at this time—at Worcester, Lincoln, the Fellows' Quadrangle at Merton—the exterior elevations are almost ignored, and design and decoration are concentrated on the courtyard. Yet they were not wholly ignored; for as the traditional plan was continued, so too was the traditional importance of the entry. The Parks Road elevation of Wadham College, built in 1610–13, reveals its date by its symmetry and partly by its slight emphasis on the ends of the façade, brought forward as shallow bays. The heaviest emphasis, however, is on the central entrance, with its oriel window and its square tower rising above the roof level. A building outside the Universities but with a similar traditional corporate role, Abbot's Hospital at Guildford, begun in 1619,[1] has the entrance as the most dominant unit of the street front. The influence of taste and of the general manner of design was strong enough to ensure that these institutions did not build in a wholly medieval fashion. Their especial and largely unchanged role in society prevented them, by its effect both on their plans and on their aesthetic and intellectual predilections, from building wholly in the prevailing mode. The result was that many of their buildings continued the forms and styles of the preceding quarter-century.[2]

[1] A. Onslow, *Life of Dr. George Abbot* (1778), p.28.
[2] As almshouses lost their community and college character, although there are exceptions such as Morden's College at Blackheath, they became merely so many

The results of a similar interaction between a functionally-determined plan and personal or general taste can be seen in the use of balustrading and cresting along the fronts of these great houses. Balustrading is used on so many houses that its appearance might appear to be dictated wholly by the opportunity it provided for using classical motifs. In fact there are strict limitations on that use which suggest that while classical fashion played its part, other fashions also played theirs; and in many cases fashion of any sort was subordinate to other considerations. There were great houses where other motifs were used along with balustrading; the initials of Bess of Hardwick at Hardwick (Pl. 3b), strapwork cresting at Wollaton. There were other buildings with cresting but no balustrading: a series of religious texts at Castle Ashby (Pl. 3a),[1] crenellation at the Schools and at Wadham College in Oxford. That it was the great size of the large houses that brought the necessity for some sort of cresting is shown by its more sparing use on minor ones. The theme was socially determined; the variations upon it by the individual's taste; and that taste by a great number of factors, a nostalgia for the old society or family pride or a liking for foreign tricks or an inexplicable idiosyncrasy.

In summary, the general design of the exterior elevations of these greater courtyard houses progresses from an asymmetrical elevation, with the main emphasis on the entrance, to a symmetrical elevation with the main entrance-piece and the ends in a coherent design; and within that design the entrance often loses its dominance and becomes one unit among its peers. The effects are achieved in the main by the use of related and contrasted masses, and this follows from the problem, rooted in native conditions, of giving symmetry and coherence to a very long façade. It is possible to derive this type of design—with the masses in the centre and at the ends—from Nonsuch, begun in 1538 for Henry VIII, and probably the most famous of all English houses in the six-

dwellings under one roof and often abandoned the courtyard plan. For many illustrations and plans of almshouses see W. H. Godfrey, *The English Almshouse* (1955).

[1] At Audley End the Earl of Suffolk incorporated into the cresting of the now-destroyed principal court an apophthegm that all servants of the absolute State did well to remember: 'Sapientis est in consilio fortunam semper habere' (L. Magolotti, *Travels of Cosmo III, Grand Duke of Tuscany* (1821), p. 203).

teenth century. Such a derivation, however, has little meaning: the designers of these houses could only copy Nonsuch, if copy it they did, because they had the same problem, and they had that because they had the same type of house. This does not mean that every element of their design was determined by the plan and function of these buildings; clearly there are great differences between Nonsuch and Burghley and Audley End, but in their use and disposition of architectural masses these houses are alike.

Courtyard houses have, however, both an interior and exterior aspect, and even in the largest courtyard the amount of space is limited, and the use of great projecting masses is both practically inconvenient and aesthetically overpowering. Emphasis must therefore be more or less in the same plane as the elevation and must be obtained by linear patterning and by decoration. It may also be obtained by a greater height, but here again there is a limit to the height that is aesthetically appropriate. In these circumstances such a feature as the 'frontispiece', a highly decorated entry from outside the building into the Hall or its lobby, played an important part in the architecture of the time. On the frontispiece classical elements could be used to the best effect, for emphasis could be obtained by columns and pilasters that stood out sharply from the main elevation, not solely because of their bulk but also because of their differing quality. Such early examples as that at Kirby (1572) (Pl. 6b) and Burghley (1585) are placed upon boldly projecting porches, crowned with decoration that rises above the height of the main elevation. The ultimate form of the frontispiece in great courtyards is seen not in any buildings for private individuals, but in the Oxford colleges, such as Merton, Wadham, and St. John's, and in the Schools, all erected in the early seventeenth century. Like some of their predecessors, they all rise above the general height of the building, but unlike most of them they are of very slight projection. They achieve their effect not by their bulk, not so very much by their height, but by their decoration. And that decoration is enhanced, as it is not at Burghley, for example, by its qualitative difference from the rest of the building, by its being the only classical element in a 'Gothic' or traditional façade (Pl. 21).[1]

Similar changes occur in the H and half-H houses of the period. The early ones, Montacute, or Doddington or Condover, completed in 1598, generally emphasize the centre of the elevation within the wings with a porch, of great projection and carried up above the height of the main façade. This has little decoration and, except on the entrance floor, where there are the inevitable flanking columns to the doorway, nothing at all like a frontispiece. After the turn of the century frontispieces in these houses became very common[1] and the decoration gradually crept up the whole of the porch front. At Charlton, Kent, it is not confined to the ground story; the first story also has its columns and the second story is richly ornamented. At Bramshill (1605–12) there is an even more elaborately decorated example, with the ornament applied equally richly on all three stories (Pl. 7b).

The intention behind this usage in the great courtyard houses and in houses on an H and half-H plan is illustrated by a consideration of the use in some smaller houses. North Cadbury Court (c. 1581) and Newton Surmaville, built a full generation later, were houses whose main façades had no wing returns to obtain emphasis from, and their fronts were punctuated by two bay projections equidistant from the ends (Pl. 9). One of these was the entrance-porch, and it was a canon of contemporary taste that it should be emphasized; but to emphasize it overmuch would make it differ sharply from its twin, and offend against the other canon—of symmetry. Caught in this contradiction, the designers of these houses compromised as best they could: they gave the entrance some emphasis, but eschewed that which a frontispiece would have afforded. This contradiction between symmetry and the need to emphasize the entrance is also shown by Burton Agnes (1600–3) and Chastleton, begun in 1602. Each has a very small courtyard and therefore a not very long façade. Each has two bay projections along the elevation, spaced at equal distances from the ends. Adhering strictly to the demands of symmetry, the entrance is put, not in the front, but at the side of one of the bays, where it

---

[1] They were sometimes added, as at Browsholme, Yorks., to existing façades, T. L. Parker, *Browsholme Hall* (1815), pp. 1–10; *Yorkshire Archaeological Journ.* xx (1909), 464–7.

is invisible from the exterior. Symmetry is therefore not offended if it is more highly decorated than any other part, and so a magnificent frontispiece is placed upon it. Thus symmetry is maintained, the entrance is, at least formally, highly emphasized, and the fashions of the great are triumphantly followed.

Comparatively short elevations were unable to achieve the easy mass rhythm either of the courtyard houses with their terminal towers and central entrance tower or of the H and half-H houses with their flanking wings and central porch. Therefore their builders either avoid frontispieces, as at North Cadbury and Newton Surmaville, or they accommodate them by a trick which in effect renders them almost purposeless. Within the large courtyards frontispieces were a necessary ornament; in the H and half-H houses they were a useful reinforcement of the emphasis; in others they were an embarrassment.

H and half-H houses show some resemblance to the courtyard houses in their side elevations as well; for these, generally accommodating a Long Gallery, are often very long and have that at least in common with a courtyard elevation. Sometimes, for example at Charlton (Pl. 26), they are punctuated with towers, but in general, as at Doddington, only a shallow projection is used or else, as at Montacute, an oriel is considered sufficient.

This avoidance of towers and similar projections was not due to any dislike of them, or to a differing view of the need for architectural emphasis. Rather, it was that the form of these houses supplied its own punctuation, in the deeply projecting wings on either side of a recessed central front. In some cases, at Charlton, Hatfield, and Quenby, and formerly at Wimbledon (Pl. 2a), the roofs of the wings are kept low and out of sight and an impression of a cliff-like mass is given. At the very late Quenby no balustrading or cresting is used to crown the elevation, and the effect of mass is seen here in its boldest form (Pl. 17b). These, however, were exceptions. Wimbledon and Hatfield were among the biggest houses of their period and were built by men very close to the court. Such men were more likely to abandon vernacular practices, and so they used gables in the early period of the courtyard house more frequently than later on. At Burghley, the Hall (begun *c.* 1556) has a large gable, but in the later building gables are rigorously avoided. At Gorhambury, as an eighteenth-century water-colour shows, the entrance front of the original building of 1563–8 has two large gables flanking a smaller central gable; the gallery wing added in 1577 at the end of that front dispenses with them as far as possible. With the appearance of the H and half-H houses the gable came back, for the gable was one of the best-known and most impressive methods of ending a roof-line; but even among these houses the larger ones, as the examples given above suggest, often strove to hide their gables or else to minimize them.[1]

A comparison of Montacute and Doddington with the nearly contemporary smaller houses of Bishop's Hull (*c.* 1586) and King-ston Maurward, completed in 1591, illustrates this tendency. At Montacute the wing gables are of the ornamental 'Dutch' type, and above the porch and between the wings are modest semicircles of stone linked by balustrading. At Doddington this hesitancy in gable treatment was even more marked, and the wings were emphasized by a mere stone semicircle, a trick that is half-way towards the flat-topped manner of Wimbledon and Quenby.[2] The contrast with Bishop's Hull and Kingston Maurward (Pl. 10*a*) is clear. There the compositions are dominated by the large straight wing-gables, which at Bishop's Hull stand out not only by their size and boldness, but also by the absence from the wing front of any fenestration apart from a small two-light window in the gable itself. The difference between the two treatments—of Doddington and of Bishop's Hull—is the result of the differing conceptions of men to whom the gable was an embarrassing conse-quence of the plans of their houses, and of men to whom the gable was an element that could be made to play its part in the design.

It is necessary to emphasize this point because houses like Kings-ton Maurward and Bishop's Hull are not mere buildings in which

---

[1] To some extent this absence of gables from the larger houses may be due to removal by later generations; the towers of the north front at Hatfield, for example, appear to have been gabled originally; L. Stone in *Arch. Journ.* cxii (1955), 124.

[2] The wings of the entrance front at Doddington are now finished in the Wimbledon and Quenby manner; the original treatment can be seen in J. Kip and L. Knyff, *Britannia Illustrata* (1708), p. 63.

design is of little importance. On the contrary, their main fronts have a very careful symmetry, and the gables do not intrude into that symmetry and are not irrelevant to it, but are used to emphasize it. These houses are thus very different from such earlier ones as Holcombe Court and Sandford Orcas, where gables are used, not in a symmetrical composition, but with a fine careless disregard for symmetry at all. There the gable is a structural feature that is content to be that and nothing else; in the later houses it is one that has considerable aesthetic thought spent upon it and is made to play its considered part in a deliberate design.

This progression, however, towards treating the gable as part of the design was not achieved all at once, and in the last thirty years of the sixteenth century the increasing consciousness of the aesthetic problem presented by gables often showed itself in attempts at decorating them. At Eastbury, built about 1572, the gables on all the elevations are finished with elaborately moulded brick finials at the sides and apex; at Water Eaton, Oxfordshire (c. 1585), those on the main front have obelisk finials and corbelled kneelers. At Wakehurst Place and at Gravetye, both in Sussex and built in the 1590's,[1] the gables are heavily loaded with decoration, with elaborate ball finials with jewel ornament at Wakenhurst, and with finials carried on scrolled and triglyphed brackets at Gravetye.

This decorative treatment was, however, a false trail, and the true path was towards an increasingly subtle rhythm in the placing of similar and of contrasting gables. At Loseley, Surrey (1562–8), the siting of different sized straight gables has become complex; two large gables on the wings flank the composition, and between them are two smaller ones with three yet smaller in the intervals between these four (Pl. 11a). That their relationship was intended to play a major part in emphasizing the unity of the design is shown by the contrast between their symmetrical placing and deliberate rhythm and the asymmetry and irregularity of the fenestration. Often straight-sided gables were used by themselves until the end of the period, but it became increasingly common to use them in conjunction with curved gables, and to use curved

---

[1] W. H. Blaauw in *Sussex Archaeological Collections*, x (1858), 166–7; V.C.H. *Sussex*, vii. 165–6.

gables, either similar or with contrasting silhouettes, alone. In general, although curved gables are to be found at Montacute and on the exterior of Kirby, they occur late, and in many districts, particularly in the stone districts, hardly appear at all; and when they do appear in these parts are nearly always on fairly large houses, with many gables. For this there were good reasons. Where straight-sided gables are used alone they can be made to vary only in size or in the amount of decoration lavished upon them; but the practice of heavily decorating gables declined about the turn of the century, and it was not always convenient or possible to vary gable sizes. In such circumstances the necessary variety of treatment could be obtained by the contrasted use of straight-sided and curved gables, or of curved gables with contrasting profiles. This is not to say that curved gables were invented or introduced for this purpose, but that their potentialities in this way helped them to spread.

Although the use of related gables became widespread around 1600, it had appeared in some houses many years before: Barrington Court and Loseley have already been referred to. Yet, probably because of its complexity, the Loseley formula was generally eschewed in later years. At Condover straight gables are used over the wings and between the wings and the central porch, but the porch itself is emphasized with a curved gable flanked by two small obelisks. At Burton Agnes the straight gables of the wings and the central portion are contrasted, not with curved gables, but with strapwork cresting over the projecting porches. This, however, was a somewhat unusual variation of a manner which, without ever ousting the use of straight gables alone, became increasingly common in the smaller houses and persisted to a very late date. It is, of course, the plan of the H or half-H house which very largely determines this use of five related gables along a front, and as late as 1625 Stibbington Hall in Huntingdonshire follows the same system as Condover.

Not every house, however, was built on an H or half-H plan, and the increasing skill of the builders of the smaller houses is seen by their use of gables to provide architectural effect along elevations in which they got no help in achieving emphasis from projecting wings. A comparison between North Cadbury Court and Newton Surmaville (Pl. 9) is of interest here. Both houses are in Somerset, and both have two large bays along the main elevation but no terminal wings or projections. At North Cadbury four small identical gables are arranged regularly along the roof, but have no relation to the bays and the first two stories and play little part in punctuating the design. At Newton Surmaville the four small gables have become three large ones sited to occupy all the sky-line between and flanking the two bays and, by this considered relationship, unifying and punctuating the whole front. This was not a trick that was known only in Somerset. Moyns Park in Essex, of uncertain date but probably built at some time between the building of the first two, solves a similar problem in a similar manner. It is in this that the smaller houses contrast with many of the later larger houses such as Holland House or Apethorpe (*c.* 1623), whose builders never got beyond the banality of putting along a roof-line as many small and often over-decorated gables as they could pack in.

At the same time, these non-courtyard houses with their shorter elevations and greater relative height, and with their roof-lines emphasized by gables, were able to deal better with the aesthetic problem that chimneys presented to those who insisted upon symmetry and classicism. In the greater houses, at first, as at Hampton Court, the convenient medieval habit was continued of putting chimneys where they were wanted, and aestheticism was conciliated by lavishing decoration upon the shafts. Even in later years shafts were often highly decorated: at Hardwick they have a double-jewel ornament, and at Somerset House in 1609–10 chimney shafts were 'polished and ranced'.[1] Such half-hearted compromises as Hampton Court shows could, however, not be used for the later great houses that consciously attempted a classical effect; and two other methods were tried. The first was to disguise the shafts as single or coupled classical columns, as at Kirby and Burghley, and in the royal buildings at Newmarket in 1619–20, where cut bricks were used in the 'Tuscan heads' of chimney shafts.[2] The second method, used at Longleat and, in combination

[1] P.R.O. E. 351–3244.                    [2] P.R.O. E. 351–3253.

with the first, at Burghley, was to hide the chimneys amidst a forest of turrets and cupolas and cresting that made up the sky-line. This method was followed, in a modified way, in a house as late as Audley End. Yet whichever method was used, the users were admitting that chimneys were a nuisance to them and that they had no answer to the problem of incorporating them into a design.

The solution was found by the builders of the smaller houses. They had, of course, the conditions for a solution at hand: the peculiar plans of their houses, often an H or half-H, the greater height and shorter length, and the confirmed use of the gable as an element in the design. They had far more chimneys to use relative to the length of the building, and they had a far shorter roof-line to string them along. Their problem, therefore, was not the insoluble one of dealing with any individual chimney but of dealing with many chimneys related to one another and to the other elements in the design. As with most problems, once it had been correctly posed it was only a question of time—in this case a short time—before human wit solved it, by concentrating the chimneys together and achieving an effect, not by any decoration placed upon them, but by their mass and its relationship with the lines of the elevation. An early example is Condover, where the chimneys are arranged in detached groups along the main axis, with a group along the axis of each wing. In later houses this became very common, and a remarkable instance occurs at Hatfield. Hatfield is a great house, but its wings, comparatively short and two and three rooms thick, permit that concentration of chimneys typical of the smaller houses. The end of each wing is emphasized by a regiment of twelve chimneys arranged, in order to get the maximum effect, parallel with the axis, not of the wing, but of the main block (Pl. 4). In great houses, however, chimneys were still not wholly welcome as an element in the façade, and it is therefore not surprising that the culmination of the use of massed chimneys is at a smaller house, Lilford in Northamptonshire, built about 1635. Thirteen chimney stacks, their length increased by the regular space between each and their unity emphasized by the continuous capping over all, occupy the centre of the roof-line and dominate the garden-front (Pl. 11b).

This, however, for all its success, was the simpler way of treating a roof-line. Another way was to relate the chimneys to one another by massing them in groups and relating these masses in turn to the other elements of the façade, particularly to the gables. A tentative method was employed at Wraxall Manor in Dorset, in the early seventeenth century, and at Poundisford Park, where the chimneys are made to issue from and to crown the gables. More frequently an attempt was made to alternate the chimneys in a rhythm with the gables. There is an early instance at Cobham Hall, and an unusual one at Batemans at Burwash in Sussex (c. 1634). Formally, Batemans has an asymmetrical front, with a large gable over a projecting wing at one end and a small gable above the porch at the other; but above that end rise six ranked chimneys, dominating the roof-line and balancing the great gable at the other end. A more regular example and one of the most successful is at Anderson Manor in Dorset, built about twelve years before. The usual three-gabled front is here held together and unified by two rows of massed chimneys occupying the space between the wings and the central porch and completing the vertical emphasis (Pl. 10b). This may be considered as a mature solution of the problem of combining all the parts of a building of the time into a unified design.

Such smaller houses as Anderson Manor succeeded better at this than the contemporary 'Prodigy Houses'. The builders of the latter, especially of the courtyard houses and to a lesser degree of the larger H type houses, were attempting to attain a classic air from essentially native buildings. This was not merely a question of putting classical decoration upon a non-classical building. It was more fundamental than that, for if we abstract the decoration —the columns, and friezes, and pediments—the contradiction still remains. It resulted from trying to treat buildings whose functions were still of a partly feudal nature in a classical fashion: an attempt which involved the designers of these long-façaded houses in the contradiction of using such non-classical elements as towers and crenellations in an attempt to obtain a symmetrical and classical effect.

It was not, however, solely this contradiction between the

function of their houses and the form they attempted to give them that led to a clash of conceptions in the façade; the ambivalent attitude of these men towards the old and the new—clinging to the one and yet striving to exploit the other—was also reflected in their architecture. Such a house as Longford used deliberately old-fashioned round towers to flank an up-to-date arcaded front (Pl. 2b). Even in the later great houses of the period the same contradictions appear. The Secretary of Cosmo of Tuscany, travelling in 1669 and judging buildings by the standards of Italy, remarked of Audley End: 'The architecture of the palace, though it was only built sixty years ago, is nevertheless not regular but inclines to the Gothic mixed with a little Doric and Ionic.'[1] Probably the writer did not mean anything very closely definable by 'Gothic', but at least he intended his readers to understand that Audley End was an unclassical house with some classical elements.

The builders of the smaller houses, on the other hand, were not in the ambiguous position of their more important contemporaries. Their social status did not render it necessary for them to build palaces, nor was a classical air of such moment to them as to men with greater pretensions. The form of their buildings allowed them to use such traditional features as prominent gables and chimneys, and their addiction to the fashionable classicism was not strong enough to hinder that use. In contrast, then, to the houses of the courtiers with such nostalgically feudal elements as towers and gateways in a generally classical design, these lesser men used traditional elements with no aristocratic connotations in a design that, but for its general symmetry, had little classical character. In so doing, they achieved, despite the smaller scale of their houses, far more integration of design than was possible in the extended elevations of the greater houses.

As the plans of the courtyard and H and half-H houses affected their design, so too did the plans of the 'double-pile' houses affect theirs. In 1600, however, these were comparatively new and rare, and the means of design of the H and half-H houses, especially of the smaller ones often erected by men of the same social status, were applied to them. Such widely scattered examples as

[1] L. Magolotti, *Travels of Cosmo III, Grand Duke of Tuscany* (1821), pp. 203-4.

Whitehall near Shrewsbury (1578–82) (Pl. 12a), the Wiltshire houses of Boyton (c. 1618) (Pl. 12b), Keevil (c. 1611), and Upper Upham (c. 1599),[1] and Toseland in Huntingdonshire (Pl. 14b) all have vernacular gables in a regular rhythm along their fronts, most of them have a deeply projecting porch, generally of two stories, and sometimes, as at Toseland and Upper Upham, flanked by bay-windows. Their chimneys are prominent and so too are their broad multi-light windows, imitating those of the long ranges of the greater houses.

There were, however, some men building on a square block plan who did not belong to the court circle but were of more wealth and standing than the builders of Keevil and Boyton, and who tended therefore in their aesthetic views to follow the lead of the builders of the greater houses. Thus they eschewed gables and instead masked the roofs with crenellations, as at Lulworth (Pl. 13a) and Bolsover (Pl. 16a), or with an abrupt stop to the façade in the Quenby manner, as originally at Wootton Lodge. At the same time they attempted to get a façade similar to that of the greater houses, with projecting bastions at Lulworth or pronounced angle-buttresses at Bolsover or projecting canted bays at Wootton. The more aristocratic nature of their houses was appreciated by a writer of fifty years ago who noted that Caverswall Castle—built on a rectangular block plan, probably by Matthew Cradock, a wool merchant of Stafford—follows its neighbour, Wootton, but in a humbler manner.[2]

The failure of these established ways, so effective in the H and half-H houses, to achieve a successful design when applied to the new type of house is shown by the simultaneous rise to dominance of the square-block plan and the disappearance of the old method of design. That method needed a great amount of room, and this was denied it by the shorter façades and the absence of wings. The

[1] H. Brakspear, 'Notes on Upper Upham Manor House', *Wilts. Archaeological Mag.* xxviii (1894–6), 84–86.

[2] *C.L.* xxix (17 June 1911), 886–95. The castellations at Caverswall appear to be modern. A view in Plot's *Natural History of Staffordshire* (Oxford, 1686) shows balustrading along the roof, and Plot's words—'not altogether unlike a castellated mansion' (p. 448)—suggest that it was not castellated. As at Wootton, the balustrading itself may not have been original.

gables and chimneys could be given no relationship to the rest of the elevation; the deeply projecting porch was inadequately balanced by the slight bay-windows, or not balanced at all, and the broad multi-light windows inherited from houses with long ranges were ill-proportioned to the shorter wall-space. The classic 'double-pile' houses, Coleshill, Thorpe Hall, the original Kingston Lacey, Eltham Lodge, and Ramsbury Manor, eschewed all of these elements, together with the bastions and crenellations of Lulworth and Bolsover.

It is possible, indeed it is usual, to ascribe the characteristics of this classic type to the Palladianism of Jones and his followers or to the Mannerism of Peter Mills or the 'Dutch' proclivities of Hugh May. It would be folly to say that such views are wrong, for clearly they contain a large amount of truth, but at the same time it is over-simplification to think that they adequately explain the appearance of these houses. In the first place these new methods of architectural design could only be applied in the mid-seventeenth century because English society had developed the English house to a point where the compact 'double-pile' and not the long courtyard and H-type plan was dominant. Palladianism and Mannerism, it must be remembered, were nothing new in the mid-seventeenth century and Holland was not one of the newly discovered territories. Many men of earlier years were well enough acquainted with these styles,[1] but only rarely, and never in building a complete 'courtier' house, did they employ them. Such styles could only be employed when the 'courtier' type plan had given way to the 'double-pile'.

Secondly, the classic type of double-pile house did not emerge out of the air; on the contrary, it has quite a long history, and a clear development can be traced in which the designers gradually abandon the old methods and approach the later manner. Such a house as Kew Palace has reduced the gable to little more than the backcloth to a dormer-window, and Forty Hall, Enfield, and

---

[1] In a letter to Sir John Holles that accompanied a loan of architectural books, the Earl of Northumberland remarked 'Paladius you have already' and gave a list of the books he was sending that includes several Mannerist authors (H.M.C. *Portland*, ix. 152).

Cromwell House (*c.* 1630) abandon it altogether and introduce the dominating overall roof of Coleshill and Thorpe Hall. The two- or three-storied porch is either reduced to one story or abandoned altogether, as at Kew and at Boston Manor (*c.* 1622–3). Further, the multi-light windows that had earlier been taken over from greater houses with long ranges become smaller and are more widely spaced. This, however, is not confined to these square-block houses; it appears, as at Hatfield, on some of the shorter elevations of the H and half-H types. It appears, too, on houses that have no possible debts to Palladianism or 'Artisan Mannerism', such as Woolmore Farm near Melksham (1631),[1] where the ground floor has a central doorway flanked by two four-light windows, but the first floor a central two-light window flanked by two small three-light ones (Pl. 14*a*). A reduction in the size of windows is apparent also at Boyton and Keevil; and Clegg Hall, Lancashire, built before 1622,[2] is wholly in the Jacobean manner but with windows of comparatively narrow proportions.[3] On the other hand, the new type had not wholly purged itself of the old, and at Coleshill the chimneys are given as much prominence in the design as at any H-type house.

These attributes of the 'double-pile' house were partly dictated by the comparative shortness of the façade, and were partly the result of the taking over of that house by men farther removed from vernacular practices than its originators. In itself this type of house is not the most important in the architecture of our period, but a study of it has the value of illuminating, by contrast, the

---

[1] Woolmore Farm is not documented at all as far as I know; the date is above the door.

[2] Garner and Stratton (*Domestic Architecture of . . . the Tudor Period*, i. 89) date Clegg Hall to 1620; V.C.H. *Lancs.* (v. 218–19) boldly risks a date bracket between 1571 and 1622. From the evidence given by H. Fishwick (*History of the Parish of Rochdale* (Rochdale, 1889), pp. 350–4), it is probable that it was built between 1610 and 1622.

[3] There were good practical reasons for reducing the size of windows. As Bacon said in the *Essay on Building*, 'You shall have sometimes Faire Houses so full of Glasse that one cannot tell where to become to be out of the Sunne or Cold'; but while courtyard and H-plan houses were being built with their long ranges and their punctuating bay-windows such practical considerations could rarely be allowed much weight, although at Bramshill the windows between the bays along the terrace front are small compared with earlier houses.

forces that brought about the development of the great courtyard and H-plan houses.

With this analysis in mind we are perhaps in a position to attempt to establish the authorship of the design of these houses. Although we have come a long way from the days when John of Padua or John Thorpe was credited with nearly every important building of the late sixteenth century, there is still a considerable amount of anachronistic speculation about the 'architects' of these houses. This is partly because some names, other than that of the owner, can often be associated with them. Robert Smithson, for example, is described on his tomb in Wollaton Church as 'Survayor and Architector to the Noble House of Wollaton'; Robert Lyminge is described in the Blickling parish register as the 'architect' of Blickling Hall;[1] Walter Hancock, the master-mason at Condover, is said, in an entry in the parish register of Much Wenlock, to have been responsible for 'most sumptuous buildings'.[2]

Just how little this meant is revealed by two incidental contemporary remarks upon the relationship between the 'architect' or 'surveyor' and the patron. Hatton wrote to Burghley upon the latter's visiting Holdenby during its building in 1579, to request him to tell the surveyor 'of such lacks and faults as shall appear' so that 'by good corrections at this time' they might be amended.[3] It is unlikely that Burghley was naïve enough to take the request seriously, but if he refrained from adverse comment it was out of deference to Hatton's feelings and not the surveyor's. The surveyor was there to carry out his employer's ideas and give his advice when he was asked for it. This at least was how John Strode, the builder of Chantmarle in the early seventeenth century, saw the matter. He referred to his surveyor, Gabriel Moore, as one whose function it had been 'to survey and direct the building to the forme I conceived and plotted it', and yet he called him 'a skilful architect'.[4] When Darrell was jeering at the constant changes of intention at Longleat it never occurred to him to blame the 'surveyors'

---

[1] J. Lees-Milne, *Blickling Hall* (1955), p. 9.
[2] 'Extracts from the Registers of the Parish of Much Wenlock', *Shropshire Archaeological Soc. Trans.* xi (1888), 15.    [3] E. St. J. Brooks, *Sir Christopher Hatton*, p. 158.
[4] *Account Book of John Strode*, Dorset County Record Office, MW/M4.

or the master-mason, or to hold anyone but Thynne himself responsible. And this interference and control of the minutest details was not an eccentricity of Thynne's; Burghley's careful supervision of his own buildings is well known; the Earl of Northumberland paid equal attention to minutiae at Syon; and Hatton, it is clear, considered that he or his friends were the ones to decide what 'lacks and faults' needed what 'corrections'.

This does not mean that the 'Surveyor' or 'Architect' had no voice at all. Mr. Lawrence Stone in his analysis of the building records of Hatfield has, I think, shown convincingly that there, and probably in any building, the views of two or three men played a part in determining the final form;[1] but the decisive voice was the owner's. Although a man like Lyminge might vow at Hatfield that he would 'never agree to' certain proposals of his colleagues, there was little that he could do except convince the owner of the justness of his views. His position is shown clearly enough in his economic relationship with Cecil, who was his employer and not his client; he worked for a weekly wage and not, even though he might receive a large gratuity from an appreciative owner, for a fee. He was still a 'mechanick', and his main function was to carry out the 'mechanical' tasks involved in building.

Such a conclusion, however, means little, for except in rare cases any architectural design has always been the result of a compromise between the wishes of the owner and of the 'architect'. The problem is therefore not mainly one of establishing this relationship, but of estimating the relative weights of the parties in it. To do this it is not enough to conduct a textual criticism of incidental references to 'surveyors' and 'architects', and an analysis of individual building accounts; it is necessary to consider the material that these provide in relation to its historical background. Now the period we are discussing is characterized by the application to building of principles and practices of design and decoration known only to those learned in the architecture and motifs of the Renaissance; but such learning in England at the time was necessarily book-learning, and few master-masons or master-carpenters had the money or opportunity to buy the books, or the leisure to

[1] *Arch. Journ.* cxii (1955), 102–6.

study them. Chapman remarked of Inigo Jones, when dedicating to him his translation of 'Musaeus' in 1616, that he was 'our only learned architect';[1] he was indeed one of the very few who had the opportunity to be learned. These opportunities were mostly open to, and almost wholly taken by, the 'courtiers' who could obtain the books and even spare the time to read the comparatively small corpus of them.

It was therefore these men, Thynne, Burghley, Northumberland, who were learned in 'architecture'. It was they who sent Shute to Italy to study classical examples; it was they who were importing the latest works from France and building up architectural libraries; it was they who, to ensure that they got what they wanted, were, like Pytts of Kyre Park, lending their masons 'Books of Architecture' to work from.[2] The building activities of the ninth Earl of Northumberland were nothing out of the ordinary, and yet he was able to lend Sir John Holles no less than eleven books on architecture by such foreign authors as Alberti, Serlio, del'Orme, Vignola, du Cerceau, and Dietterlin; and either he or Holles also owned a copy of Palladio.[3] Furthermore, not only had these men access to foreign books; they also had access, far more freely than a working-mason, to domestic exemplars. Thus Northumberland wrote to Cecil in 1603 that he was preparing to 'go and see Copthall, for now that I am a builder I must borrow of my knowledge somewhat out of Tibballs, somewhat out of every place of mark where curiosities are used'.[4] Not only, therefore, were they the 'architects' of the period, in the sense that as individuals they played the decisive part in the designs of their own houses, but they were so in the more important sense that as a class they determined the framework, and had a monopoly of the sources, of the aesthetic ideas within which the design of any great house had to be carried out. It is not accidental that at Northumberland's Syon House, where we have one of the clearest examples of an owner interested and learned in architecture, we have little evidence for an 'architect'. The building records of

---

[1] G. Chapman, *Homer's Batrachomyomachia*, ed. R. Hooper (1858), p. 211.
[2] Baldwyn-Childe, 'The Building of Kyre Park', *The Antiquary*, xxii (1890), 53.
[3] H.M.C. *Portland*, ix. 152.                    [4] H.M.C. *Cecil*, xv. 383.

Syon have been preserved for most of the relevant time, but 'the carpenter from Petworth, one John Dee, emerges as the nearest approach to an architect in Northumberland's building arrangements, coming to Syon four several times to make models for stairs, a round roof for the Great Chamber, and to set out the garden plot'.[1]

Further, this happened at a time when the practice of Renaissance architecture had brought about not only the abandonment of Gothic motifs and principles of design but of Gothic construction technique as well, and in its place had introduced one based upon classical models. This, compared with Gothic, was, in general, simple and primitive, for in building, as in other crafts that served a wide market, the later Middle Ages had far more 'know-how' than antiquity. In consequence, an ignorance of the highly skilled and painfully acquired masonry and carpentry technique of Gothic masters was no longer an insurmountable obstacle to would-be amateur designers. They could no longer be 'blinded with science' by a master-craftsman intent on getting his own way. Because of this combination of circumstances the Robert Smithsons and the Lyminges were, in fact, farther from the position of the modern architect than the Wynfords and Yeveles of two hundred years before. These latter worked within an unchallenged system of aesthetic ideas largely created by the traditions of the craft in which they had been trained, and with a technique of construction requiring a wide experience in an expert calculation of complex stresses, that no amount of book-learning, even if it had been available, could provide. The Elizabethan and Jacobean 'Surveyors' worked with aesthetic ideas that they had obtained at second-hand from their employers, and with a constructional technique, dictated by those ideas, that was obvious enough.

Perhaps the point needs no further labouring, but one should not overlook the fact that contemporary architectural historians by their deeds, if not their words, are in agreement with this conclusion. Recently Messrs. Harvey and Colvin have between them revealed to us in two monumental works the names of a host of architects and near-architects for all the centuries of English history

[1] G. R. Batho, 'Syon House; the First Two Hundred Years', *London and Middx. Archaeological Soc. Trans.* xix (1956), 13.

—with the exception of the years from 1550 to 1660. They have not, nor has anyone else, cared to mine far in that sandy soil.

The Renaissance was ultimately to create in England the artist architect; but a stage on the way was the destruction of the Gothic master-craftsman, and his replacement by the book-learned amateur and his very subordinate 'Surveyor' or 'Architect'. When the architect as we know him does appear, in the person of Inigo Jones, it is in peculiar circumstances; as a protégé of the virtuosi. They, however, were a new phenomenon in England. Such men as Burghley, Northumberland, Suffolk, and the courtiers in general, were dabblers in Renaissance art amid the intervals of a busy life, taking what pleased them, generally decorative motifs, and ignoring the rest. The virtuosi were more serious students; they were imbued with the spirit of that art and accepted its assumptions. One of these was the pre-eminent role of the artist: in architecture of the architect. Ben Jonson may have been referring solely to masque-settings, but he estimated shrewdly Jones's idea of his function as an artist when he wrote 'in design he calls it, He must be sole Inventor'.[1] Such an attitude probably puzzled and certainly annoyed Jonson, but the circle of the virtuosi was ready enough to agree with it. It was ready to do more: it was ready to encourage it; and whatever may be the truth about Jones's earlier visit to Italy, he was there in 1613 and 1614 in the suite of the Earl of Arundel, the leader of the virtuosi, and for the purpose of studying Italian and Classic models. He was probably not quite alone in this. John Smithson, as his papers in the R.I.B.A. library show, came to London from Nottinghamshire and made drawings of examples of the most advanced architecture of the time, including some at Arundel House, and probably at the expense and on the instructions of his patron, William Cavendish, later 'the loyal Duke' of Newcastle. When Sir Roger Townsend was projecting Rainham in 1619–20 his mason spent a considerable time with him on the Continent and in London, presumably looking, at least incidentally, at possible models.[2]

[1] *Tale of a Tub*, Act V, Sc. 2.
[2] H. L. Bradfer-Lawrence, 'The Building of Raynham Hall', *Norfolk Archaeology*, xxiii (1929), 93–105.

It is instructive to compare Jones's journey to Italy with that of
John Shute, who went there in 1550 at the expense of Northumberland, one of that very narrow circle who in the mid-
century produced a small amount of architecture of a purer
classicism and a deeper Renaissance feeling than anything in
England before Jones's Palladianism. That nothing came of
Shute's journey other than a belated book is not to be attributed
to any deficiencies that Shute may have had, or even to Northumberland's early fall from power, but rather to the absence of
conditions in mid-sixteenth-century England capable of fostering
the growth of a class of men, apart from the odd individual,
similar to the virtuosi. But with the scattering of these by the
troubles of Charles I's reign, and after the deaths of Jones and John
Webb, the professional 'architect' disappeared from the scene, and
amateurs reigned again for a period lasting, at a conservative
estimate, another half-century.

What has been said so far, however, applies mainly to the
houses of the greater men. There are, as far as I know, no documents that reveal the owner of a lesser house exercising the same
minute control over details that the great men exercised, or taking
the same interest in architecture. This does not mean that they had
no hand in the design of their houses. Strode's example at Chante-
marle shows that on occasions they played a decisive role, and
perhaps if more of their papers had been preserved more evidence
of this sort would be forthcoming. Yet the papers of at least one of
them have survived, those of Sir Thomas Tresham. Of all the
building 'enthusiasts' who did not belong to the court circle
Tresham is the best known, and one would expect him to have had
definite views on architecture. Yet in all the volumes of his papers
preserved at the British Museum there is no sign of any architectural interest. There are building accounts and there are pages
of mystical speculation, but not a word that reveals any knowledge
of or interest in the books and buildings that the greater men were
studying. It is therefore perhaps not accidental that among these
papers is preserved a document—the contract between Tresham
and William Grumbold the mason for the building of Rothwell
Market House—that shows the mason preparing his own design

and merely submitting it for approval.[1] As far as the evidence goes, it shows that Grumbold and not Tresham was the 'architect' of the building. Among the lesser builders this was probably a frequent relationship: an owner no more and generally less versed in contemporary architecture than his master-mason. In such a relationship it is the mason who usually has the decisive voice and is, in fact, the 'architect'. It is ironical that many of those who were making the greatest show of Renaissance art were busiest in preventing the emergence of its most typical exponent—the Renaissance artist. Those, on the other hand, who knew least about it were giving the mason-craftsmen the best opportunity to exploit the new situation and develop into artists.

These craftsmen continued and developed a native style of building, and in so doing produced an architecture which, in contrast with that of the greater houses of the period, is remarkable for its homogeneity. They were the designers who provided for men of limited means houses which achieved merit by the bold use of related masses and structural features devoid of almost any costly decoration. They were the men who knew the formula for success: making virtues of their necessities and opportunities of their difficulties.

[1] B.M. Add. Mss. 39831, No. 1.

# II

# ARCHITECTURAL DECORATION

THE distinction made between the architecture of the greater and of the lesser men applies equally to the decoration that they placed upon their buildings. As the leading figures of the absolute State, the former were more imbued with the ideas of the Renaissance and with a respect for classical learning, and revealed it in their choice of decoration. This was, however, a temporary situation, for as the sixteenth century wore on a knowledge of and an admiration for antiquity spread more widely, and the differences between the intellectual and artistic sympathies of the two groups grew less. Further, what differences there might be were lessened by a common fondness for exploiting the same forms in achieving architectural design, thereby using ornament in the same way and, as a consequence, often using the same kind.

In the reign of Edward VI and in the years immediately following there appeared, at Lacock, Sudeley, Dudley, and Longleat,[1] a style of architectural decoration which was different from anything that had preceded it and was not greatly copied by later builders. It was the work of a very small group of men, of whom the more important ended their days on the scaffold and the less important in political retirement; and its failure to spread widely was connected with but not wholly due to the fate of its initiators, Edward Seymour, Duke of Somerset, and his brother, Thomas Seymour, the Duke of Northumberland, Sir William Sharington, and Sir John Thynne. Most of their building was carried out before 1553,

[1] I have not space to argue the matter here, but I should say that I have omitted Somerset House because I am not convinced that the front that was pulled down by Chambers was erected by Somerset. As the argument of this chapter is not strengthened by its omission, and would not be weakened by its inclusion, I consider I am entitled to sit on the fence—even though it may be one of my own making—and exclude Somerset House from the discussion.

but its most important example, Longleat, was completed under Elizabeth, and for that reason their work must be considered here.

The ornament that had invaded England in the early sixteenth century was, whether directly or indirectly, of Italian inspiration; it was not classic, it was a version of Italian Renaissance art. With the increasing anti-Italianism that the rupture with the Papacy brought, it began to fall into disfavour, and in the fourth and later decades of the century it was not much used except in an occasional cartouche of arms.[1] Renaissance thought and feeling, however, were too essential components of the Tudor State and of the men who ran it to be abandoned because there was some taint of Rome about them, and so if one form of classically derived ornament was put aside another had to be found. At the same time, as a deeper knowledge of antiquity was acquired or sought, the pretensions of quattrocento decoration to be 'roman' were less easily accepted among classically learned men. Since such men were the fountain-head from which most of the others derived their Renaissance ideas, they gave a 'learned' bias to art-appreciation. This had a special effect upon architecture and architectural decoration, for this was the one art of antiquity about which it was possible in the mid-century to display any learning at all. L. Einstein remarked long ago that 'Architecture was then the only art really noticed by English travellers', and he went on to suggest why—'perhaps because of its learned side'.[2]

Learned humanists, still rare and with a considerable scarcity value, had the ear of those who had assumed control of affairs on the death of Henry VIII. Sharington and his friends and patrons may or may not have been greatly learned themselves, but they were under the influence of those who were, and the architecture that they produced is characterized by a greater knowledge of classical models than anything produced in England before the advent of Inigo Jones. It was one of that circle—Northumberland—

[1] In the last years of Henry VIII's reign there were attempts to prevent, or at least to restrict, the immigration of foreign artists, *L.P.H. VIII*, xx, pt. 1, p. 439.

[2] *The Italian Renaissance in England* (New York, 1902), p. 147. In contrast, 'At a time when painting had barely passed its zenith Hoby and Thomas passed through Italy without even noticing its existence and quite insensible to its charms'. Ibid., p. 149.

who sent John Shute to Italy to study foreign and ancient examples. In Shute's own words, he was to 'confer with the doings of the skilful Masters in architecture and also to view such ancient Monuments hereof as are yet extant'; and in the book that he published several years later he claimed to have largely followed Vitruvius's precepts.[1] Its truth or falsity is less important than the claim itself; for it reveals the attitude of these men and helps to explain the purer classicism of the work produced by them, and its close resemblance to some elements of the architecture of such learned builders as Sir Thomas Smith of Hill Hall and Dr. Caius.

Men like Somerset and Northumberland were not able to devote much leisure to the detailed study of classical antiquity, and the task of designing and controlling their buildings seems to have fallen upon one of their number. W. G. Clark-Maxwell has convincingly shown that the work at Dudley, Sudeley, and Lacock has so much in common and yet otherwise unique, that it must all be ascribed to one man; and that man he has taken to be Sir William Sharington.[2]

The character of Sharington's work can best be appreciated by comparing it with the Renaissance ornament of the first twenty to thirty years of the century. Not only is the quality of the decoration different, it is used in a different way. At Layer Marney the motifs of the often delicate ornament are the little balusters upon the window mullions, the egg and dart and guilloches of the string course, the flowered consoles of the heads of the window-lights, and the shell-cresting upon the towers. These are used light-heartedly, not only with no attempt at correctness, but in conjunction with Gothic forms and even with the intention of producing a Gothic effect. The egg and dart and the guilloches are placed immediately above a corbel-table of cusped two-centred

[1] *The First and Chief Grounds of Architecture* (1912).

[2] 'Sir William Sharington's Work at Lacock, Sudeley and Dudley', *Arch. Journ.* lxx (1913), 175–82. Mr. Douglas Simpson, however, has been able to show resemblances between the details of these buildings and the drawings in Shute's book, and has called him the architect, 'Dudley Castle: The Renaissance Buildings', *Arch. Journ.* ci (1944), 119–25. I speak of Sharington as though he were the architect, but I do not exclude the possibility that he owed much or even all of the architectural expression of his ideas to Shute.

arcading, the consoles of the window-lights are so contrived that the lights appear, from a short distance, to have cusped ogee heads, and the shell-cresting of the towers is a gayer form of crenellation. In Sharington's work the air of gaiety is absent; in its place is an obvious attempt at correctness, and even austerity. Decoration is not lavished over the whole of a building but confined mainly to such features as doors and windows. Where, as in the Conduit House on Bowden Hill, near Lacock, ornament is used along the whole face it is merely a plain dentil course beneath the eaves. Sharington avoids the elaborately decorated mullions of Layer Marney and is content merely to mark the main intersections of mullions and transoms with a simple roundel, and although he too puts consoles parallel with the plane of the walling into the window-heads, they are of classical profile and avoid any suggestion of Gothic forms (Pl. 15a). Consoles also appear on the interiors of his windows, plain at Dudley, scrolled at Lacock (Fig. 12), and carry or pretend to carry the sill. His doorways are all flat-headed with classical entablatures and brackets.

The Marian reaction of 1553 broke up the circle for which this architecture had been carried out and helped to ensure that the style should gain no wide hold in England. It did not, however, wholly end it, for its basis was not merely a personal liking of the Seymours and Northumberland, but rather a bias engendered by a respect for classical scholarship and a pride in membership of those still select circles for whom it had a meaning. When his retirement from political life allowed Sir John Thynne to build at Longleat he built, although very much later, in the manner of his old friends; but so too in the 1560's and 70's did such learned men as Caius and Smith.

Thynne's work at Longleat belongs in time to the ten or twenty years after Elizabeth's accession, but in spirit to Sharington's epoch, and it is not only on grounds of style that one may reckon Thynne as Sharington's follower. His determination to achieve *la pierre juste*, his 'beating down windows for this or that fault, they knew not why or wherefore' that Darrell jeered at,[1] shows him to have

---

[1] For 'Wild Will' Darrell's scorn of the activities of his fellow Wiltshireman see above, p. 33.

been, like Sharington, a man with a very precise aesthetic intent. Further, the letter from Sharington to Thynne, which has been so often quoted to establish Sharington's relationship with Dudley and the role of Chapman, the carver, shows that Sharington gave advice to Thynne and sent him 'patterns' for some of his work.

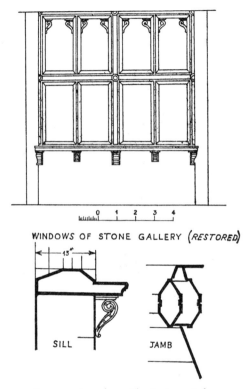

WINDOWS OF STONE GALLERY (*RESTORED*)

SILL          JAMB

FIG. 12. *Lacock: a Sharington window*

Although the decoration at Longleat has dropped even those faint signs of the early Renaissance, such as the roundels at the mullion intersections and the consoles at the heads of the lights that Sharington still preserved, it is in the Sharington manner. Its quality is such—and it is in this way that it belongs so clearly to Sharington's epoch—that it is only by its mullioned and transomed windows that Longleat betrays its Tudor origins (Pl. 18*a*). The decoration is remarkable not only for its quality but for its disposition as well, for it covers the whole of the main face of each front, and the shallow bays that project from it. Longleat differs from its predecessors in having none of the exuberance and gaiety of the early Renaissance; it was also to differ in the abundance of its ornament from most of its successors.[1]

Another house that may be included in this small group of learned mid-century architecture is Hill Hall in Essex, built by Sir Thomas Smith (d. 1578), a notable classical scholar. Hill Hall has been greatly altered, but the courtyard, which dates from about 1575, appears to have preserved its original character. It has mullioned and transomed windows separated by attached columns of a Doric order below and Ionic above. As Dr. Pevsner has pointed out, the metopes and triglyphs of the Doric order are incorrectly spaced, but nevertheless the whole is an attempt at a correct and severe classical effect.[2] Chronologically Hill Hall is long after Sharington's work, but it belongs, as its builder belonged, to the same age.

A similar time-lag is evident in the work of Dr. Caius at Gonville and Caius College, Cambridge. Like Smith, Caius was a learned classicist although, unlike Smith and the Sharington circle, he had leanings towards Roman Catholicism.[3] His work, like theirs, shows a determination to achieve correctness, and the Gate of Virtue, built some time after 1565, is severe and plain, despite the classically modelled angels in the spandrels of the arch (Pl. 19a).

Although the 'Sharington Manner' is almost confined to these buildings, nevertheless correctly classical motifs appear upon some other houses of the third quarter of the century, but in a way

[1] At Sherborne, Gloucs., the wing that was probably built by Thomas Dutton (d. 1581), a friend of Sharington and not unknown to Thynne, seems to have shared some of Longleat's features, M. Girouard in *C.L.* cxx (1956), 954.

[2] N. Pevsner, *Buildings of England—Essex* (1954), pp. 353–5.

[3] Thomas Byng, Vice-Chancellor of the University, writing to Burghley on 14 Dec. 1572, referred to an inventory of 'much popish trumpery' that had been found in the college and that he laid to Caius's charge (B.M. Lans. Mss. 15, No. 64). Over six years earlier Matthew Parker, then Archbishop of Canterbury, told Burghley that he had received reports that Caius was an open 'Atheist'—a contemporary smear-word used by every religious party to describe all others—and asked for action to be taken against him. He was probably speaking figuratively, but his words have a very tempting application, when he said 'I like not the stones that are builded by such impiety' (ibid. 8, No. 70).

that can be described as the grafting of the ornament of the Sharington circle on to the practice of the earlier period. The motifs of the early Renaissance are eschewed; in their place appear classical orders, more or less correctly proportioned and with all their attributes. They are used, however, in the same way

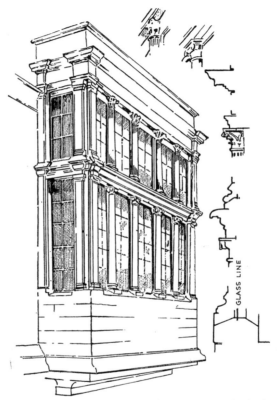

FIG. 13. *Broughton Castle: oriel of 1554 and detail of columns*

as the earlier ornament was used; as decoration applied in a completely unclassical manner. At Broughton Castle in Oxfordshire the oriel of 1554 has quite correctly superposed Ionic and Corinthian columns and pilasters, of good proportions and with their entablatures (Fig. 13). Taken in themselves, little fault could be found with them, but they are used as no classical column was ever used, as window mullions. At Deene Park (1549–72) fluted columns were similarly used in a very broad window (Pl. 18b). This use of columns at Broughton and Deene Park is essentially the same practice, although the forms are different, as the use of flat mullions covered with elaborate Renaissance motifs at Layer Marney. A common variation of this unclassical use of classical forms occurred at Sir Nicholas Bacon's Gorhambury, a building with all the usual Tudor details, such as windows with four-centred heads to the lights and returned labels, and with no hint of classical decoration anywhere except on the porch in the court-yard. The porch was a highly classical composition with Doric and Ionic columns, a finely moulded pedimented cornice adorned with statues, and with more statues in niches. In itself it was well enough, but its purpose and its relationship with the rest of the building robbed it of its character. In some houses the situation is reversed and non-classical elements are intruded into a classical framework. At Moreton Corbet (Fig. 14), built before 1579, on the porch of Leicester's Gatehouse at Kenilworth (c. 1570), and very much later at Houghton Conquest,[1] correctly classical columns have heraldic beasts carved upon their podiums, and Doric orders complete with triglyphs and guttae have the metopes filled with heraldic badges and emblems.

The use of Sharington ornament without the thorough-going Sharington manner reveals the significance of this learned mid-century architecture: that it was patronized by the greatest 'Statists' of the time and, with very little exception, by them and their associates alone. The immediate causes of this have been suggested above, but it is necessary to go farther and ask why the Seymours and Northumberland were more susceptible than later men to the charms of a learned architecture, and why their rule was so brief. Whether from conviction or a misjudgement of the times or an amalgam of the two, they followed in Church and State a radical policy that went far beyond anything that the politically powerful classes were ready to accept. At the same time they had destroyed the more advanced radicalism of Kett's followers, and therefore—it has been the fate of many radicals—

[1] The land on which Houghton House was built was granted to Mary Sidney, Countess of Pembroke, for life by James, and at her death in 1621 she had built 'two lodges' there (H.M.C. 7th Report, Appendix, p. 250). The date of the grant, according to the D.N.B., was 1615.

the only force that might have protected them from their enemies on the right. The results were the Protector's speedy fall from power and subsequent execution and Northumberland's failure to gain any help in his attempts to thwart the Marian *revanche*.

FIG. 14. *Moreton Corbet*

In art they followed a similar course and favoured a radical classicism that was too advanced for all but a few of their countrymen to accept. There is a striking parallel between their politics and their patronage. Their buildings were the outcome of the interaction between their ultra-Renaissance and ultra-Reformation ideas and the emphasis upon 'learning' of the small corps of professional classicists who were an essential part of the State machine.

The negative aspect of the Sharington manner, however—the avoidance of quattrocento motifs—was not peculiar to the Sharington circle. These motifs, although most popular with the great in earlier years, had not been confined to them but had appeared, for example at East Barsham, upon some smaller houses. In the middle of the century such houses were built with little or no classical decoration, and even larger ones, when not distantly echoing Sharingtonian motifs, show an almost exclusive use of sub-Gothic and Tudor ornament. At Cowdray, Sussex, the west range with the hall and porch was built apparently by the Earl of Southampton some time before 1543. In the vaulting of the porch delicate arabesques and human heads are introduced, and on its face there is a sculptured panel with flanking enriched pilasters, all in the manner of the Renaissance work of the period. But the part completed in the second half of the century, after the house had passed from Southampton's possession, is in a wholly native style. Loseley (Pl. 11a) and Hoghton Tower in Lancashire, both built in the 1560's, are completely devoid of classical, and indeed of almost any, decoration.

Yet quattrocento ornament did not wholly disappear, and its survival in odd places throws some light upon its significance. Caius's Gate of Virtue has already been mentioned as an example of the Sharington manner, but Caius was also responsible for the nearby Gate of Honour (c. 1573) in a very different style. This is highly decorated, and without achieving the light-hearted effect of some of the decoration of the early years of the century has many of its most characteristic motifs: the roundels in high relief, the perspective masoned arch, the decorative panelled pilasters, all in conjunction with a four-centred head to the entry (Pl. 19b). Although Caius died before the gateway was completed, there seems little doubt that it was built to his design, and its nature calls for some explanation. In the Gate of Virtue Caius was following the same principles as the other 'learned amateurs' and erecting a severely classic building, far removed in spirit from the early Renaissance decoration. In the Gate of Honour he reverted in part to the earlier style, although with difference enough to mark his greater scholarship. It has been suggested earlier that Sharington and his circle were debarred from such a style by their anti-Roman prejudices. Caius was not. He may not have been a Roman Catholic but, as the articles found when his rooms were searched in 1572 showed, there was some ground for suspecting him of 'Romish' sympathies. He was therefore not inhibited by religious antipathy from building in the earlier style, and he was also able, by his learning, to build in a style similar to that of Sharington and Smith.

A comparison with Caius's work can be found at Dingley Hall, Northants. (c. 1558–60), where the motifs of the early Renaissance are found in combination with Gothic details, but the severely classical features are absent. The builder was Edward Griffin, Attorney-General to Queen Mary, and his religious and political views are not in doubt, for on the porch is the inscription 'Ano 1558 In the Rayne of Felep and Marey. After Darkness . . . cometh light.' Dingley reveals the decoration that a man with Catholic views but not, as far as we know, learned in classical architecture, found congenial. His work shares with that of Caius Gothic and early Renaissance features; it lacks the architectural learning that is another feature of Caius's work; it contrasts absolutely with the learned and austere architecture of Sharington and his ultra-Protestant friends and employers.

It must not be imagined, however, that a connexion between religious views and aesthetic appreciation was an immutable law. It was only a tendency, and among men who were not so aesthetically conscious as Sharington and Thynne early Renaissance motifs continued to be used, and often in connexion with other motifs. At Kirby, where the giant order in the courtyard is derived by Sir John Summerson from Écouen, and much of the ornament from the works of Serlio, Shute, and Blum,[1] there are reminiscences of the earlier fashion in the decorated pilaster buttresses of the central bay of the north face of the courtyard and in the porch of 1572 (Pl. 6b). A resemblance between Kirby and Dingley Hall has been noticed by Sir John, who has suggested that it originates from the probable employment at Dingley of Thomas Thorpe, the master-mason of Kirby. But what has not been sufficiently

[1] 'John Thorpe and the Thorpes of Kingscliffe', Arch. Rev. cvi (1949), 291–300.

emphasized is that the resemblance between the two houses is confined to the use of early Renaissance ornament at both, and the great difference between the two is that at Dingley this type of ornament predominates, while at Kirby it is subordinate. It is not enough to answer that Kirby is more than a decade later, for so too is Caius's Gate of Honour, which has as much of this ornament as Dingley.

One cannot from this and from the characteristics of the Sharington school draw the conclusion that Catholics and Protestants consciously used architectural ornament as a religious manifesto, or fought out their battles in the realms of aesthetics, but that religious opinions, because of the Italian origins of Renaissance art, often coloured aesthetic predilections. Thus the builders of the mid-century avoided earlier motifs because there was a taint of Rome upon them, and were unable to follow Sharington far because Humanism was still largely the preserve of learned professionals; in consequence they fell back upon native sub-Gothic and Tudor ornament.

By the last quarter of the century the struggle with the Counter-Reformation was more intense, and anti-papal feeling and propaganda, intensified by Continental refugees, had grown fiercer, and was meeting with a fiercer response, often organized by refugees fleeing the other way. 'Each year the stories each group brought became more horrifying and better authenticated. By the 1570's there were enough undeniable or plausible ones to keep partisanship on both sides at white heat.'[1] One result of this was a cessation of those journeys to Italy that had earlier been common among the wealthier classes. When Sir Thomas Hoby was at Naples in 1550 he was put to some trouble to avoid the great number of his compatriots,[2] and even a merchant's son like John Lok was visiting Venice in 1553–4 as part of his education.[3] But before long Roger Ascham was publicly deploring the visits of young noblemen and

[1] G. Mattingley, *Renaissance Diplomacy* (1955), pp. 200–1.
[2] 'The Travels and Life of Sir Thomas Hoby Knt.', ed. E. Powell, *Camden Miscellany*, x (1902), 37–38. Hoby's decision to go south from Naples was partly from a desire to see the country but 'also to absent myself for a while out of Englishemenne's companie for the tung's sake'.
[3] E. G. R. Taylor, *Late Tudor and Early Stuart Geography* (1934), p. 24.

gentlemen to Italy as likely to improve their minds very little and damage their religion very much.[1] In the later years of the century interest in Italy declined rapidly, and of the twenty-four books on European countries published in England between 1583 and 1625 only four deal with Italy, and of these two are devoted to anti-papal Venice.[2] From this an important consequence followed: that the increasing influence of Humanism in England in the last years of the century was not paralleled by an increased interest in or appreciation of Italian or pure classical architecture.

This affected decoration in several ways. There were no aesthetic considerations powerful enough to hinder the building of the long wings and main blocks that the advantages of the H and half-H plans were encouraging, and it was easy, almost necessary, to achieve an effect upon these by concentrating ornament at a few places. Since it was being used upon buildings of no pronounced classical character, and since there were in any case no widely recognized classical standards, that ornament could be given, without incongruity, almost any current form; but the concentration of it, with the intent of emphasizing components of the structure, helped to put a premium upon bold rather than upon delicate motifs and workmanship. Further, a style that accommodated a variety of forms from diverse sources was welcome because it also allowed the easy insertion into ornament of the most favoured motifs of all: the coats-of-arms, crests, badges, and other heraldic devices that a host of new men, in an effort to give themselves a patina of age, were multiplying in every artistic medium.[3]

[1] *The Scholemaster*, ed. D. Whimster (1934), pp. 65–68.

[2] E. G. R. Taylor, op. cit., p. 42.

[3] From 1530 onwards Heraldic visitations became commoner and began to acquire a new character, and the Heralds were in the habit of visiting the nobility and gentry in their homes and checking 'evidences' which included heraldic displays upon buildings, tombs, stained glass, &c. (A. R. Wagner, *Heralds and Heraldry in the Middle Ages* (1939); A. W. Vivian-Neal, 'The Visitations of Somerset 1573, 1591', *Somerset Archaeological Soc. Trans.* lxxxiv (1938), 59–70; P. Styles, 'The Heralds' Visitation of Warwickshire 1682–3', *Birmingham Archaeological Soc. Trans.* lxxi (1953), 96–134.) *The Art of Limming*, a slim volume published in London in 1573 and reissued many times, has been taken by some commentators as evidence of a contemporary interest in art-technique; in fact, as its matter and title-page reveal, it was intended as a technical guide for amateur heralds.

Before discussing the concentration of ornament it is necessary to make another point and to correct the prevailing impression that the architecture of the period is lavishly decorated, that, to quote a modern writer, Elizabethan and Jacobean craftsmen applied 'a mass of extraneous ornamentation to the outside surfaces of country houses'.[1] In fact these houses are, in general, severely plain, and just how plain may be appreciated by a consideration of the south front of Castle Ashby, where a Palladian screen of Charles I's time is flanked by the late Elizabethan wings and appears ornate in comparison (Pl. 3a). This plainness increased as the H plan superseded the courtyard plan in which, as at Kirby and to a less degree at Burghley, considerable decoration was lavished upon the courtyard, in contrast with the bareness of the external elevations.

The mistake arises from a failure to understand that although much of the ornament of the late sixteenth century is indeed 'applied', it is applied with an artistic purpose: to emphasize the elements of the general design. Nowhere is this more clearly seen than in those very features that are so often criticized on the score of over-ornamentation, porches, and frontispieces. These are, it is true, often loaded and over-loaded with ornament, but generally they are on façades that have little other ornament. Instances are numerous: Cobham, Gayhurst (Pl. 20), Charlton, Bramshill, Aston Hall (1618–35). Further, the less that they project from the main face and achieve emphasis by their mass, the more highly decorated they are. That they are intended to contrast with the rest of the front is shown plainly enough in the Schools Quadrangle elevation of the Bodleian Library (Pl. 21a), where the frontispiece is distinguished not only by the lavish decoration upon it and the plainness of everything else, but also by the deliberate difference between its wholly Renaissance details and the sub-Gothic form of the windows of the rest of the building.

This concentration of decoration in conjunction with the waning of the Italianate styles leads to a great diminution in the use of columniated façades. The lavish use of pilasters and engaged columns, as at Longleat and at Moreton Corbet or on the wing at

[1] J. Lees-Milne, *Tudor Renaissance* (1951), p. 49.

Dingley Hall, or the use of columns as mullions and window jambs, as at Deene Hall, becomes less frequent.[1] There are notable exceptions to this, but except for Wollaton, which is in a class by itself, they are only seeming exceptions. Burleigh has columns along all the courtyard elevations, but they are columns that perform a function in supporting the arches of the loggia, and may be contrasted with the purely decorative function of the columns at Kirby and Hill Hall. The ornate façade at Longford is in essence an extended frontispiece between the two great terminal bastions. At Castle Ashby, Cobham, Condover, Doddington, Montacute, Wimbledon, and Worksop decorative columns are either absent or appear only upon a frontispiece or porch.

The demand for concentration of ornament helped to rob windows too of much of their decoration. However plain the humdrum early Tudor style had been, it had usually afforded cusped or uncusped depressed heads to the lights or more or less elaborate labels; in many houses of the end of the century windows were denied not only the elaborate columns of Broughton and Deene Park, but even this native enrichment. This was partly due as well to a liking for the contrast between the plain walling and the great areas of glass that the huge windows of the time provided. The well-known rhyme about Hardwick Hall—'More glass than wall'—has more than a hint of pride in it, and a contemporary described Kenilworth with approval as 'a day time, on every side, so glittering by glass'.[2] Where such effects were aimed at, or even achieved by accident, decoration upon windows themselves was likely to be little. In some houses of the time the windows retain their ornament, but it is generally above the heads alone and not upon mullions or jambs. At Montacute, at Brereton, and in many East Anglian houses the openings are surmounted by low

[1] Wakehurst in Sussex is a very late example of the use of columns as mullions and window jambs.

[2] J. Nichols, *Progresses of Queen Elizabeth* (1823), i. 472. Although it began to decline in the early seventeenth century this liking for great areas of glass went very deep and continued among some men for a long time. It is indeed not Hardwick but Astley Hall, Lancs., of the 1660's that is, in Muthesius's words, 'the most striking example of this window-mania' (das auffallendste Beispiel dieser Fenstersucht), *Das englische Haus* (Berlin, 1908), i. 51.

pediments, at Cobham by strapwork and at Hinchinbrooke in 1602 by strapwork, balustrading, and a cartouche of arms. At Cobham and Hinchinbrooke, however, the decorated windows are in projecting bays, and their ornament is intended not so much for their decoration as for giving emphasis to the structural unit of which they form part.

In the smaller houses the pattern is similar but in one way more intensified and in another more belated. The builders of these were, on the whole, little concerned with keeping abreast of the aesthetic and intellectual advances of the age and under no great impulse to exhibit an acquaintance with classical art forms. At the same time the design of their buildings made even more use of related masses and of the aesthetic possibilities of structural units than did those of the greater men. In consequence, the plainness and concentration of decoration that is so observable on so many of the greater houses is even more marked in the smaller. There is a great number of such houses, of varying size and importance, where decoration, if present at all, is confined to a cartouche of arms above the columns of the entrance. Bishop's Hull, Kingston Maurward (Pl. 10a), such Gloucestershire houses as Doughton Manor and More Hall, Cadhay and Sydenham in Devonshire, all of the last quarter of the century, are well-known examples.

Ornament disposed in this way, as a means of heightening the effect of a structural unit or of providing the emphasis that the structure was unable to afford, was necessarily related not to the components of the building but to the effect of the building as a whole. It had, therefore, only one necessary characteristic, that it should be obvious and striking, and this, while not dictating its nature, militated against the correct or delicate classical ornament of earlier years and in favour of a coarse and licentious form of it. It was in these circumstances that the close political and economic relations with the Low Countries played a great part in the formation of English decorative style: not by creating, but by providing a ready satisfaction for, a native demand. That demand was met by an influx of refugees and by the importation of Flemish pattern books and of the works of de Vries and Dietterlin.[1]

[1] The north Europeans who had the kindest reception in England—Shute, De

This tendency to a concentration of ornament has been noticed by Wüsten, who considers it to be the English form of Mannerism: 'The basic organising principle of Mannerism in English Architecture consisted in this; to pile up at a few places a surfeit of Mannerist ornament and effects, while the rest of the building was relatively free from dissonances and even a predilection for an *amor vacui* was often apparent.'[1] It is not clear from this whether it is the concentration of ornament or of Mannerist ornament that is significant. If the first meaning is intended then there is, by all the current definitions of the term, no compelling reason to regard the practice as evidence of Mannerism; if the second, then it was the nature and not only the concentration of ornament that was important. But since this concentration was a characteristic of English architecture of the period and the concentration of Mannerist ornament only a particular form of it, this amounts to no more than saying that Mannerism in this context consisted of using Mannerist ornament. One can call that use 'Mannerist' if one likes, but since architecture was at the same time rejecting many Mannerist forms and using many non-Mannerist ones, it is more useful to see this as one aspect of a general readiness to employ any forms that were suitable to the prevailing manner of design, and to employ those forms alone. In this connexion it is useful to consider the Thorpe and Smithson Collections.[2] They contain a large number of elevations of identified and unidentified buildings; of the latter, some may be drawings of buildings that have disappeared without record, but others are clearly original designs. Not one of the more florid and 'Mannerist' elevations of

Vries, Dietterlin—had no corpus of architectural work to their credit. On the title-page of his book Shute called himself a 'Paynter' as well as an 'Archytecte', was described on his tomb as a 'painter-stainer' and was known to Haydocke as a miniaturist; De Vries and Dietterlin were mural painters and decorators. It was because of this that they went down so well; their 'decorator's' conception of Renaissance architecture and ornament best answered the problems of English builders of the time.

   [1] 'Das Grundgestaltungsprinzip des Manierismus in der englischen Architektur bestand darin; an wenig Punkten eine überreiche Fülle manieristischer Ornamente und Effekte zu häufen, während die übrigen Teile des Baues relativ frei von Dissonanzen waren und sogar oft eine Vorliebe für ein *amor vacui* in Erscheinung trat', *Die Architektur des Manierismus in England* (Leipzig, 1951), p. 225.

   [2] In the Soane Museum and the R.I.B.A. Library respectively.

either Thorpe or Smithson can be identified or be shown ever to have been executed. It is possible that future research will alter this impression, but until it does we must conclude that the wilder extravagances of Flemish designers, although well enough known to and experimented with by men like Thorpe and Smithson, were not congenial to the patrons of the time. Indeed, until English architecture had reached a certain level, even the more restrained designs of de Vries were not widely accepted; and although he published in the mid-century, what copying there was from foreign sources before the 1580's was, with the exception of such an obvious import as Gresham's Royal Exchange, of Italian and French rather than of Flemish models. Dietterlin's work, on the other hand, appeared in 1598[1] at a more opportune moment and had an almost immediate welcome.

Jan Vriedeman de Vries first published in the late 1550's and early 1560's, and his books went through several editions in the next fifty years. His manner of decoration, with its extravagant strapwork, its grotesques, and its contorted attitudes, is important for our purpose, but more so is the theory on which it was based. In *Architectura* he stated his plain view that Vitruvius or any other authority may be flouted when the conditions within a country demand it; in his own words—'accomoder l'art à la situation et nécessité du pais plus que oncques a esté besoing aux Anciens'.[2] He was specifically referring in this context to design but he applied his principles to decoration as well; in fact he was far more restrained in his architectural design than in his decoration, and attempted at least to give his buildings, taken as a whole, a classical composition.

Wendel Dietterlin differs from de Vries in two important ways. The first is that he is not concerned with architecture at all, but with applied decoration; throughout his oddly miscalled book *Architectura* there is not one design for a whole building. The second difference, resulting from the first, is that his columns

---

[1] It is possible that something was known of Dietterlin in England before 1598, for although the complete five books of *Architectura* were not published until then, at Nuremberg, a Part I was issued at Stuttgart in 1593 and a Part II at Strassburg in 1594.

[2] *Architectura ou Bastiment prins de Vitruve* (Antwerp, 1577), Section 'Dorica'.

have little function, and his terms and caryatides are far less weight-bearing members than freestanding figures. As a German writer has remarked, his pillars and columns derive from the forms of Alsatian joinery and are not conceived as masonry at all.[1]

In conjunction with this, he takes the strapwork and grotesques of de Vries to new heights, or depths, of perversion of classical motifs. But it must be noted that Dietterlin was not copied indiscriminately by English craftsmen; on the contrary they showed a very selective attitude towards his work. His principles, or lack of them, and his use of classical structural elements as pure decoration, with their consequent debasement into forms no longer even pretending to be classical columns, were followed readily enough, but, as Sir John Summerson has pointed out, his extremely contorted decorative forms were rejected.[2] From Dietterlin, as from de Vries, English builders took not the tortured 'Mannerist' elements but rather the bold and coarse technique.

Because of this the ornament of the time, although wholly 'Flemish' in the sense that it follows de Vries' precepts and accommodates art to native needs, and largely Flemish in its choice of motifs, is in no way wedded to Flanders or restricted to northern European sources, but is, on the contrary, extremely eclectic. Wollaton, which is in so many other ways exceptional, is in this respect an excellent example of the Elizabethan practice of taking decorative motifs from all over Europe and mingling them unrestrainedly. Various writers have analysed its individual parts and, although they disagree about certain details, they mostly see Venetian lendings in the heads of the hall windows and in the dies of the ground-floor pilasters, French in the tourelles of the central tower and in the plan, Flemish in the strapwork cartouches, and Serlio and de Vries and du Cerceau elbowing one another out of what space is left[3] (Pl. 8).

[1] M. Pirr, *Die Architectura des Wendel Dietterlin* (Gräfenhainichen, 1940), p. 81.

[2] *Architecture in Britain 1530–1830* (1953), p. 45.

[3] See, for example, Summerson, op. cit., pp. 33–35; Lees-Milne, *Tudor Renaissance*, p. 113; M. Whiffen, *Elizabethan and Jacobean Architecture* (1952), pp. 37–38. Dr. Pevsner, in addition, has found room there for a trace of Gothic revival, *Arch. Rev.* cvii (1950), 147–53.

Wollaton, although an extreme case, does not stand alone. At Longford such French forms as the double arcade, the anse-de-panier arches of the ground floor, and the pedimented gables are mingled with coarse Flemish terms and strapwork. At Burghley there is the same contrast between the character of the stone staircase, of the courtyard, and of the frontispiece, and that of the great obelisk that surmounts the frontispiece. At Cobham the porch reveals French influence, but the strapwork above the windows of the exterior is Flemish. Often, as in the triglyphed and arabesqued friezes of Montacute and Condover and the geometrical patterning of Rushton Hall, there is nothing but the English craftsman's version of classical ornament. At Brereton Hall (Pl. 6a) the decoration, with its coarse brackets and balusters and strapwork panelling, has a Flemish air, but the motifs within the panels and the undistinguished floral ornament are in an English manner. Occasionally, as in the nail-head frieze of the upper story at Montacute, the decoration is without any classical or foreign connotation. It is, I think, because of this that writers are nearest the mark when they refer to Wollaton, *tout court* and without any attempt at a refined analysis of its individual features, as a pre-eminent example of the Anglo-Flemish style of decoration. In its amount and dispersal of ornament Wollaton is a freak among its contemporaries, but in its mingling of motifs it is the clearest illustration of the attitude towards decorative detail of the great builders of the time.

After 1600 Flemish motifs became increasingly extravagant, and this, as the frontispieces at the nearly contemporary Charlton, Bramshill, and Northumberland House show, was less the result of ignorance than of a deliberate perversion of classical rules. In earlier frontispieces the main element was often a series of classical orders which at least attempted correctness. At Charlton (Pl. 26), and at the later Aston Hall, the lavishly decorated columns have curving and contorted outlines; at Bramshill (Pl. 7b) they taper downwards, a trick common enough in joinery but absurd in brick or stone. The now-demolished Northumberland House had an ornate frontispiece with similar details.[1] Examples of the

---

[1] *L.C.C.S.L.* xviii (1937), 10–16, pls. 4, 5.

unemployed caryatides of which Dietterlin was so fond may be seen flanking the centrepiece of the gatehouse at Burton Agnes and pretending to bear the weight of the frieze above them with bunches of fruit (Pl. 22). This usage must be sharply distinguished from that of Montacute, of freestanding figures in niches making no pretence of being anything other than sculptural ornament.

The extent to which some of the builders of the early seventeenth century turned away from the attempted classicism of their predecessors can be measured by a comparison of the gatehouse at Burton Agnes, built about 1610, with those at Tixall (1580) (Pl. 13b) and at Lostock near Bolton (1590).[1] At Tixall the archway is flanked by superimposed Doric, Ionic, and Corinthian orders, each carrying a frieze that continues along the main wall-face, and the building is surmounted by balustrading. Lostock is essentially similar. The Burton Agnes gatehouse has work-shy caryatides in place of ordered columns and is surmounted by cresting that has no classical character at all but is a form of crenellation; its style is noticeably different from that of the slightly earlier frontispiece at the same house. The same change is revealed in the altered nature of parapets and gables and, when it was present, of decoration upon the heads of windows. Balustrading was increasingly superseded by strapwork or geometrical patterning, or religious or patriotic texts; pediments and labels above windows by strapwork, as at Wothorpe; and curvilinear gables that had been rare before 1600 became commoner, and occasionally, for instance at Dorfold, had further decoration placed upon them.

Despite the prominence of this type of decoration it was not, in the early seventeenth century, the only or even the most significant form. Of more importance because of its contribution to later developments was the emergence of a more restrained and knowledgeable style that had some affinities with French originals, some with Italian, and was the precursor, one might almost say the experimental stage, of Jones's Palladianism. This style is to be regarded as an early sign of the emergence of the virtuosi; and, as one would expect from their highly articulate feelings about art, it was accompanied by a great deal of praise of foreign models.

[1] E. Baines, *History of Lancashire* (1836), iii. 108.

Literary references show that there was a quite conscious admiration of French taste. Henry Peacham wrote, 'I know not whether in all Europe any buildings may for majesty and state be compared with those of France ... they being the best architects of the world.' He singled out the work of Francis I and Henry IV at the Louvre, the Tuileries, Fontainebleau, Blois, Amboise, Villiers-Cotterets, Charleval, and Vincennes.[1] Thomas Coryate joined with Peacham in praise of the Louvre, the Tuileries, and Fontainebleau and interestingly enough, in view of its supposed connexion with Somerset House, added Écouen—'a most magnificent Pallace'.[2] Balthazar Gerbier, acting as an artistic adviser and agent to the Duke of Buckingham, wrote in 1624 from Paris, 'all the folks here are so fine and so magnificent and curious in their houses'.[3] Jones himself, though for what reason is uncertain, had at least taken the trouble to visit Chambord.[4] That there was more to this than a mere literary attitude, that there was a deliberate copying of French models, is shown by the Royal Accounts for Somerset House for 1610–11. An entry appears there, of a kind that had never appeared before: '32 french lights', and a description of them.[5] Further, there is the use of a type of window that contemporaries, with whatever justification, thought of as 'French'. The accounts for Somerset House make it clear that the distinguishing marks of the 'french lights' were a surround projecting considerably from the wall face, supporting brackets, and a frieze or slight apron below the sill. There were perhaps similar windows on the Strand Exchange,[6] and they are to be seen at Hatfield, at Houghton Conquest, and, in conjunction with Flemish features, at Wothorpe.[7]

Praise of things Italian was less forthcoming, but it was clearly in the air. Coryat vowed that he would rather have lost the gift

[1] *The Compleat Gentleman* (1622), pp. 204–8.

[2] *Crudities* (1611), pp. 19, 24–27, 38–40.

[3] G. Goodman, *The Court of James I*, ed. J. S. Brewer (1839), ii. 342–3.

[4] For Jones's travels in or through France see J. A. Gotch, *Inigo Jones* (1928), and J. Lees-Milne, *The Age of Inigo Jones* (1953).        [5] P.R.O. E. 351-3245.

[6] This depends upon how far Smithson's drawing in the R.I.B.A. Library can be trusted.

[7] Built by Thomas Cecil, first Earl of Exeter, before 1622 and, according to a pleasant tradition, that he might be 'out of the dust when his great house at Burghley was sweeping', Camden, *Britannia*, ed. Gough (1806), ii. 292.

of the four best manors in Somerset than foregone a sight of Venice.[1] When John Smithson was in London in 1618–19, making drawings of doorways and windows that appealed to him, he knew enough to label them 'Italyan'.[2] In doing so, he was, at a considerable distance, following the lead of Jones and Arundel and Wotton. The distance, however, must be stressed, for while the ultimate result of this trend was to be Jones's Palladianism, nevertheless many men, in fact the majority, who were prepared to indulge in a liking for French or Italian forms or motifs were unable to go as fast or as far as the more aesthetically conscious and orientated virtuosi.

This is suggested not only by the narrowness of the circle that patronized Jones in the years that followed the beginnings of the Queen's House at Greenwich, but by the evidence that is beginning to accumulate of designs and possibly of executed work by him in the ten years before. Mr. Lees-Milne has recently given us reasons for believing the temple-like portico with three superimposed orders at Houghton Conquest to be his work.[3] Mr. Stone has drawn attention to the payment of £10 to Jones for 'drawinge of some Architecture' at Hatfield in 1610, inferring that this may refer to the south front there,[4] and has further shown that a drawing at Worcester College, Oxford, is very likely his design for Cecil's 'New Exchange' of 1608–9.[5] Assuming that these attributions are correct,[6] we can see a consistent course of events. The Worcester College drawing is the earliest of these; it is the closest to Jones's mature style; it was not carried out. At Hatfield he either tried much the same style, again with the same lack of success, or curled his lip from the start and turned out a typical Jacobean design. At Houghton Conquest, where he had another five to ten years of

[1] *Crudities*, p. 291.
[2] For Smithson in London see Gotch, *Inigo Jones*, and 'Development of House Design in the Reigns of Elizabeth and James I', *Journ. R.I.B.A.* xvi (1909), 41–69.
[3] *Age of Inigo Jones*, pp. 105–9.          [4] *Arch. Journ.* cxii (1955), 118.
[5] *Arch. Journ.* cxiv (1957), 108–12.
[6] Attributing buildings to Jones has been as popular a game as attributing pictures to Zuccari and Gheeraerts, and has been played in the past with the same lack of success. Mr. Lees-Milne and Mr. Stone seem to me to play it very convincingly, but then I am a contemporary of theirs and was hammered on the same anvil.

virtuoso propaganda to assist him and, one supposes, a more malleable client, he was able to come closer to his own conception of architecture. This sequence makes it reasonably clear that any buildings earlier than 1618 that can be shown to be by Jones are not so much examples of his early manner as of his forced surrenders to or his reluctant compromises with his yet unregenerate patrons.

The new interests expressed themselves in various ways. One of the most obvious is the increasing use of the loggia, which had long been known in England but had never become common. Hatfield and Charlton in Wiltshire are examples on a grand scale, but there are many more, such as Bramshill and Cranborne (Pl. 23), where a loggia, however small, is incorporated in the building. This common use of loggias and the employment of piers and columns that it necessitated, retarded the decline of the classical column, not only as a structural member but also as an element in the design. Although houses with loggias had plain walling above the arcade there are some, Hatfield and possibly Cecil's 'New Exchange' in the Strand,[1] where columns or pilasters were carried upon and continued the punctuation of the piers.

Approaching somewhat closer to the developed Palladianism of Charles I's reign is the use of 'Italyan' doors and windows. Instances may be seen at Bolsover, where the main door has the rustication and pedimenting, and the windows have the proportions, that Smithson labelled 'Italyan' (Pl. 16a). The gatehouse that was formerly at Clifton Maybank[2] has many Jacobean features, but its general design, with a recessed columniated front between flanking pavilions surmounted by attics, is wholly untypical of the period and is more 'Italian' than anything else. The temple-like portico of three superimposed orders at Houghton Conquest is another example. In the years following Jones's first Palladian buildings,

[1] There is some doubt about the pilasters at the New Exchange. They are shown in Smithson's drawing, but a late seventeenth- or early eighteenth-century one shows a plain wall face above the loggia, *L.C.C.S.L.* xviii (1937), 94–96, pl. 58. There had, however, been considerable alterations to the 'upper part' in 1638 and 1639, L. Stone in *Arch. Journ.* cxiv (1957), 119.

[2] The Clifton Maybank Gatehouse was removed to Hinton St. George, Somerset, in 1800, A. Oswald, *Country Houses of Dorset* (1934–5), pp. 24–25. It is illustrated by Oswald, pl. 60, and in J. Hutchins, *History of Dorset* (1st ed. 1774), ii. 460–1.

Blickling has windows of Italian proportions, with architrave and pediment (Pl. 24). At Stanway, built about 1630, the gatehouse has several such 'Italian' details, and the gateway into the garden is rusticated in a manner similar to that at Arundel House. This treatment must be distinguished from that at houses like Morton Corbet or Kirkstead, where the windows have retained their broad proportions and the pediment is in consequence a low one, and merely another classical motif mechanically applied to a space that is unsuitable to it.

Side by side with this new 'Italianism', and partly in sympathy with it, may be seen a minor revival of the 'Italianism' of nearly a century before. At Chilham Castle, Kent—whose plan is supposedly copied from the Villa Farnese—there is a corbelled oriel similar to that at Hengrave Hall; a rather plainer example occurs at Hartwell House in Buckinghamshire (Pl. 7a) and there was similar corbelling at Northumberland House.[1] These were tentative steps in the direction of, but, it must be emphasized, still very far away from, Jones's mature style. In all the houses mentioned the motifs are mingled with other forms—the purely native flanking turrets at Hatfield and Houghton Conquest, the crenellations at Bolsover, the Flemish decoration at Wothorpe—in a way that reveals that it was ornament that was changing rather than the character of the architecture as a whole. But yet the character of architecture was changing in part; the 'Italyan' windows at Bolsover, and windows of similar proportions elsewhere, could be happily introduced only because of the shorter elevations that sufficed for 'double-pile' ranges and square-block plans.

In the houses of lesser men ornament never reached the fully-fashioned Anglo-Flemish style of the greater. In some of these lesser houses in the late sixteenth century the type of classical ornament that had appeared earlier on the greater lingered on. At Barlborough (c. 1583–4) and at North Cadbury (Pl. 9a) there is the shell cresting seen long before at Layer Marney and Dingley, and at North Cadbury and at Wakehurst the jambs of windows were still treated as classical columns. At the same time these houses often have some of the less florid motifs of their greater

[1] *L.C.C.S.L.* xviii (1937), pls. 4, 5.

contemporaries, generally in conjunction with other styles. At Wakehurst, for example, sub-Gothic forms and forms derived from the greater houses of the mid-century are mingled with the nail-head ornament of Montacute, and similar decoration, but less of it, is found on the related house at Gravetye.

It is within this context that the use of Gothic and sub-Gothic motifs in the later years is best understood. Their peculiarity is not that they were often but that they were very variously used: upon lesser houses, upon greater, upon churches, and upon university buildings. This is sometimes called a 'survival' and sometimes a 'revival'. It was in fact both, and it could only be revived by some men because it had survived amongst others. It had done this in two ways; through its unconscious use by men to whom its idiom was still natural, and in a conscious admiration of its aesthetic qualities by others who also knew something about contemporary art. John Norden, who was as well acquainted as any man with the great houses of the Elizabethans, admired the 'beauty and curious contrived work' of Henry VII's chapel, echoed Leland's 'Orbis Miraculum', and thought it a 'mirror' of art and architecture.[1] Stephen Powle, a man of Calvinist sympathies and of wide enough taste to be greatly impressed by the tomb of Henri II at St. Denis, wrote to his father from the Continent in 1581:

I finde nothing in frannce of sutch thinges as be obiectes to the sight more worth the notinge then there monasteries and churches. The which for stately buildinges, curious Imadgry and verietie of relickes is equall with any other parte of Europe whatsoever. In travelinge from Calais to Paris I beheld nothinge so mutch to be observed as the Church of Amiens in Picardie and of St. Denis in the Isle of frannce.'[2]

This appreciation of the aesthetic appeal of Gothic was the basis of its deliberate use, and the intention was either to advertise the religious functions of the building, or to give it an archaic air, or to emphasize a particular feature by the contrast of its ornament with the classical character of all the rest. Of these the first is by far the

[1] *Speculum Britanniae . . . Middlesex* (1593), pp. 43–44.
[2] B. M. Lans. Mss. 100, No. 19.

most significant and there is more point to it than is generally allowed.

It is sometimes argued that churches continued to be built in a Gothic style because a church was by tradition a Gothic building. This, however, is plainly inadequate, for so, until the Renaissance, were all buildings. The explanation is rather to be sought in the fact that Gothic was, as far as contemporaries knew, the only current style that was a native English growth. To many, treading a narrow path between Geneva on the one hand and Rome on the other, Gothic ornament was a symbol of their national Church that, by amazing luck or by the inscrutable designs of Providence, had preserved the Apostolic Succession among God's Englishmen. When the new library was being built at St. John's College, Cambridge, in 1623 the windows were deliberately given a Gothic form, and the Bishop of Exeter wrote to the Master to express his opinion that 'the old fashion of church window' was 'most meet for such a building'.[1] A library, of course, is not a church, but a library in a university college in the early seventeenth century was still mainly a repository for sacred learning and had a markedly ecclesiastical character. For all their bitter fights, the religious factions in England then had much in common, and Milton spoke to a wide audience when he vowed to

> . . . love the high embowèd roof
> With antick pillars massy proof.

There could be no greater mistake than to imagine that churches and chapels were built with Gothic ornament from a mere mechanical following of the old ways. Gothic ornament still possessed an intellectual and emotional content and blended, or attempted to blend, national feeling with religious piety. Nevertheless, because it was used in this fashion it employed the forms that had been used earlier, and wholly failed to develop; and it could only be used because of the untrammelled practice of contemporary designers, who saw no incongruity in combining constituents of diverse origin and had not lost all knowledge of Gothic work.

No better examples of the deliberate use of Gothic for its religious

---

[1] R.C.H.M. *City of Cambridge*, pp. 196–7.

associations can be found than the Oxford colleges of the early seventeenth century. In the ranges of chambers and in the halls the lights of the windows have generally a four-centred arch or a flat head or else, as in the Hall at Wadham, tracery that is little more than disguised strapwork. But in the chapels, as at Lincoln (Pl. 16b) and Jesus, an almost pure Perpendicular tracery is used, and in the former this contrasts strongly with the four-centred heads of the lights of the nearly contemporary range of chambers. A similar contrast between the full or would-be full Gothic character of the chapel windows and the sub-Gothic character of those of the domestic ranges is found at Abbot's Hospital in Guildford. It is found also in some of the greater houses that revived the private chapel, such as Hatfield and Charlton, and here the contrast is between an attempt at a full Gothic effect in the chapel and a wholly non-Gothic effect in the rest of the building. In the churches of the period, which, although rare, are commoner than for a century before, the main architectural features are almost wholly Gothic. The church at Groombridge in Sussex, built in 1623—and traditionally in thanksgiving for the failure of the projected match between Prince Charles and the Roman Catholic Spanish Infanta— is almost indistinguishable in all but its plan from one of the late fifteenth century. Only the porch betrays the date and is in a contemporary 'Jacobean' style (Pl. 25b). A similar contrast between the Renaissance ornament applied to the porch and the Gothic, or sub-Gothic, character of the rest of the building occurs at the somewhat earlier church (c. 1611–14) of St. Michael at Theydon Mount, Essex.[1] A church porch had still a markedly secular character and the medieval habit of using it to transact business in lasted until the end of our period,[2] and it was therefore sometimes treated differently from the rest of the church.

The second type of deliberate usage is far less common and is wholly confined to the building, at about the turn of the century, of a number of castles—Lulworth, Sherborne, Bolsover—with a

[1] N. Pevsner, *Buildings of England—Essex*, pp. 352–3.
[2] In an agreement of 1624 between Sir Paul D'Ewes and Jan Jansen, of St. Martin-in-the-Fields, payment for the erection of a tomb in Stowlangtoft Church was to be made in the church porch, B.M. Harl. Mss. 98, No. 15.

rectangular and keep-like plan and form. The castellar air given by the plan and height is added to by romantic diminutive bastions at Lulworth (Pl. 13*a*), and crenellations, in place of a parapet or balustrade, at all three. At Longford, too, something of this character was given by the great bastion towers at the three corners of the building.

Longford is also an example of the third usage. The bastions of the entrance front there are not flanking an ordinary Elizabethan range, but a short and highly ornamented façade, in form an extended frontispiece, that runs between and is contrasted with them (Pl. 2*b*). It is again at Oxford, however, that the practice is clearest. The contrast between the often full-blown Gothic of chapel windows and the sub-Gothic of domestic ranges is paralleled by that between both of these and the wholly Renaissance ornament of the dominating frontispieces. The point was made earlier, when the Schools Quadrangle frontispiece (Pl. 21*a*) was cited as an example of emphasis; here it is not the emphasis itself that is at issue but the manner of obtaining it by the clash of motifs of wholly different style and origin.

There is, however, a further point to be made. At a time when the builders of great houses were indulging in frontispieces with the perverted ornament of Bramshill and Charlton, Oxford was erecting the purest examples of exercises upon the classical orders. Nowhere, not even at Hatfield, is there anything to compare with the five superimposed orders of the Schools Quadrangle, and the frontispieces at Merton (Pl. 21*b*) and Wadham are not far behind it. The contrast, therefore, is not, as it might well have been in the great houses, between Gothic and classicist but between Gothic and a would-be learned form of classical ornament.

It is tempting to suggest that this unique combination appeared at Oxford because the University was still a largely religious institution and yet a repository of the New Learning. In that case, however, one must explain why the same combination is not so apparent at Cambridge. It would be easy, but insufficient, to attribute this to the ending by about 1600 of the great expansion and rebuilding that had gone on there for a century. In fact, even in the early seventeenth century considerable additions were being made to some colleges, with ample opportunities for the clapping-on of a frontispiece if one had been desired.

The explanation is rather to be found in the answer to another question: why did the expansion of Cambridge slacken and that of Oxford accelerate just about this time? One may perhaps explain it this way: the State was moving rightwards in religion at a time when Cambridge had gained something of a Puritan reputation, and just as the suspicion of Lollardry at Oxford had led to the expansion of Cambridge in the fifteenth century, so now the whiff of Puritanism from Cambridge was diverting patronage to Oxford.

The greater weight of Puritanism at Cambridge affected the architecture there. Because Puritans were more fiercely anti-Italian and were more uncompromisingly English they tended—in the absence of any compelling social pressure—to adhere to a traditional style of building and to avoid foreign motifs. Thus the great Jacobean frontispieces of Oxford are unknown at Cambridge. Indeed the only consistently Renaissance architecture at Cambridge prior to the accession of Charles I is in the work of Caius and the doorway traditionally ascribed to Sir Christopher Wray at Magdalene; Caius certainly had 'Romish' sympathies and Wray was far removed from the Puritan camp. Even in later years, when something, but not enough, had been done to purge Cambridge, its architecture never approached the Italianism of Oxford as revealed in the Botanic Gardens gateway, the porch at St. Mary's, and the now destroyed gatehouse of Magdalen.

Puritanism affected Cambridge architecture in another way: by confining it not merely to the traditional but to a particular form of the traditional style. The early seventeenth-century architecture of Cambridge is largely—the deliberate taking down and stone-by-stone rebuilding of King Edward's tower at Trinity is exceptional —in the sober and humdrum sub-Gothic of many smaller houses of the period. At Oxford, by contrast, there was 'a taste for the more showy and eccentric features of Tudor Gothic such as the fan vault'.[1]

It is by comparison with this deliberate self-conscious use of Gothic in some of the greater houses and at Oxford that its use

[1] R.C.H.M. *City of Oxford*, p. xxii.

elsewhere can be best appreciated. The unstudied use of Gothic is well illustrated at a minor house of some pretensions, at Barlborough, where the string course is so managed that it runs up above the windows of the main face to form a label. At Kingston Maurward (Pl. 10a) the mullions and jambs of the windows of the main front have pure Perpendicular bases. At Sydenham (Devonshire) the semicircular arched doorway has a flat moulded head with sub-Gothic foliage in the spandrels. The windows at Wakehurst and at the much later Chantmarle (Pl. 17a), which was not begun until 1612, have four-centred heads to the lights. In these houses, and in many others which retain such sub-Gothic features as returned labels above the windows, these forms are mingled indiscriminately with various kinds of Renaissance decoration, or are used in a building with a rigidly Renaissance symmetry.

It was not only in distinctive uses of Gothic that the greater and lesser houses differed. The latter reflected in the early seventeenth century a marked disposition to avoid the 'French' and 'Italian' motifs and even the more exaggerated forms of the 'Anglo-Flemish' style. Thus although there was a general tendency among all men to abandon the classical columns flanking the entry, this led in the minor houses not to the use of the contorted pilasters and decoration of Bramshill and Charlton but to the almost complete absence of decoration at all. This is illustrated by a comparison of the porch of North Cadbury with its flanking columns and that of Newton Surmaville, where they are conspicuously absent (Pl. 9). Such early seventeenth-century Dorset houses as Chantmarle, Wraxall, Wynford Eagle, Edmondsham, and Anderson Manor, which all have porch entrances with semicircular heads and without flanking columns, are typical. They contrast with a late sixteenth-century Dorset house like Tyneham, where the entrance has a pedimented head and bracket, and with Water Eaton, where it has flanking Tuscan columns. This was, of course, only a tendency and not a law, for there are instances of the use of classical columns in these houses in later years and they had not always been present earlier.

Where columns are still used in a late house such as Hanford Hall (c. 1624), the decoration applied to the entrance has no hint of the

Bramshill manner, but is of the older character, with plain flanking pilasters surmounted by a low flat pediment. Houses such as Shipton Hall and Madeley in Shropshire, with the decoration confined to low pediments above the entrances, are in the same vein. At Llanhydrock in Cornwall, the gatehouse, built as late as 1651, has blind arcading, and windows flanked by columns in the manner of eighty years before, and the columns themselves have resemblances to those at Cotehelstone.

It is, I think, possible to show that, contrary to the popular view, Elizabethan and Jacobean architecture is, on the whole, remarkable not for the abundance but for the scarcity of its applied ornament. At the same time it is beyond dispute that no matter what results an analysis may achieve, these buildings, and especially the later ones, give a general impression of being highly decorated; and the apparent contradiction calls for some explanation.

The answer lies largely in the advent to fashion of brick as a building material. Although it had been used by the very greatest in the early sixteenth century, it suffered an eclipse with the coming of the Renaissance, and nearly all the houses of important men between 1550 and 1590 had been built of stone. Some of the exceptions have significant features. Gorhambury was partly built of brick and flint, but some of the original plastering over the front still remains, and the half-inch projection of the window-surrounds from the main face show that it was always intended to be plastered. Rather similar treatment can be seen at Bisham. In the royal building accounts there are many references throughout the late sixteenth century to the covering of naked brickwork and the simulation of stone.[1] As late as 1642, Fuller, while recognizing the virtues of brick, was inclined to prefer it for utilitarian rather than aesthetic reasons—'freestone, like a fair complexion, soonest waxeth old, while brick keeps her beauty longest'.[2]

Nevertheless, by the turn of the century brick was well established. Aubrey, writing not so long after Fuller, said, although with considerable exaggeration, that Lord Chief Justice Popham, who

[1] E. Mercer, 'The Decoration of the Royal Palaces from 1553–1625', *Arch. Journ.* cx (1954), 150–63.
[2] *The Holy State* (1642), p. 168.

died in 1607, 'first brought in brick building in London (scil. after Lincoln's Inn and St. James)'.[1] The general truth behind the exaggeration, however, is not confined to London, but covers a wide area. In part this use of brick may have been the result of a recognition of the material's qualities, in part a lesson learnt from the Low Countries, but undoubtedly it helped to solve the problems of would-be builders who were, on the whole, less wealthy individually than their predecessors and less able to make quarries of monastic buildings, although the earlier importance of these as a source of cheap materials can be over-rated.[2]

The ornamental value of brick lay mainly in its colour and range of tone, and cut and gauged brick for decoration is hardly known at all before the end of our period. A new appreciation of the colour of the material is revealed in the royal building accounts which show that the practice of covering or disguising brickwork gave way in the early seventeenth century to one of heightening its natural colour by 'pencilling', 'russetting', or 'red-colouring' it.[3] Allied to this, although favoured rather in the lesser than the greater houses, was a revival of the habit of decorating a building by picking out patterns, generally diaper, in a different, darker brick. It is perhaps an exaggeration to call this a revival, for the practice had never wholly died out, but it became commoner in later years than it had been earlier, and spread, tentatively, to some great houses. Thus it is used far more thoroughly at North Mimms and at Quenby (Pl. 17b) than it had been at the earlier Eastbury, where it is confined to a diamond pattern on some of the gables; and although found at such an imposing late house as Dorfold it is confined there to the upper stories. The effect aimed at may be judged from Ralph Symons's 'upright' for the building of Second Court at St. John's College, Cambridge, in 1598[4] (fig. 15). At Anderson Manor the

[1] *Brief Lives*, ed. O. L. Dick (1949), p. 246.

[2] Loseley, for example, is often said to have been built of the ruins of Waverley Abbey, but it is clear that most of the stone for it was dug in the quarry. It was only 'white stone', and ashlar from the Friary at Guildford, that More considered worth plundering, J. Evans, 'Extracts from the Account Book of Sir William More', *Archaeologia*, xxxvi (1854), 294–310.

[3] E. Mercer in *Arch. Journ.* cx (1954), 150–63.

[4] R.C.H.M. *City of Cambridge*, p. 194b.

common diaper pattern is avoided, and instead, every third course is in a darker brick. Such patterning was obviously popular, and it is probable that attempts were made to obtain it cheaply; and for this Symons's 'upright' provides some curious evidence. No diapering is now visible in Second Court and there is nothing to suggest any wholesale disturbance of the brickwork. It could, of

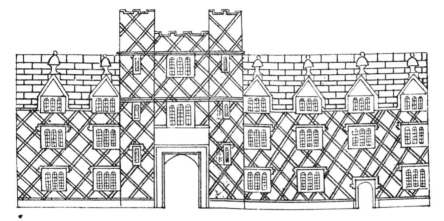

FIG. 15. *St. John's College, Cambridge. 'Upright' by Ralph Symons*

course, be argued that Symons's intention was abandoned in the course of building, were it not that David Loggan's engraving, first published in 1690, shows the Court with diaper patterning upon it.[1] There is no reason to think that Loggan invented this, and we must conclude that it was there in *c.* 1690 and has since vanished. But if it were in brick of a different colour, then it would not vanish; it might, however, if it were only painted on. Now there is an entry in the accounts, upon completion of the building, for 'painting' the brickwork.[2] This may, of course, refer to something else, although it is hard to suggest what else, but if it can be referred to the patterning, then the contradiction between the present state of the building and Loggan's independent confirmation of Symons's 'upright' vanishes, and we have a further instance

[1] *Cantabrigia Illustrata*, ed. J. W. Clark (Cambridge, 1905). I have to thank Mr. Denys Spittle for drawing my attention to Loggan's engraving.
[2] R.C.H.M. *City of Cambridge*, p. 194.

of the fondness for diaper patterning and, in a new way, of the habit of painting and colouring brickwork.[1]

More important than a heightening of the colour of the brick-work, or the use of different colours, was the contrasting of the red brick with white or whitened stonework. This was an effect easily achieved by the use of brick for the main walling and of stone for dressings, quoins, string-courses, parapets, window and door-surrounds. Moyns Park is an early example of this and Wimbledon was another. Later examples are numerous, but Hat-field and Charlton may be singled out. At Hatfield there is a con-trast between the red brick of the walling and the white stonework of the quoins, and, on the south front, of the façade and frontis-piece. At Charlton, which Mr. Whiffen has called 'the Jacobean style at its most mature',[2] the practice is taken farther with the patterned quoining not only of the main walls but also of the window-bays, and the plain but heavily emphasized stone string-courses at three levels (Pl. 26).

It is, however, clearest at some of the lesser houses, which lack even such limited applied ornament, for instance upon the porch, as that seen at Charlton. Here, as in its general design, Anderson Manor is a classic example. Apart from a raised keystone to the porch entrance and ball finials upon the gables its decorative quality is wholly obtained by the contrast of the red and purple brickwork with the white quoins, window-dressings, string-courses, and copings of the plinth and gables (Pl. 10b). In a house of even less pretensions, Woolmore Farm, there is the same total lack of applied ornament and the same use of materials to give a decorative quality (Pl. 14a). That these 'studies in red and white' were quite conscious creations and were striven after even when no stone at all was used is shown again by the royal building accounts. Those for James I's

[1] Painted diaper may have been quite common. It is odd that on many, if not most, houses with brick diaper the patterning begins and ends in both dimensions in a quite arbitrary way, as though its use at any particular stage of building depended solely upon the availability of the burnt bricks. Men of the time were no fonder of sporadic patches of decoration than we are today, and this usage suggests that they were not as worried as we should expect by the irregularity of the brick diaper, because they could, if necessary, complete the patterning in paint.

[2] M. Whiffen, *Elizabethan and Jacobean Architecture* (1952), p. 63.

houses at Newmarket and Royston refer to the 'russetting' or 'red-colouring' of the main wall-faces and the 'white-finishing' or 'laying with finishing mortar' of the brick window-jambs and fascias.[1] This deliberate colour contrast was not restricted to buildings in which brick was used. The builders of Gorhambury and Bisham attempted to hide the flint; those of Lake House, Wiltshire (*c.* 1600) (Pl. 27), and of the bastions at Longford used it in conjunction with white stone to obtain a bold chequer-work pattern; at Stockton House (Pl. 15*b*) in the same county the two materials were used in alternate courses to give a banded effect. These practices had, of course, been common enough upon minor domestic buildings and upon churches in flint-and-stone producing areas, but their appearance upon houses of some importance and of conscious aesthetic design was new.

Whatever view may be taken of their aesthetic success, Jacobean designers achieved in these houses a complete integration of ornament and structure: an integration in which ornament was almost wholly provided by emphasizing the qualities of the materials used in the structure. In design, Jacobean houses are the fruit of a long growth, and the same is true of their mode of decoration; that mode is the result of a continuous development in which applied ornament is increasingly subordinated to, and finally eliminated from, the structural design.

From this distance of time it is possible to see the development of ornament, as of general design, as the outcome of a long-sustained conflict between opposing forces. On the one hand were the aesthetic ideas of the Renaissance that the absolute State had indirectly brought into England; on the other was the native environment of men who were on the whole and almost until the end of our period the active or quiescent supporters of that State. This environment expressed itself in their religious and social predilections, in the form of their buildings, and in the material at hand. The conflict resulted at times in a forced compromise, at times in a happy agreement, but in the end in the almost total victory of native needs in building over every Renaissance canon of design and ornament but that of symmetry. In so doing it

[1] E. Mercer in *Arch. Journ.* cx (1954), 150–63.

produced, although temporal and social distinctions can be discerned, an architecture that was remarkable for its homogeneity.

To this there are, however, two important exceptions: the work of the Sharington circle and of Inigo Jones and his patrons. Both of these were the productions of men who were in control of the State machine but were isolated politically from the classes that were the most important potential supporters of the State. Charles I, the greatest of all the patrons of the aesthetics that Jones and the virtuosi propagated, ended where Somerset and Northumberland ended, on the scaffold of political defeat. Yet the parallel is less significant than the contrast. The Sharingtonians isolated themselves from their potential supporters by pushing on too fast with the new social and political developments; the virtuosi and their master by clinging too long to the old. But while the advanced politics of the former were reflected in advanced art, the retarded politics of the latter were not accompanied by a retarded art. Humanism had done its work by then. It was no longer the intellectual expression of the absolute State but the climate of opinion of all educated men. Instead of a small group of professionally learned men there was now, potentially, a whole class able to appreciate not merely the decorative motifs but the artistic intent of the Continental Renaissance. In contrast with Hoby and Thomas in the mid-sixteenth century, English visitors to the Continent in the early seventeenth, such as Robert Treswell in Spain in 1604[1] and Sir George Chaworth at Brussels in 1621,[2] were taking a considerable interest in painting. William Trumbull, when Resident Agent at Brussels slightly earlier, apparently spent a not inconsiderable amount of his time in viewing, procuring, and safeguarding pictures for himself and his friends.[3] The title of Peacham's book *The Compleat Gentleman*, in contrast with Castiglione's *Courtier*, is a mark of the change.

Nevertheless, there were forces militating against the development that was latent in the situation. The point has been made that the

[1] *A Relation of . . . the Journey of . . . Charles Earle of Nottingham . . . to the King of Spaine* (1605).

[2] 'Diary', ed. A. J. Kempe, *Loseley Manuscripts* (1835), pp. 420–87.

[3] H.M.C. *Downshire*, iv. 71, 147, 256, 508, 515.

virtuoso, unlike the Castiglione courtier, was 'a gentleman no longer connected with the Court, and characterized by an inexhaustible and disinterested curiosity in every branch of culture'.[1] But this is a description of what might have been, not of what was, in the early seventeenth century. In practice, for the reasons sketched in the Introduction, the virtuosi were straitly tied to the court, and this tie was a fruitful source of impediments to the spread of their ideas. Those who disliked the State's policies tended to vent their spleen upon the virtuosi's tastes. Not everyone perhaps grew indignant at the high-handed treatment of the parishioners of St. Gregory's in pursuance of a royal scheme to give a Palladian look to St. Paul's, for not everyone was affected; but the Commissions of 1620 and 1631 for raising money for that scheme—and over £100,000 was collected between 1631 and 1643[2]—were another matter. They placed the financial burden for Jones's ideas upon wealthy and influential circles and helped to establish an emotional link between the new art and royal extortion. In the course of a venomous attack on the memory of James I and his courtiers, Francis Osborne went out of his way to jibe at Arundel for his collection of marbles and statuary and at Charles I for having similar interests.[3]

It is necessary to stress the interaction of these two factors—the new level of Humanism in England and the policies followed by the State—for the failure to appreciate it has led Dr. Per Palme into a one-sided political explanation of the introduction of Palladianism. In his view the Whitehall Banqueting House was erected in a revolutionary style as a sign and in celebration of the expected triumph of the Spanish Match, and from this beginning Palladianism spread.[4] I think it would be sufficient to controvert such an idea by a mere statement of the obvious truth, that men's aesthetic tastes are not so shallow that they change at a breath because of a political *rapprochement* with a former enemy; but there

[1] L. Salerno, '17th Century English Literature on Painting', *Journ. W.C.I.* xiv (1951), 236-7.

[2] R. Newcourt, *Reportorium Ecclesiasticum Parochiale Londinense* (1708), i. 4

[3] *Traditional Memoyres of the Raigne of King James* (Oxford, 1658), p. 58.

[4] *Triumph of Peace A Study of the Whitehall Banqueting House* (Stockholm, 1956).

are more historical arguments. Neither the Spanish Match nor the Banqueting House came into the world Minerva-like. Both had a long gestation. The *rapprochement* with Spain was only one aspect of the Crown's estrangement from the country, and its consequent tendency to seek alliance with anti-popular forces. And the manner of the Banqueting House was neither so new nor so unique as Dr. Palme suggests. Quite apart from the Queen's House at Greenwich, which had at least been begun by 1616 at the latest,[1] the signs of the introduction of a new art were apparent in many media long before either the Banqueting House or the Spanish Match had been seriously projected. There is indeed a connexion between the two, and if the Palladianism of the one was popularly associated with the other, then that may have contributed to preventing the style from spreading widely. This connexion, however, was not a simple and direct one of cause and effect; rather both were the result of a long and many-sided historical development.

Their dependence upon the court prevented the virtuosi's success from being anything but brief and narrow; but that dependence was a temporary phenomenon, while the success itself was based upon intellectual advances that were irreversible. Thus the very appearance of the virtuosi was itself a guarantee that English artists would one day achieve a better status and English art a higher level.

[1] P.R.O. E. 351-3389.

# III

# INTERIOR DECORATION

THE forms of interior decoration, although varied, were parallel in development and need to be discussed as a whole. The interaction between Renaissance sympathies and fashions and the native environment, which determined the manner of architectural decoration, operated here in different circumstances and with different results. Social needs, although requiring in some houses a Great Hall and a Long Gallery, made very few other demands upon the nature of a room, and in consequence ornament had a far greater role and was more profusely used. It is to the interiors of Elizabethan and Jacobean houses that the general view, that this architecture is overloaded with decoration, properly applies.

Invariably in the earlier years and commonly until the end, a great amount of ornament was spread evenly in an overall patterning, often paid for by the yard, upon the whole surface. This repetitive patterning, and the method of paying for it, was nothing but a continuation of medieval practice; what was new was the employment of different motifs. By the 1580's a style had been formed which was notable for its abundance of motifs, for its grotesques, strapwork, terms and caryatides, jewel ornament, obelisk pinnacles and plain and interlaced arcading. It was the style known to contemporaries as the 'antique' and well described by Peacham as 'an unnatural or unorderly composition for delight sake, of men, beasts, birds, fishes, flowers, &c., without Rime or reason, for the greater variety you show in your invention the more you please.'[1]

Paintwork was the commonest method of decoration: and it was ubiquitous. Every surface that was free of tapestries or wall hangings and that could be reached with a brush was painted, either in

[1] *The Gentleman's Exercise* (1612), p. 50.

simple colours or with patterning. Only a few instances need be given. At such a very neglected royal house as Woodstock the 'fret' of the plaster ceiling was coloured in 1595.[1] Woodwork was not only painted in a colour different from its natural appearance, as in the Long Gallery at Westminster in 1580–1, but often with patterning, as at Shire Hall, Wilmington, Kent (*c.* 1591),[2] and on the strings of the staircase at Astonbury, Herts.[3] Stone doorcases were frequently painted, even those in Inigo Jones's Banqueting House. The patterning was often in a monochrome, but where there was no patterning, and even sometimes where there was, bright colours were used. In the royal accounts, and, for example, in the expense account of George Levens, Sir Thomas Tresham's steward,[4] such items as vermilion, ochre, indigo, and the primary colours occur constantly.

Apart from mere colouring there was a great amount of painted decoration. It had many forms, and F. W. Reader—on whose work any discussion of the subject must lean heavily—distinguishes nine types, including figure subjects.[5] However, the eight other types can best be discussed together under one head as patterning. The wall-surface to be decorated was usually divided into a main filling and a frieze, which might vary considerably in depth. Throughout the period, but less obviously so in the later years, the frieze had more pictorial quality than the filling, which was generally treated wholly as patterning. At a house in Market Street, Saffron Walden, where the decoration is probably of the mid-sixteenth century,

---

[1] E. Mercer, 'The Decoration of the Royal Palaces from 1553 to 1625', *Arch. Journ.* cx (1954), 150–63. When the sources for royal examples mentioned in this section are not documented they will be found there.

[2] E. Yates in *Arch. Journ.* lxxxvi (1929), 111–12.

[3] As most of the woodwork and plasterwork is found in, and is generally an integral part of, the houses of the period it is often dealt with by the authorities cited on page 15, n. 1. Only where there is some reason for disagreeing with their conclusions have I documented examples discussed by them.

[4] B.M. Add. Mss. 39832, f. 114.

[5] Mr. Reader's articles in the *Archaeological Journal*, vols. lxxxix, xcii, xciv, xcviii, are the invaluable basic corpus of published material. To them should be added P. M. Johnston's article in vol. xxxvii, N.S., of the *Journal of the British Archaeological Association*. To avoid a forest of footnotes I have only exceptionally documented examples discussed there.

the filling consists of delicately interlaced conventional floral designs, while the frieze, although itself a patterning, introduces moustachioed human heads. As the urns and amorini and grotesques of 'antique work' became better known they too sometimes appeared in the filling which, as at Elmstead Hall, Essex,[1] might become indistinguishable in subject-matter from the frieze (Pl. 25a).

The popularity of 'antique work', however, did not wholly oust a more native style of geometrical ornament and naturalistic floral designs. The elaborate foliage and beasts in a very medieval manner formerly at High Sunderland, Halifax,[2] or the more exotic but still partially medieval beasts and flowers of The Old Flushing Inn at Rye (c. 1547)[3] are not found in the second half of the century, but the naturalistic floral tradition died harder. In the Guest Chamber at No. 3 Cornmarket, Oxford (c. 1580), the geometrical patterning of the filling is enriched with delicate paintings of English flowers, Canterbury-bells and wild-roses, and with conventional late-medieval grape-bunches (Pl. 28). Very similar motifs were used again, at some time after 1572, at Peke's Farm, Chiddingly, Sussex. The panels, painted during James I's reign, in the Crown Hotel at Aylesbury and the filling, with a date of 1600 or 1606, at Dedham in Essex[4] preserve the same usage to a less degree and avoid the conventionalized 'antique' style. In some cases— houses in Market Street and in The Close at Saffron Walden— although the motifs have become conventional, the execution still retains a delicacy and thinness of line similar to that of the earlier examples.

Geometrical patterning too was continued throughout the period. In many designs it was combined with something else— No. 3 Cornmarket, Oxford, has already been mentioned—but there was much decoration that was purely geometrical. It took the form of circles connected by diagonal, vertical, and horizontal bands at The Priory at Thaxted. At Paramour Grange in Kent a

[1] G. M. Benton in *Essex Archaeological Soc. Trans.* N.S. xxi (1937), 340-2.
[2] Now in the Bankfield Museum, Halifax.
[3] P. M. Johnston in *Sussex Archaeological Collections*, l (1907), 117-24.
[4] G. M. Benton in *Essex Archaeological Soc. Trans.* N.S. xxii (1940), 148-9.

design, executed in 1603, of interlaced octagons enclosing hexagons and what appear to be carrots has been shown to be a remote and wholly misunderstood imitation of the ceiling of Wolsey's Closet at Hampton Court; and in or about 1600 the same design was used at Barham's Manor House in Suffolk.[1]

In combination with any of these forms and either in the filling or in the frieze might be found religious or patriotic or moralizing texts. Some happy men combined all the qualities in these, and on an old house in Weymouth, pulled down in 1821, was written the verse:

God save our Queen Elizabethe, God send her happy dayes,
God grant her grace to persewir in his most holey wayes An Dom 1577.[2]

The Old Rectory House at Cocking, Sussex, had the walls painted with texts from the Bishops' Bible of 1570. At Bridgefoot House, Kelvedon, in Essex, there was painted over a fireplace a text from the Geneva Bible of 1560.[3] When alterations to Glastonbury House in Smithfield had been completed in 1587 the painter sent in his bill for 'painting beams in the great chamber and writing verses about'.[4] This, however, was the more popular aspect of the matter. In higher circles there was a liking for more learned and esoteric themes. Paul Hentzner commented on the Gallery at Whitehall with its 'variety of emblems on paper cut into the shape of shields with mottoes';[5] they impressed John Manningham so much in 1601 that he described them at length in his diary.[6]

Wainscot was, at first, almost invariably in small panels, and was often highly decorated: with lion-masks at Brenchley Parsonage, Surrey, c. 1573, with moulded geometrical patterns on some of the shorter wall-surfaces at Hardwick. Inlay was not uncommon; at Gilling Castle the panels were richly ornamented with interlaced patterning and floral decoration in holly, and the panelling from Sizergh Castle, now in the Victoria and Albert Museum, has inlaid arcading. The effect was sometimes imitated

[1] G. M. Benton in *Antiq. Journ.* x (1930), 255–6; N. Lloyd, ibid. xi (1931), 169–70.
[2] *Salisbury and Winchester Journal*, 28 May 1821.
[3] F. Roe in *Conn.* lxxxv (1930), 18–25.    [4] B.M. Eg. Mss. 2599, No. 9.
[5] *A Journey into England in the Year 1598*, ed. H. Walpole (1757), p. 29.
[6] 'Diary of John Manningham', ed. J. Bruce, *Camden Soc.* xcix (1868), 3–5.

in paint, and in 1597–8 the Sergeant Painter was paid at the extravagant rate of ten shillings a yard for painting wainscot at Oatlands with 'draughts of gold and silver of marquetry'. Imitation cartouches and panelling were often painted upon woodwork, and those in the Kederminster Library in Langley-Marish Church appear to be as late as 1626.[1]

The plaster ceilings of the second half of the sixteenth century were generally covered with a great amount of repetitive ornament, intricately and geometrically patterned with ribs whose deep sections continue Gothic forms and whose disposition is reminiscent in early examples, as in the hall at Collacombe Barton, Devon, of late Gothic vaulting. Pendants at the rib intersections added to the ornamental effect; at first, as at Melcombe Bingham and Loseley, they were little more than floral bosses in obvious imitation of the bosses of wooden ceilings, but as plasterers grew more ambitious the pendants became more elaborate, and at Herringston (Pl. 29) and Dorfold (c. 1620) they take the form of openwork lanterns along the ridge of the barrel-vaulted ceiling. The panels formed by the ribs were often filled with plaster decoration, with royal or family badges, or with the well-modelled birds and beasts of Melbury House (Pl. 30b). By about 1600 the plaster ribs were becoming broader and shallower and a fondness for curvilinear patterning and strapwork was showing itself.[2] At the same time the running tendrils and floral motifs of wall-painting were imitated, as at Michaelchurch Court, Herefordshire, in 1602, and at Burton Agnes, where the Long Gallery ceiling had a series of six scrolls of roses running its whole length[3] (Pl. 35a) and that of the Oak Room is covered with a honeysuckle design.

In the early years of the seventeenth century this diffuse manner of design began to give way to one which treated a surface as an architectural whole and accommodated ornament to its proportions. With this was introduced a set of motifs, of which the most noticeable are correctly classical architectural features: panelling in

[1] E. Clive Rouse in *Records of Bucks*. xiv (1941–6), 50–69.

[2] As late as 1615, however, a pattern-book of geometrical designs was partly intended for plasterers; see W. Gedde, *A Booke of sundry draughts* . . . (1615–16).

[3] C. J. Richardson, *Architectural Remains* . . . (1838), pl. xviii.

the form of blind window-openings with pediments and hipped and eared architraves, perspective masoned arches, columns and pilasters used, not as a decoration to break up a wall surface, but to frame an ornamented space. One of the commonest symptoms of the change is the replacement of the coarse and profuse 'jewel-ornament' by the elegant and isolated 'carrot-drop' or split baluster. There was, too, a minor revival of the less exuberant motifs imported in the early sixteenth century. Perspective arches and the use of columns and pilasters to frame a piece of decoration are known to have been present at Nonsuch. Motifs that had been introduced in a slightly earlier period and long since neglected were revived. The ceiling at East Riddlesden Hall (c. 1640)[1] is a copy of that of Wolsey's Closet at Hampton Court, and the early seventeenth-century studio ceiling at Canons Ashby and one at Little Strickland Hall, Westmorland (Pl. 30a), are imitations of that at the Chapel Royal, St. James's. This revival is neither accidental nor insignificant. Its causes are to be sought directly in the new manner of design which eschewed 'unorderly com-position' and found itself in sympathy with the motifs used in those very rare early houses—all traditionally associated with foreign artists—in which a considered design is apparent in interior decoration. Its significance is that for the first time Renaissance motifs are used by English artists not for their intrinsic decorative qualities but for their general propriety.

The process is most clearly seen in the development of wainscot, and the first sign of the change is the increase in the size of panels that occurs in the late sixteenth century. In the Great Chamber at Gilling Castle, built in the last years of Elizabeth's reign, the area from floor to frieze is covered by three tiers of fairly large panels instead of the usual five, six, or seven of small ones. The interlaced arcading above large panels of wainscot from Sizergh Castle is a nearly contemporary example of the same tendency. By the early years of the next century even larger panels were being used: some at Burton Agnes are 8 feet high by 6 ft. wide, and some at Hatfield and Dorfold are only slightly smaller.

An increase in the size of the panels, although of significance,

_____
[1] M. Jourdain, *English Decorative Plasterwork* . . ., p. 37.

was yet decoration in the old unorganized manner, carried out, or capable of being carried out, by the yard, and it still preserved the most distinctive characteristic of early panelling: that, apart from a frieze and perhaps a low skirting, it was generally as undifferentiated vertically as it was horizontally and unrelated in either dimension to the proportions of the surface it was covering. At the turn of the century, for instance in the small Dining-room at Montacute and in the Ball-room at Knole, attempts were made to proportion the wainscot not to the height but to the length of the wall by introducing pilasters that broke up the space into large vertically divided areas (Fig. 16a). In the Great Chamber at Chastleton (c. 1602) the panelling is divided into a deep base, a main field, and a frieze, with the design of the base sharply distinguished from that of the field and the field divided by pilasters, each upon a podium, into large self-contained areas (Fig. 16b). Essentially, the innovation at Chastleton that permits the break-up of the wall-space in both directions is the introduction of what is, in effect, a dado. The point is of importance not only for our period but for later years as well, for whatever changes English panelling underwent in the following centuries, the dado was rarely absent from it.

The dado, however, was introduced not for its own sake but as a result of treating panelling architecturally. By this I do not merely refer to the use of pilasters or columns—they are to be found easily enough at Knole and Burton Agnes and on the Cuckfield screen— or to the use of architecturally-derived motifs, but to a manner that breaks up the wall-surface into distinct areas whose proportions are determined by those of the columns or pilasters: into a frieze that is related to the entablature, a main field related to the height of the drum, a dado related to the podium, and all three areas sharply defined.[1] What is involved can be understood by considering what did not happen at Knole; each pilaster there has its podium, and the bottom panel is related to it, but that panel is distinguished in no way from those above, is not even divided

---

[1] This development was hinted at, but not followed up and dated to a rather later period, by Margaret Jourdain (*English Decoration and Furniture*, p. 42; *English Interior Decoration*, pp. 16–17) and Nathaniel Lloyd (*History of the English House*, p. 7).

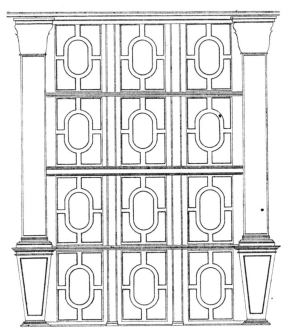

*a. Diagram of panelling at Knole*

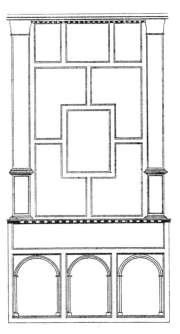

*b. Diagram of panelling
at Chastleton*

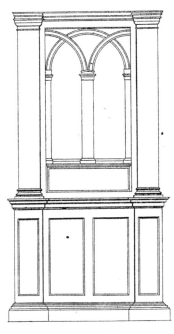

*c. Diagram of panelling
at Tissington*

Fig. 16.

from them by a more pronounced moulding, and the panelling runs uniformly and uninterruptedly from floor to frieze.

Chastleton shows perhaps the first, but not the full signs of the new manner; that is to be seen in the Drawing-room at Tissington (*c.* 1613 (Fig. 16*c*)), the nearly contemporary panelling of the Hall at Whitehall, Shrewsbury,[1] the White Parlour at Holland House (*c.* 1624), and at Kew Palace (1631).[2] At all of these the podium, and with it the lowest division of the panelling, is proportioned to the pilaster upon it, the moulding that marks the division between the base of the pilaster and the podium is heavily emphasized as a true dado rail, and the panelling beneath is different in size or shape or patterning or motif or all four from the panel or panels of the main field. Even where, as at Kew, that field is still divided into many small panels or, as in the Red Room at Tissington, has interlaced arcading, the threefold vertical division of a shallow frieze, a deep main field, and a shallower but still deep dado is the basis of the design. Even on the screen at Audley End, which uses not columns or pilasters but terms, the frieze is related to the human bust, the field to the term, and the dado to the podium, and each is different in design and ornament from the others (Pl. 31). The architectural nature of the new decoration is emphasized by the decreasing use in panelling of coloured inlay and marquetry, a not uncommon technique in the later years of the sixteenth century. In the early seventeenth century, although the practice was still followed at Gawthorpe,[3] it rapidly lost popularity, but only in panelling; in furniture, where there is little question of architectural treatment, as distinct from the use of applied architectural motifs, inlay continued to be fashionable up to the middle of the century.

Relating the panelling to the columniation did more than determine the height of these three divisions; it helped to determine, or at least to influence, their length as well. There is a minimum limit

[1] For Whitehall I accept the date that H. A. Tipping argues for in *English Homes*, part 3, i, pp. 139–46.

[2] J. Charlton, *Kew Palace* (1956).

[3] J. P. Whitaker (*History of the Parish of Whalley* (Blackburn, 1801), p. 319) gives a date of 1601–5 for Gawthorpe. It is more or less confirmed by 'The House and Farm Accounts of the Shuttleworths', part 1 (*Chetham Soc.* xxxv (1856)), and by the date 1603 on an overmantel in the gallery.

to the permissible spacing of properly proportioned columns or pilasters that rise, with podium and frieze, from floor to ceiling. It had been possible at Knole to break up the area between the main pilasters with slender pilaster-strips and revert to a system of many panels arranged in vertical rows, but the architectural feeling that was producing the new manner militated against the use of such un-architectural things as pilaster-strips. Instead the area between the pilasters often grew wider, and the main field became more or less square. Although this space was still sometimes filled with a number of small panels, nevertheless its size and proportions facilitated a different manner, and the inclination, paralleled in wall-painting, was to treat it as an organized whole: at Chastleton, with a central panel ornamented with a double-arch within surrounding and subordinate panels, at Tissington, with a central panel flanked by its own diminutive pilasters and surmounted with strapwork cresting, in the White Parlour at Holland House, with a central architectural composition within plain moulded panelling. The concentration of interest is apparent, and where the wall was too short to allow more than one of these broad divisions, it was, one may say, treated as the object of a single non-repetitive design.

It would, however, be incorrect to give the impression that this concentration was universal, even in the last years of the period. On the contrary, it appeared in few houses, and even then was confined to the more important rooms or to some of them; at Holland House, for example, the very elaborate and costly panelling of the Gilt Room was carried out in the old way, with no attempt at organized design. In ecclesiastical buildings, despite the occasional exception like the chapels at Knole and at Lincoln College, Oxford, the old manner continued unchallenged throughout the period. The Screen and fittings of 1616 in Croscombe Church, Somerset, with their elaborate strapwork and cresting, and the Screen, dated 1614, to the Freke Chapel in Iwerne Courtney Church, Dorset, are the developed form of the style of the previous forty years. The Screen in Wadham chapel, with its gadrooned arcading, arabesques, lion-masks, and strapwork, is in the same vein (Pl. 32a), and that of 1631-3, in St. John's Church, Leeds, has no trace of the new motifs or aesthetic approach.

From about 1600 the signs of an attempt at a concentration of interest and avoidance of the usual patterning become more obvious in painted decoration. A comparison of Peke's Farm and No. 3 Cornmarket, Oxford, with Nos. 61 High Street, Amersham, and 55 High Street, Hoddesdon, illustrates this. In all of these houses the painted decoration is on timber-framed walls. At the first two, both of *c.* 1580, canvas was stretched over the timber uprights and the space between, and an uninterrupted repetitive patterning painted upon it. At the other two, where the decoration is twenty to thirty years later, the uprights were exposed to view and semi-circular arches with imposts and brackets painted upon them to simulate arcading. The uprights are about 2½ feet apart, and so, while the scheme of decoration is still repetitive, it is less so than in the usual close-set small panels and painted decoration. As wainscot was given a concentrated interest, with the use of larger panels, so too was its painted imitation, and at 'Denmark House' (Somerset House) in 1618–19 a wall in a gallery was painted 'in four several parts', each 7½ feet high and from 1½ to 3 feet wide. At Bolsover the large panels of the Star Chamber (*c.* 1621)[1] are each painted with a single full-length figure, the nearly contemporary panelling that is now at Astley Hall, Lancashire, is of similar nature (Pl. 37*a*),[2] and the now-destroyed 'Portrait Chamber' at Stanford Court, Worcestershire, was wainscoted in large panels with three-quarter length portraits of members and connexions of the Salwey family painted upon them.[3]

The painting of ceilings was mainly confined to picking out the ribs or emphasizing the details of the plasterwork, but not every ceiling was ribbed, and some that were not had elaborate painted decoration upon them. Unfortunately few of these have survived and we are mainly dependent upon records for our knowledge of them. There is, therefore, no certainty about this form of decoration, but it seems likely that here too there was a tendency towards a unification and concentration of interest. Thus the

[1] R. W. Goulding, *Bolsover Castle* (Oxford, 1928).
[2] R. H. Blackburn in *C.L.* cxviii (Nov. 1945), 1214.
[3] W. Niven, *Old Worcestershire Houses* (1873), pp. 18–19; T. E. Winnington in *Associated Architectural Socs. Reports*, viii (1865), 166–9.

canvas ceiling of the old Banqueting House at Westminster was painted in 1584–5 in a repetitive pattern of 'diamonds, frutage and other kinds of work'. The same ceiling was repainted in 1603–4 in a wholly different manner, the central part with 'work called the clouds' and the rest with the royal arms and architectural motifs. That this was a treatment that regarded the surface as an artistic whole is suggested by a comparison with Vaughan's early seventeenth-century description of a ceiling in a room at the Globe Tavern which was 'painted overhead with a cloudy sky and some few dispersed stars'.[1] The fashion was by then not uncommon, for there still exists at West Hall, Folke, Dorset, a ceiling painted in a similar manner.[2] At Gorhambury the Gallery ceiling was painted at some time after James I's accession with busts of classical heroes and 'Greek and Roman Emperors'.[3]

The same liking for a concentration of effect is reflected in figure subjects and landscape painting. From the early sixteenth century there are several important large-scale mural figure subjects, varying from such comparatively accomplished works as those of Carpenters' Hall and Mildenhall Manor to the crude figures of the Nine Worthies at 61 High Street, Amersham. After about 1550 such large-scale figures disappeared for nearly half a century. Yet figure painting did not wholly disappear in the late sixteenth century; it was used generally in friezes or in small panels within the general patterning. *The Story of Tobit* at the White Swan, Stratford on Avon (*c.* 1580), is in small panels within a deep frieze, and set within a larger area of flowers and conventional landscapes. The probably contemporary *Dives and Lazarus* at Pittleworth Manor is of small scale, and set within the general patterning. *The Prodigal* at Knightsland Farm, South Mimms, probably somewhat later than the other two, is in a narrow frieze above plain panelling (Pl. 34), and the *Four Ages of Man* at West Stow Hall in Suffolk is on a fireplace overmantel. The 'very artistic paintings and correct landscapes' of English and European towns and counties and the 'armorial bearings and domains' of every gentleman-landowner of

[1] *Works*, ed. L. C. Martin (Oxford, 1914), i. 10.
[2] R.C.H.M. *West Dorset*, p. 112.
[3] Aubrey, *Brief Lives*, ed. O. L. Dick (1950), p. 14.

England that the Duke of Wirtemberg saw at Theobalds in 1592 seem, since all the apartments were 'adorned with beautiful tapestries and the like',[1] to refer most probably to a painted frieze comparable with that of Gilling Castle.

By the early seventeenth century it was not unusual to paint a whole wall with one or more large-scale subjects, often figure subjects or landscapes. In the Gallery at Grove House, Essex, all the wall surface, and not merely a frieze, was covered with scenes of rural life in twelve large compartments, and bore the date 1617.[2] At Eastbury seascapes were painted within a perspective arcading;[3] in the east range of Walnut Tree Court at Queen's College, Cambridge, there is an arcade in fake perspective[4] and at Rothamsted arcading, with the shell-niches so beloved of early seventeenth-century masons and the large panelling of the period, is painted with a *trompe d'œil* effect.[5] In 1621 the walls of the King's Withdrawing Chamber at Whitehall were painted in four equal squares showing the Four Parts of the World and the Four Seasons. A chamber in the Globe Tavern was described by Vaughan as 'painted . . . on the sides with Land-scapes, Hills, Shepheards, and Sheep'[6] and in 1623–4 the ceiling and walls of a room at Theobald's Lodge were painted with 'landskips, frutages and divers kinds of beasts'. The figure paintings of the last years of the sixteenth century at Stodmarsh Court, Kent,[7] are intermediate between the small-scale and large-scale subject, with figures symbolic of the planets and scenes from the story of Actaeon and Diana. Some of the panels are still small—one is only 3 feet by 2 feet—but the others are larger and nearly life-size. At Harvington Hall, Worcestershire, the figures

[1] W. Rye, *England as seen by Foreigners* (1865), pp. 44–45.

[2] *Gent. Mag.* ciii, pt. 2 (Nov. 1833), pp. 393–4.

[3] T. H. Clarke and W. H. Black, *Eastbury Illustrated* (1834); *L.C.C.S.L.* xi, 'Eastbury Manor House'.

[4] The range was built in 1617–19 and the decoration is probably contemporary, R.C.H.M. *City of Cambridge*, pp. 177–8.

[5] The battle-scene on the frieze above the arcading may well be of the late sixteenth century; see C. E. Keyser in *Proc. Soc. Ant.* xix (1901–3), 51–54, and H. C. Andrews in *East Herts. Archaeological Soc. Trans.* xi (1940–4), 146–9. The arcading itself is in a different style, at a different level of competence, and has no organic connexion with the frieze.          [6] *Works*, ed. L. C. Martin (Oxford, 1914), i. 10.

[7] T. H. Lehfeldt in *Archaeologia Cantiana*, xxxi (1915), 54–60.

of the Nine Worthies are also life-size,[1] and those of James I, Henry IV, and the King of Spain at Gorhambury were so described by Aubrey.[2]

Yet the concentration of painted decoration after about 1600, although real enough and in line with the development in other media, is in one way a by-product of something else. It seems likely that the increasing fashion for textile hangings and the wider use of wainscot had greatly reduced the demand for large-scale domestic murals by the mid-sixteenth century. Although the accounts of the Office of Works show that the Sergeant Painter was occasionally employed in the later years of the century on the 'repair' of old murals, neither he nor anyone else was employed on new ones. It is noticeable that when discussing wall-decoration Harrison fails to mention murals: 'The wals of our houses on the inner side be either hanged with tapestrie; arras worke or painted cloths, wherein either diverse histories, or hearbes, beasts, knots and such like are stained.'[3] Even in lesser houses the greater use of wainscot was obliterating old wall-paintings, and presumably reducing the demand for new. At the Golden Cross at Oxford a wall-painting of the mid-century had been largely hidden by panelling before 1594,[4] and in the Old Flushing Inn at Rye early sixteenth-century painted decoration was covered by panelling in about 1600.[5] By then, however, the peak demand for painted cloths was apparently over. Very few of these have survived and it is probable that they disintegrated quickly. In 1598 Stow remarked that 'the workmanship of stayning'—the technique used upon painted cloths—'is departed out of use in England'.[6] In

---

[1] At Harvington, as at Rothamsted, it is, I think, necessary to disentangle work of two periods. H. R. Hodgkinson (*Birmingham Archaeological Soc. Trans.* lii (1938), 1–26), although regarding all as of the late sixteenth century, admits a difference of style between the *Nine Worthies* and the rest of the painted decoration; Miss E. M. Moore (*Archaeologia*, lxxxviii (1940), 281–8) while not explicitly saying as much implies that the former are of the early seventeenth century, a view that I follow here.

[2] *Brief Lives*, ed. O. L. Dick (1950), p. 14.

[3] Introduction to Holinshed's *Chronicles* (2nd ed. 1587), p. 187.

[4] E. Clive Rouse in *Oxoniensia*, xx (1955), 84–89.

[5] P. M. Johnston in *Sussex Archaeological Collections*, l (1907), 118–19.

[6] *Survey of London*, ed. C. L. Kingsford, ii. 3–4. See *O.H.E.A.* viii. 78 for a revival of painted cloths in the 1630's.

consequence there was a short period when walls in houses of some pretensions were occasionally left bare; just how short it was may be judged from the wainscot at Bosworth House, Wendover, which is of only slightly later date than the painted representation of early seventeenth-century cartouched panelling that was found beneath it.[1] This, however, occurred at a time when a new manner of design was working in favour of a concentration of interest, and when the trained craftsmen of the Painter-Stainers Company were finding employment upon painted cloths less easy to come by, and in consequence large-scale murals of some competence reappeared after a lapse of half-a-century.

In plasterwork, as in joinery, the new manner revealed itself in the first place in the use of larger panels and in a variation in their sizes and shapes. As the desire to portray scenes and human figures grew and was paralleled by the growing skill of the craftsman, so the panels swelled to the size of those at Boston Manor and Blickling (Pl. 33a). This trend, still a repetitive patterning but on a larger scale, culminated in *The Labours of Hercules* on a ceiling at Emral Hall, Flintshire, which was probably built as late as 1650.[2]

There are also a number of early seventeenth-century ceilings in which the interest is concentrated by limiting the amount of decoration. One at Wilderhope, Salop, dated 1602, has an elaborate motif in the centre and scattered and simple decoration elsewhere. At Limbury and Througham, both in Gloucestershire, there are ceilings divided into large compartments, each with simple decoration concentrated at the corners and in the centre. The Trout Room at Daneway, in the same county, has a leaf-boss centrally and a proportioned pattern of squares and circles arranged around it against a plain field.[3] At Sir Peter Paul Pindar's house in Bishopsgate the ceiling of the chapel had a great amount of strapwork decoration upon it, but strapwork that radiated from, and gave

[1] *Records of Bucks.* xii (1927–33), 225–38.

[2] *C.L.* xxvii (Feb. 1910), 270–9. A date in the late seventeenth or early eighteenth century is suggested by the R.C.A.M., *Flintshire*, ii. 116. Emral Hall has been demolished.

[3] C. Hussey in *C.L.* cxi (Jan. 1952), 32–35, dates the 'High Building' at Daneway, in which this ceiling is, to 1600–20.

emphasis to, a central roundel with a figured scene.[1] At Kew Palace an otherwise plain ceiling has a single emblematical figure in the centre.

A concentrated effect was sometimes brought about as well by the reintroduction in the form of trabeations of the beams that the vogue for elaborately plastered ceilings had only recently eliminated from English rooms. These broke up the surface by their very presence and usually divided it lengthwise into a central and smaller flanking compartments. In the 'King James Room' (c. 1603–8) at Knole the ceiling is divided by shallow plastered beams; rather deeper beams break up the nearly contemporary ceiling at Speke Hall and occur in the small Drawing-room at Apethorpe, in a room at Daneway, at Limbury, at Calgarth Hall, Windermere, and were formerly at East Riddlesden, Yorkshire, and at Park Hall near Oswestry (Pl. 36a). Upon these ceilings the interest is generally concentrated in a central compartment, for example, the great panel at Apethorpe or the figure of Neptune at Park Hall. Within the lesser compartments themselves what interest there is is concentrated at the centre. The compartments of the ceiling of Jones's Banqueting House were painted by Rubens with scenes from classical mythology. That, of course, is usually regarded as a foreign import, and so it was; but it could only be imported because its trabeations and painted compartments provided a solution to the problems that native designers were beginning to meet.[2]

The new manner of decoration also ensured that the deep plaster friezes of some late sixteenth-century houses should not be widely imitated. Shallow friezes of the type in Wolsey's Closet at Hampton Court continued throughout the period and varied only in their decoration, changing from Wolsey's early Renaissance ornament to the family badges of moorhens and mulberry trees at Loseley and to the strapwork and grotesques of Clarkson's Hall at Mansfield Woodhouse. After the mid-century as plasterers

---

[1] C. J. Richardson, *Architectural Remains*, pt. 1, appendix, pl. 3.

[2] This general development was partly offset by the contemporary practice— springing from the same aesthetic origins—of copying some of the motifs and designs of the purer Italian imports of the early-mid sixteenth century, a practice that is revealed in the ceilings already mentioned at Canons Ashby, East Riddlesden, and Little Strickland.

became more ambitious they attempted to cover more of the wall-surface, and some friezes became very deep and elaborate; those at Gilling Castle and at Levens, Westmorland, are well-known examples. But they are small beer compared with the great friezes at Plas Mawr, in the Sitting-room at Beaudesert (c. 1570–80), and in the Presence Chamber at Hardwick New Hall. Here the plasterers had things all their own way and covered the whole upper half of the wall-surface: with conventional designs, heraldic badges, and terminal figures at Plas Mawr, with life-size terminal figures at Beaudesert, with hunting-scenes and figures of Spring and Summer in high relief at Hardwick (Pl. 36b). By the early seventeenth century, however, this practice, which divided the wall into two more or less equal horizontal areas, was being superseded; friezes as deep even as that at Gilling Castle became less common as the desire for properly proportioned columniation upon the wainscot reduced the area between the top of the entablature and the ceiling to very narrow limits, and sometimes, as at Park Hall and Boston Manor, eliminated it altogether.

Despite all the painted decoration, plaster-work, and joinery, the most striking feature of an Elizabethan or Jacobean room was generally the chimney-piece. The growth in its importance and its later change in character is an epitome of the general development, and it is perhaps as well to establish at once that highly ornamental chimney-pieces were not a direct consequence of the Renaissance; on the contrary, Renaissance ideas at first probably militated against them. While fifteenth and very early sixteenth century fireplaces are uncommon, many of those that survive have abundant decoration, such as the elaborate quatrefoils of a fireplace at Tattersall Castle and the decoration upon one in the wholly Gothic Abbot's Parlour at Muchelney. Early mid-sixteenth-century pieces in a Renaissance context are generally less decorated. In the Abbot's Parlour at Thame the wall-space above the opening is undifferentiated from the rest of the room, which is in a mélange of Renaissance and traditional styles. The later assembling of linenfold panelling running uninterruptedly above the opening in Wolsey's Closet at Hampton Court, and also seen in a room at Boughton Malherbe, suggests that the overmantels had no original decoration.

There are some early to mid-sixteenth-century houses—Barrington Court and Poundisford Park, for example—in which no over-mantel of much before 1600 survives, and at Loseley chimney-pieces were inserted during the early seventeenth century into a house of the 1560's. However, as English houses became residences and the fireplace, which had been absent from many houses in the Middle Ages, became a standard fitment, so the importance of the chimney-piece as a self-contained centre of decorative interest grew.

The change from no emphasis to a vast amount came very quickly, but a short stage in the mid-century in which the over-mantel was acquiring importance can be discerned. At Mapperton, Dorset, there is a chimney-piece of c. 1550–60 with a plaster over-mantel decorated with Renaissance baluster shafts and vases (Pl. 33b). In an upper room at Longleat there is one of c. 1570[1] with considerable decoration around the opening but a comparatively unimportant overmantel, and chimney-pieces with similar slight overmantels occur at Upper Upham Manor (before 1599),[2] in Wiltshire. The speed of development is demonstrated at Sizergh Castle. Two early examples there, of 1563 and 1569, are highly ornamented but narrower, lower, and far less dominating than one of 1575 and another, undated but flanked by terms, of the later years of the century. At Mapperton and at Longleat the comparative lack of importance of the overmantel is partly due to the low ceiling of the room it is in, but by the 1570's English rooms were beginning to be 'well belighted' and 'hy roofed' in the way admired by Laneham at Kenilworth,[3] and so the last remaining check upon the hegemony of the chimney-piece had gone. As early as 1571 the piece in the Smoking-room at Deene Park, with its opening flanked by pilasters and its overmantel with three highly orna-mented panels, is beginning to attain to the dominance that was to characterize later examples.

This dominance was achieved in two ways, by sheer size or by

[1] C. Hussey in *C.L.* cv (Apr. 1949), 866. It should, however, be mentioned that Dr. Pevsner considers this piece to be of the late seventeenth century.

[2] H. Brakspear in *Wilts. Archaeological Mag.* xxviii (1894–6), 84–86. The similarity between the Longleat and Upper Upham examples was pointed out many years ago by C. Hussey in *C.L.* li (July 1922), 888–95.

[3] J. Nichols, *Progresses of Queen Elizabeth* (1823), i. 472.

abundance of ornament, and often by both. The stone piece of
1599 at Cobham impresses by its great height, width, and projection. Some of those at Hatfield, with their great width and heavy
columns and mouldings, owe part of their effect to their size. The
'colossal' quality of these productions is emphasized by the use of a
giant order of Doric columns to flank the opening and overmantel
in the Drawing-room at Dorfold, and of giant fluted pilasters in
the Dining-room at Temple Newsam. An unorganized abundance
of ornament reveals itself in a medley of classical columns and
pilasters, caryatides, terms, gadrooning, strapwork, jewel ornament, cusped and plain arcading, and richly patterned inlay. Such
a comparatively minor piece as that in wood at Church Farm,
Wolvercote, Oxfordshire, has arabesques, caryatides, arcading, and
a decorated frieze. The chalk fireplace in the Drawing-room at
Loseley has an opening flanked by fluted columns, a rusticated and
vermiculated surround, and, above, six elaborately decorated panels
with terms (Pl. 35b). The overmantel in the Old House at Sandwich has panels flanked by clustered columns, made of compressed
shavings, that break forward from the main plane and support
heraldic beasts, while above and below are friezes decorated with
inlay. The chimney-piece in the former Long Gallery at Barlborough is equally elaborate: its overmantel, flanked by caryatides
on ornamented bases, has a central shield of arms with two other
shields below held up by the figures of a man and two women.[1]

These enormous and ornate chimney-pieces went on to the end
of our period and beyond, but they no longer went alone. In the
last years of the sixteenth century a new manner appeared, in which
size and splendour were still present, but ornament was simple and
sparse, and interest was concentrated. The piece at Cobham already
mentioned is immense, but its decorative effect is achieved not
with innumerable carved figures and motifs but by the use of broad
areas of coloured and contrasted marbles. There are similar fireplaces at Bramshill and, each with a single central figure, at Hardwick New Hall (Pl. 38a), and plaster overmantels of similar

[1] Mr. Oswald's arguments about the overmantel in the Hall at Burton Agnes,
whether he is right or wrong in his conclusions, are testimony to the unorganized
mode of decoration of these pieces; see *C.L.* xciii (June 1953), 1886–9.

simplicity of ornament, each with one theme only, at the Old Hall (Pl. 38b). At first, however, it is more the concentration of interest than simplicity of ornament that is apparent here, although the one helped to bring about the other. The overmantel of c. 1575 in the Senior Common Room at University College, Oxford, is divided into three panels and is lavishly ornamented with caryatides, gadrooning, arcading, and figured scenes, while that of about fifty years later in a room at Lincoln College has a single panel with an eared and hipped architrave and broken pediment. In the Carved Parlour at Crewe Hall the overmantel had a single scene,[1] although the subject, *The Idle and the Industrious*, could have been better shown in two. At East Quantockshead there are four overmantels in four different rooms, each with one scene from the life of Christ: a contrast with Burton Agnes, where the original lower stage of the Hall overmantel has four scenes of *The Wise and Foolish Virgins* in adjacent panels.

The concentration of interest, however, led to a simplicity of ornament in overmantels, partly by depreciating extraneous and multifarious decoration, and partly as a result of the same concentration, already referred to, in panelling. It is necessary to make this latter point, because the appearance of the great stone and marble pieces often carried out by foreigners—as de Whitt at Cobham,[2] William Cure at Somerset House,[3] Maximilian Colt at St. James's,[4] at Hatfield,[5] and, possibly, at Charlton[6]—are not to be explained merely as the irresistible and self-explanatory conquest of English art by 'Flemish influence', but rather as the quick exploitation by foreign craftsmen, parallel with that in sculpture, of the opportunities that the new trend in English taste was providing.

[1] C. J. Richardson, *Old English Mansions*, 2nd series (1841), n.p.

[2] Letters to Lord Cobham from his steward in 1601 refer to a contract to be made with de Whitt for two chimney-pieces and make it seem likely that he had done similar work for Cobham before (*Cal. S.P. Dom. 1601-3*, pp. 139, 46). The piece of 1599 in the gallery at Cobham, therefore, may well be de Whitt's work; but that he was also responsible, as Mr. Lees-Milne suggests (*Tudor Renaissance*, p. 91), for the porch of 1594—five years earlier and in a wholly different style—is much less certain.

[3] P.R.O. E. 351-3248.

[4] Ibid. 3244.

[5] H. A. Tipping, *English Homes*, part 3, ii, p. 322.

[6] R.C.H.M. *East London*, p. xxxv.

Indeed, those at Hardwick, which appear to be the earliest examples, were probably by an Englishman, Thomas Accres.[1]

That trend, which was treating wainscot architecturally and introducing simple architectural motifs into it, treated overmantels in the same way. Thus there appear chimney-pieces devoid of the mass of ornamentation of earlier examples, and with their decoration provided by one or two architectural motifs: the simple panelling at The Priory, Tottenham, the probably closely contemporary blind window openings with pediment and architrave or simple strapped ovals of the examples from Lime Street, London, now in the Victoria and Albert Museum, the variations upon the common cipher and square motifs of wainscot of an overmantel in a bedroom at Billesley Manor, Warwickshire.[2] In most cases the panelling of the overmantel, although similar to that of the wainscot, is more elaborate. In the Breakfast Room at Tissington, however, it is merely different, and in the White Parlour at Holland House the complete control exercised by the general design is apparent, for the decoration of the main central bay of the overmantel—a pedimented arch with a monogram—was not even a variation but merely a repetition of that of the wainscot of the rest of the room.

The Breakfast Room at Tissington and the White Parlour at Holland House are plain symptoms of a change in the nature of the overmantel and of the decline in its importance as a feature of ornamental value in its own right. In the most extreme manifestation of this, in the minor rooms at Charlton and in important rooms at Anderson Manor, it vanishes altogether. In greater rooms it remains a centre of interest by becoming the frame for another work of art. It seems likely, for example, that Cecil's mosaic portrait on the overmantel in the Library at Hatfield was always intended for its present or for a similar position (Pl. 39a). It was sent from Venice by Wotton in 1610, while Hatfield was still

[1] C. Hussey in C.L. lxiv (Dec. 1928), 934–42.

[2] Billesley Manor, or a 'great part' of it, was 'new built' by Sir Robert Lee (Dugdale, Antiquities of Warwickshire (1656), p. 540). Lee came into possession before 1619 (D.N.B., Trussell, John); he died in 1637 ('Visitation of Warwickshire 1682–3', Harl. Soc. lxii. 70).

building, and was executed from a portrait by de Critz that Cecil had sent to Wotton, presumably for the mosaic maker to work from.[1] The overmantel of *c.* 1630 at Wynford Eagle, Dorset, with its painted landscapes, and those in the Brown Gallery at Knole, in the Drawing-room at the Charterhouse, and in the Long Gallery at Westwood Park, which frame an easel portrait, may not have been originally intended for their present purpose, but their nature made it easy to adapt them to it. When Balthazar Gerbier wrote to Buckingham from Paris in 1624 commending the French manner, 'the best paintings are before the chimney . . . they always put the principal piece over the chimney . . .',[2] English treatment had already reached a position from which it could, if wanted, follow this lead.

Despite the dominance of the chimney-piece in general, it was not often of much elaboration or size in the Hall. Pieces with unimportant overmantels or none at all were usual and the most decorated feature was the Screen. As the character of great houses changed, the Hall lost its original purpose but took on a new one, that of providing an imposing first impression of the interior of the house. In this the Screen had an important role, for it could be made the vehicle of an abundance of decoration or of a display of learned taste. The Screen of 1581 at Cuckfield Park, Sussex, is a highly decorated structure that dominates the Hall, and those of 1562–73 in the Middle Temple and of 1617–18 at Jesus College, Oxford, are elaborately ornamented examples from the beginning and end of the period. Even in a one-story Hall such as that at Bramshill the Screen is exploited for a display of intricate decoration.

That decoration is the main purpose of these screens is shown by the abandonment at Hatfield and Audley End of the double entry from the screens-passage, preserved in the college halls because of its practical convenience. However, as ornament became simpler and the concept of a pure Entrance Hall spread more widely, the Screen began to disappear or to lose all of its original character, even where a Hall and separate entrance lobby were still preserved. In a smaller house such as Bolsover it disappeared completely.

[1] H. A. Tipping, *English Homes*, part 3, ii, pp. 342–3.
[2] G. Goodman, *The Court of James I* (1839), ii. 342–3.

In a larger house like Montacute the Screen of *c.* 1600 (Pl. 32*b*) and at Longleat of *c.* 1603[1] is little more than an arcade, and the late Screen at Swakeleys, Middlesex, with a large central opening flanked by two smaller ones, is nothing more. Thus even in a house with both Hall and entrance lobby the disappearance of the Screen or its conversion into something quite different had been made possible, and in some cases had been brought about, by the end of Elizabeth's reign.

Nevertheless, magnificent Screens, loaded and overloaded with ornament and rising nearly to ceiling level, were still being erected in the first quarter of the seventeenth century, generally in the houses of the very great: of Salisbury at Hatfield, of Suffolk at Audley End, of Sackville at Knole. In many ways these men were showing an appreciation of the most up-to-date art in England of the time; indeed even on the Screen at Audley End with its profusion of coarse terms and strapwork there are perspective masoned arches in the most advanced style (Pl. 31). Yet in general these Screens, compared with those at Hardwick and Montacute, have little sign of the new restrained manner. There cannot be much doubt that such huge structures, sited in a Great Hall to which they added effect, were intended as a demonstration of the social position of their owners and retain their archaic character for that reason. It is a generally accepted view that the Great Hall and the Screen disappeared because they had lost all function. In fact, they disappeared when, having lost any utilitarian purpose, they were robbed of their value as monuments of grandeur and bearers of ornament by a change in architectural taste. It was not merely a functional but a certain sequence of social, functional, and aesthetic development that banished them from the English house.

The decline of the Hall and the increase in importance of the Long Gallery and Great Chamber, invariably on an upper floor, were the main factors in developing the staircase, for they made it necessary to provide something more than the long straight flight of stone steps between two walls or the winding 'vice' of earlier years. Here, too, the change was a gradual one. As late as 1590–7 a

[1] C. Hussey in *C.L.* cv (Apr. 1949), 1928.

plain straight flight between two walls was built at Hardwick New Hall, at Castle Ashby vices were provided at the ends of the long wings, and in a plan of *c.* 1595 for rebuilding Beaufort House, Chelsea, there are no fewer than seven vices in external turrets, besides a spacious well staircase in the main block.[1] In many quite late houses, for example Chastleton, although the 'vice' was abandoned, staircases were still placed in external turrets, and as late as 1625 Bacon was recommending them at all the four corners of a courtyard house.[2]

Despite Bacon's precepts, however, the vice and its more elaborate descendant, the staircase turret, were disappearing as such houses themselves disappeared. In the compactly planned house of the early seventeenth century there was no need for a great number of staircases, and by the end of the period the vice had become so unnecessary and inconvenient that George Herbert used it in a well-known line, 'Is all good structure in a winding stair?', as a symbol of the conceits and affectations of a school of poetry that he had little sympathy with.

Because ease of access to the newly important upper floors was a major consideration, the new type of staircase was distinguished by its breadth, its easy ascent, and its frequent landings. Such stairs, if they were not to take up a great amount of space, could not be built as one long flight, but had rather to be built around a central well or in a dog-legged form. Examples occur soon after the middle of the sixteenth century; there is a famous one of stone at Burghley, but later they were almost invariably of wood. The great weight of stone staircases and the consequent need for supporting walls precluded the dog-legged form, and for the well form necessitated a central core of masonry. The use of wood and of thin treads and risers in place of solid blocks for the steps obviated the need for that and for walls on both sides, and, with the weight of the stair carried by strings and newels, allowed the side next to the well to be open to it.

[1] A. W. Clapham and W. H. Godfrey, *Some Famous Buildings* (1913), pp. 86–87.
[2] *Essays*—'On Building'. E. F. Seckler (*Arch. Rev.* cix (May 1951), 301–3) dates Bacon's views on staircases to 1598. Bacon first published some essays in that year but this one did not appear until 1625.

In the early years of the seventeenth century the staircase developed very quickly into the type of Hatfield and Knole. Placed in
a prominent position, generally near the Hall and sometimes set off
with an arcade before it, as at Knole, Temple Newsam and Rushton,
it was of straight flights with many landings, open on the side away
from the wall, and lavishly decorated.[1] The massive newel was often
the most prominent member and the most elaborate. Its sides were
adorned with all the motifs of the time: with foliage and trophies at
the Charterhouse, with strapwork at Benthall Hall, with an imitation of rusticated stonework at Holland House. It was nearly always
surmounted with carved finials, in the shape of acorns at Tissington, plain ball-finials at Cranborne, carved foliage, pierced pinnacles, and seated lions at Charlton, and heraldic beasts with shields
at Knole (Pl. 39b). Occasionally, however, the craftsman breaks
away from such banalities and produces some of the finest examples
of the contemporary carver's art. The well-modelled putti by John
Bucke[2] at Hatfield, playing musical instruments and throwing
balls, are lively and accomplished variations upon the stock theme
(Pl. 41). One of the best examples must have been at Bacon's house
at Verulam, where on every newel was 'some prettie figure, as of a
grave Divine with his booke and spectacles, a mendicant Friar etc.
not one thing twice'.[3] The newels on the upper flights frequently
had elaborate pendants beneath them, often in the form of inverted
urn finials but quite frequently in the same fashion as the openwork
pendants of the timber roofs of the sixteenth century.

Further decoration, apart from the newels, was provided by
balustrading, of which the turned baluster and the cut and generally rake-moulded baluster were the main types. It is difficult to
say which is the earlier, and the cut and pierced balusters of Oakwell
Hall (c. 1583) may be weighed against the symmetrically turned
ones of late sixteenth-century date at Clifton House, Clifton Maybank, Dorset, and both compared with those at Chastleton which

[1] For an interesting alternative view of the development of the staircase, but
one which tends to consider it apart from all the other elements of a house, see Seckler's
article quoted in the preceding note.
[2] L. Stone in *Arch. Journ.* cxii (1955), 121-2.
[3] Aubrey, *Brief Lives*, ed. O. L. Dick (1950), p. 13.

are cut to a turned form. By the early years of James's reign both types had developed rapidly; the first tending to become asymmetrical and elegant, and the second increasingly elaborate, generally unpierced, except in such unpretentious examples as that at Glasgow Stud Farm at Enfield, highly decorated and with the mouldings raked to follow the rise of the stairs. Cut balusters had many variations: at Charterhouse there are pilasters with grotesque busts which spring from keyed and rusticated arches; at Charlton, diminishing columns with Doric, Ionic, and Corinthian caps; at Boston House, diminishing pilasters carrying an arcade.

At about the end of the period there appeared at such houses as Aston Hall and Benthall Hall staircases in which the space between the handrail and the string was filled not with balustrading but with strapwork patterning (Pl. 40a). At Rawdon House, Hoddesdon (c. 1622), the balustrade of the landing has two panels filled with carved scenes showing Samson and Delilah and musicians playing instruments, and that of the stairs is filled with a strapwork design. The staircases of the 1630's at Cromwell House and Ham House, with their elaborate panels with trophies of arms, are well on the way to the manner of the third quarter of the century.

Subject-matter and iconography too were common to all forms of interior decoration at any given time, but they differed sharply from those of easel-painting and they were not of predominantly classical derivation. They had three main sources: the classics, the new scientific interest, and religion; and the last was far and away the most important.

The preponderance of religious themes had a threefold cause. In the first place, and of minor significance, was the continuity, parallel with that of the manner of design, of medieval subjects and attitudes. A house of comparatively late date in the Butterwalk at Dartmouth, for example, has a plaster ceiling with the formerly popular Tree of Jesse. On the chimney-piece in the Hall at Burton Agnes is a scene, to quote the latest writer upon it, 'in the tradition of a medieval Last Judgment'.[1] More important was the wider knowledge of the Bible brought about by the Protestant attitude towards it and its consequent translations into the vernacular.

[1] A. Oswald in *C.L.* cxii (June 1953), 1889.

Biblical subjects, familiar enough in medieval typology, were now used by the Reformers with a more directly didactic purpose: Daniel in the Lions' Den at Stockton House, Wiltshire, Tobias at Langley's, Essex, Samson and the Gates of Gaza in the Old House at Sandwich. It was, however, the intellectual climate of the time, which still based ethics, although no longer politics, upon an appeal to religion, that played the greatest role. This was common to both Catholics and Protestants; when Richard Haydocke translated Lomazzo's *Trattato dell' arte* . . . he was careful to leave out the original's defence of 'images', but included, and emphasized in a marginal note, its view of the moral purpose of art.[1] Protestants, however, regarding Salvation as the responsibility of the individual without the intervention of saints or priests, tended to introduce a moral element into every action of daily life; Milton's famous line, 'As ever in my great Taskmaster's eye', and George Herbert's poem *Elixir* are equal examples from extreme and moderate Protestant opinion. In consequence iconography and subject-matter had a pronounced ethical and moralizing character which determined both the predominance of biblical themes and the marked partiality for a particular selection of them.

This restricted the use of classical themes not merely negatively by preferring those from the Scriptures but positively by censoring many subjects from Greek and Roman mythology and history. Antiquity is a quarry from which many edifying lessons may, no doubt, be obtained but it is one in which Christian moralists mine often with difficulty and sometimes at their peril. In late sixteenth-century England many classical themes were damned in their own right; many more were compromised by their past association with Italian art. Ascham's condemnation of almost everything in Italy as dangerous to the morals of the otherwise incorruptible English[2] and Peacham's later complaint of the 'lewd art of many foreign prints' and the 'abominable ends' of their 'wicked makers'[3] reveal a widespread and long-lived determination to keep the more

[1] *A tracte containing the artes of curious painting* (Oxford, 1598), preface; G. P. Lomazzo, *Trattato dell' arte della pittura* (Milan, 1584), proemio.
[2] *The Scholemaster*, ed. D. C. Whimster (1934), pp. 65–80.
[3] *The Gentleman's Exercise* (1612), pp. 9–10.

pagan aspects of classicism out of our island Eden. The resulting
avoidance of classical in favour of biblical subjects is seen on a
chimney-piece at Boston Manor, Middlesex (*c.* 1623), where the
grotesques and scrolled ornament of a design by Abraham de
Bruyn have been faithfully copied, but the original central subject,
Perseus with the head of Medusa, has been expelled in favour of
the Sacrifice of Isaac.[1]

This ethical bias had a further consequence: New Testament
themes, until the later years, are rare. When they appear earlier it is
because of the ease with which they can be used to point a moral:
Dives and Lazarus, the Prodigal Son, the Good and Bad Steward.
The emphasis is on what the individual, with Divine guidance,
can do for himself and not, as in contemporary Catholic art, on
what Christ and the saints have already suffered for him. Earthly
life, with Salvation as its prize, is seen as a fight to be fought or a
task to be done. This is shown clearly enough when classical themes
do appear, for the most popular of all was the Labours of Hercules,
and on an overmantel at Levens, Westmorland, he is pointedly
associated with that mighty warrior and worker for the cause,
Samson.

Moral fervour also goes a long way to explain the innumerable
emblematic figures, mostly of the Virtues, on overmantels, friezes,
and ceilings. These may be regarded as the translation into plastic
art of the popular collections of maxims and emblems of the time.[2]
It was the habit for students to cull from the classics lists and
examples of stock themes, such as 'Piety', 'Faith', 'Old Age and
Youth', and to use them to illustrate various morals.[3] The best
known of these collections, Baldwin's *Moral Philosophy*, was 'the
most popular of all books deriving from antiquity' and went
through at least thirteen editions between 1547 and 1600.[4] It was

[1] M. Jourdain, *English Interior Decoration* (1950), pp. 8–9, pl. 29.

[2] For an early example of the link between emblems in literature and in art see G.
Clutton, 'An Emblem by Holbein for Erasmus and More', *Journ. W.C.I.* i (1937–9),
63–66.

[3] R. R. Bolgar, *The Classical Heritage and its Beneficiaries* (Cambridge, 1954), pp.
272–5.

[4] H. B. Lathrop, *Translations from the Classics into English* . . . (Madison, U.S.A.,
1933), p. 310.

probably from such a source that the painters of such moralizing wall-paintings as that on the theme of 'Age and Youth' at West Stow Hall, Suffolk, drew much of their inspiration. Before long the maxims were being illustrated with fanciful personifications of the virtues and vices in, for example, Geoffrey Whitney's *A Choice of Emblems* of 1586 and Peacham's *Minerva Britanna* of 1612.[1] Books like these had a wide influence and direct copying from them was not uncommon. Some of the figures on a ceiling at Blickling are taken directly from *Minerva Britanna* (Pl. 33a); at Hawsted Hall in Suffolk a small wainscoted closet was painted with forty-one emblematical pictures from Claudius Paradin's *Heroical Devises* and Gabriele Simeoni's *Purtraitures or Emblems*,[2] and there are carved scenes on the overmantel and frieze in the Summer Room at University College, Oxford, from Alciati's *Emblematum Liber*.[3]

Yet all these, although the most obvious, are far from being the only pieces in the pattern. While some classical themes were not welcome to all men, there was no general conflict between religion and the study of antiquity and there are many instances of their appearance without any moral or abstract quality at all: Orpheus at Haddon Hall, the Dryads at Broughton Castle, Psyche and Cupid at Hill Hall, Jupiter and Danae at Charlton. It will be noticed, however, that such examples are rather to be found in the houses of the greater than the lesser men, and it is on this basis that one may draw a distinction between the iconography of the two groups. Where the gentry and merchants tended to concentrate on biblical subjects with some use of the less pagan aspects of classical learning, the courtiers divided their attention fairly equally between the Bible and all aspects of the classics. Thus the Cupid and Psyche at Hill Hall is accompanied by The Destruction of Sennacherib and Hezekiah before the Temple; the overmantel in the White Drawing-room at Charlton has a scene of Perseus with the head of

---

[1] For the importance of emblems see Rosemary Freeman, *English Emblem Books* (1948).

[2] J. Cullum, *History of Hawsted* (1784), pp. 134–9, 145; J. Nichols, *Progresses of Queen Elizabeth* (1823), i. 124–5. The panels are now at Christchurch Mansion, Ipswich. Paladin and Simeoni were published abridged in a single volume in English in 1591.

[3] P. C. Bayley in *University College Record* (Oxford), iii (1958), 192–201; iv (1959), 252–6. I have to thank the Editor for drawing my attention to these articles.

Medusa but the fireplace frieze has the Triumph of Christ; at Bolsover the Elysium Room has figures of the Olympians and the Heaven Room of the ascending Christ. Houses of any pretensions rarely had mural decoration, but it is noticeable that in those that had, Hill Hall, Hulcott Manor, and Stodmarsh Court, the illustrations of classical themes contrast sharply with the almost invariably biblical and moral subjects of such small houses as Knightsland Farm, South Mimms, and the Swan Inn at Stratford-on-Avon.

The period is, however, characterized not only by the rediscovery of certain aspects of the classics and of the Bible but also by the first beginnings of modern science, in which the English played a considerable role. Gilbert and Norman were making discoveries in magnetism; British mathematicians were in the forefront of the new developments;[1] and Harvey was investigating the circulation of the blood. A minor industrial revolution was going on and was demanding the investigation of scientific problems in mining and metallurgy. Further, the Tudor State was one of several and the Tudor dynasty had potentially dangerous rivals; in consequence its military needs also played a part in scientific development.[2] When founding his college in 1575 Gresham made provision, for the first time in England, for professorships of Geometry and Astronomy;[3] in 1583 a chair of Mathematics and Natural Philosophy was endowed at Edinburgh, and between 1619 and 1621 chairs of Geometry, Astronomy, and Natural Philosophy at Oxford. The epoch-making achievements of British science still lay far in the future, but already a realization of its potentialities was abroad, and was given conscious expression in Bacon's formulation of a programme to be sponsored by the State for subduing Nature by scientific discoveries.[4] One result of the land settlement

---

[1] For the suggestion that English mathematicians helped to clarify Bruno's views see J. G. Crowther, *The Sciences of Energy* (1954), p. 38.

[2] See, for example, R. T. Gunther in *Archaeologia*, lxxix (1929), 55–72.

[3] For the significance of Gresham's College see F. R. Johnson in *J.H.I.* i (1940), 413–38.

[4] See B. Farrington, *Francis Bacon* (1951). The connexion between Science and the State in this period is important, for it played a part in the development of the virtuosi. It is true that a bias towards science by English Puritans has been amply demonstrated by R. K. Merton ('Science, Technology and Society in 17th century England', *Osiris*,

consequent upon the spoliation of the monasteries was the great number of books on rational husbandry and on land survey that appeared in the sixteenth and early seventeenth centuries. At the same time the Tudor State, to function properly, required something of an inventory of its subjects and their possessions, and this was provided by the writings of such antiquaries, topographers, and surveyors as Leland, Camden, and Norden, and in the maps of Saxton and Speed.

This scientific interest, and in particular its English bias towards the sciences connected with Navigation and land-survey was reflected in various ways in the plastic arts. This reflection was, of course, conditioned by the prevailing art theory and practice, and because emblematic themes were popular it often appeared in an emblematic form. Thus in the Dining-room at South Wraxall there are emblematical figures of 'Geometria' and 'Arithmetica' and at Burton Agnes and Stodmarsh Court of the 'Four Planets'. At Theobalds, however, there was a ceiling that was, in its way, an attempt at a scientific model of the Heavens. The Duke of Wirtemberg thus described it in 1592: 'it contains the twelve signs of the Zodiac so that at night you can see distinctly the stars proper to each; on the same stage the sun performs its course which is, without doubt, contrived by some concealed ingenious mechanism'.[1]

These elements—State needs, scientific interest, and social position—worked together towards one end and found artistic expression at Theobalds, Gorhambury, and Gilling Castle. At Theobalds there was 'depicted the Kingdom of England with all its cities, towns and villages, mountains and rivers', and 'correct landscapes of all the most important and remarkable towns in Christendom'.[2] In the Hall at Gorhambury there was a

iv (1938), 360–632) and S. F. Mason ('The Scientific Revolution and the Protestant Reformation', *Annals of Science*, ix (1953), 64–87, 154–75), but their evidence is drawn mainly from the membership of the Invisible College and the Royal Society, from a time, that is, when the absolute State had been destroyed. In earlier years scientists had usually been dependent upon the court; Dee, Borough, Norman, Gilbert, Harriot, and Harvey were all patronized directly by the Crown or by its leading courtiers.

[1] W. Rye, *England as seen by Foreigners* (1865), pp. 44–45.
[2] Ibid., p. 45.

wall-painting of Ceres introducing the sowing of corn with the text *Moniti Meliora*. (Instruction brings Progress)[1] and at Gilling Castle a painted frieze, with the arms of all the gentry of Yorkshire hung upon trees.

The scientific advances did not in any way introduce discord into the prevailing ideology; on the contrary, religion, the classics, and the sciences were joined in a general harmony. This is very marked in the attitude towards the Bible and the classics of Francis Bacon, whose avowed intention was to introduce a new scientific method and a new logic. It has been shown that in medicine, for example, despite the progress made, there was no significant clash with religious doctrine.[2] While it is true that Marlowe may have been an Atheist—although the evidence comes mainly from a government informer—one of a profession notorious for their indifference to truth—he was, if so, a very lone figure. The general assimilation of all branches of knowledge and ethics is revealed by the overmantel now at Chipchase Castle with its *mélange* of personifications of the Five Senses and the Four Elements, the signs of the Zodiac, classical gods and goddesses, the Virtues, emblems of the Four Continents, and scenes from the Bible (Pl. 37*b*).[3] In more learned circles a similar concord prevailed. The series of roundels of 1616–18 in the Painted Gallery at the Bodleian Library represents the history of secular and divine learning, and includes not only the men one would expect to see in such a parade but Dante and Petrarch (or Boccacio) and modern mathematicians and cosmographers like Tycho Brahe and Mercator (or Ortelius) and Copernicus.[4] The reception accorded to Copernicus illustrates both the widespread interest in science and the absence, at first, of any serious conflict between it and religion. His views were not universally accepted but then the main advantage of the Copernican over the Ptolemaic hypothesis was that it simplified the mathematics of the subject; the system of Tycho Brahe, however, which

[1] Aubrey, *Brief Lives*, ed. O. L. Dick (1950), pp. 12–15.

[2] P. H. Kocher, 'The Idea of God in Elizabethan Medicine', *J.H.I.* xi (1950), 3–29.

[3] The overmantel at Chipchase may not have been made in England (G. Nares in *C.L.* cxix (1956), 1365), but it suited English taste.

[4] J. N. L. Myres in *Bodleian Library Record*, iii (Oct. 1950), 82–91, (Aug. 1951), 201–7, iv (Apr. 1952), 30–51.

remained geocentric, did as much. Until Kepler had introduced the concept of elliptical orbits and the telescope had revealed the phases of Venus, the arguments for and against Copernicus's views were about equally balanced, as Bacon pointed out. The hypothesis won acceptance most easily among mathematicians, but it was not confined to them, and its wide currency is amusingly revealed by the change that came over the hyperboles of flatterers of royalty, comparisons of the monarch with the *primum mobile* giving way to comparisons with the sun.

The upper classes' appreciation of their social position and of its dependence on the Tudor land settlement and the Tudor State was the reason also for the unprecedented display of royal arms and badges in so many private houses. Doubtless sycophancy and the desire to pay a fulsome compliment to the Sovereign had its part in this, but not all men were sycophants, and the ubiquity of these symbols of the Tudor dynasty, probably the commonest single motif, must be attributed to a genuine attachment to the Sovereign as the symbol of the State and the status quo. But this attachment had a further consequence. The Tudor Monarchy was an absolute monarchy and one of the ways of maintaining it was to propagate absolutist ideas and a respect for former absolute States. The frequent occurrence of busts and representations of the Roman emperors, from da Maiano's series at Hampton Court in the 1520's to those at Gorhambury a century later, is the expression in art of those ideas. The popularity of the emperors was, of course, partly because of their character as an aspect of classical antiquity, but it was not wholly on that account, for other aspects of antiquity— The Gracchi, even Brutus—were not in favour at all. The absolute Imperial State was admired; the oligarchical Republic was ignored.

What has been said so far applies to the whole period, but in the early seventeenth century new themes appeared. Paintings of the type at Theobalds and Gilling Castle, with their shields of arms and general character of a mural 'Debrett', give way to more purely landscape representation, although still with an obvious social content of a 'stately house' or of figures of gentlemen and gentlewomen. Simple painted arcading is superseded by competently drawn architectural pieces in fake perspective. This was taken over in part from the scene-painting of court masques, and one of the first known instances occurred under Jones's direction, upon a stage erected in Christ Church Hall for James's visit to Oxford in 1605.[1] Most important of all is the increased fondness for New Testament themes and often for those not of a moral but of a devotional and even ecstatic nature. At the Court House, East Quantockshead, Somerset, there are four overmantels of *c.* 1629 with scenes from the Life of Christ: 'Christ and the Children', 'The Entry into Jerusalem', 'The Ascension', 'The Deposition'. On a fireplace at Charlton there is 'The Triumph of Christ' and at Bolsover 'The Ascension' again; at the Charterhouse 'The Last Supper' was painted on an overmantel. These are subjects of a type that had been unknown in England since Elizabeth's accession. Often they are associated with other long-forgotten or rejected subjects; the Apostles, for example, appear at the Charterhouse and, together with saints, at Bolsover, and were intended at Cecil's New Exchange.[2] Their frequent occurrence at this time contrasts strongly with the inscribed apology for their appearance upon the Cornwall Triptych of 1588 in Burford Church, Salop.[3]

This new subject-matter followed closely upon the first signs of a new manner of design and coincided with the thorough-going development of that manner by a particular group of men. The new matter and the intensification of the new manner are the reflection in interior decoration of the aesthetic consciousness and the High Anglican sympathies of the virtuosi and of the conditions that were producing them. The virtuosi, indeed, carried out a consistent campaign against the old style. Peacham, it will be remembered, criticized the 'antique' as 'unnatural', 'unorderly', and 'without Rime or reason'; Wotton condemned its 'medlie and motlie Designes' as fit only for friezes and borders;[4] Jones pronounced that ornament should be composed 'with decorum, according to the use and order it is of'.[5] Nature, Order, Reason;

[1] B.M. Harl. Mss. 7044, No. 8.
[2] L. Stone in *Arch. Journ.* cxiv (1957), 112–13.
[3] C. Hussey in *C.L.* cxii (Dec. 1957), 1310–13.
[4] *The Elements of Architecture*, ed. S. Prideaux (1903), p. 78.
[5] J. Lees-Milne, *Age of Inigo Jones* (1953), p. 53.

these were some of the abstract and sophisticated slogans with which the virtuosi attacked the old art and, by importing into them their own concrete conceptions of what was natural, orderly, and rational, propagated the new.

It is with this general development in mind that one must approach the most important example of the interior decoration of this period—the murals at Hill Hall, Essex. They consist of scenes from the story of Cupid and Psyche, and of 'King Hezekiah before the Temple Door' (Pl. 40b) and 'The Destruction of Sennacherib's Army'. They are drawn life-size, with considerable classical architectural detail and with a skill far above that of the general run of wall-paintings of the period. The subjects from the Cupid and Psyche story are framed within painted borders of hanging fruit swags and flowers and are copies of engravings by The Master of the Die. The Old Testament subjects are in borders with classical architectural details.

Hill Hall was begun by Sir Thomas Smith after 1568,[1] and Dr. Pevsner has dated these paintings to about 1570 and Mr. Reader to about 1580. The agreement of such authorities might seem to have settled at least their late sixteenth-century origin, but this unanimity is based implicitly upon arguments that are far from conclusive: that the most probable date of the paintings is that of the erection of the building and that this probability is increased by the equal probability that subjects of such consciously classical choice are to be attributed to the taste of the learned classicist who built Hill Hall. Such an argument is often a good one, but here its two components may be mutually exclusive. Hill Hall was not finished at Smith's death in 1577[2]—the courtyard, in fact, seems not to have been begun until 1575[3]—and though it is arguable that the murals were painted while building was going on, it is equally arguable that they were not. It is this that makes Dr. Pevsner's date of 1570 not impossible but difficult. Mr. Reader, in preferring a date of 1580,

---

[1] N. Pevsner, *Buildings of England—Essex*, pp. 353-5.

[2] In his will Smith left £20 to be paid to his 'architect', Richard Kirby, as soon as the house was tiled and all carpentry work done (J. Strype, *Life of Sir Thomas Smith* (Oxford, 1820), p. 171).

[3] It is possible indeed that the building itself was not begun until 1575; see N. Pevsner in *Arch. Rev.* (May 1955), p. 307, n. 4.

presumably after the completion of Hill Hall, was apparently trying to avoid this difficulty, but in doing so he created another, for
this supposes that the paintings were carried out after Smith's
death, and yet half the argument for a late sixteenth-century date
depends upon Smith's personal taste.

The importance of Smith's classical learning in this context,
however, can be exaggerated. Deep learning is one thing, and a
taste for the arts another. Smith may have been devoted to classical
literature and mythology, but if he was, his devotion was not
reflected in his library. In an inventory of 1566 his many books are
listed under several headings: 'History', 'Natural Philosophy',
'Theology', 'Mathematics', 'Medicine', 'Grammar and Poetry'.
Of these the last section is the shortest, and within it grammar has a
marked preponderance over poetry. He had, it is true, some works
of Vitruvius, but then architecture, and especially Vitruvius, was to
a man of Smith's era a matter of learning rather than of art; indeed
these books are catalogued under 'Mathematics'.[1] The subjects that
Strype enumerates as objects of interest to Smith reveal, as the
library does, a man of affairs with strong utilitarian and scientific
interests.[2] Smith, in fact, was one of those, like Cheke, of whom
R. R. Bolgar has said: 'One cannot help suspecting that their
scholarship was largely a means to an end. Croke had made the
point that a study of the classics would fit a man for public affairs
and Cheke had plainly taken him at his word.'[3] Classical learning
alone, in short, while it would predispose a man to, was no proof
of, a deep interest in classical literature or in its representation in
Renaissance art.

If, however, there is little reason to think that Sir Thomas's
artistic taste must lie at the back of these paintings, there is even
less to attribute them, as Mr. Reader's argument does, to his heir,
Sir William Smith. He had spent all his mature life, until he inherited at the age of thirty, in the Irish Wars, and we need not
suspect him of any learned artistic tastes whatever. Sir Thomas
himself clearly did not, for he left all his books on his death to
Queens' College, Cambridge, 'because he saw none of those that

[1] Strype, pp. 274–81.                          [2] Ibid., pp. 159–67.
[3] *The Classical Heritage and its Beneficiaries* (1954), p. 314.

should succeed him for a long time were like to take to learning'.[1]
The history of the building and our knowledge of Sir Thomas
Smith and his heir present no overwhelming arguments, therefore,
for accepting the date of 1570–80. Other considerations give some
reason for rejecting it. If classical learning and travel in Italy were
capable in the late sixteenth century of producing a demand for
such works in England then, since Smith was not the only man
with those advantages, there should be other examples in the
houses of his contemporaries. They may come to light in the future,
but they have not done so yet.

It can, of course, be argued that all this matters little, for the
paintings are obviously 'freaks'. Perhaps they are, but if they are,
then what becomes of the 1570–80 dating? Freaks are by definition
outside of the normal sequence of development, and as freaks these
may belong to any decade in the seventy years that followed the
beginning of Hill Hall. Before one applies the 'freak' label—which
is, in effect, to abandon the problem—it is necessary to ask whether
they can be better fitted into another period than the late sixteenth
century. In some ways they can. The Old Testament scenes are
set in borders of twisted columns very similar to those of the painted
arcading at Eastbury. The competence of these paintings can be
equalled elsewhere, for example in the seascapes at Eastbury, and
while their manner is not so easily paralleled it reveals a taste for a
sophisticated form of Continental art that is far more characteristic
of the virtuosi than of Sir Thomas Smith's era. The use of a stencil
for the borders, unknown in domestic mural decoration in the late
sixteenth century, suggests that they are of the early seventeenth,
which has produced other examples of stencil work.[2] What is of
greatest importance, however, is that the Hill Hall paintings are
large-scale and occupy nearly all of the wall-surface from floor to
ceiling. There is nothing comparable in any other big house of the
late sixteenth century, for the contemporary habit of covering

[1] Strype, p. 156.
[2] J. F. A. Roberts has argued that the use of a stencil in 1580, forbidden by the
Painter-Stainers' Company in 1582, implies foreign workmanship (*Burl. Mag.* lxxviii
(1941), 86–92). However it does not, for what is yet to be proved is that the paintings
are of the late sixteenth century.

every inch of space with hangings, wainscot, and plasterwork discouraged, if it did not forbid, such huge murals. In the early years
of the next century, when painted cloths had gone out of favour,
walls were sometimes left bare and in consequence murals similar
to those at Hill Hall are found in other houses.

It would be idle to pretend that there is any certainty in the
matter, and new discoveries may prove Dr. Pevsner and Mr. Reader
to have been brilliantly right. Nevertheless on the present evidence
the Hill Hall paintings can be placed in the late sixteenth century
only on the assumption that they are freaks; if placed in the early
seventeenth they can be fitted, with some reservations, into a
coherent sequence of development. For this reason the later date is,
at the moment, to be preferred.

The increase of wealth expendable upon their comforts that came
to some classes in the sixteenth century and that revealed itself in
the unprecedented design and decoration of houses was reflected
also in the furnishings of the time. Domestic furniture became not
only more plentiful but more comfortable and elaborate as well.
The four-poster bed with a panelled tester or canopy above and a
highly decorated head-board became common, at least among the
well-to-do; the once lonely chair appropriated to the master of
the house acquired companions and upholstery, and by the early
seventeenth century children's chairs were being made. In addition
to the great 'table-dormant' and the trestle-tables in the Hall other
and more specialized types began to appear, such as draw-tables
and smaller games tables; and cupboards and presses became commoner and more ornamental. In general this new and elaborate
furniture was made of oak, but walnut was not uncommon among
the wealthy, and ash and beech were occasionally used.

The decoration upon furniture was an adaptation of that upon
panelling and upon wooden overmantels, an adaptation in which,
from the nature of the case, general design was of smaller moment
and applied ornament, in consequence, of greater. Carved enrichment, of arabesques, strapwork, arcading, caryatides, terms, and
columns, was applied in profusion. The legs of tables and the
supports of bed-testers were often given a curious bulbous outline
—with gadrooning or other decoration—which has become the

hall-mark of the developed style. This, however, was only the extreme form of the general practice of ornamenting structural members, seen, for instance, on an open court-cupboard in the Burrell Collection which has the front supports in the form of caryatides at the top and heraldic beasts with shields below. The same feature is seen upon many of the turned or 'thrown' chairs, which appear to have a West Country origin, where every structural member is covered with turned ornament.

More striking than this carved and turned decoration, and more expensive, was that carried out in inlays of coloured woods, generally of holly or bog oak but sometimes of other woods such as cherry and on one occasion at least in bone.[1] This practice was not confined to oak furniture; a bed in the Victoria and Albert Museum that once belonged to the Corbet family is of walnut inlaid with holly and bog oak (Pl. 42). The use of contrasting woods in one piece of furniture was not confined to inlay, and a frieze, bracket, or other carved decoration might be carried out in walnut while the rest was in oak.

The head-board of a bed or the solid back of a chair were favourite places for inlay. The subject-matter was often of the same character as the floral scrolls and birds of a chair of c. 1600 in the Victoria and Albert Museum (229–1898) or the floral patterning of a cupboard in the Hart Collection. A fashionable theme, paralleling some overmantels, was an architectural composition in perspective, and that of the Great Bed of Ware, in the Victoria and Albert Museum, with swans on an ornamental lake before a building in perspective, is similar to the overmantel in the Senior Combination Room at St. John's College, Cambridge. A bed at Berkeley Castle, elaborately decorated and with two small figures in the round set within the pedestals of the posts as in an aedicule, has upon the head-board, flanking the arms of James I, inlaid figures of Justice and Mercy.

The highest development of inlay, however, is found upon the ornamental chests and presses that served, among other uses, the purposes of modern wardrobes. An example in the Victoria and

[1] See A. Vallance, *Art in England during the Elizabethan and Stuart Periods* (1908), p. 98.

Albert Museum is inlaid in holly and bog oak with marquetry designs of domed and turreted buildings (Pl. 44*b*). Southwark Cathedral has a chest, probably of *c.* 1588, elaborately decorated with inlaid vases of flowers in the main panels, carved blind windows complete with moulded sills and architraves within an imitated masonry surround in the smaller ones, and inlaid views of buildings in the base. The fondness for architectural scenes and motifs was not confined to inlay work or to domestic furniture; a pulpit of a date prior to 1636[1] from St. Katherine's Hospital, Regent's Park, has six perspective architectural scenes upon it in low relief.

Not everyone, however, could afford a great amount of inlay or of carving and sometimes the effect achieved in these techniques was attempted in paint. The head-board of a bed belonging to Mr. L. G. G. Ramsay has two framed panels with painted architectural compositions, and a chest in the Victoria and Albert Museum (W27–1913) is painted with vases of roses, tulips, and carnations. Few painted examples survive, but one may suspect that they were once common.

Although there was no great change in furniture throughout the period, nevertheless signs of a new style, or at least of a lighter construction that would bring about a new style, were apparent. Earlier, whatever the timber used, furniture had been heavy and solid. Chairs, with the exception of those called from their form X-chairs, had high solid backs, partly as a protection from the draughts that blew then through English houses even more viciously than now. Beds had heavy posts, often with a panelled wooden canopy, and high and heavy head-boards; tables were massively framed. In later years chairs often lost their high and solid backs and acquired the lighter framing of later styles. X-chairs themselves became commoner and their special feature, the upholstered seat, is used upon other types, such as the light 'farthingale' chairs of the early seventeenth century that allowed fashionable ladies to sit down in their cumbersome clothes with comfort and complacency. Beds, too, became less massive; the panelled tester was increasingly displaced by one of fabric and the bed-posts,

[1] R.C.H.M. *West London*, p. 89.

with less weight to bear, became slighter. The tables-dormant continued to be heavy, but other and special types, games tables and gate-legged tables, became common and, because they needed to be more movable, were more lightly framed. The slighter framing and the reduction of the amount of timber to bare essentials eliminated many of the earlier opportunities for ornamentation, and in this way helped to bring about the pre-conditions necessary for the different style of later years.

Another result of the greater amount of wealth available in the sixteenth century for domestic spending was a widespread import of foreign tapestries, mostly for wall-hangings but occasionally as cushion and table covers and as hangings and covers for beds.[1] They were of two main types: those with large-scale figure subjects in a Renaissance manner on biblical and classical themes, and 'verdures', which were floral designs with occasional birds and beasts or heraldic roundels or cartouches among the foliage. Closely related to verdures were the popular scenes of hunting and of other aspects of the rural life of the upper classes.

Throughout the period these foreign tapestries had the field mainly to themselves, but about 1560 an attempt was made by William Sheldon to set up an English manufactory on his estates at Barcheston[2] (Warwicks.) and later at Bordesley (Worcs.).[3] Under the technical direction of Richard Hickes and his son Francis the enterprise continued into the early years of the seventeenth century, at least until 1611 if the *Four Seasons* at Hatfield are Sheldon work. Sheldon's aim, it has been said, 'was obviously that of providing sound and useful hangings, often in evidently English taste, for the local county families'.[4] Indeed the Sheldons never succeeded in ending or restricting the import of foreign tapestries

[1] It is usual and useful to distinguish between tapestry hangings, carpets, and embroideries. These categories, however, are not absolute; many hangings and some carpets were embroidered, some cushion- and table-covers were worked in tapestry, and some in the 'Turkey-work' that is the method of manufacture of most carpets. As long as this is remembered, however, the threefold division is a convenience in discussion.

[2] J. Humphreys, 'Elizabethan Sheldon Tapestries', *Archaeologia*, lxxiv (1925), 184.

[3] E. A. B. Barnard and A. J. B. Wace, 'The Sheldon Tapestry Weavers and their Work', *Archaeologia*, lxxviii (1928), 257, 261.

[4] G. Wingfield Digby in *Conn.* cxxix (1952), 10–11.

and it is doubtful whether they ever achieved more than a very local market for their larger pieces. Those whose provenance is at all clear are the maps of Worcestershire (frontispiece), of Oxfordshire and Berkshire, and, in fragments, of Gloucestershire that belong to the Bodleian, and the hangings and cushion-covers of c. 1595, that were formerly at Chastleton, a few miles from Barcheston. *The Seasons* at Hatfield were woven, as the armorials upon them show, for Sir John Tracy of Toddington, Gloucestershire, who had, like Ralph Sheldon, married into the Throckmorton family.[1] There is nothing of any size that was certainly woven for anyone farther away or of higher standing, and the reputation of the manufactory was not enough to win from a foreigner the famous commission for a set of tapestries to commemorate the defeat of the Armada.

The larger Sheldon products failed to impress the most important buyers of tapestries, the very wealthy, partly no doubt on account of their defects but also because of their qualities. Their art was of a very homely sort, paralleling in many respects that of the more popular art forms, the engravings and mural paintings in lesser houses. The county maps have pictorial renderings of parkland, towns, and buildings, and borders with fruit and flowers. Figure subjects are small-scale and retiring. The scenes from Ovid and from the Story of Judah, that were formerly at Chastleton, and the figures of the Virtues on a piece at Sudeley Castle are set within medallions and cartouches in a field of floral designs, birds, and beasts. A cushion cover in the Lever Art Gallery has figures of Faith, Hope, and Charity beneath arcades and against a landscape background set within a border of parkland scenes, beasts, and foliage. The first are in the tradition of the minor mural painting of the time, with its small-scale figured friezes or inset figure-subjects against a field of floral or patterned decoration; the second, although the figures are of more importance, is within the same tradition and may be contrasted with the hangings of the Virtues on the Screen at Hardwick where bolder figures are set beneath arcades that are intended as realistic representations of masonry setting off, and not absorbing, the figure-subject.

[1] Barnard and Wace, op. cit., p. 303.

*The Seasons* at Hatfield, which alone of probable Sheldon work have large-scale figures, are very different in conception. They are copied from engravings by Martin de Vos and the figure-subjects are the main element in the composition. Yet, quite apart from the clumsiness of the figures themselves, the details and workmanship are very much in the Sheldon manner, with borders set with innumerable roundels and medallions, many of whose subjects are taken from Whitney's *Book of Emblems*.[1]

Although their large pieces were probably never of a standard to impress the very great, there is some evidence that the Sheldons turned out for them, or at least for some of them, small-scale work of a higher quality. Certainly their manufactory was not unknown at court, for in 1571 Leicester was commending it to the citizens of Warwick as an example of local initiative in finding work for the idle poor.[2] In 1592 armorial pieces were probably being supplied for Hardwick.[3] Cushion covers woven in silk and wool and of finer workmanship than the larger pieces may well represent the kind of work that the Sheldons did for those who preferred, and could afford, to go to foreign sources when they wanted large hangings.

Apart from the Sheldon products there appear to have been no large tapestries made in England before the setting-up of the Mortlake manufactory in 1619. The Mortlake tapestries, however, until well beyond 1625 can hardly be regarded as products of English art. The workmen were foreign, the designers were foreign, and the themes were supplied from foreign sources. They are important as a symptom of the changes in English art, but they were, initially, as much imports as if they had been manufactured overseas.[4]

Carpets, like tapestries, were widely imported into England during the period and, again like tapestries, provoked a small amount of native work, less than a dozen important surviving examples in all. The Leicester Inventory of 1588 refers to a 'Turquoy carpett of Norwiche work'[5] and that of the Countess of

[1] A. F. Kendrick, 'The Hatfield Tapestries of the Seasons', *Wal. Soc.* ii (1913), 93–94.
[2] Humphreys, op. cit., p. 184.
[3] W. G. Thompson, *Tapestry Weaving in England* (1914), p. 57.
[4] See *O.H.E.A.* viii (1957), 124–31.
[5] J. O. Halliwell, *Ancient Inventories* (1854), p. 147.

Bedford of 1602 to a Turkey carpet 'of Englishe makinge'.[1] Apparently not all English carpets were produced by professional weavers, for the same inventory mentions 'Two Wyndowe Turkey Carpettes of my owne makinge',[2] a phrase that suggests that large pieces and not merely cushion covers were worked by leisured ladies.

'Turkey-work' was the generic name for the method of knotting short lengths of wool on to a loosely woven fabric, and the English examples are readily distinguishable because they used hemp instead of the silk of the Eastern manufacturers for the warp and woof. Further, Eastern weavers beat down the individual knots in the course of working and so got about one-third more into the warp than transversely, and English workers copying an Eastern example knot for knot produced a more elongated pattern.

The distinctive feature of English work lies not in these technical differences but in its style of ornament. Although at first they copied Eastern examples both in pattern and in colour-scheme, English weavers began before long to disregard their mentors. They avoided the hot reds and contrasting sombre colours and showed a preference for cooler and fresher tints, for green, blue, yellow, and white. The Gorhambury carpet of 1570 has a dark blue field with a pattern predominantly in greens and yellows. The pattern itself is a simple diaper with floral elaborations and with the royal arms flanked by those of Harbottle and the Borough of Ipswich with the date in the centre. The border has a pattern of honeysuckle between oak-stems. Even the Buccleuch carpets of 1584 and 1585, which are copies of imported work and have a red field, make great use of bright greens, blues, and yellows.

The culmination of this tendency is seen in the Hulse carpet, formerly in the Victoria and Albert Museum and now at Breamore House, Hants. It has an apple-green ground upon which is a pattern of running tendrils with roses, honeysuckles, pansies, pomegranates, grapes, hyacinths, with butterflies and caterpillars between. The border has a white ground with black spots and a more conventionalized floral pattern (Pl. 43). Unlike most English examples it has neither heraldry nor inscription but merely the date, 1614.

[1] C. E. C. Tattersall, *History of British Carpets* (Benfleet, 1934), p. 41.
[2] Ibid., p. 41.

This carpet and its close relatives at Knole, with motifs that parallel much of the wall-painting and some of the plasterwork of the time, reveal how quickly and thoroughly a native style established itself.

Like tapestries, embroideries were used in a number of ways, but less often as wall- and bed-hangings than as table, cushion, and pillow covers. Unlike tapestries they were not, on the whole, the work of professionals but of amateurs, generally of the women of the upper classes. Those at Hardwick are the work of Mary Queen of Scots, of the Countess of Shrewsbury, and of their attendant ladies; skill with the needle was a highly rated accomplishment and the most important pieces of embroidery of a famous needle-woman, Dorothy Selby, were reproduced in stone upon her monument at Ightham. Probably in consequence of this feminine—and, in the circumstances of the time, unlearned—background, embroidery was little affected by Renaissance motifs or pattern books but drew largely from the old illuminated manuscripts and from such popular native works as Topsell's *History of the Beasts*, Gerard's *Herbal*, and Whitney's *Emblems*.

Embroidered table and floor carpets sometimes copy Turkey-work patterns; an example in the Victoria and Albert Museum (T41–1928) has a border based upon the Cufic lettering of Caucasian carpets, but even here the Turkey-work colours are avoided and blues, greens, and yellows are prominent. Often, as in the St. John of Bletso carpet (Victoria and Albert Museum), the treatment is similar to that of the naturalist floral design of the Hulse carpet of 1614 at Breamore. Cushion covers generally have a central subject, often heraldic, within a floral border; that to which Mary Hulton affixed her name has a blue-purple ground with the arms of James I centrally in a surround of sprigs and tendrils with grape bunches, hyacinths, marigolds, and two birds (Pl. 44a). This fondness for a floral design is also apparent upon pillow-cases, together with a marked liking for an overall pattern in which coiling tendrils form a circle that encloses a single flower. Pictorial subjects were not uncommon and the 'Genesis' set of pillow-covers in the Victoria and Albert Museum has a series of scenes from the Old Testament.

Together with furniture and textiles, gold and silver plate, in the form of salt-cellars, ewers, flagons, and cups, became common in prosperous Tudor households. In this as in so many other media, foreign borrowings, although conspicuous, were mainly restricted to decorative motifs, and the fantastic forms of Continental silver-smiths were rarely copied. The Gibbon Salt of 1576, in the possession of the Goldsmiths' Company, has four Ionic columns, surmounted by little cupolas, around a central pillar of rock-crystal with a figure of Neptune; it is one of the most elaborate survivals and although one or two pieces of greater fantasy are known from inventories there is nothing to suggest that they were of English workmanship. More typical is the Mostyn Salt of 1586 (V. & A.), of conventional round form and heavily decorated with lion-masks, fruit, flowers, and beasts. In later years the native fondness for naturalistic floral designs, so evident in wall-paintings and textiles, ousted the earlier grotesques and the heavy masses of fruit and flowers in favour of simpler forms and less crowded ornament. Pictorial representation was sometimes attempted, and in 1588 Burghley presented the Queen with a piece of gold plate engraved with Frobisher's ship, the *Triumph*.[1] By the early seventeenth century, engraving, rather than chasing or embossing, had become popular and a cup of 1611 in the Victoria and Albert Museum has alternate bands of strapwork and of engraved hunting-scenes. Plate was one of the very few crafts that retained an ecclesiastical market, and the Elizabethan church settlement gave work to such local silversmiths as the Stratfords of Dorchester in producing communion cups to replace chalices. There was much activity in this in the second decade of Elizabeth's reign and in such counties as Dorset, Gloucestershire, Sussex, and Yorkshire the majority of Elizabethan communion cups are of the years between 1568 and 1578. These cups are of a common form; a curved foot, a knop on the stem, a bowl in the shape of an inverted bell, and a domed cover. Variations sometimes occur, and the cup at Shipton Gorge in Dorset has a bowl shaped like a wine-glass. Decoration is generally no more than a band of engraved strapwork or foliage around the foot, the bowl, and the cover.

[1] A. J. Collins, *Jewels and Plate of Elizabeth I* (1955), pp. 590–1.

# IV

# PAINTING

'And art made tongue-tied by authority.'

SHAKESPEARE: *Sonnet lxvi*

T HE most important form of easel-painting in England in this period, both in amount and in contemporary estimation, was portraiture. There were, however, other forms and they are best dealt with first. One of the commonest, and it is not surprising in an age when classical learning was spreading widely, was Greek and Roman story and mythology. A surviving example is the *Ulysses and Penelope* (*c.* 1570) formerly at Castle Howard, which may have been painted in this country but which appears more likely to be an import of the Fontainebleau School, and was ascribed by Dimier to Primaticcio;[1] and another is a double-scene from the same story at Hardwick. There is evidence for the former existence of many more. The *Andromeda* for which 'Arnold the Painter' was paid by the Office of Revels in 1572[2] may have been no more than a piece of stage scenery, but in the inventory of the pictures of the Earl of Leicester taken in 1588 there occur such paintings as 'One of Cupid and Venus' and 'Diana bathying hirself with hir Nimphes';[3] and in that of the Earl of Somerset of 1615 several 'great tables' of 'Venus and Cupid', 'Bacchus', 'Ceres and Venus', and 'Venus and Adonis'.[4] That any of these is of native origin is most unlikely; on the contrary, they are illustrations of the need of some few men for a respite from portraiture, and of the inability of any native painter to satisfy it.

[1] L. Dimier, *French Painting in the 16th Century* (1904), p. 184. Sir Anthony Blunt is inclined to accept this ascription: *Art and Architecture in France 1500–1700* (1953), p. 65.

[2] A. Feuillerat, *Documents relating to the Office of Revels to Queen Elizabeth* (Louvain, 1908), p. 175.

[3] *Notes & Queries*, 3rd ser. ii (1862), 201–2, 224–6.

[4] *The Loseley Manuscripts*, ed. A. J. Kempe (1835), pp. 407–8.

Perhaps commoner, certainly more typical in their utilitarian intention, and often of English workmanship, were the historico-propaganda pieces that carried on the tradition of Holbein's Whitehall murals of Henry VII and Henry VIII, and the frescoes portraying the latter's military exploits. The best known of these is the painting at Sudeley Castle by Hans Eworth, in which a seated Henry VIII is flanked on the one side by Mary and Philip of Spain with a figure of Mars, and on the other by Elizabeth with 'Peace' and 'Plenty'. It is possible that by the early seventeenth century this type of picture was widely popular. There is in the possession of the Society of Antiquaries a curious diptych painted, according to an inscription on the frame, 'by John Gipkyn for Henry Farley' in 1616. The two panels show Old St. Paul's in a dilapidated and in a renovated state, and pamphlets published by Farley in 1616 and 1621 make it plain that the painting was intended to be presented to James I as an eloquent petition for the restoration of the building.[1] In 1625 the East India Company was commissioning a painting of the massacre of Amboyna as a piece propaganda against their Dutch rivals. It was of sufficient public importance to draw forth a Dutch protest and a royal reprimand to the Company and the painter with orders to abandon it.[2] Outside our period in date but not in origin is the painting, probably by one of the Percevals of Salisbury, commemorating the Gunpowder Plot, at New College, Oxford, an elaborate composition divided into many scenes and with much symbolism, intended to celebrate the triumph of Justice and James I over the wicked.[3] It is of interest because in its form it copies the temporary structures erected for a pageant or a royal visit and sometimes illustrated in engravings,[4] and because its iconographical scheme was drawn up by Richard Haydocke, himself a designer if not an engraver of brasses. It is probable that there was a widespread taste for such

[1] H. Farley, *The Complaint of Paules to all Christian Soules* (1616); *St. Paules Church her bill for the Parliament* (1621).

[2] *Unpublished Papers of Sir Peter Paul Rubens*, ed. W. N. Sainsbury (1859), pp. 351–2.

[3] L. G. W. Legg, 'On a Picture commemorative of the Gunpowder Plot', *Archaeologia*, lxxxiv (1934), 27–39.

[4] See the illustrations in Stephen Harrison, *The Arches of Triumph Erected in honor of . . . James the First* (1604).

subjects, but one that was rarely able to express itself in easel-painting. Of a similar nature, because they have a story to tell, are the scenes from the life and death of Sir Henry Unton, in the National Portrait Gallery (Pl. 46).

Superficially similar but in conception very different are such 'occasion pieces' as the *Visit of Queen Elizabeth to Blackfriars* at Sherborne Castle and the *Meeting of the English and Spanish Pleni-potentiaries* (Pl. 48) (N.P.G.). They are not, in fact, representations of scenes or occasions so much as group-portraits. The *Pleni-potentiaries* is obviously a group-portrait, and the painter of the *Visit* was far more concerned with an accurate representation of the Queen and her courtiers than with expressing the bustle and movement of a royal procession.

There are some allegorical or symbolic paintings, but here too the portrait bias is evident. Such paintings of Elizabeth as the 'Ermine' and 'Rainbow' at Hatfield are far more portraits with symbols than anything else, and even Eworth's *Sir John Luttrell* at Dunster Castle, with its subject wading in a shipwreck-sea and communing with a deity, is primarily a portrait and only second-arily an allegory. The two companion panels of the *Perfect Wife*[1] of half-a-century later were doubtless meant to inculcate a valuable lesson in feminine behaviour, but the use of two pictures, of an older and of a younger woman with different facial features, show that portraits either of a first and second wife or of a mother and daughter are intended. Eworth's *Elizabeth and the Three Graces* of 1569, at Hampton Court, in which the Queen astounds none but the simple by awarding the prize to herself, is partly a portrait and wholly a piece of flattery of an individual. This interest in persons to the exclusion of almost everything else, of which the deification of Gloriana is the extreme example, is rarely absent. It is revealed in an amusing way in a picture in which no human being other than a groom appears, that at Hatfield of the white horse which Elizabeth rode at Tilbury and later gave to Cecil, a picture that is not to be re-garded as evidence of an interest in nature, or even in horses, but in anything connected, however obliquely, with a famous individual.

[1] Reproduced by M. K. Martin in 'Some Pictures by Marcus Gheeraerts the Younger', *Burl. Mag.* xxv (1914), 137-44.

There is also some evidence of a taste in restricted circles for genre painting. The Leicester inventories include 'a picture of a froe selling fruytage', 'Tenn smale pictures of Dutch women', a devise made by Hubbard on cloth of 'a butcher and a maide buying meate'; and in the Lumley inventory (1590) there is an item of 'a great table of a Dutche woman selling of fruyte'.[1] Somewhat similar in its interest in the affairs of ordinary people is Hofnagel's *Marriage Feast at Bermondsey*, now at Hatfield. Leicester's collection contained also some of the *galanteries* that were popular in France in the mid-century; at Kenilworth there were two pictures of Poppaea Sabina and at Leicester House one of 'an old man looking on his booke, and a Ladye by him entysing him from it'. These were probably of the type of the *Poppaea Sabina*, now in the Roth Museum at Geneva, and of the picture in Rennes Museum of a veil-clad woman hesitating between an old and a young man. It is perhaps not an unworthy suspicion that some of Leicester's and Somerset's pictures from classical mythology were more *galanteries* than anything else, for such obviously amatory subjects as 'Venus and Cupid', 'Diana and Actaeon', 'Diana and her nymphs bathing' are commonest among them; and the Castle Howard *Ulysses and Penelope* has more than a hint of the Fontainebleau style of elegant semi-pornography.

In contrast to this form of aristocratic entertainment, religious paintings were not uncommon in these collections. In Leicester's possession were such works as *Christ calling Peter out of the Custom House* and *John the Baptist preaching in the Wilderness*. At Lumley there was 'a great table of the birthe of Christ' and 'a table of Dives and Lazarus'. A painting of *c.* 1570, now in the possession of Mr. Derek Sherborn, shows a human figure representing the soul ascending past a multitude of moral perils to Heaven (Pl. 45).

It must be emphasized that there is no reason to suppose that any of these, with the exception of Hubbard's *Butcher and Maid* and Hofnagel's *Marriage Feast at Bermondsey*, was painted by an Englishman or in this country. The genre pictures of 'Dutchwomen' and 'froes' are certainly imports from the Low Countries, the *galanteries* appear to be of French origin, and there is no known

---

[1] For the Lumley inventory see *Wal. Soc.* vi (1918), 15–50.

religious picture that can be ascribed to an English painter or to the
'English period' of a foreign painter. Mr. Sherborn's painting was
certainly carried out for an English patron, but its authorship and
provenance are unknown, and despite its form it is more of a
morality than anything else.

Apart from the examples already mentioned and some others
like them, all the easel-painting of the period is portraiture, in
marked distinction from the range of subject-matter in the other
arts of the time. A comparison between the Armada *Elizabeth*
and the Armada Tapestries that hung in the old House of Lords
shows the great difference in approach to the same subject of the
easel-painters and of other artists.[1] The tapestries consist of
episodes from the running fight with the Spanish fleet; the painting
has a dominating seated figure of Queen Elizabeth with small inset
panels of a scene from a naval battle. The one is a commemoration
of an historical event, the other a portrait with a reference to the
event.

An understanding of this near-monopoly by portraiture must
be sought in the peculiar circumstances in which English painting
developed in the early and mid-sixteenth century. There appeared
in England at that time, almost simultaneously and in more or less
direct association, an absolute State based on a landowning class,
the religious doctrines of the Reformation, and the intellectual
changes of the Renaissance. The new type of landowner was not,
in many cases, any wealthier than his predecessors, but unlike them
he was debarred, as the subject of an absolute State, from spending
his wealth upon armies of retainers to win or maintain for him a
national or local power. He spent it, instead, upon keeping up a
'port' and in looking after his comforts. One such comfort was to
place tapestries, generally imported, and other hangings upon the
formerly bare or painted walls of many rooms; and, in consequence, to reduce the demand for domestic murals. At the same
time there was practically no demand for church murals as the
doctrines of the Reformers enforced a 'decent plainness' upon

[1] The Armada Tapestries perished in the fire that destroyed the old Houses of
Parliament. Their appearance, however, is preserved in John Pine's engravings published in 1739 and reissued in 1753.

religious buildings. The results of this double blow were twofold. The painter was robbed of two of his most important opportunities and was placed, as a member of a now crowded and almost redundant craft, in a very weak position against his prospective customers and patrons. The major field for the display of large-scale figure and narrative painting was closed and the tradition and prestige of such painting greatly weakened.[1]

In this situation the Humanist ideas of the Renaissance presented the painter with almost his only opportunity, but with a very limited one. The stress on the individual that was the most revolutionary concept of the period entailed, for all its liberating influence, some severe restrictions. It considered 'an interest in mankind to be an interest in persons, history to be a pageant of heroes'[2] and religion a matter of direct communication between a man and his Maker. It was this negative aspect that was eagerly seized on by the contemporary monarchies, who saw in the glorification of the individual a sanction of their absolute control of the State, and by their courtiers, who looked on the Sovereign's glory as the guarantee of their position and their position as the basis of his power. In England, where the dynasty's legal title was as dubious as its supporters' moral claim to much of their land, it was especially welcome. This ideology of the most important patrons of the time had a threefold effect on easel-painting. An interest in persons demanded that they should be subjects of painting, and portraits therefore multiplied. The view of history as a 'pageant of heroes' led to a demand for portraits, real or imagined, of the famous dead and the far-away living, and to a lack of demand for 'historical' paintings, of events in which no particular hero participated. The more private nature of religion and the consequent attitude towards 'idolatry' eliminated any great desire for paintings of biblical subjects or of individual saints and Madonnas. With the painters in too humble a position to express whatever objections they may have had, and with the narrative traditions of mural painting exerting no influence, the easel-

[1] For a similar view of portraiture in France of the later Valois State see Irene Adler, 'Die Clouet', *J.K.S.W.*, n.f. iii (1929), 201.

[2] Barrows Dunham, *Man against Myth* (1948), p. 62.

painting of the period was, in essence, a reflection of the ideas of the absolute State and its creatures and creators.

Before this view can be maintained, however, there are some weighty objections to be overcome. It has been held that painting, even portrait-painting, had a decorative purpose and was intended as a part of 'the furnishings and embellishments' of a house.[1] There is some evidence that appears to support this, for when, in 1599, Hilliard agreed to paint a portrait of the Queen for the Goldsmiths' Company the picture was to hang in the house 'as an ornament'.[2] But if this is a correct assessment, then it raises the quite insoluble problem of why the other decorative arts—woodwork, plasterwork, hangings, murals—were allowed a wide variety of subject-matter while easel-painting was restricted to portraiture. It would seem to be nearer the truth that any decorative value that easel-painting had, and certainly the gorgeous costume-pieces were decorative, was a by-product of its main function of recording an individual. In the introduction to his translation of Lomazzo's *Trattato dell'arte* Haydocke listed several functions of painting, but 'ornament' and 'delight' were not among them.[3] A decorative intention seems to have played little part in the hanging of pictures. It is true that the evidence for this comes mainly from the end of the period, but, as far as it goes, it is strong. On his visits to Titchfield and Wilton in 1635 Lieutenant Hammond recorded pictures nowhere but in the Long Gallery and in his description of other rooms mentioned only 'the arras'.[4] In Ben Jonson's *Poetaster* of 1602 Albius instructs his wife to hang 'no pictures in the hall nor in the dining-chamber but in the gallery only for 'tis not courtly else'.[5] There are exceptions to this. In Somerset's inventory several pictures are recorded in the 'bowling alley'. They are, however, all classical or religious subjects and

[1] C. H. Collins Baker and W. G. Constable, *English Painting in the 16th and 17th Centuries* (Paris, 1930), p. 4.

[2] W. S. Prideaux, *Memorials of the Goldsmiths' Company* (1896), i. 98.

[3] Richard Haydocke, *A Tract containing the Artes of Curious Painting Carving Building* (Oxford, 1598), p. iii.

[4] 'A Relation of a Short Survey of the Western Counties made in 1635', ed. L. G. W. Legg, *Camden Miscellany*, xvi (1936), 43, 66.

[5] *The Poetaster*, II. ii.

there is not a portrait among them. Such a restriction of portraits to one room, the room where the family strolled and guests were entertained, suggests that they were not regarded in general as a form of decoration but more as the votive images of a State and Ancestor cult.[1]

It may also be objected that it is one-sided to consider the painting of an age as solely determined by the patron's tastes, for the artist too has a say in the matter. But the men who painted the most typical portraits of the Elizabethans and Jacobeans were not artists, they were craftsmen. By this I do not intend any denigration of their potential talents but a definition of their social status. Before the artist as a social phenomenon can appear, the man who not only reflects but plays a major part in creating the aesthetics of his time, a particular combination of social and intellectual conditions is necessary. These conditions were present in Italy, but they were not yet present in England. Dürer's well-known letter to Pirckheimer from Venice in 1506 reveals the contrast between the position of the Italian artist and of his German counterpart: 'hie bin ich ein Herr, doheim ein Schmarotzer'—('here I am a gentleman, at home a hanger-on').[2] An English Dürer would have said the same but more bitterly, for developments in England were lowering rather than raising the status of the painter.

The tasks on which they might be employed emphasize that easel-painters were regarded as ordinary craftsmen. George Gower, who already had a reputation as a portrait-painter, was in 1581 made Sergeant Painter, with the function of supervising the decoration, almost wholly repetitive patterning, of the Royal palaces.[3] John Matthew of Nottingham was entrusted by the Earl of Rutland with the 'newe paintinge of divers pictures and hanging of the same in the longe gallerye' and in 1591-2 was employed by the same patron on the very ordinary job of 'painting the tombes

---

[1] By the end of the period this was, of course, no longer true of the aesthetically enlightened. Wotton (*Elements of Architecture*, ed. S. Prideaux (1903), pp. 78–79) and Gerbier (see above, p. 120) reveal very different views on the placing of paintings.

[2] *Albrecht Dürers schriftlicher Nachlass*, ed. E. Heidrich (Berlin, 1910), p. 149.

[3] For the kind of work generally carried out under the direction of the Sergeant Painter see E. Mercer, 'The Decoration of the Royal Palaces from 1553 to 1625', *Arch. Journ.* cx (1954), 150–63.

at Bottesford'.[1] Sampson Strong, whose works between 1596 and 1610 included Founders' portraits for New College, All Souls, and Christ Church, was being paid a few shillings in 1605 and 1607–8 for colouring doors and organs at the last college.[2] Conversely many men who must have spent most of their time on murals or painted cloths for 'the common sort', or else on mere colouring, were considered competent to turn out a good portrait. A whole incident in *Arden of Feversham* turns upon the undoubted ability of an artisan in a small country town to do so. Nor was this dramatic licence. Old Sir Gervase Holles was painted in 1626 by 'a workeman, (the best yt was then in the country)', i.e. in the neighbourhood, and 'that piece, (though performed but by an ordinary hand) was very like him'.[3] That there was indeed an unofficial craft organization among the better known painters is shown by the intimate connexions between the Gheeraerts, the de Critzes, and the Olivers; by the family firm of the Percevals of Salisbury; by the succession from generation to generation, from Marcus Gheeraerts the Elder to Marcus the Younger, from Troilus to John to Emmanuel and John de Critz, from Isaac to Peter Oliver, from Nicholas to Lawrence Hilliard.[4] As late as 1622 Peacham felt it necessary to assure his readers that painting was not a 'base' occupation[5] and Hilliard had earlier lamented that miniaturists were 'needy artificers'.[6]

The last point, however, needs elaboration, for it has been asserted that Hilliard in so doing was following the example of Italian theorists and attempting to raise the status of the painter, or, at least, of the miniature-painter, the limner.[7] If this were so it

[1] H.M.C. *Rutland*, iv. 404–5.

[2] R. Lane Poole, *Catalogue of Oxford Portraits*, ii (Oxford, 1926), pp. xi–xiii; W. G. Hiscock, 'Notes on some Christ Church Portraits', *Oxoniensia*, xi (1946–7), 147–51.

[3] 'Memorials of the Holles Family', *Camden Soc.* 3rd ser. lv (1944), 125.

[4] The family connexions of the Gheeraerts, de Critzes, Olivers, and other painters of the period are well laid out in E. K. Waterhouse, *Painting in Britain 1530–1790* (1953), and E. Auerbach, *Tudor Artists* (1954). For the Percevals see C. Haskins, *Salisbury Corporation Pictures and Plate* (Salisbury, 1910).

[5] Henry Peacham, *The Compleat Gentleman* (1622), pp. 105–6.

[6] Nicholas Hilliard, 'The Art of Limning', ed. P. Norman, *Wal. Soc.* i (1912), 15–16.

[7] John Pope-Hennessy, 'Nicholas Hilliard and Mannerist Art Theory', *Journ. W.C.I.* vi (1943), 89–100.

would suggest that the dominance of the patron was not complete and that painters were at least fighting against it. But the conclusions that Hilliard drew from his lamentations shows that this is a misunderstanding of his complaint. He does not argue that limners should be recognized as gentlemen, but that none but gentlemen should be allowed to 'meddle with limning'.[1] The difference is profound. This was not an attempt to raise the status of his colleagues but to set himself apart from them and climb above them. His remarks do not contradict but emphasize the low social standing of limners and 'picture-makers'. And that standing changed little throughout the period. Balthazar Gerbier in an undated letter, probably written about 1625, indignantly repudiated the taunts of his enemies that he 'was but a painter the other day', and protested that he was 'never a painter' until he entered Buckingham's service.[2]

Theoretical considerations alone, however, rarely prove a point, and it is necessary to consider the position of some of the indisputable artists of the time, such immigrants as Holbein, Eworth, and Ketel. The change in Holbein's style from the Humanist serenity and breadth of his earlier period to the stiller and colder manner of his later years is well known. On a lower level and at a later date the style of Hans Eworth undergoes a parallel change. Yet the work of both men, moulded overseas as artists in the European tradition, stands out from the common level of English painting. Frey has noted that the quality in Holbein which Irene Adler has called a 'fast grausame Objektivität' never disappeared from his work,[3] and Eworth never completely degenerated into a painter of Elizabethan costume-pieces. For all the pressure of their patrons' taste, Holbein to a large degree and Eworth to a less preserved their artistic integrity and purpose. But what the English upper-classes had to bear with from an artist of the stature of Holbein they were little prepared, and in course of time became less prepared, to tolerate from other men. It is probably not an

---

[1] 'Art of Limning', pp. 15–18.

[2] G. Goodman, *The Court of James I*, ed. J. S. Brewer (1839), ii. 392.

[3] D. Frey, *Englisches Wesen in der bildenden Kunst* (Stuttgart, Berlin, 1942), pp. 244–5.

accident that Cornelis Ketel, whose *Frobisher* and *William Gresham* have other qualities than those of the costume-piece, left England after a few years' stay. No other painter of any note remained as long, and no professional English painter challenged the prevailing style. At the end of the period Sir Nathaniel Bacon, an amateur, developed a style and above all a subject-matter very different from that of the professionals. But Bacon was a country gentleman who did not have to make his living from his art or to care about the taste of patrons. Conversely, Inigo Jones, a man of no less talent but not endowed with means, after beginning his career as a 'picture-maker'[1] quitted that limited calling for a field in which he could exercise his genius. The examples of these two— melancholy in one way, encouraging in another—reveal that it was not a lack of potential artistic talent in England which limited the art of the time, but that the dominance of patrons with a limited vision denied potential artists the chance of developing their talents.[2]

There is a third factor that must be considered as a possible determinant of the nature of Elizabethan and Jacobean painting; the influence upon English patrons of Continental, specifically of Mannerist, art and art-theories. Hilliard's miniatures, the frozen portraits of English courtiers, the linear technique used in them, and the translation by Haydocke of the work of a leading Mannerist theorist, Lomazzo, have been taken as evidence of a general domination of English painting by Mannerism. The similarities between English portraiture and Mannerist portraiture are clear enough; but equally clear are the differences between English painting and Mannerist painting. Mannerism was very much more than a style of portraiture coupled with a preference for a linear

[1] For Jones as a 'picture maker' see H.M.C. *Rutland*, iv. 446.
[2] It has been shown by Dr. Auerbach (*Burl. Mag.* xci (1949), 166–8) that Hilliard painted at least one portrait 'in great'; and it is possible that both he and Oliver painted a great many. One would like to see the point established, for its implications are in themselves evidence enough to prove the frustration of potential talent by the dominance of contemporary patrons. Hilliard and Oliver were undoubtedly men of immense talent, but if they did do much painting 'in great' then the complete absence of any corpus of work above the common level demonstrates plainly that in that field they were as little able to exercise their abilities as the other professional painters.

rather than a plastic technique. It was an art that showed both by its slavish copying and its wilful defiance of the canons of the past its deep roots in the Italian Renaissance. It was simultaneously rigidly disciplined and wilfully licentious, elegant and farouche, pornographic and ecstatically religious, lost in the 'other world' of antiquity and yet vividly conscious of the horrors of the sixteenth century. It was the art of men of splendid talents and a glorious tradition robbed of their heritage, by the necessities and accidents of European history, at the very moment that they were about to enter upon it. It was the art of a tortured and often despairing society. Of all its varied aspects only the formalized linear portrait is found in England. But it is wholly inadequate to define that portrait as a product of Mannerism; it was specifically a product of one of the factors in the formation of Mannerism, the absolute State and its ideology. In England there were no such disappointments for artists, for none had risen from the ranks of the craftsmen-painters to be disappointed, and despite the burnings at Smithfield, the atrocities of the Irish Wars, the horrors of the Slave Trade, and the unending misery of the Enclosures, life for the articulate sections of the population was very different from life in the greater part of western Europe. Englishmen knew nothing of foreign armies or of civil and religious wars, and for those who could afford to commission paintings the period was one of increasing prosperity. They were, in fact, already developing that smug attitude towards the Continent, compounded of pity and contempt, that has been one of their most enduring and least endearing characteristics. An 'Entertainment' written by John Lyly for Elizabeth's visit to Bisham in 1592 makes great play with a contrast between English carts laden with corn, English rivers flowing with fish, English grass feeding fat cattle, and Europe's carts laden with armour, her rivers flowing with blood and her people feeding, like cattle, on her grass.[1]

In these circumstances Mannerist art had little or no appeal. Even when Englishmen knew and praised Mannerist artists they picked on aspects of their work which the artists themselves would

---

[1] Lyly, *Complete Works*, ed. R. W. Bond (1902), i. 475.

not have considered very important. In the *Winter's Tale* Shakespeare says of Giulio Romano, 'had he himself eternity and could (he) put breath into his work (he) would beguile nature of her costume so perfectly he is her ape'.[1] Nevertheless, while the accidents of history preserved England from many of the misfortunes of sixteenth-century Europe, she was still part of Europe and the Tudor State was a fairly typical absolutism of the European pattern. The qualities of the stiff and formal portraits that Mannerist painters produced for the European courts were therefore not wholly unwelcome in court circles in England. In that sense, and only in that sense, was English painting under Mannerist influence. Mannerism did not create the English portrait of the period, but Mannerist portraiture was congenial to English taste because it served men whose tastes were, in one respect, similar to those of English patrons.

The first demand of this taste was not the portrayal of the individual in his own right but as the symbol or servant of the absolute State, and therefore this portraiture has not only a monumental function but a social function as well. On the one hand it has an aspect of 'effigies domesticated', to use Mr. Piper's phrase, on the other a concentration on the outward signs of rank and office that reaches its full development in the 'costume-pieces'. By either route it arrived at a representation of the individual from which all individuality other than the mere facial features had been processed away, a representation which called for nothing more than a surface likeness. In a dialogue from yet another 'Entertainment' to Queen Elizabeth in 1598 a poet is made to say to a painter 'so shallow are we both, that the Painter must spend his colors in lymning attires, the Poet in commending the fasshions'.[2] The writer intended, on the surface at least, nothing more than a conventional and fulsome compliment to the inexpressible virtues of the Queen. In fact he made a shrewd analysis of the cause of the 'shallowness' of English painting: the glorification of the absolute monarchy and its servants. For such an end the means of a hard,

[1] *Winter's Tale*, v. ii.
[2] *Queen Elizabeth's Entertainment at Mitcham . . . 1598*, ed. L. Hotsen (Yale, 1953), p. 27. Hotsen attributes this to Lyly.

linear outline was obvious and easy; and in its technique, as well as in its conception of portraiture, English painting was in no need of instruction from Continental Mannerists. It has indeed been pointed out that it is perhaps precisely because of its use of a primitive and traditional linear technique that 'the Elizabethan State portrait rivals and sometimes surpasses the work of Bronzino and Mor in turning the likeness of a human being into an icon-like image'.[1]

The literature of the time, although far from presenting a comprehensive reflection of aesthetic ideas, does much to confirm this estimate of the nature of painting. Haydocke referred specifically and at length to its monumental function when listing the pleasures of amateur painting: 'not only a grace to health but also a contentment and recreation unto Sickness, and a kind of preservative against Death and Mortality: by a perpetuall preserving of their shapes, whose substances Physicke could not prolong, no not for a season'.[2] Shakespeare's views on painting were probably no better and no worse than anyone else's. Despite the praise of the Poet in *Timon of Athens*, that a picture 'tutored nature', it is reasonably clear that to Shakespeare painting was a close imitation not so much of nature as of men in society. In the same scene Timon says, 'The painting is almost the natural man: / For since dishonour traffics with man's nature / He is but outside: these pencilled figures are / Even such as they give out.'[3] Even a member of the Sidney circle— Fulke Greville—in comparing language with painting said, 'For as of pictures which should manifest / The lief, we say not that is fineliest wrought / Which fairest simply showed, but faire and like.'[4] Peacham put the matter quite simply; painting, he said, is 'only imitation of the surface of nature'.[5] There were pictures, notably some of the portraits of the Queen, in which nature was not left to speak for herself but was helped out by a considerable amount of flattery of the sitter's features, but this apparent de-

---

[1] M. Jenkins, *The State Portrait, its Origin and Evolution* (U.S.A. College Art Association, New York, 1947), p. 24.

[2] *Artes of Curious Painting etc.*, p. iii.                    [3] *Timon of Athens*, I. i.

[4] Fulke Greville, *Collected Works*, ed. A. B. Grosart, ii (1870), 47.

[5] *Compleat Gentleman* (1622), pp. 105–6.

parture from the rule emphasizes its intention. In an age when beauty of physical feature was considered a mark of nobility, was an almost essential qualification for an ambassador[1] and a desirable quality in a scholar,[2] this 'tutoring of nature' was merely another way of indicating the status of the painter's patron.

The types of portrait common in the period can all be shown to stem from the prevailing ideas on the individual and the State. That aspect of contemporary thought that saw history as 'a pageant of heroes' is plainly reflected in the appearance of portrait galleries of famous men. Such collections as those revealed by the Leicester and Lumley inventories were quite catholic in their range and mingled, with an apparent lack of discrimination, friends and foes, co-religionists and heretics, Englishmen and foreigners.[3] The practice continued throughout the period and as late as Charles I's reign Lord Lothian's agent in Paris was writing about 'thirty-two pictures of noblemen and others' in France which his master desired.[4] Sometimes a deliberate series of historical portraits was collected or painted, such as that which Sir Edward Hoby commissioned of all his predecessors in office when he was Governor of Queenborough Castle[5] or that of benefactors and distinguished members at Peterhouse College, Cambridge.[6] The most impressive of all such series is that recently discovered upon the frieze of the Picture Gallery at the Bodleian, painted between 1616 and 1618 and illustrating with around two hundred portraits the history of secular and divine learning.[7]

The subjects were not necessarily drawn from the long dead or

---

[1] G. Mattingley, *Renaissance Diplomacy* (1955), p. 215.

[2] R. Ascham, *The Scholemaster*, ed. D. C. Whimster (1933), pp. 32–33.

[3] The inventory taken at Greenwich of the collection of Anne of Denmark reveals the same diversity; see O. Millar, 'Abraham van Doort's catalogue of the collection of Charles I', *Wal. Soc.* xxxvii (1958–60).

[4] Mary Hervey, 'Notes on a Tudor Artist—Gerlach Flicke', *Burl. Mag.* xvii (1910), 148.

[5] Waterhouse, *Painting in Britain 1530–1790*, p. 25.

[6] R. J. Willis and J. W. Clarke, *Architectural History of the University of Cambridge* (Cambridge, 1886), i. 64–68.

[7] J. N. L. Myres in *Bodleian Library Record*, iii, No. 30 (Oct. 1950), 82–91; iii, No. 32 (Aug. 1951), 201–7; iv, No. 1 (Apr. 1952), 30–51. These, of course, are murals and not easel-paintings, but their form and conception are wholly that of the easel-painters.

even the very famous living. Anybody in the news had his chance of widespread pictorial representation. Lord Herbert of Cherbury relates that on his return to England in 1610 after some romantic escapades on the Continent he was 'in great esteem both in court and city; many of the greatest desiring my company'. However pleasant they may have found his company they desired his silent presence as well. The Earl of Dorset commissioned a copy of a portrait of Herbert that Larkin had painted, and hung it in his gallery. Anne of Denmark obtained another copy and Lady Ayres got Isaac Oliver to make a miniature from a copy of Larkin's work.[1]

The extent to which portraits of men in the public eye proliferated is shown by an analysis of those of the Wriothesley Earls of Southampton. Of the first Earl, who died in 1550, a K.G. and Lord Chancellor, three portraits are known and there is reason to suspect the former existence of at least three more. The second Earl (1545–81) was not a public figure, was never made a K.G., and was suspected of Roman Catholic leanings. There is only one known portrait of him and no reason to think that there were once more. The third Earl (d. 1624), who 'won distinction as a courtier, as a soldier, as a promoter of colonial enterprise and as a lover of learning', is commemorated by around thirty portraits. After allowing for the great increase in portraits as the period progressed, the discrepancy between the number of portraits of the first and third Earl on the one hand and of the second on the other is still striking; and the difference is made more striking and simultaneously explained by an analysis of the dates of the portraits of the third Earl. Only one can be certainly dated to before 1603 while twenty are certainly after; and it was in 1603 that Southampton's fortunes changed. In that year after a long period of disgrace, at first for his clandestine marriage with Elizabeth Vernon and later for his connexion with Essex's plot, he was liberated from the Tower, created a K.G., made Captain of the Isle of Wight, and launched on his public career. As a result, portraits of him multiplied.[2]

[1] *Autobiography*, ed. Sidney Lee (1906), pp. 68–69.
[2] R. W. Goulding, *The Wriothesley Portraits* (Oxford, 1920), pp. 35–43.

Such portraits cannot be wholly distinguished from 'State' portraits. In the early sixteenth century it was common for courts that were contemplating marriage alliances to obtain 'likenesses' of the intended victims. Holbein's portrait of Christina of Denmark is one of the best known examples. In later years sovereigns often exchanged portraits and an ambassador taking up residence abroad often presented his master's portrait upon arrival, or was presented with a portrait of the Sovereign to whom he was accredited. In 1606 John de Critz was paid for three full-lengths of James, Queen Anne, and Prince Henry, that were to be sent to the Archduke of Austria.[1] Kings had subjects as well as brothers, and portraits were often bestowed on them as a mark of favour, and some of the portraits of James that Van Somer painted were given to English courtiers.[2] The traffic was not all one way, however, for James commissioned portraits of some of his greater subjects. In 1620 Mytens was paid £26 for a picture of the Earl of Nottingham 'made by his Ma⁵ command'[3] and in 1625 he received £130 for several pictures of 'diverse noble personages'.[4]

At a lower level courtiers imitated their king and commissioned portraits of one another and presented their own. In 1598–9 Robert Peake painted several portraits of the Earl of Rutland, of which one was intended for 'Mrs. Mary Ratcliffe', of the family of the Earls of Sussex.[5] In 1607 John de Critz was paid for portraits of Salisbury that were intended for the Constable of Castile, the French and Venetian Ambassadors, and Lady Elizabeth Gilford; and he had painted or had been commissioned to paint for Salisbury a portrait of the Countess of Oxford.[6] Among the upper classes these 'State' portraits had a function somewhat similar to that of visiting cards fifty years ago; their presence in a man's house underwrote his social position.

[1] R. Lane Poole, 'The De Critz Family of Painters', *Wal. Soc.* ii (1913), 45–53.

[2] P. Cunningham, 'New Materials for the life of Paul van Somer', *Builder*, xxii (1864), 417.

[3] Now in the National Maritime Museum.

[4] P. Cunningham, 'New Materials for the life of Daniel Mytens', *Builder*, xxii, pp. 309–10; C. C. Stopes, 'Daniel Mytens in England', *Burl. Mag.* xvii (1910), 160–3.

[5] H.M.C. *Rutland*, iv. 417.

[6] R. Lane Poole, 'The De Critz Family of Painters', *Wal. Soc.* ii (1913), 45–53.

There was, however, a more intimate aspect to portraiture. Many men who were not courtiers had their 'likenesses' taken, and the courtiers themselves were not always on parade. In consequence there was a great amount of painting in the nature of a 'family record', and just as 'State' portraits approximated in some fashion to Victorian visiting cards, so these served a purpose somewhat similar to that of the family album. It is not always possible to distinguish between the two kinds. Some of the examples listed above may have been presents to relations or to friends, as the picture of herself by Larkin that Anne Clifford, Countess of Dorset, sent to 'my cozen Hall' certainly was.[1] It is noticeable that the inventories of the period draw a distinction between pictures and 'pictures of a smaller scantling'. Professor Waterhouse has suggested that the 'large miniature', the panel of about sixteen inches square, may have been the form common among the gentry.[2] I should like to modify that and suggest that small panel pictures were almost universal among the gentry and other classes who had fewer 'state occasions', and were common among courtiers in their 'off duty' moments, as mementoes for their family and friends. The absolute sizes of these paintings are not significant, for sizes increased as time went on, but there was at any given moment a distinction between larger and smaller pictures. In general there are very few portraits of minor people that in any decade are as large as many of the portraits of courtiers of the same time. Yet the portraits of courtiers are not all the same size. It is noticeable that the portraits of Burghley, for example, fall into two main groups, of larger and of smaller pictures, although in both he is generally invested with all the regalia of his office. The much restored picture in the Bodleian in which he is riding on a mule is in a class by itself.[3]

One of the most obvious intentions behind much of this painting was to provide a memorial for the already or soon-to-be dead. The

[1] *Diary of Lady Anne Clifford*, ed. V. Sackville-West (1923), p. 84. By a misreading or a misprint the name is there given as Sarkinge.

[2] Waterhouse, *Painting in Britain 1530–1790*, p. 17.

[3] For Burghley's portraits compare, for example, those in the National Portrait Gallery with the smaller pictures in the Earl Beauchamp and Raveningham Collections.

portrait, possibly of William Stoke, now at Worcester College, Oxford, with its prim inscription, 'Pro Memoria et non pro Vana Gloria', is an eloquent example. A great number of portraits, too great for coincidence, bear the year of the sitter's death, and are probably immediately posthumous works or posthumous copies of an earlier original. The painting of Elizabeth Drury from Haw-sted House is dated 1610, the year of her death, and is unusual in showing the sitter half-lying on her side on a couch, a pose which recalls, and was probably meant to recall, the reclining attitude of many of the funeral effigies of the time.[1] Indeed some men had nothing more than a painting for their monument. At Lydiard Tregoze a St. John monument takes the form of a wooden triptych with painted life-size figures of the family. A similar monument, dated 1588 and signed by an almost unknown Melchior Salaboss, commemorates three generations of the Cornwall family at Bur-ford, Salop.[2] The monument of Ralph Maynard (d. 1613) in St. Albans Cathedral is a large-scale mural with the dead man painted in the kneeling position of many contemporary effigies.

Sometimes the intention appears to be to establish a lien on the future. The portrait of the Earl of Surrey, who was executed in 1547, exists in four versions, at Arundel, Castle Howard, Knole, and Parham (Pl. 50). It has a riddling Latin motto, *Satis super est*, and the arms of Howard, with the descent through Thomas of Brotherton from Edward III, prominently shown. If questions were asked, and they were, it could be explained away as meaning nothing more than 'There is enough above', his heavenly reward is enough; the other meaning, however, was probably the intended one, 'There is enough left over', his descendants are still alive, with its many and far-reaching implications. The picture has more sig-nificance than is generally realized. In content it may be compared with two Scottish examples: that at Darnaway Castle of the corpse of the murdered Earl of Moray with the legend 'God Revenge My Caus' (1591) and that at Holyrood of the murdered Darnley with kneeling figures of his family praying for vengeance (Pl. 47). In

[1] Illustrated in J. Cullum, *The History and Antiquities of Hawsted* (1784), p. 146.
[2] The Cornwall triptych is fully described and illustrated by C. Hussey in *C.L.* cxii (Dec. 1947), 1310–13.

Scotland, where the magnates still went their merry feudal way, their politics and their painting little removed from the Middle Ages, incitements to private redress were expressed in crude pictures.[1] In England, where the State had instilled into the greatest some respect for its authority and into painting some appreciation of Renaissance art, such sentiments were dissembled and hidden beneath a sophisticated elegance. But not everyone saw the future as the avenger of the present. More pathetic than the *Surrey*, for its feeling is of a commoner and higher nature, is the portrait of Sir Henry Crofts, from Richinghall, painted in the year of his death, wherein he is shown with his right arm about the neck of his only child and with the motto, in Latin, 'My only hope'.

This, however, was only one aspect of the family record. There are a number of paintings of parents and their children. One of these, that of Lord Cobham and his family, exists in two versions. The first, at Longleat, is dated 1567 and shows six children. In 1568 another child was born and so an up-to-date record was obtained by copying the 1567 picture and adding the figure of one more child.[2] This is a close parallel to the contemporary French practice of copying a portrait of a few years before and ageing the features of the sitter.[3]

There are also portraits of 'a man in his vocation', the lesser man's version of the State pictures of the great. Such are those of Francis Hervey, at Ickworth, holding in his hand a tasselled hauberk to mark his position as Gentleman Pensioner to Queen Elizabeth,[4] of Rowland Lytton, at Knebworth, a gentleman-volunteer in Leicester's expedition to the Low Countries in 1585-6, holding a tilting-lance, the badge of the volunteers, and of

[1] The Darnley picture was commissioned in London in 1567 (R.A. *Catalogue of an Exhibition of British Portraits* (1956-7), No. 21) and presumably not without the knowledge of the English authorities. They, however, were quite likely to welcome in another country a situation that they would not tolerate in their own.

[2] L. Cust, 'The Painter HE (Hans Eworth)', *Wal. Soc.* ii (1913), 35.

[3] L. Dimier, *Le Portrait en France au XVI<sup>e</sup> siècle* (Paris, Brussels, 1924), i. 69-72.

[4] For Hervey's picture see Farrer, *Portraits in Suffolk Houses*, pp. 210-11; see also J. L. Nevinson, 'Portraits of Gentlemen Pensioners before 1625', *Wal. Soc.* xxxiv (1954), 1-13.

Captain Thomas Lee (Tate Gallery), an Elizabethan thug employed in the Irish Wars, with his military accoutrements and with naked thighs, legs, and feet—'the get-up of a *Hybernus Miles . . .* and obviously well-adapted for bog-trotting'.[1] From about 1625 onwards there is a series of portraits of Captains of the Trainbands, each with the ceremonial leading-staff that proclaims his rank;[2] and by 1633 it was worth the while of a foreign painter to visit a remote country town to draw the portraits of the leading citizens and their wives.[3] The writer of the *Entertainment . . . at Mitcham* of 1598 was exaggerating when he complained that 'now every Citizen's wife that wears a taffeta kirtle and a velvet hatt . . . must have her picture in the parlour',[4] but his outraged snobbery had given him a clear vision of the future.

The inscription on the now lost double-portrait of himself and 'Red Rover' Strangways that Gerlach Flicke painted when they were in prison together in 1554 sums up the intention of most of the portraiture of the time: the insistence on the facial likeness, on the vocation or status of the sitter, on the memorial nature of the work.[5] Translated from the Latin the inscription runs 'Such in appearance was Gerlach Flicke when he was a painter in the City of London. This he painted from a mirror for his dear friends that they might be able to remember him after his death.'

The nature of English painting around the year 1550 was also partly determined by its history during the quarter-century before. The work of Holbein and later of the Netherlander Guillim Scrotes, formerly Court Painter to Mary of Hungary, and of the German, Gerlach Flicke, had developed three distinguishable types of portrait. There was first the type deriving from Holbein: the full-length figure, generally in a frontal pose with straddled legs against a more or less plain background. The unsigned *Earl De la Warr* in the Tate Gallery must be regarded as continuing the Holbein tradition. The less accomplished *Young Man in Red* at Hampton

[1] E. K. Chambers, *Sir Henry Lee* (Oxford, 1936), pp. 190–1.
[2] J. L. Nevinson, 'Captains of the Trainbands', *Conn.* cxli (Apr. 1958), 159–62.
[3] B.M. Eg. Mss. 784, f. 189 (Diary of William Whiteway of Dorchester, Dorset).
[4] *Queen Elizabeth's Entertainment at Mitcham . . . 1598*, p. 27.
[5] Illustrated in *Conn*, xlv (1916), 163–4.

Court, not set against but dominating over a landscape background, and the *Sir Thomas Gresham* of 1544 at Mercers' Hall may not even have been painted in England but were clearly intended for an audience familiar with that tradition. There is a second type, represented by the *Earl of Surrey* already mentioned, which is attributed to Scrotes (Pl. 50). In these the forceful stance of the Holbein full-length is replaced by a Mannerist elegance, not to say languor, of pose against a background of classicist architectural accessories. A third type is that represented by Flicke's *Unknown Nobleman* of 1547 now in the Edinburgh Gallery, and the *Archbishop Cranmer* of 1548 in the National Portrait Gallery. Here the subject is placed well forward in the picture and against a plain background or a photographically painted interior. The characterization is bold and the details presented in a Holbein-esque style.

From this position English portraiture developed under Elizabeth and James in three stages, with the divisions occurring about 1570 and the end of the sixteenth century. The first stage is dominated by the Fleming, Hans Eworth, who came to England in the late 1540's and worked here at least until 1573.[1] There are over thirty portraits signed by him, most of them dated, and he is unique among the painters of the period in having a securely authenticated corpus of work.[2] For that reason alone he is an extremely important figure, for in his work it is possible to see the development of an artist in the conditions of the time over a long period. His earliest extant portraits are those of Sir John Luttrell and Capt. Thomas Wyndham (Pl. 49*a*), painted in 1550. The first is a portrait-allegory in the full Continental Mannerist tradition, in which Luttrell, waist-deep and naked in a shipwreck sea, raises his arm to a naked figure of Peace in an inset panel. The allegory has several layers of specific but now largely obscure meaning. The inscription modernized runs, 'More than the rock amidst the raging seas the constant heart no danger dreads or fears', and

---

[1] To prevent any cavilling, I should, I suppose, make it clear that by 'Eworth' I mean the painter who signed with the monogram HE.

[2] For a catalogue and discussion of most of Eworth's work—and much else besides —see L. Cust, 'The Painter HE (Hans Eworth)', *Wal. Soc.* ii (1913), 1–44.

reveals what is doubtless the primary meaning. Although the figure and features of the subject are painted with some force and individuality the picture is mainly important for revealing the type of thing that Eworth could turn his hand to when asked. It is significant that he seems never to have been asked again. The *Wyndham* is a straightforward portrait, in which a plain soldier is shown half-length and full-face beneath a tree, with his military accoutrements by him, as though caught in an off-duty moment between battles, and with no attempt at a courtier-like presentation. The face has considerable characterization, depth, and plasticity, and the expression and pose have an air of suppressed vigour, which is yet different from the rather blatant force and aggression of Flicke's *Unknown Nobleman*.

These two paintings are crucial to a consideration of Eworth, for they show the fashionably Mannerist and yet quite powerful portraiture with which he began his English career. Very soon, however, he abandoned his early position: the influence of Holbein could not be wholly disregarded and is to be seen in the *Lady Dacre* of 1554 at Ottawa, where Eworth's tenseness has been modified into a Holbeinesque solidity, and a photographically realized background is introduced. Further, the portraits that Anthonis Mor was painting for the Hapsburg courts in which, without descending to flattery, he invested his gorgeously apparelled sitters with an aloofly dignified, sometimes imperious air, were of a type to make some appeal to English courtiers. At some time in the mid-century Eworth painted the so-called *Sir Henry Sidney* (Lord De L'Isle and Dudley) in a style that approaches that of Mor, whose influence is apparent again in the *Queen Mary* of 1554 at the Society of Antiquaries. But reminiscences of Holbein or attempts at imitating Mor were incidentals in his development; more fundamental and decisive was the taste of his patrons for a stiff likeness. As early as the *Lord Maltravers* of 1557 (Duke of Norfolk) he is showing the first signs of painting the flat costume-pieces of the Elizabethan period. To judge from his known works Eworth got few commissions from the very great until the 1560's and this change was therefore retarded by his work for such unfashionable people as Lady Dacre and the Duchess of Suffolk, whose taste still ran to the portrait types of an earlier age. In two pictures of the Duke and Duchess of Norfolk painted in 1562–3 Eworth signalizes his emergence into his final manner, a manner in which the figures are of little importance, the facial expression is uninteresting, and the main concern is with the costume and the armorial tapestry of the background (Pl. 49b).

Yet to say that much and no more of Eworth would be grossly unfair. He was, at bottom, an artist trained abroad and his individual vision never wholly deserted him. It is possible to find the restrained energy of the *Wyndham* portrait and a tenseness of portrayal even in works of his latest period; in Sir Harold Bowden's *Unknown Lady* (of 1558), in the *Unknown Lady* (1563) at Holyrood, and in the *Joan Thornbury* (Pl. 51) of 1566. All these are pictures of women, and it is a peculiarity of Eworth that in his later years his female subjects are more individualized and have more force than his men. The companion panels of 1560, in the possession of Dame Dehra Parker, exemplify this point.[1] The man's portrait, while still well-modelled and with some individuality, is a long way below the *Wyndham*. The lady's, however, is not; here, as in those mentioned above, is a woman with lively features and a tense energy. It is not to be supposed that Eworth had a peculiar talent for painting women, for he did at times paint equally good portraits of men, or that the women of the age were, taken as a whole, more forceful characters than their lords and masters. Rather it may be suggested that because of their low status as a sex, whatever their rank, their portraits were less subject to 'state' influences and a painter was, on some occasions, allowed a freer rein.

The other works of the period—nearly all of them anonymous —fall into three main types, which may for convenience be labelled the 'post-Flicke', 'Eworth', and 'Elizabethan' types. The use of the term, the 'Eworth' type, for example, does not imply any connexion with Eworth or his studio, but merely a closer resemblance to Eworth's known work than to anything else. And the distinction between the types is not absolute, for, as has been said, Eworth himself approaches the 'Elizabethan' type in his later work. The 'post-Flicke' School, which attempts to continue Flicke's continuation

[1] Exhibited at R.A. Winter Exhibition 1950–1, Catalogue, nos. 53, 57.

of Holbein's solidity, and sometimes of his psychological insight, is represented by the *Sir George Somerset* and *Sir Charles Somerset* of 1566 (Duke of Beaufort). In them there is a bold presentation of a half-length figure, set solidly, with some facial modelling and an almost brutal realism. The type had not wholly disappeared a decade later and the *Sir Nicholas Bacon* (1579) at Raveningham is a very late example. Faint elements of the style are present in the *Lady Lumley* (1563) by Stephen van der Meulen, and are not wholly absent from Eworth's *Lady Dacre*. But these paintings, and particularly the two *Somersets*, are more decorative in intention than, and without the depth of, Flicke's work and are beginning to resemble the 'Elizabethan' school.

The 'Eworth' types—most of which have at some time been ascribed to Eworth himself—are distinguished by a more sensitive and elegant air, an occasional use of Mannerist architectural background and some concentration on decorative costume-detail. The *Man of the Tichborne Family* (1559) (Lord Leconfield) and the *Thomas 2nd Baron Wentworth* (Pl. 52*b*) are examples of this style. The more courtly full or three-quarter length pose, the softer modelling, the more refined facial features, and the conventional pilasters of an unreal space of the background mark them off sharply from Flicke's style, and relate them closely to Eworth's *Sir Henry Sidney*. In a similar but more symbolical vein is the *Edward Courtenay, Earl of Devon* (1553), in which a three-quarter-length figure of considerable delicacy is set under the impost of an arch and before a ruined keep, in reference to Courtenay's recent liberation from the Tower by Queen Mary. The out-of-doors setting and the symbolism of the background—as distinct from the placing of unrelated symbols about the sitter—are touches reminiscent of the early Eworth, while the well-bred pose and features link the picture with those just mentioned.

Similarities with the style of Eworth may be noticed in the two known works of the Fleming, Stephen van der Meulen: the portraits of Lord and Lady Lumley at Lumley Castle. The first is dated 1563, and the second is presumably its twin. Van der Meulen is, as far as can be judged, another Eworth, a foreign artist labouring to please his English patrons but never wholly losing his original

Antwerp manner. Both the Lumley portraits have a decorative aspect, but this is less noticeable than in the later works of Eworth; both are still a long way from the flat 'Elizabethan' style, and have some character in the expression. The solidity of the *Lady Lumley* has already been mentioned; by contrast the *Lord Lumley* has, without the Mannerist background, the features of the 'Eworth' type, and a hint of the influence of Mor. The influence is to be seen again, though at a great remove, in the portrait of the Earl of Leicester in the National Portrait Gallery, in which the stance and imperious air recall Mor's *Philip II* and *Donna Juana* in the Royal Collection.

The third type, the forerunner of the two-dimensional Elizabethan portrait, is aesthetically beneath these, but is of the most significance in the years between 1550 and 1570. Yet it is in those years not so very common in its pure form, and is to be seen more as an increasingly obvious element of the other styles. A comparison between the *1st Baron Wentworth* of 1547 and the *2nd Baron* of 1568 (Pl. 52) is illuminating. Both have been ascribed by a competent and learned critic to Eworth and both have similarities with his style.[1] But the later painting, although in accessories and pose it appears to be an attempt at an imitation of the earlier, is noticeably flatter in technique, less bold in presentation, less sure in pose, and more decorative. It is on the way to the 'Elizabethan' style. Such portraits as the *Richard Holford* (1567) from the Holford Collection and the now lost *Countess of Lincoln*[2] (1560) are almost in the style of the last years of the century.

The common name for that style, 'the Elizabethan costume-piece,' indicates its exaggerated emphasis on the details of the gorgeous dress of the sitter. The portaits of the Queen herself are notorious for their display of finery but the same intention is apparent in the less ostentatious pictures of lesser mortals. A good example is the *Sir Edward Hoby* of 1578 (Pl. 53*b*), formerly at Bisham Abbey, which obtains considerable decorative effect by the rich colour contrasts of the white doublet trimmed with silver, the maroon ribbon about the neck, the black hat with gold ornament, and the pale green background broken by a brightly painted shield-

[1] L. Cust, 'The Painter HE', *Wal. Soc.* ii (1913), 35.
[2] Illustrated in *Wal. Soc.* ii, pl. xxiii.

of-arms. In an age when the apparel oft proclaimed the man such emphasis is not surprising, for it was with man in his social position that the portraiture of the time was concerned. There is, indeed, evidence in the *Portrait of a Lady* (1576) in the Tate Gallery[1] of the repainting and alteration in the sitter's lifetime of her costume but not of her features. The phenomenon was not confined to England; it has been noticed in contemporary French painting.[2] Such an emphasis precluded any life or movement in the sitter and reinforced the tendency initiated by other factors, to paint in a flat and linear manner; indeed some of these pictures are more decorative patterns than portraits.

The lifelessness of this art is most apparent in the treatment of the only portions of the human body whose existence was recognized, the hands and face. The tenseness of some of Eworth's women sitters is derived not only from the facial features but from the often clasped or moving hands. In later work the hands are invariably still, holding a wand of office, or some other symbol of the sitter's rank, or a pair of gloves, or dangling loosely at the sitter's side. Hands, of course, were merely an embarrassment to the painter of a costume-piece, but the face was of prime importance. Yet because it was the face not of a man but of the holder of an office or a founder or representative of a family it was denied individual expression, given a timeless air, and painted very much as a hard flat outline. By the middle of the seventies the conception of a portrait as a State or family record had almost ousted any individual approach. It is not accidental that some of the earliest paintings in which this effect is apparent are such family groups as those of Lords Cobham and Windsor (1567 and 1568), the Judd Memorial painting (1560) in the Dulwich Gallery, with its accessories of corpses, candles, and 'All that makes death a hideous show', and the Bacon family picture of 1578 at Raveningham, which is almost a painting of a funeral monument. Examples of individual portraits in the same manner are numerous; the half-length of Henry Cary, Lord Hunsdon, is typical (Pl. 54*b*). Cary is turned a quarter-left, his left hand at his waist, his right holding a white wand. He is

[1] Formerly in the National Gallery; No. 4811 in *Catalogue of the British School* (1946).
[2] L. Dimier, *Le Portrait en France au XVI*ᵉ *siècle*, i. 68–69.

dressed in a black doublet and cap, both trimmed with gold and silver lace, a white ruff and ruffles, and a gold jewelled chain, all set against a plain dark-grey background. The face is almost without modelling or expression and with no other mark of individuality than its physical features.

Hand in hand with this, the background accessories of earlier years —the furniture of a room, a landscape seen through a window, the tapestry or cloth-hung walls of Eworth—are often replaced by objects wholly unrelated to the space in which the subject is set but expressive of his rank. The most obvious and commonest of such symbols were coats-of-arms placed above the sitter's shoulders or around the edge of the picture. Their siting mattered little, for neither they nor the sitter were represented as in an actual space. An extreme example is the picture in the National Portrait Gallery of Christopher Hatton as Chancellor of Oxford University, a portrait in which the person is lost amidst a confusion of shields-of-arms, complimentary and punning verses, and symbolic animals (Pl. 54a). Rarely can any man have shown so much respect for an office and so little for its holder as the painter of this picture, yet he was merely taking the typical portraiture of the period to its ultimate conclusion.

At the same time the bust and the half-length portrait became increasingly common. This was in part due to the greater amount of painting being commissioned by minor people and for or by personal friends of the greater. It was, however, also a result of a fondness for a likeness that led to a neglect of all parts of the body but the face. It was paralleled in monumental sculpture—although at a later date because a stronger tradition had to be overcome— where the bust began to be used as an alternative to the effigy.

The painter who typifies the portraiture of the years after 1570, although his skill is well above the average, is the Englishman, George Gower. Gower is an interesting phenomenon for he was, like Sir Nathaniel Bacon later, a man of the gentry. Unlike Bacon, he seems to have needed or to have desired to turn his artistic talent to financial account; as he tersely expressed it, 'skill revives with gain'.[1] In consequence his work is as patron-dominated as that

[1] Inscription on his self-portrait in the possession of Earl Fitzwilliam.

of his craftsmen contemporaries; but because he had not, presumably, been trained in their workshops, it retains an individual character. He is known at present by five portraits; of Sir Thomas and Lady Kitson, in the Tate Gallery (Pl. 55a), and of Sir Francis and Lady Willoughby (Lord Middleton), all of 1573, and the self-portrait of 1579 (Pl. 55b).[1] He was apparently painting a portrait of the Earl of Rutland in 1576,[2] and the *Sir Thomas Cornwallis* (*c.* 1577) at Audley End is probably his.[3] All the elements of contemporary portraiture are to be found in his work: the decorative patterning, the linear and flat effect, the plain background enriched with coats-of-arms, with, as far as is yet known, a concentration on the bust or half or three-quarter length. Yet there are differences between his work and that of most of his contemporaries. The *verlorene Blick*, the timelessness, the lack of expression is not so marked; instead there is some attempt at portraying character. The linear quality is less obvious, his faces show some modelling, although in a sharp and angular fashion, and the emphasis on decoration and costume is not quite so great.

Apart from Gower there are about twenty men recorded in contemporary documents who painted or may have painted portraits. One of them is a certain Hubbard, who painted Lady Leicester and her son in 1584,[4] but none of whose work has yet been identified. Another is Sir William Segar, or else his brother Francis, who in 1590 probably painted the *Earl of Essex* in the National Gallery at Dublin.[5] One of the Segars also worked in miniature,[6] and to another miniaturist, Rowland Lockey, has been plausibly attributed the National Portrait Gallery's version of the family of Sir Thomas More.[7] Arnold Bronkhorst was appointed painter to

---

[1] J. W. Goodison, 'George Gower, Sergeant Painter to Queen Elizabeth', *Burl. Mag.* xc (1949), 261–4.

[2] Ibid.          [3] D. Piper in *Conn. Period Guide: Tudor*, p. 54.

[4] *Notes & Queries*, 3rd ser. ii (1862), 224–5.

[5] D. Piper, 'Hilliard, Segar and the Earl of Essex', *Burl. Mag.* xcix (1957), 224–31; 299–303; for further possible works by Segar see also E. Auerbach, *Nicholas Hilliard*, pp. 271–81.

[6] See below, p. 214.

[7] O. Kurz, 'Rowland Lockey', *Burl. Mag.* xcix (1957), 13–16. Between 1608 and 1613 he was frequently employed by Sir William Cavendish on large-scale portraits; see E. Auerbach, *Nicholas Hilliard*, pp. 254–6.

James VI of Scotland in 1580,[1] but until recently nothing was
known of his work. However a signed portrait of Lord St. John of
Bletsoe, dated 1578, has lately come to light.[2] Of the rest of the
known names it may be said that so little other than the name is
known that they are as empty of content as those in a telephone
directory.[3] An exception can be made for two foreigners, Jerome
Custodis and Cornelius Ketel. There are three known works by
Custodis, all painted in 1589: *Sir John Parker*, at Hampton Court,
and *Lord Chandos* and his daughter *Elizabeth Bridges*, both at
Woburn. The last has some charm and delicacy of execution, but
the subject—a young girl of fourteen, later to be a court beauty—
is one which lends itself to charm, and Custodis's other two portraits are in no way distinguished. Ketel, who was in England from
1573 to 1581, is a painter of a higher class and of some interest for
he appears to have tried to break away from the prevailing manner.
His *Unknown Youth* (1576) at Parham Park is in Eworth's later
style, but the *Frobisher* of 1577, in the Bodleian, has considerable
movement and energy, and the *William Gresham* (1579) (Pl. 53a)
is in a bold and solid style, more in keeping with Dutch portraiture
of the time. Ketel seems to have been mainly patronized by merchants. The *Frobisher* is presumably that for which he was paid £5
by the Company of Cathay after Frobisher's return from his
voyage to seek the North-West Passage in 1576. He was paid at the
same time for several large and small pictures of an Eskimo that
Frobisher brought back with him, and for pictures of two officers
of the Company; and he was paid £6—the largest single sum— for
a painting of a most unusual subject, Frobisher's ship, the *Gabriel*.[4]
He finally quitted England for presumably more congenial patrons
in Amsterdam.

The visit of Federico Zuccari, who was here for a few months in

[1] Waterhouse, *Painting in Britain 1530–1790*, p. 29.

[2] Now in the possession of the Hon. H. Lawson Johnston. Possible works by Bronkhorst are discussed by E. Auerbach, *Nicholas Hilliard*, pp. 265–71.

[3] The names and sparse biographical details of a great many men who are known
to, or who may, have painted easel pictures are to be found in the appendices to Dr.
Auerbach's *Tudor Artists*.

[4] C. F. Cooper, *Proceedings of the Record Commission* (1833), pp. 75, 560; *Bodleian
Library Record*, vi (1960), 579.

1575,[1] requires something more than a mention. He was the most distinguished foreign artist to come to England in the years between Mor and van Dyck, and, if the attributions of owners could be trusted, the busiest ever. In fact, however, all that certainly survive of whatever works he may have executed while in this country are two drawings of Elizabeth and of Leicester, in the British Museum. These are of importance, for it has been suggested that the background symbolism of the former had some influence upon later portraits of the Queen,[2] and that the latter influenced the pose and accessories of courtier full-lengths.[3] This may be true, but even so the effect was peripheral, mainly upon accessories, and at the best it did nothing more than force on a development that was already latent in English painting.

Gower was appointed Sergeant Painter in 1581 and attempted soon afterwards, but apparently without success, to get for himself and his successors in office a monopoly of royal portraits 'in great'.[4] That he should think he had a chance of such a *coup* suggests that he had already painted the Queen and in a way that won her approval, but none of her known portraits has so far been identified as by his hand. It seems likely that this is because royal portraiture was the extreme example of the 'State' portrait in which the dictates of the patron's conception of the art were absolute and allowed for very little variation from the norm. It is a curious fact that while the short reigns of Mary and Edward VI have produced a considerable number of royal portraits, and the last thirty years of Elizabeth's reign a multitude, the first eleven years of her reign have produced very little and almost nothing of any worth. This is not to be explained by invoking the draft proclamation of 1563 which prohibited the manufacture of unauthorized portraits until the Queen had sat to 'some connyng painter',[5] for there remains the problem of why she had not sat earlier and why she apparently

[1] See R. Strong in *Journ. W.C.I.* xxii (1959), 359–60.

[2] D. Piper in *Conn. Period Guide: Tudor*, p. 53.

[3] E. K. Waterhouse, 'The Palazzo Zuccari', *Burl. Mag.* lxix (1936), 133–4; *Painting in Britain 1530–1790*, p. 26.

[4] The draft patent, which included a monopoly of royal miniatures for Hilliard, was printed by Sir Frederick Madden in *Notes & Queries*, 1st ser. vi (1852), 237–9.

[5] *Cal. S.P. Dom. 1547–80*, p. 232.

waited so long afterwards before sitting. From a statement by Hilliard we know that Elizabeth was strongly in favour of a linear manner of painting,[1] and it is likely that it was not until about 1570 that English painting had developed to the stage of producing a painter to suit her taste, and that her taste contributed to the formation of the style that dominated English portraiture after 1570.

The portraits of the Queen in the next twenty years are little different from the general style except for their greater use of applied symbolism. The 'Pheonix' and 'Cobham' portraits in the National Portrait Gallery are better but typical examples of the painting of the period. The 'Ermine' portrait of 1585, in which an ermine as a symbol of virginity is painted on the sleeve of the dress, is an example of this symbolism, which is merely applied to a portrait and is not, as in Eworth's *Sir John Luttrell*, an essential part of the picture. The cult nature of these royal portraits is illustrated by that at Arbury. Against a background of a patterned cloth a three-quarter length is painted in a wholly flat style, with a triangular composition of the figure with its veil and ruff giving on the whole the appearance of an icon. There are two portraits, however, that stand apart from the rest: that signed M.G.F. at Welbeck and another at Siena. In both Elizabeth is painted full length against a Mannerist background of an architectural prospect with a group of courtiers in the distance. The location of the Siena portrait hints that it may have been intended from its inception for a Continental owner and its character suggests a Continental origin.[2] The Welbeck panel is presumably by either the elder or younger Marcus Gheeraerts. The elder Gheeraerts was more active in England as an engraver than as a portrait-painter—there is, in fact, no known English portrait by him—and the younger, if he was the artist, must have painted the picture at a very early stage in his career. Whichever Gheeraerts is preferred as the author of the Welbeck panel, it may be supposed that these two pictures were the work of men not greatly experienced in Elizabethan portraiture, and that they owe their characteristics to this unusual origin.

[1] 'Art of Limning', pp. 28–29.
[2] It has been attributed by Dr. Wittkower to Zuccari; F. Saxl and R. Wittkower, *British Art and the Mediterranean* (Oxford, 1948), p. 39, pl. 4.

It is in connexion with the Queen's portraits that the important question of the relationship between painting 'in great' and miniatures is best discussed. It has been said that the 'great' portraits are but 'blown-up miniatures in conception',[1] that 'the miniature set the style for oil painting and started a typically English school.'[2] On the other hand there is the view that 'there is not any established connection between Elizabethan painting on the scale of life and Elizabethan miniatures'.[3] While both these views have an element of truth, both must be regarded as inadequate. The likeness between the linear technique of Hilliard's miniatures and that of larger paintings, the appearance of important portraits of Elizabeth contemporary with or shortly after Hilliard's miniature of 1572 in the National Portrait Gallery (Pl. 73a), the similarity between the facial type of his miniature and that of the *Cobham* (Pl. 56a) and *Pelican*[4] portraits of *c.* 1575: these are the not insignificant facts on which the first view is based. But they are not the only facts. Painting 'in great' was developing towards the Elizabethan style long before Hilliard appeared on the scene; and while his manner is indeed a linear one, his miniatures are not invariably flat, and many that are have acquired that quality from the unintended fading of their colours. Even if his work were the same in all respects as that of the painters, the correspondence would still fall short of proving that theirs was influenced by his, or of proving or disproving the converse. It must be remembered that a linear technique is no more inevitable in miniature than in large-scale painting: in Hilliard's own lifetime Isaac Oliver was turning out miniatures with considerable modelling and shadow. If there is linearity in Hilliard's style then that itself calls for an explanation, and the explanation demands an analysis of the forces that were simultaneously causing miniatures and oil-paintings to resemble each other in some ways and differ in others. These forces were not the creation of any one man, and if Hilliard had never existed English painting would have gone in the direction that it went; but that is not to say

[1] D. Piper, *Conn. Period Guide: Tudor*, p. 54.
[2] E. Auerbach, *Tudor Artists*, pp. 131–2.
[3] Waterhouse, *Painting in Britain 1530–1790*, p. 19.
[4] The 'Pelican' Elizabeth is now in the Walker Art Gallery, Liverpool.

that it would have followed exactly the same road. In some cases, it is clear, there is a direct relationship between a miniature and a dependent painting, and it may be allowed that some of Hilliard's miniatures played a part in determining some features of some of Elizabeth's portraits and, thereby, of Elizabethan portraiture. They did not 'set a style' or 'start a school' but they had some effect upon the Elizabethan style and school.

It will perhaps be felt as a relief to turn from a consideration of the common Elizabethan painting to a small group of works that is outside the general development, and of these the portrait at Raveningham of Sir Henry Nevill (Pl. 58) is outstanding. Nevill is seated between a fluted marble column and a pilaster in the background, his head outlined against a dark panel and his figure, set with the breadth of an early Holbein, placed fully and roundly in its setting. The life and expression of the well-modelled features and the actuality of the figure and its pose are in complete contrast with the costume-pieces of the period, and it is not surprising that the work has been ascribed to a foreign artist. It is, however, not wholly unique. The portrait of Edward Grimston (1590) at Gorhambury is a less ambitious production but with a very similar technique and effect. There is also a painting of uncertain date, and known in two versions, said to be of Sir Anthony Wingfield (d. 1562), in which the background and the trick of a panel against which to outline the head is almost exactly reproduced. It is, however, far inferior in execution to the Nevill portrait.

There are some curious but apparently accidental family connexions between these pictures. Nevill married a Bacon girl, Grimston's descendants came into possession of the Bacon property, and Nevill's picture was originally at Spixworth Park labelled *Sir Henry Wingfield*. But one indisputable common circumstance of all these portraits is their connexion with the Eastern Counties. Very tentatively, I would suggest that the Nevill and Grimston portraits are by an English amateur free both from the training of the workshops and the dictates of fashion and acquainted with the work of such Netherlands artists as Marten de Vos and Ars Pieters. It is possible that he copied the accessories of the Nevill portrait from the earlier *Wingfield*, in which the artist had attempted, by his use of a panel taking the outline of the sitter's head, to combine a Mannerist architectural background with the plain silhouette-taking background of the developing Elizabethan style.

In the last years of her reign and with the growth of the 'Elizabethan legend' as an increasing political necessity, the portraits of the Queen began to lose all touch with reality and to become either fantasy paintings or cult-icons. Even the last verisimilitude, the faithful rendering of the features, is intermittent, and some portraits indulge in unashamed face-lifting. The fantastic portrayal of the features in these, and of the features and costume in the *Rainbow* portrait at Hatfield, are typical of one aspect of royal portraits in the last few years of the reign (Pl. 56*b*). Typical of another is the *Ditchley* painting (Pl. 61), in which the Queen is seen full-length, standing on a map of England, with a lowering but fitfully bright sky above: an expression of the awe-inspiring, all-powerful, and all-wise sovereign of the legend. Such a portrait as that at Corsham Court, with its symbolic figures of Death and Time hovering over the aged Queen and reminding men of her mortality, is out of the usual run and is probably posthumous.

Royal portraits affected those of the greater men, which became more hieratic and stately and more often of life-size in full and three-quarter lengths. These were not an innovation in the 1590's, but they became far commoner then. The full-lengths of Sir Henry Lee and of Essex in Garter robes, both from the Dillon Collection, of Essex by a sea-shore (Pl. 60) and of the Earl of Sussex in armour (Pl. 62*a*) are typical of the portraits of important people in the last years of Elizabeth's reign, and were the forerunners of those of the early years of the next century. These full-lengths were novel in two ways: in their vast numbers, often of quite minor people and reflecting the increase in the numbers of court hangers-on, and in the abandonment of the plain silhouette-taking background and, instead, the placing of the figure in a real space. The ornamental shields and inscriptions that sufficed to fill the background of a bust or a half-length were inadequate to a full-length. At first perhaps the lack was not felt, for the 'Garter' portraits of Essex and Lee have plain backgrounds, but there are signs of a change in the Woburn *Essex* and in the portrait of Capt.

Thomas Lee (1594), in both of which the figure is at least placed against a landscape background.

By the early seventeenth century it was usual for a full-length figure to be placed in a setting, and generally in an interior. Of the interiors little need be said. In contrast to the idealized Mannerist columns and pilasters of the mid-sixteenth century these are made up of contemporary furnishings: baize-covered tables, chairs, and cushions, Turkey carpets or matting, and the only out-of-the-way property is often a heavily-draped curtain across part of the background. The exterior backgrounds are less common but more significant for they develop into the romantic-cum-courtly background of Mytens and van Dyck. The Woburn *Essex* and the *Capt. Thomas Lee* are not greatly different from such pictures as the so-called *Mary Queen of Scots* in the National Portrait Gallery and the very early *Young Man in Red*, in which the figure is looming before rather than standing in a landscape. There now begins, however, a series of portraits wherein the subject is placed not against a distant scene but in a rural setting, a wood, a park, a garden. The picture, now in the Metropolitan Museum, New York, of Prince Henry accompanied by a boy of the Harrington family at the end of a successful stag hunt in a forest is, if the date 1603 is to be trusted, a very early example; but it was a popular one, for there is another version at Hampton Court in which Henry's companion is a Devereux (Pl. 62*b*). The *Lady Tanfield* (Pl. 57*a*) and the so-called *Arabella Stuart* (Hampton Court) are examples of this type, in which, however, the subjects are in masque costume and the background may be intended merely as a stage-setting;[1] but the so-called *Elizabeth of Bohemia* from Wroxton Abbey and the *Lady and Child* in the Birmingham Art Gallery (Pl. 57*b*) have no such connotation.

It was not only technical considerations that determined the development of these backgrounds. The same necessity of indicating the rank and position of the sitter that influenced Elizabethan portraiture was also present in Jacobean. But Jacobean courtiers

[1] For the popularity of landscapes on the scenic back-cloths of masque-settings see Henry and Margaret Ogden, *English Taste in Landscape in the 17th Century* (University of Michigan Press, 1955), pp. 21–22.

were commoner birds than Elizabethan and only a small proportion of them held an office that could be conveniently indicated by a symbol, or had fought in the Wars and could represent themselves for the rest of their lives as soldiers. They had only their social standing to boast of; their position not as men of affairs but as men of breeding, men possessing those indefinable qualities with which, in the absence of any real virtues, most aristocracies like to endow themselves. The background setting—the elegant curtain, the expensive carpet, the richly-covered table, the cushioned chair—were therefore important in placing the sitter in surroundings which automatically indicated his rank.

The exterior setting is to be referred to the different character of the patrons of the time compared with their fathers, landed proprietors spending some of their time on their estates and part at court rather than busy men of State with great landed possessions, and these rural backgrounds are the first expression in easel-painting of an interest in landscape that was already partly revealing itself in murals and was later to reveal itself on canvas. The later development of these backgrounds tends to support this view. By the 1620's there was a type of portrait—Geldorp's *2nd Earl of Salisbury* with Hatfield in the background (Pl. 64a), the portrait of Sir Thomas Holte with Aston Hall in the background[1]—in which the subject is placed in an actual locality, and one which refers directly to his position in life. Van Somer's *Anne of Denmark* in front of Oatlands is perhaps the best-known (Pl. 59) and the Cowdray portrait of Sir William Pope with a courtyard in the background may be an unrecognized example. This is, of course, not unconnected with the contemporary pride in magnificence of building, and the accurate inset drawing of New College that Sampson Strong included in his imaginary portrait of Wykeham in 1596 is an early foretaste, naturally in a medieval Oxford manner, of a later courtly practice. The method could be applied to interiors, and Myten's portrait of Lord Arundel in his sculpture gallery (Duke of Norfolk) is a direct translation of it.

[1] The Aston Hall portrait is an eighteenth-century copy (A. Oswald in *C.L.* cl (1953), 554–5), possibly, as Oswald suggests, of an engraving but more probably of a now lost original.

The intention of these portraits inevitably affected the pose of the subject. Universally at first and commonly until the end of the period, the sitter was painted in a stiff and lifeless attitude, generally standing, three-quarter face, with one foot hugging the other, the hands dangling lifelessly or placed unconvincingly upon a table or a cushion, and the clothes, of men and women, denying the existence of a body beneath them. The portrait of the fifth Earl of Sussex (Pl. 62a) and the *Lady Russell* by Gheeraerts of thirty years later (Pl. 67) are examples of this stock pose. But although this remained common an equally still but more elegant, even languid, pose began to appear. Early examples are the portrait of James I leaning against a table, now in the National Maritime Museum, and the full-length at Helmingham of Ludovic Stuart, Duke of Richmond and Lennox (Pl. 66). The picture of Elizabeth Drury reclining on a couch has already been mentioned as an example of an 'effigy domesticated' but it is, of course, a domestication of the elegantly reclining effigy that was common at this time in monumental sculpture. There is at times, too, an almost direct imitation of the elegant tricks of the mid-sixteenth-century Mannerists, as in the portrait of Mary, Countess of Pembroke at Knole, in which the sitter has been given a neck as long as a Burmese beauty's. From the 1620's elegance became common and is to be found in some of the possible works of van Somer and the indisputable work of Mytens. It must be stressed, however, that these two painters did not form this taste; they gave it—until the coming of van Dyck —its best expression and thereby helped to spread its appeal.

Of the painters who contributed to this there is, apart from some meagre biographical details and payments for mostly unidentified pictures, exasperatingly little to be said. Up to about 1616 there were four men who may be judged, either by the position they held, the persons they painted or the fees they received, to have been the leading painters of the day. They are John de Critz, Sergeant Painter, Robert Peake, painter to Prince Henry and later Sergeant Painter, the younger Marcus Gheeraerts, described as 'His Majesty's Painter', and William Larkin, who seems to have held no official position but who was, at least by 1617, commanding the same fees as the others. By de Critz, it may be said at once, there is no certainly known work, but the mosaic of Robert Cecil at Hatfield was carried out from a portrait by him and it would be unreasonable to deny that he probably painted the portrait of Cecil there now.[1] Peake is known for certain by the portrait of Prince Charles of 1613 in the Old Schools at Cambridge.[2] Gheeraerts, who was at one time in danger of being as overworked by the attributionists as Zuccari, is known possibly by the Welbeck *Queen Elizabeth*, very probably by the *Barbara Gamage and her children* at Penshurst, and indisputably by the *Duke of Würtemberg* at Hampton Court (1608), *Lady Russell* at Woburn, *Lucy, Countess of Huntingdon* (1623), and the *Mrs. Anne Hoskins* of 1629.[3] He also painted whatever was on the portrait of Camden in the Bodleian before it got into its present state. Larkin very probably painted the oval bust portraits of Sir Thomas Lucy and Lord Herbert of Cherbury[4] at Charlecote Park. Apart from these, there is the possibility that Isaac Oliver painted large-scale portraits as well as miniatures, but the recent attribution to Larkin of the Charlecote portraits has robbed him of two of his most likely runners.

With so little proven work, it is clear that attempts at disentangling the *œuvre* of any of these men are extraordinarily difficult. And the position is complicated because three of them, de Critz, Gheeraerts, and Oliver, had close family connexions; and de Critz had two sons and Oliver one who followed their fathers' profession. How far they had separate workshops or how far they collaborated with one another is wholly unknown and this introduces a further difficulty, for it makes the use of a Morellian method very uncertain. The attempt to isolate studio-tricks—the placing of a cushion

[1] The work of John de Critz and his sons is discussed by R. Lane Poole in the article already cited, *Wal. Soc.* ii (1913), 45–53. This and the articles by Finberg and Cust mentioned below are well documented but their attributions are not to be trusted.

[2] A. J. Finberg, 'An Authentic Portrait by Robert Peake', *Wal. Soc.* ix (1920–1), 89–95.

[3] R. Lane Poole, 'Marcus Gheeraerts, Father and Son, Painters', *Wal. Soc.* iii (1914), 1–8: L. Cust, 'Marcus Gheeraerts', *Wal. Soc.* iii (1914), 9–45. For Gheeraerts' signed painting of Mrs. Hoskins see R.A. *Catalogue of an Exhibition of British Portraits* (1956–7), No. 30. The *Lucy, Countess of Huntingdon*, signed and dated 1623, was exhibited at the R.A. in 1938.

[4] J. Lees-Milne, 'Two Portraits at Charlecote Park', *Burl. Mag.* xciv (1952), 352–6.

upon the arm of a chair, the almost metallic drawing of a curtain, the use of individual studio 'properties'—is an uneasy one if these may come from one studio serving several men or from several closely connected studios. Nevertheless it might still be possible to isolate Peake and Larkin, but unfortunately their known or probable work has little that sets it indisputably apart from anyone else's. These men are, in their own way, as much a reflection of the tastes of their patrons as their immediate predecessors were. They can be distinguished from their predecessors and successors, but it has not yet been possible to distinguish them with certainty from one another.

By 1616, however, a new trend was apparent in English painting, revealing itself in a class of intimate portraits wherein the sitter is caught not perhaps in an unguarded but in a private moment. The best known of these is the painting at Welbeck, called *Frances Howard*, of a lady before a dressing-table, clad in an open night-rail and brushing her long hair, a work notable not only for its subject-matter but for its freedom from the general flatness and stiffness of the time. The portrait of Lady Anne Rich (*c.* 1620) (Pl. 65*a*) and those of Elizabeth Vernon, the runaway-bride of the third Earl of Southampton, at Welbeck and Boughton are in a similar vein. In their own way these are parallel with the *Lady Tanfield* and the *Lady and Child* at Birmingham, with their rustic settings; they are intended to catch a moment in the private life of the subject and not merely to perpetuate a public figure or a family patriarch.

Linked with these are a number of portraits of considerable delicacy and charm which have many echoes of earlier miniatures. The so-called *Lady Catherine Jermyn* of 1614 is almost a translation into large-scale painting of such a miniature as that of the so-called *Frances Howard* of *c.* 1595 by Isaac Oliver, a translation in which the impersonal air and the sightless gaze of earlier portraiture is replaced by the sitter's 'secret smiling'. In the National Portrait Gallery there is a picture of an unknown lady (Pl. 65*b*), of the same date as the *Lady Jermyn* and, although rather less intimate, in the same vein and with the same pose, and accompanied by a motto—No Spring till Now—which both in sentiment and lettering recalls those of some of Hilliard's miniatures.

It may be suggested that these pictures, some of whose qualities are continued later in such works as Gheeraerts' *Mrs. Anne Hoskins* and the portraits of Cornelius Johnson, are the result of the inter-action of two factors: the increase in affection between the members of a family at this time that has been noted by several writers, and the loss by the miniature of much of its earlier quality of privacy and intimacy.

At this time, too, the flat and linear style of early portraiture became less common. It never wholly disappeared, and the work of Cornelius Johnson, who belongs to the Carolean rather than the Jacobean era, can often be distinguished from that of his contem-poraries by its lack of weight and solidity. The appearance of a more solid and volume-conscious manner may be partly explained by the use of the full-length in a real space, a practice that set problems of depth and plasticity that the half-length or bust against a background could avoid. In the main, however, it must be ascribed to a change in the taste of patrons, or rather to an increase in the number of patrons with a taste for and an appreciation of modern art, to the appearance of the virtuosi. Such books as Peacham's *Graphice*, written specifically as an aid to amateur painters, reveal that some among the wealthier classes were in-dulging in pursuits for which their fathers had no inclination.[1] The activities of men like Sir Nathaniel Bacon, Francis Potter,[2] and Peacham himself are instances of this. Some of them attained a high level of skill. A certain Bilford, one of Sir Henry Wotton's 'prin-cipal gentlemen', was considered by Wotton—not a mean judge—to be the equal of Isaac Oliver,[3] and between 1614 and 1623 a court official, Sir James Palmer, was also painting miniatures.[4]

---

[1] For an analysis of the virtuosi, who were the leaders in these activities, see W. E. Houghton, 'The English Virtuoso in the 17th Century', *J.H.I.* iii (1942), 51–73, 190–219. The wholly different attitude towards the arts in earlier years is brought out by Ruth Kelso, *The Doctrine of the English Gentleman in the 16th Century*, University of Illinois Studies xiv (1949).

[2] Aubrey, *Brief Lives*, ed. O. L. Dick (1950), pp. 247–9.

[3] Bilford or Belford is mentioned in Thomas Coryate's *Crudities* (1611), p. 236, and in John Chamberlain's *Letters*, ed. N. E. McClure (Philadelphia, 1939), p. 312. He is probably the Mark Belford who was a limner in Prince Henry's service in 1612, Auerbach, *Tudor Artists*, p. 152.

[4] See Graham Reynolds in *Burl. Mag.* xci (1949), 196–7.

When Sir Francis Kynaston founded the Museum Minervae in 1635, to provide a broader and more up-to-date education for gentlemen than the Universities were capable of, painting was included in the curriculum along with riding, music, architecture, modern languages, and natural science.[1] Even those who were far from being virtuosi were influenced by this development. Sir Gervase Holles, who died in 1627 at a ripe age, told his young grandson that 'he would have a gentleman have some knowledge of all the artes' even though 'it did not become him to be excellent in any of them'.[2]

The arrival in this country in 1616 of Paul Van Somer and, by 1618, of Daniel Mytens,[3] brought about a development in English painting that was latent in this situation. Trained in the school of portraiture that centred on Miereveld, they possessed qualities that enabled them to produce the type of portrait that was now wanted in court and State circles. They were able to paint with the depth and plasticity that the full-length in a real space demanded, they were able to give their subjects the freer, more impressive and up-to-date poses of the Dutch school, and to infuse into them a greater sense of personality than the earlier picture-makers had achieved. The earliest known English work by Van Somer—*Anne of Denmark before Oatlands* (Pl. 59)—although stiff in handling, has all of these qualities in some degree, and in conception is more grandiose than anything seen in England for a long time. His other known or plausibly attributed works—of which the most important are the *2nd Earl of Devonshire with his son*, and the *Countess of Devonshire with her daughter* (both 1619, Marquess of Ailesbury), *Thomas, Lord Windsor* (signed and dated 1620, at Cardiff),[4] and the *Countess of Oxford* (*c.* 1621, Marquess of Ailesbury)—are in a less ambitious but similar vein. Abraham van Bliejenberch, who was

[1] E. G. R. Taylor, *Late Tudor and Stuart Geography* (1934), pp. 98–99; *D.N.B.* reference to Kynaston.

[2] 'Memorials of the Holles Family', *Camden Soc.* 3rd ser. lv (1944), 125–6.

[3] Most of the known facts about Van Somer and Mytens are to be found in the articles by Peter Cunningham and C. C. Stopes previously cited. For further facts and for some about Van Bliejenberch see Waterhouse, *Painting in Britain*, Auerbach, *Tudor Artists*, and M. Whinney and O. Millar, *English Art 1625–1714*.

[4] Discussed by J. Steegman in *Burl. Mag.* xci (1949), pp. 52–53.

here for a short time, shows himself in his *Robert Ker, Earl of Ancrum* (1618), and *3rd Earl of Pembroke* (Earl of Powys) to be a painter of the same class.

Van Somer's career in England was short—he was dead by January 1622—but Daniel Mytens was here for a long time. His main achievement is more a Carolean than a Jacobean phenomenon and has been fully dealt with by Mr. Oliver Millar.[1] His work in this country, or for English patrons, before 1625, such as the signed *3rd Earl of Southampton* of 1610 and the *Earl and Countess of Banbury* (*c.* 1617) attributed to him by Mr. Millar, marks an advance upon Van Somer in its sense of personality, assurance of pose, and illusion of depth.

Although these painters raised English portraiture to a new level, there is, nevertheless, no sharp break between their work and that of their immediate predecessors. By the middle of the second decade of the century the native-born or native-domiciled painters had reached the stage represented by the National Maritime Museum's *James I* and the *Ludovic Stuart* at Helmingham. Van Somer, and Mytens later, and last of all Van Dyck developed further the qualities that already existed in embryo in the full-length of the early years of the century.

There was, however, one artist who stood apart from this development and whose greatest talents came to fruition precisely because of his unconcern with the general preoccupation of English painting, the amateur Sir Nathaniel Bacon who died in 1627 at the age of forty-one. As far as it can be said of any artist in England at the time, Bacon was born lucky; his means were ample and therefore he was not made to cramp his talent to suit a patron's taste, and he grew to maturity just when the virtuosi were making art a respectable and even fashionable employment for gentlemen.

As a portrait-painter Bacon is not greatly different in kind from the best of his contemporaries, although his self-portrait at Gorhambury reveals a greater subtlety and breadth of colouring, a more clearly seen and solidly realized space, and a greater power of characterization than they had then achieved. It is typical, too, of the originality and independence of the man that his portrait of

[1] *English Art 1625–1714.*

his wife is in profile (Pl. 68) in startling contrast to anything that had been seen in England for three-quarters of a century, and in a style very different from the medallion-manner of Oliver's profile miniatures. But although four of his six remaining works are portraits, Bacon was not primarily a portrait painter at all. Even in his full-length self-portrait at Gorhambury (Pl. 64b) the careful insistence on such matters as the texture of the wall in the background and the objects on the table reveal other interests. His largest surviving pictures are *The Cookmaid* and its companion (Pl. 69), both now at Gorhambury, and he is known to have painted 'ten great pieces in wainscot of fish and fowle'. The two Gorhambury pictures are perhaps the finest painted by an English artist in the seventeenth century. They are remarkable for their vivid but balanced colouring, for their accomplished composition and for a command of detail and a realism in its expression that hardly any painter before had attained. The figure of the cookmaid—'the first real woman to appear in British art'—has a solidity and a verisimilitude unequalled in England since Holbein's early period, and a warm humanity that was unique. Bacon must have been well acquainted with Continental art, with Caravaggio and the school of Utrecht, and he made good use of his knowledge, but he produced in these two paintings an amalgam that is wholly individual. It would be too much to say that they are essentially English, for there is nothing else in England to compare them with, but for all their knowledge of European art they are not foreign importations.[1]

It is fitting to end a survey of painting of this period with Bacon not only because he is incontestably its greatest figure but also because he is, by being its least characteristic, its most revealing artist. His career, by its contrast with theirs, underlines the restrictions which hampered and stultified the professional painters. Further it illustrates at the same time both the widespread influence and the limitations of the virtuosi. There can be little doubt that it was they who created the climate that allowed Bacon to combine

[1] The known facts about, and a penetrating appreciation of, Bacon are given by Bernard Denvir, 'Sir Nathaniel Bacon, Some Notes on a Significant Artist', *Conn.* cxxxvii (1956), 116–19.

a gentleman's status with an artist's activities. Bacon shared many of the virtuosi's interests, but he was not of the court and produced in consequence an art of a very different kind from theirs. Indeed it would appear that they failed to appreciate his distinctive qualities.[1] This is clearly seen in Peacham's commendation of him: 'Nor can I overpasse the ingenuitie and excellency of many Noble and Gentlemen of our owne nation herein, of whom I know many; but none in my opinion who deserveth more respect and admiration for his skill and practise herein then Master Nathaniel Bacon . . . not inferiour in my judgement to our skilfullest Masters.'[2] Rarely has one man more mispraised another than in these comparisons. The aestheticism of the virtuosi was a very dim light to see Bacon's work by, for they were men with advanced views but yet tied to the State and little able to understand an art that was not. In practice their encouragement of painting was little more than a refining of court-portraiture that culminated in the elegant and accomplished flatteries of Van Dyck. These traits in their make-up explain both their attack upon the older court art and their inability to foster a new one in native soil. Bacon is thus a most important artist; not only for his own merits, not only for the significance of his relationship with the professional painters, but even more for his revelation of the weaknesses in the position of the virtuosi that ultimately frustrated their efforts.

[1] W. E. Houghton (*The English Virtuoso*, pp. 205–11) establishes—as far as such a point can be established from literary sources alone—that the virtuosi, or at least the earlier of them, had a view of painting that was not so greatly different from that of their uninformed contemporaries and predecessors.

[2] *Compleat Gentleman* (1622), p. 106.

# V

# MINIATURES

MINIATURE-painting, or limning as it was then
called, was a highly esteemed art in England in this
period, and its leading practitioners, Nicholas Hilliard
and Isaac Oliver,[1] had a great reputation not only among their own
countrymen but even in France. Each has a corpus of work which,
despite some uncertainty about the frontier territory between the
two, is well-founded and long-established. Further, it is and always
has been beyond dispute that their work is of great merit, and that
they are at least the equals in their field of any foreign artist of the
time. All these qualities distinguish them sharply from their contemporaries among the large-scale painters, and an explanation
of this is essential to an understanding of the English miniature in
the late sixteenth and early seventeenth centuries. It is possible, of
course, to attribute the contrast solely to the greater artistic talents
of Hilliard and Oliver, but such an explanation is inadequate. It
must be pointed out that the difference lay not merely in inborn
qualities—if it lay there at all—but also and more significantly in
the opportunities of exercising and developing them. The restrictions that stultified the latent talents of the painters bound the
limners less tightly; more, it was precisely because the painters
were so restricted that the limners got their opportunities to produce works of merit. The stiff expressionless 'physiognomies' of
the large-scale painters were the price that the Elizabethans paid
for the exquisite productions of Hilliard.

The work of a Danish scholar, Dr. Colding, has greatly altered
the general view of the development behind the English miniature.
In particular, by emphasizing and illustrating far more concretely
than any of his predecessors the miniature's origin in, and depend-

[1] Hilliard was born in 1547 and was buried on 7 Jan. 1619; Oliver was born *c.* 1565
and died in 1617. For a full biography of Hilliard see E. Auerbach, *Nicholas Hilliard*
(1961).

ence upon, the art of the goldsmith Dr. Colding has enabled us to understand how well suited it was to fulfil the purpose demanded of it in England at the beginning of Elizabeth's reign.[1] Miniature-painting, in the sense in which it is applied to works of this period, means working in water-colours or gouache upon a surface of calf skin or vellum. The method was perfected in medieval book illumination, and its intimate connexion with goldsmith's work is shown by the way in which the illumination is intended to enhance the lavishly applied gold leaf. The backgrounds of such illuminations were almost invariably of an ultramarine, and the colours most favoured were ruby reds, fresh yellows, and emerald greens. As late as about the year 1600 Hilliard, although by then he was the champion of a nearly lost cause, was insisting that these and murrey, all of which he linked with the precious stones, were the only perfect colours and the only ones fit for limning.[2]

By the end of the fifteenth century the illuminators of the Flemish School were beginning to produce limnings that were not set in a book at all but existed independently as small pictures. These early cabinet miniatures of the late fifteenth and early sixteenth centuries show a direct descent from the 'histoires' of the illuminated manuscripts. At the same time the small roundels, often with individual portraits, that had been used in the decoration surrounding the larger illuminations began, as in the *Guerres Galliques* of c. 1520, to be used by themselves as the only illumination on a page of manuscript, and the jewelled reliquary-lockets that had often held religious miniatures were increasingly used to hold portraits. With the advent of the Reformation they were used in Protestant countries for little else, and religious illumination upon liturgical books, of the kind carried out by Horenbout for Wolsey, disappeared.[3] Apart from the decoration of the initial letters of official documents,[4] it was as a 'portrait box' that the miniature was mainly known in England by the end of Henry VIII's reign,[5]

[1] T. H. Colding, *Aspects of Miniature Painting, its Origins and Development* (Copenhagen, 1953).

[2] 'The Art of Limning', ed. P. Norman, *Wal. Soc.* i (1913), 37.

[3] H. Paget, 'Gerard and Lucas Hornebolt in England', *Burl. Mag.* ci (1959), 396.

[4] For a full discussion of these see E. Auerbach, *Tudor Artists* (1954).

[5] The point needs some emphasis, for this was not, even in the sixteenth century,

and its rapid rise to esteem was largely due to this new content, aided by the English fondness for the rich materials that were a consequence of the miniature's origin amongst the goldsmiths.[1]

The iconography of the English miniature under the Tudor and early Stuart sovereigns is very similar to that of large-scale paintings. There is the occasional religious scene, such as the *Solomon and the Queen of Sheba*, attributed to Holbein, at Windsor, and the *Trinity* that Lavinia Teerlinck gave as a New Year gift to Queen Mary in 1556. There is a record of a miniature, also by Lavinia Teerlinck, of 'the Quenis Matie and many other personages', a large miniature of an aristocratic *fête champêtre* by Isaac Oliver at Ledreborg Castle, and a few subjects such as *Diana* and a *Head of Christ* (Pls. 72e and 74c) by the same artist. In later years Peter Oliver was widely engaged on making miniature copies of the most highly esteemed Italian paintings. Although his work and some of his father's is of importance as a symptom of the change in the nature of miniatures in the early seventeenth century, all of these are insignificant in number compared with the portraits.

This preoccupation with portraiture is alone common to the miniature and to the oil-painting in our period, but in earlier years there had been other similarities. English miniature-painting was a comparatively flourishing importation under Henry VIII, who, according to Hilliard, had several limners in his service. One of these was Lavinia Teerlinck and another was Luke Horenbout, traditionally Holbein's instructor in the art. Nothing remains of Lavinia Teerlinck's achievements[2] and until recently nothing was known of Horenbout's, but he is now being tentatively connected

the inevitable form of the miniature. In contrast with English development the work of the Italian and deeply Catholic miniaturist, Giulio Clovio (1498–1578), remained very largely of a religious nature; see the list of his works in Vasari's *Lives* (A. B. Hinds' translation 1927), iv. 244–9.

[1] An Italian visiting England in 1497 and referring to relics and vestments at Canterbury remarked with scorn that 'Everyone considers them very wonderful owing to the lavish use of gold and precious stones, which all Englishmen boast of continually.' C. V. Malfatti, *Two Italian Accounts of Tudor England* (Barcelona, 1953), p. 31.

[2] For Lavinia Teerlinck's now lost works see Auerbach, *Tudor Artists*, pp. 91, 188. She is first referred to as the 'King's Paintress' in 1546 and continued to receive her annuity from the Crown until her death thirty years later (ibid., pp. 105, 187–8).

with a body of work.[1] These and all the rest had what was in one respect the ill-fortune to be Holbein's contemporaries. Anything that they could do that great artist could do better, and it was inevitable that once he had turned his hand to limning he should excel in that art as he excelled in all others. For that reason and also because Hilliard declared himself to be the imitator of 'Holbein's maner of limning'[2] it is necessary to consider briefly the character of Holbein's miniatures.

In a revealing comparison between Holbein's oil-painting of Anne of Cleves in the Louvre and his miniature of her in the Victoria and Albert Museum, Dr. Colding has convincingly shown that Holbein's technique in limning is that of the goldsmith-illuminators.[3] The gold border and the use of gold for details of dress and jewellery, the clear, almost transparent blue background, the light colours, the careful brushwork: these traditional methods of illumination are found in the miniature but are absent from the oil-painting. But it is never enough to discuss Holbein's art in terms of technique alone, and it may be doubted whether Dr. Colding is on firm ground in denying any similarity, other than pose and dress, between the two works. Rather, however formally correct this view may be, the conclusion of Mr. John Pope-Hennessy that 'as a whole the miniature remained for Holbein . . . a small painting' is a more important truth.[4] The effect and intention of Holbein's miniatures is the same as that of his large paintings, the fixing, within a sharply defined outline and with the utmost clarity, of the personality of the sitter. His *Mrs. Pemberton* (V. & A.), which Mr. Carl Winter, almost in an understatement, has called 'the greatest miniature ever painted in England',[5] differs not at all, technique and scale apart, from his larger works. This similarity in subject-matter and in treatment between large- and small-scale painting is, however, not a peculiarity of Holbein's. The

[1] An attempt to identify Horenbout's work was made by Mr. Graham Reynolds in *Conn. Period Guides: Tudor* (1956), pp. 128-9; and see the article by H. Paget referred to on p. 191, note 3.
[2] 'The Art of Limning', p. 19.     [3] *Aspects of Miniature Painting*, pp. 21-22.
[4] *A Lecture on Nicholas Hilliard* (1949), pp. 13-14.
[5] 'The British School of Miniature Painters' (1948; reprinted from *Proc. Brit. Acad.* xxxiv. 7).

817207                                    O

miniatures now attributed to Horenbout and such known works of Simon Benninck as the *Unknown Man* of *c.* 1525 in the Louvre and the *Self-portrait* of 1558 in the Victoria and Albert Museum have all the qualities, including, in the latter example, the defined space or distant landscape against which the sitter is placed, of the searching realism of the more advanced portraiture of the age. The limners, and especially Holbein, had succeeded in producing in a different medium the aesthetics of contemporary oil-painting, in particular of the court portrait.[1] It was a considerable achievement, but it was to be short-lived.

The development of oil-painting in England from the humanity and breadth of the early Holbein to the formalized linear state portrait of the years around 1600 has already been traced. The development of the miniature in the same period is different in almost every respect. While the technical difference between the two arts made their later divergence possible, that alone cannot wholly explain it; for earlier the two techniques had produced a similar art and continued to do so until about 1570. Lavinia Teerlinck continued to receive her annuity from the Crown until her death in 1576, and although the miniature of the Trinity that she presented to Queen Mary and the group portrait of 1563 are lost, their subject-matter and probably 'cabinet' character would seem to relate them more to earlier than later miniatures. A recent acquisition by the Victoria and Albert Museum is a miniature dated 1549 of a woman, half-length, in which the modelling, form, and stance have affinities with Eworth's work (Pl. 73d). The *Queen Elizabeth* or, as it is sometimes called, *Lady Jane Grey* at Windsor is considered by Mr. Graham Reynolds to be an early copy by Hilliard of an Eworth original.[2] Such other early miniatures by Hilliard as that of the Duke of Somerset and the Portland *Queen Elizabeth* are great paintings in little, and their connexion with large-scale painting is emphasized by the one being almost certainly a copy of an earlier large-scale original and by the other

[1] Mr. Winter has made the most recent serious attempt to establish a corpus of Holbein's miniatures, 'Holbein's Miniatures', *Burl. Mag.* lxxxiii (1943), 266–9; see also P. Ganz, *The Paintings of Hans Holbein* (1950).
[2] *English Portrait Miniatures* (1950), p. 17.

having a large-scale copy or prototype at Warwick Castle. Even outside of portraiture, miniatures seem to have been closely related at this time to oil-painting. In 1556 Nicholas Lyzard, the Sergeant Painter, presented Mary with 'a table painted with the Maundy',[1] and one of the few non-portrait miniatures known, of somewhat later date than Lyzard's painting, appears also to be a representation of a Maundy.[2] The evidence is clearly slight, but what there is of it suggests that until about 1570 the miniature had not emancipated itself from the convention of oil-painting.

Its emancipation was brought about by the intensified exploitation of it, in reaction against the increasingly State and public nature of oil-painting, as a private art, as an intimate personal secret.[3] Such a view of the miniature is strongly suggested by the literary evidence. Most of the miniatures of the early sixteenth-century Italian, Giulio Clovio, were of devotional subjects, but those that were not were almost all, as Vasari remarked, 'of lords, friends and ladies that they (his employers) have loved'.[4] Sir James Melville's well-known story of Elizabeth's reluctance, whether real or conventional, to allow him to see the 'little picture' of her then favourite, and suspected lover, Leicester, illustrates the private and personal aspect of the miniature.[5] Hilliard considered the greatest feat of limning to be not merely the delineation of the sitter's features but the expression of that 'grace in countenance by which the affections appear', the revelation of those 'lovely graces', 'wittye smilings,' 'stolne glances'[6] that are the pleasures of intimacy. Limning, he considered, was 'for the service of noble persons very meet in small voloms in privat manner for thecm to have the portraits and pictures of themselves, their peers, . . .'.[7] In Marlowe's *Edward II* the close relations between the King and Gaveston are emphasized by their exchange of miniatures when they have to part.[8] This concept of the peculiarly intimate nature of the art

---

[1] Auerbach, *Tudor Artists*, pp. 91–92.
[2] T. M. Wood, 'The Beauchamp Miniatures', *Studio*, lxxi (1917), 85.
[3] Cf. Irene Adler, 'Die Clouet', *J.K.S.W.*, n.f. iii (1929), 224.
[4] *Lives* (Hinds's translation), iv. 229.
[5] *Memories of Sir James Melville of Halhill*, ed. A. F. Steuart (1929), p. 94.
[6] 'Art of Limning', p. 23.
[7] Ibid., p. 16.                                        [8] Act I, Sc. iv.

persisted long after Hilliard and Oliver were dead. When Buckingham was away in Madrid in 1623 his wife, irked at the separation,
implored him to send her his picture 'well done in little' for 'since
I must be barred of the principal I must feed, as new lovers do,
on the shadow'.[1] The connexion between limning and lovers was
emphasized as late as 1641 by Sir Kenelm Digby when he recognized, although not without advancing a cynical explanation for it,
that 'Cavaliers . . . are ever more earnest to have their mistresses'
picture in limning than in a large draught with oyle colors.'[2]

Literary evidence on such a point, however, cannot be conclusive
by itself; it must be taken in conjunction with the surviving
miniatures and oil-paintings. When these are considered as a whole,
it is noticeable that while both forms are largely confined to portraiture their subject matter within that field is vastly different. The
usual limning is not a representation of a statesman, a soldier, a
court-favourite in all his regalia, but of a lover, a mistress, a wife,
an intimate friend. A very great proportion of them, far greater
than among oil-paintings, are of young men and women shown
in all the freshness of youth, and these, as Mr. Graham Reynolds
says, are generally the best.[3] Like the oil-painters, the limners used
a great deal of symbolism, but of a very different kind. Instead of
badges of rank and office, or references to worldly achievements,
they filled their works with symbols of unrequited love, with
uninhibited fancies, and with now unfathomable allusions. One of
Hilliard's best known miniatures is of a man clad in a shirt against
a background of flames and fingering a locket (Pl. 63a); another is
of an elegant youth with more than his share of what was then
regarded as beauty, leaning against a tree amidst conventionalized
rose-briars, with a latin inscription meaning 'My praised faith
brings my pains' (Pl. 63b).[4] There are, of course, 'State' miniatures
to be found but, with the exception of those of Elizabeth (Pl. 73a
and b), they are overwhelmingly of the years after 1590 by which
time the Elizabethan miniature, as we shall see, was changing into

[1] G. Goodman, Court of James I (1839), ii. 280.
[2] Letter to Toby Mathew, B.M. Add. Mss. 41,846, ff. 56–57.
[3] Nicholas Hilliard and Isaac Oliver (V. &. A. Handbook (1947)), p. 15.
[4] Both of these are in the V. & A.

something else. Further, although the miniatures of Elizabeth are, in a sense, 'State' portraits they are far more expressions in art of the high-flown emotional relationships, real or pretended, that existed between Elizabeth and her courtiers and were well fitted to the prevailing concept of the miniature.[1]

This gulf between limning and painting, the private nature of the one and official nature of the other, itself calls, however, for an explanation, for the patrons who called the tune to the painters called it as loudly to the limners; perhaps more loudly, for miniatures, often in a jewelled setting, were thereby much more expensive than paintings and were, in general, beyond the pocket of any but the wealthy or spendthrift. Hilliard, as we have seen, considered they were 'for the service of noble persons,' and that limning 'tendeth not to comon men's usse'.[2] As Professor Waterhouse has said, 'Hilliard's miniatures were for the very rich only'[3] and, at least until the death of Elizabeth, the 'very rich' meant, in practice, the nobility and courtiers. The explanation of these men's simultaneous patronage of restricted formalized large-scale painting and of the exquisite and sensitive works of Hilliard is to be found in the contradiction underlying the ideology of the Tudor State and its supporters. The positive and most immediately striking aspect of the age is the universality of talent of its greatest figures. This is the epoch of 'a host of authentic geniuses', of men who combined in one body the qualities of the courtier, soldier, scholar and of the poet, musician, and natural scientist as well. Such a flowering of human potentialities was not the happy result of genetic mutations in the preceding generation but was fostered by a deliberate State policy at a time when opportunities were almost limitless and knowledge and resources very scanty. Even so early it was impossible to maintain a modern State with medieval notions; to keep itself in being the absolute State of the sixteenth century had to nurture and employ a great number of men trained in and

[1] For examples of the fantasies that were woven around Elizabeth and of the attitudes that were engendered see Frances A. Yates, 'Queen Elizabeth as Astraea', *Journ. W.C.I.* x (1947), 27–82, and E. C. Wilson, *England's Eliza* (Harvard, 1939).

[2] 'Art of Limning', p. 16.

[3] 'The Decline of the Miniature', *Penguin Parade*, 2nd ser., No. 1, pp. 46–47.

permeated with the New Learning and all its implications. Tudor
courtiers were, and had to be, not only men of affairs but men
abreast or ahead of contemporary thought in all its aspects,[1] and
this, because of the nature of the Tudor State, involved them in an
aesthetic dilemma. As men of affairs, as buttresses and beneficiaries
of the Tudor dynasty, they developed a public art in which the
glorification of the individual as a servant of the State and monarch
destroyed all individuality; but the interest in human personality
and the individual that they acquired from their participation in
the most advanced culture of the time was too strong and too
genuine to be stifled, and what it could not express in a public art
it had to express privately. For that expression it found the miniature ready to hand.

Around the year 1550 the aesthetic of the miniature and of the
oil-painting had marked similarities, but there were potentialities
of privacy in the one that were not in the other. There was, however, more than this. The miniature combined its quality of a
personal and private possession with the decorative traditions of
goldsmith's work and the restrictions upon a wholly realistic
presentation that its small scale determined. As Sir Kenelm Digby
said, 'the limner then were as much to blame if he meddled with
any defects, when the good will take up all his stroakes, as the
painter would be to leave out any deformity, since he hath room
for all'.[2] Its amalgam of all these qualities allowed the miniature
to be the expression in art of the feeling behind such literary productions as *Arcadia* and *Euphues* and the whole cult of Elizabeth:
a reaction against the stifling atmosphere of the absolute State that
expressed itself not in an escape from reality, but in an idealization
of it. In the fifty years between Mary's accession and Elizabeth's
death these qualities were developed, primarily by Hilliard, to
a point where limning and painting had almost nothing in common. It is therefore not correct to see the Elizabethan miniature,

[1] For the deliberate policy of fostering the new culture as a training for State
functionaries see R. R. Bolgar, *The Classical Heritage and its Beneficiaries* (Cambridge,
1954), ch. viii; F. Caspari, *Humanism and the Social Order in England* (Chicago, 1954);
Eleanor Rosenberg, *Leicester as a Patron of Letters* (New York, 1955); P. N. Siegel,
'English Humanism and the New Tudor Aristocracy', *J.H.I.* xiii (1952), 450–68.

[2] B.M. Add. Mss. 41,846, ff. 56–57.

as Mr. Pope-Hennessy sees it, as a 'Byzantine mirror for the Caesaropapism of the age'.[1] Rather, one must emphasize that, unlike oil-painting, it is not a direct reflection of 'Caesaropapism', but a reflection of the reaction of one aspect of the ideology of the time against the ironically anti-individual effects that the 'Caesaro-papist' aspect of the same ideology was producing.

By about 1570 the development of State-influenced portraiture had established an almost complete monopoly for the Elizabethan costume-piece and it was at that time that Hilliard burst into his personal style and, without altering its technique, in fact by limiting himself to its traditional technique, gave the miniature a new content. I think it is probable that Hilliard was quite well aware of what he was doing. He declared himself to be an imitator of Holbein's 'maner of limning',[2] and, although the phrase is vague, it is reasonably clear that he meant by it what we would call 'technique'. There is no reason to disagree with him on the point, but it must be stressed that in fact it was not merely Holbein's but the goldsmith-illuminators' technique that he was continuing: the blue background, the colour-scheme related to precious stones, the lavish use of gold, the light flesh colours, and the avoidance of shadowing. He did however employ some methods that were peculiar to Holbein and not general to all miniaturists, in particular the firm outline and the subtle modelling of the sitter's features by the use of deeper flesh tints. But he employed these to a totally different end, and thereby sundered his art from Holbein's and, for that matter, from Benninck's and Horenbout's. The aim of his art was not, like theirs, to portray an individual with all possible clarity nor, like that of his painter contemporaries, to record a visage and the status of its owner, but to reveal the most charming and winning aspects of a personality. He might well have taken for himself the motto on some old sundials—'I tell none but the pleasant hours'. There is a passage, unfortunately too long for quotation in full, in which he nearly says as much: 'The curious drawer' he says must 'catch thesse lovely graces, wittye smilings and thesse stolne glances which suddenly like lightning pass and another countenance taketh place' and must call 'thesse graces one

[1] *A Lecture on Nicholas Hilliard*, p. 29.        [2] 'Art of Limning', p. 19.

by one to theire due places.'[1] In such miniatures as his self-portrait of 1577 (Pl. 73c), the portrait of his wife (1578), of Leonard Darr in 1591 (Pl. 73f), of Mrs. Holland in 1593 (Pl. 72d) and Mrs. Mole (c. 1605), the effect of this method can best be seen.[2] They are all idealized presentations of their subjects, catching, with a liveliness of facial expression, an individual mood and creating a sense of intimacy.

The aim, however much desired, would have been unrealized if it had not happened that the technical possibilities of achieving it were present in the miniature. In the first place, despite its temporary aberration in the early sixteenth century, it was an art-form that had developed with, and whose technique encouraged, a highly decorative aspect. The pinks and carnations of the flesh tints, the light, generally blue, background, the fresh bright colours, the lavish use of gold ornament and lettering, the brilliance of the counterfeit jewellery; all these lay ready to Hilliard's hand. He enriched them with a wide use of decorative symbols and with a precise and yet free rendering of costume details and hair to enhance the graces of his sitters, so that even the most intractable cases could be saved by beauties not their own. Secondly, and of more importance, the miniature allowed scope for the idealization that was the motive of Hilliard's art. Mr. Pope-Hennessy has remarked that he 'remains from first to last the exponent of an anti-representational art';[3] his intention is to create an effect, not to render realistically what he sees. This intention could be achieved because of the small scale of the miniature. Some writers have been at pains to demonstrate that the term 'miniature' referred originally to the technique—to the use of 'minium' or red lead—and not to the size of the painting, and have upbraided the layman for imagining that a miniature must be small. However, for our period at least the layman is wiser than his teachers, for the most important quality of the Elizabethan miniature was only possible because of its small size. As Digby said, the limner, by the very

---

[1] 'Art of Limning', p. 23.

[2] The *Self-portrait* and the *Mrs. Holland* are in the V. & A.; the *Leonard Darr* and *Mrs. Mole* are in the possession of the Duke of Portland and Lord Wharton respectively.

[3] 'Nicholas Hilliard and Mannerist Art Theory', *Journ. W.C.I.* vi (1943), 99.

restrictions under which he worked, could exercise a considerable choice in rendering the varied aspects of what he saw, and because of that choice could, if the call was made, break free from the dominance of the aesthetics of the oil-painters. He could, within limits, paint as much or as little of physical reality as he liked and could, as Hilliard did, consider the capture of a fleeting expression to be the true aim of his art.[1]

This has provided the basis for the charge against Hilliard of 'flatness of presentation'. It has been vigorously rebutted by many writers, beginning with Philip Norman, the editor of the *Art of Limning*, and the accusation can no longer be pressed as strongly as it once was. It can be shown that there are many Hilliard miniatures with considerable modelling, for example, the *Unknown Man, aged 24* of 1572 (V. & A.) (Pl. 73e), the *Leonard Darr*, and many more, such as that of his wife (V. & A.), in which the flatness is the accidental result of the fading of the flesh tints. But for all that, there is some basis for the charge. It would not perhaps be fair to lay very much stress on Hilliard's own words, for they were written when he was being seriously challenged by the rival technique of Oliver and, humanly enough, he stated his views in a sharp and one-sided manner. It may also be admitted that in many of his works in which flatness is most apparent the essential Hilliard is diluted by elements of the State art of the oil-painters. Yet such miniatures as the *Young Man amidst Briars* and the portrait of 1586 of a man of the St. John family (Duke of Portland) are flat not only by comparison with Oliver's later chiaroscuro but by comparison with Holbein's work. In many others, even the most modelled, the details are often linear patterning: the curls at the sides of the temples in his own self-portrait, the cartwheel ruffs of many of his sitters, and the costumes—such as those of an *Unknown Lady* in the Fitzwilliam Museum, and of *Mrs. Holland*—that appear to be covering not a human body but a piece of cardboard. While recent critics have been right, therefore, to correct the mistaken over-emphasis by their predecessors on the linear quality of Hilliard's art, the opposite mistake of denying it altogether must also be avoided; for it tends to obscure the two most important influences on his style.

[1] 'Art of Limning', p. 23.

  The first, the illuminator's tradition, is responsible for his denun-
ciation of those who overshadow, who 'smut' their work, and
thereby break away from the only colour scheme that, in his
opinion, is valid for miniatures. The second, the intent of presenting the 'grace of countenance', of shadowing 'sweetly', of shadowing 'as though it were not shadowed at all', reinforces the first in
discouraging bold modelling, and in combination with it emphasizes the decorative, formalized character of all details. This
linear quality in his work is to be seen as one symptom of its
conventionalized nature. The hands of his sitters, for example, are
never modelled, as Oliver's are, but drawn quite formally, and
those of one could be substituted for another without any noticeable incongruity. The roses and briars that surround his famous
*Young Man* are not intended as an imitation of reality but as
decorative symbolic patterning. The flowers and symbols that
sometimes adorn his costumes are shown not as affixed to but as
painted upon the dress. All these are signs of a deliberate avoidance
of reality, of an art that is concerned, despite Hilliard's own words,
not to 'imitate nature' but to idealize it. In that idealization the
linear character of the style plays an important part.

  Inevitably the qualities of Hilliard's art have been ascribed to
foreign influence; to France in particular, to 'Mannerism' in
general. The case for French influence has been stated by several
writers and ably argued by Mr. Pope-Hennessy,[1] but there are
considerable difficulties in the way of accepting it. Hilliard was, as
far as is known, never in France before 1576 and yet his essential
style is already present in the *Unknown Man* of 1572. In France he
was 'competently mayntayned' by the duc d'Alençon,[2] who presumably would not have patronized an English miniaturist if he
had thought there were equally good French ones. What little we

  [1] In the two articles already cited. The assumption of French influence is made by
Mr. Graham Reynolds in *English Portrait Miniatures*. Mr. Winter in 'Hilliard and Elizabethan Miniatures' (*Burl. Mag.* lxxxix (1947), 175–83) showed a disposition to agree
with that view but in a slightly later work—*The British School of Miniature Painting*,
quoted above—he tended, following Irene Adler, to consider any similarities as due to
'Zeitstil'. Dr. Colding flatly rebuts any suggestion of French influence (*Aspects of
Miniature Painting*, p. 84).
  [2] N. Blakiston, 'Nicholas Hilliard as a Traveller', *Burl. Mag.* xci (1949), 169.

know of Hilliard's stay in France suggests that in fact there were not. One of the jobs on which he was engaged was to do again two miniatures that had been bungled twice, by a Frenchman and a Fleming.[1] Contemporary French opinion regarded him as 'l'un des plus excellens [painters] dont on aye mémoire, au moins en petit volume'.[2] Indeed the French valuation of their own miniaturists seems, at the time of his visit, to have been low. Quite apart from the significance of that visit, it is noticeable that there are very few French miniatures of the late sixteenth century. In contrast there are a great number of self-sufficient crayon drawings, and it is these, in Dimier's view, and not miniatures that held the esteem of French cognoscenti at the time.[3] It would be rash to say that there was nothing that French limners could teach Hilliard, but it is doubtful if the French themselves thought there was very much.

Yet such arguments can only suggest that the influence of French miniaturists upon Hilliard was insignificant; the proof must be found in a comparison of his work with theirs. And here it must be said that it is not enough to point to certain qualities of Hilliard's work, such as 'sweetness' and 'grace', as a proof of French influence. Even if these have always been present in French art, and there is little enough trace of them in French painting of the time, they have never been a French monopoly. A more concrete instance has been found in the portraits of the 'Preux de Marignan' in the *Guerres Galliques*. Certainly, they have affinities in some respects with Hilliard's work; but they have closer affinities with the miniatures of Holbein and of the reputed Horenbout. There are no traits common to Hilliard and the 'Preux de Marignan' that are not also found in Holbein, and since it is very doubtful whether Hilliard knew the one and certain that he knew the other, it is reasonable to accept his word that he was a follower of Holbein and not of the artist of the 'Preux de Marignan'. It is arguable, of

[1] E. Auerbach, 'More Light on Nicholas Hilliard', *Burl. Mag.* xci (1949), 166–8.

[2] E. P. Goldschmidt in *Times Literary Supplement*, 9 Aug. 1947, p. 403.

[3] The self-sufficiency of the crayon portrait in France in the late sixteenth century is emphasized by L. Dimier, *Le Portrait en France au XVI<sup>e</sup> siècle* (Paris, 1924), ch. 11, 12; and by Irene Adler, 'Die Clouet', *J.K.S.W.*, n.f. iii (1929), 204.

course, that Holbein himself was a follower of that artist, although Dr. Colding gives good reasons for not thinking so,[1] but that is a problem of the formation of Holbein's style, not Hilliard's.

The miniatures of the younger Clouet have also been championed as an influence upon Hilliard; but here one is at a loss to understand how these often hard and sometimes brutal portrayals in the manner of a great painting can be compared with Hilliard's work. In fact, an example which has been taken to illustrate the argument—the comparison of Clouet's full-length *Charles IX* with Hilliard's *Sir Anthony Mildmay* (*c.* 1595)[2]—goes a long way towards disproving it. The *Mildmay* is a work in which the full-length treatment, the setting of the subject in an actual space, the pose and the accessories of rank, all in the manner of a painting 'in great', are alien from the idealized presentment of Hilliard at his best (Pl. 70). If this is indeed an example of Clouet's influence then it is evident that the majority of Hilliard's works are not. There is, indeed, nothing essential in Hilliard that can be regarded as specifically due to French influence and, in the words of a later Frenchman upon a vaster theme, 'Nous n'avons pas besoin de cette hypothèse-là.'

The influence of 'Mannerism' upon Hilliard or, more precisely, the presence of 'Mannerist' elements in his work, is a more difficult problem. Much has been made of some of his remarks in the *Art of Limning*, of his expressed agreement with many of Lomazzo's precepts, and of his commendation of such a Mannerist engraver as Lambert Suavius.[3] Thus he agrees with Lomazzo's criticism of Dürer's rules of proportion, with his theory of light and shade, his emphasis on line, and with the doctrine that the painter must enter into the emotions of his sitters. But that is only a part of the truth. A study of the *Art of Limning* is in itself sufficient to arouse a certain uneasiness about the validity of applying the Mannerist label to Hilliard. For all his commendation of Mannerist engravers

[1] *Aspects of Miniature Painting*, pp. 27–31.

[2] In the Cleveland Museum of Art, Ohio.

[3] The view, which has now become orthodox, of Hilliard as a pupil of Mannerism was first developed by Mr. Pope-Hennessy in 1943 in his article, quoted above, in the *Warburg and Courtauld Journal*.

he reserves the greatest praise for Dürer, one of their favourite targets, and considers the copying of his engravings the best possible training for a miniaturist.[1] He emphasizes the point by avowing himself a disciple of Holbein. This harping on the two great figures of the 'German High Renaissance' cannot be dismissed by citing verbal similarities between Hilliard's treatise and Lomazzo's *Trattato*. If the similarities were complete and the divergences nil they would still, by themselves, prove little. Theories of art-creation have to be expressed in abstractions, and abstractions are intellectual confidence-tricksters; they can mean different things to different men, and a likeness of expression is no guarantee of a likeness of meaning. It is not, therefore, enough to compare Hilliard's words with Lomazzo's, rather Hilliard's work must be compared with that of the Mannerists.

Such a comparison reveals most important differences. Hilliard's colours are not theirs, and neither is his use of light and shade with its delicate flesh-tinting. He makes great use of line, but his line, however clear and firm, has none of the hardness of such a painter as Clouet. There are, of course, elements in his art that have affinities with Mannerism: the anti-representational tendency, the elongation of form and the use of the oval for a framework, the hardness of light in his miniatures of Elizabeth. But these can be shown to derive directly either from the function of the miniature or from the effect upon it of English 'State' painting. The resemblances are not due to any Mannerist 'influence' but to elements common to the English and European situation. Because of these Hilliard might well agree with something that a contemporary Continental Mannerist said, but he did so because his own English experience had led him by another route to a similar conclusion. If a study of the *Art of Limning* shows anything it shows this. In the first place, it is generally agreed that Hilliard knew Lomazzo only in translation, and Haydocke's translation did not appear until 1598, when Hilliard's greatest achievements were well behind him. Further, the references to Lomazzo are far from those of a disciple; rather their whole tone conveys the suggestion that Lomazzo, bright fellow, shares some of Hilliard's views. When discussing,

[1] 'Art of Limning', p. 37.

for example, the correct use of shadowing, the point which he was most concerned to establish, he says 'Paulo Lomatzo maintaineth mine oppinion, more then any other that ever I hard.'[1] To Hilliard Lomazzo's name was a handy weapon in his fight to establish in theory the methods of miniature painting that he had employed in practice throughout his life. Those methods, deriving from the use of the goldsmith-illuminator's technique to produce a private painting for the State-ridden products of Humanism, were being challenged by Oliver, and the *Art of Limning* was intended as an early *Apologia pro Vita mea*, as a counter-attack in the form of a defence.

The Elizabethan miniature was out of date by the time that Hilliard wrote. It is true that occasionally, as in *Mrs. Mole* and Lord Derby's *Elizabeth of Bohemia* (Pl. 72*b*), Hilliard sputtered with his old brilliance, but miniature-painting after the turn of the century was very different from what it had been in the years after 1570. In one way it was the very achievement of the Elizabethan miniature that brought about its eclipse. Its obvious mastery in comparison with oil-painting gave it a much greater esteem, and some patrons, in a vain attempt to have things both ways, tried to get from the miniature not only its own qualities but those of large-scale painting as well. This was revealed quite exceptionally at first in those portraits of the Queen in which not only the linearity but the background of a red curtain or hanging are symptomatic of the influence of great painting. By the end of the 1580's the influence is more apparent. Dating from *c.* 1585 there is a whole series of full-lengths by Hilliard and by Oliver in which not only the rectangular form and the full-length presentation but also the prosaic accessories of the defined space in which the subject is placed reveal that a great painting in little is being attempted. Such works as Hilliard's *Sir Christopher Hatton*[2] (Pl. 74*b*) and *Sir Anthony Mildmay*, and Oliver's *The Brothers Browne* culminate in the latter's *Richard Sackville, Earl of Dorset*, painted in 1616, a costume-piece in miniature that reproduces even the metallic

---

[1] 'Art of Limning', p. 30.
[2] The *Hatton* and *Sackville* are in the V. & A.; the *Browne Brothers* in the possession of the Marquess of Exeter.

folds in the curtain of some contemporary large-scale portraits (Pl. 71). In these paintings it is not the full-length subject that, by itself, marks the break with the Elizabethan tradition—for Hilliard's *Young Man amidst Briars* is a full-length—but the attempt at a record of the sitter amidst the accessories of his rank and social position. The big full-lengths are the most obvious examples of this trend, but it can be seen in the monotony and lack of inspiration of many of the miniatures by Hilliard, or a pupil, of James I and his family. It is revealed by the reappearance of the practice of making a miniature from a painting or other representation of the subject. Towards the end of the century Hilliard was employed, as he had not been for nearly forty years, on producing such works, in this case of the Tudor sovereigns; and Isaac Oliver produced a miniature of Lord Herbert of Cherbury not from the man himself but from a portrait of him by an oil-painter.[1] The miniature was losing its private personal character; it was showing signs of becoming a record of persons of importance. Hamlet refers scornfully to the way in which people who had previously slighted Claudius hastened to buy his 'picture in little' after he became king.[2]

By the time of Charles I the concept of the miniature as an oil-painting in little was dominant. It is shown in the employment of Peter Oliver on the copying of some of Charles's favourite large-scale paintings in a miniature form that permitted them to be taken around by the King wherever he went. A striking component of Edward Norgate's *Miniatura*, written some time in Charles's reign, is the discussion of landscapes and landscape backgrounds.[3] Although Hilliard occasionally painted a landscape background—for example in the full-length *Earl of Cumberland*—it is clear that he considered it a piece of inessential nonsense not worth mentioning in his treatise. Landscape was beginning to come into its own in English oil-painting when Norgate was writing; its entry into limning was only possible because the conception of the miniature had changed. But Norgate's book reveals also the abandonment by

[1] Lord Herbert of Cherbury, *Autobiography*, ed. Sidney Lee (1906), pp. 68–69.
[2] *Hamlet*, II. ii.
[3] *Miniatura or the Art of Limning*, ed. M. Hardie (Oxford, 1919), pp. 35, 43–54. The passages on landscape appear to date from the 1640's.

miniaturists of their traditional colour-scale and the adoption of that of the oil-painters. Nothing could be further from Hilliard's practice but more in line with theirs than Norgate's remark that while the background of a miniature could be of any colour, it is 'most . . . laid with darke and sad colour to sett of the picture'.[1] From Norgate's words and Peter Oliver's works it becomes clear that the miniature had partly lost its old function and its old form. Its brief Elizabethan flowering during the period of its release from the hegemony of the large-scale portrait was passing during the last years of Elizabeth's reign and was over by the time of Norgate and Peter Oliver. In the intervening years the struggle between the new form and the old is revealed in the works of Isaac Oliver.

The return of the miniature to captivity occurred, however, after a long development in which its connexion with the illuminator's art had become tenuous. It did not, therefore, return to its old status of dependence in aim and independence in technique but to a status in which both aim and technique were determined by oil-painting. This did not mean that the early seventeenth-century miniature was a little brother of contemporary English portraiture, for the changes that were occurring in society were affecting miniatures and oil-paintings unevenly. By the last decade of the sixteenth century the public acceptance of the power of the State, arising from the harmony between all the supporters of the Tudor settlement and expressed in the intellectual dominance of the courtiers and State functionaries, was less absolute than before. With the defeat of the Armada the need for national unity under the Sovereign was less, and disagreements were coming into the open. The Puritans were moving into opposition, Peter Wentworth was expiating in the Tower his insubordination in the Commons, and before long Essex was to attempt a minor *fronde* against the Queen. Even those who had no quarrel with the régime were finding the Elizabeth legend more difficult to maintain. Elizabeth herself as she grew older resembled Gloriana less, and flatteries that may well have been paid originally as a free benevolence began to look like a forced loan; with the accession of a canny but uncharming Scot the discrepancy between the flatteries and

[1] *Miniatura*, p. 34.

the facts became inescapable. The equilibrium between a public acceptance of the all-pervading power of the State and a private attempt to escape from it that had been the basis of the Elizabethan miniature was over, and there occurs a change that is paralleled in literature, away from a spiritualized, graceful, other-worldly fantasy towards an earthy, sharp and forceful critique of life, towards an art that concerned itself less with Arcadia and more with England.

At the same time the demand for miniatures was probably widening as more men were attempting to imitate the fashions of the aristocracy. In 1601 Hilliard, writing to Cecil and probably glancing at Oliver, referred to limners who had 'pleased the common sort exceeding well'.[1] As Hilliard considered that miniatures were for 'princes and noblemen' it may be assumed that he was here reluctantly recognizing an innovation that he disliked. It was probably the influence of this 'mass market' that played a large part in the tendency to abandon the expensive jewellery that had set off so many earlier miniatures. Even such an important figure as the Earl of Rutland paid Hilliard only £3 in 1603 for a miniature of his new king, James I,[2] a price that makes it certain that little but the limning was provided. The abandonment of the setting meant the loss of a large part of the miniature's decorative value, and that simultaneously gave the miniature more of the character of a great painting in little and made the development of a more realistic style the easier. Just as some of the courtiers helped to hasten the decay of the Elizabethan miniature by charging it with a role for which it was unfitted, so the 'common sort', attempting to get all its excellencies while robbing it of its most important decorative adjuncts, helped to destroy what they had originally wished to preserve.

Painting, however, was far less affected by the change. It had a public function and that function was not diminished but enhanced by any disturbance of the political and intellectual status quo. The more the régime was publicly attacked by its opponents and privately criticized by its supporters, the more necessary did the glorification of its representatives become; and although the ways

[1] H.M.C. *Cecil*, xi. 306.          [2] H.M.C. *Rutland*, iv. 444.

of achieving this might change, the intention remained, and prevented any deep realism of presentation in large-scale painting. It
was not, therefore, from that source that miniaturists had anything
to get in adapting their technique to a new aim. Rather they turned
to contemporary Dutch and Flemish large-scale portraiture, which
had a similar aim and was able to provide them with the models
they needed. This source was more open at first to the refugee
craftsmen than to English limners, and it was the son of a refugee,
Isaac Oliver, who was to be the chief exponent of the new style.
Oliver, of a French goldsmith's family and connected by marriage
with the de Critz and Gheeraerts circle,[1] is, if not the disciple, the
fellow believer of Goltzius. As Lugt has said, 'Son œuvre a absolu-
ment le même caractère que les portraits si spirituellement gravés
de son contemporain hollandais Goltzius.'[2]

Through all the changes that Oliver's art underwent in the
thirty years between his first known work and his death in 1617
it remained that of the large-scale painter on a small scale. In his
development there are three more or less clearly defined periods,
of which the first extends to the middle of the last decade of the
sixteenth century. In these few years in which he had not thrown
off all the precepts of the illuminators he combined a realism of
presentation and a virtuosity of depth and modelling with a general
dependence upon the traditional miniaturist colour-scale. His
earliest known works, the *Man aged 59* (1588) and the *Unknown
Youth* of the same year (Pl. 74e),[3] are wholly free of Hilliard's
dependence on line and convention of detail, and are in the manner
of contemporary Dutch and Flemish portraiture, with deep
shadowing, a sense of volume, and an instant and realistic presentation of the sitter. There is a splendid series of portraits of about the
same time, of which two easily accessible examples are the unidentified men (Nos. P37–1941 and P50–1941) in the Victoria and
Albert Museum. The series can be seen to culminate in the *Self-*

---

[1] The known facts of Oliver's life have all been brought together in Auerbach,
*Tudor Artists*, pp. 179–80.

[2] F. Lugt, *Le Portrait-Miniature illustré par la collection de S.M. la Reine des Pays-Bas*
(Amsterdam, 1917), p. 14.

[3] In the possession respectively of H.M. The Queen of the Netherlands and of
Mr. Brinsley Ford.

*portrait* belonging to the Earl of Derby (Pl. 74*a*) in which the bold and dramatic presentation and the powerful characterization of the subject has produced a masterpiece that differs both from the work of Hilliard and from that of the Continental portrait painters. At times his delineation is mercilessly real, and the unfinished portrait of Queen Elizabeth (V. & A.) (Pl. 72*c*), in which the faint defects of age are revealed in the brightest of lights, is the complete antithesis to Hilliard's work. Yet in this period Oliver's colours are still the traditional limners' colours, with the broad area of the blue background contrasted with the black or dark colour of the clothes, and both intended to show up the carnation tints of the features, the bright greens, reds, yellows, and whites of the sitter's jewels, ribbons, and laces, and the gilt lettering of the legend. Even where the field is grey, as in the portrait of Essex at Windsor Castle, the same colour-scale is apparent.

There is, however, even in this early period a symptom of the new qualities of the later Oliver. It used to be remarked that the main difference between Oliver and Hilliard was the modelling of the one and the lack of modelling of the other. It should, however, be said that they both model, but in different ways; Hilliard by the use of modulated flesh tints, Oliver by dark shadowing. The one method is that of a man held firmly in the illuminators' colour tradition, the other of one preparing to break away from it. From about the time of his visit to Italy in 1596 Oliver turns decisively to the colour schemes of the oil-painters. His backgrounds are increasingly laid in what Norgate called 'darke and sad colours': the grey of the Essex portrait, the darker grey of the profile portrait of Anne of Denmark at Windsor Castle, the very dark brown of the *Lady in Masque Costume* (Pl. 72*f*) in the Victoria and Albert Museum. He did not wholly abandon the traditional blue background—it occurs in a miniature of Elizabeth of Bohemia—but when he did use it he often broke up its area. Thus in the *Unknown Lady aged 50* (V. & A.), the outlines of the headdress are painted in a lacy black that reduces the background to almost negligible proportions. His flesh tints are no longer in shades of carnation, but contain a considerable amount of grey. Instead of the bright simple colours that Hilliard used for costumes and costume decorations there is on the one hand a great use of pink, mauve, and orange, and on the other of dark shades of green, blue, and red, and of a yellow that is nearly brown. Even the ruffs of his sitters are denied the brilliant whiteness of earlier years and are given a pale brown tinge, almost as though they had been slightly scorched in the ironing.

Besides the change of colours there is also a change in the use of colour. In Hilliard's and in Oliver's early work the colours used are few and they are not in combination but in contrast with broad areas of one colour splashed vividly with another. In his later miniatures Oliver attempts to combine very small areas of toned-down colours into a whole. The effect can best be understood by comparing the Victoria and Albert Museum's so-called *Sir Arundel Talbot* (Pl. 74*d*), painted in 1596, with the *Lady in Masque Costume*. The colour scheme of the first is in three sharply defined parts: a large area of blue background, an area almost as large of the near-black costume, and between the two the pale flesh colours of the face tinged with the light brown beard and greying hair and with the white of the ruff. In the second the dark brown of the background shades into the dark grey of the headdress and the brown of the hair, the costume is broken up into small patches of opaque colour and even the jewels upon it are painted in a dead light. This last is an extreme case, but the same method can be seen elsewhere, in the profile portrait of Henry, Prince of Wales (Fitzwilliam Museum), and in the choice of an opaque claret colour for the jewel upon the dark costume of the *Lady aged 50* already mentioned.

Oliver's last phase is more difficult to date and define than the other two; it becomes noticeable about the end of the first decade of the century, and is marked by a loss in actuality and realism. It is perhaps not fair to cite the doubtless routine portraits of Anne of Denmark and the royal family, but the change may be seen in the *Unknown Man* (*c.* 1610) belonging to Lord Harlech and the *Lady Hunsdon* (*c.* 1615) in the Victoria and Albert Museum. It is very clear in the profile miniatures of Anne of Denmark, Prince Henry, and George Villiers, in which the desire to produce the effect of a classical bust in a cameo has superseded the former intention of actuality. It is apparent again in the full-length *Richard*

*Sackville* where, in contrast with the much earlier full-length at Windsor known as *Sir Philip Sidney*, the effect of a large-scale costume piece is deliberately aimed at. The *Sackville* is important because, although in its character of a copy of a costume-piece it is highly untypical, it is an indication of the divergent tendencies then present in Oliver's art. It is also an example of the new attempt in Oliver to infuse an elegance into his miniatures, for example into many of those of Anne of Denmark, and into the profile miniatures. Elegance was not a quality native to Oliver's art or even one which he had earlier acquired. In such miniatures as the so-called *Frances Howard Countess of Essex* (c. 1595)[1] and the *Lucy Harrington* of ten years later he achieves an almost Hilliardesque grace. In these later years, however, when he abandons his matter-of-fact vision and follows Hilliard in heightening the qualities of his sitters, what he adds is not grace but its synthetic substitute, elegance.

The blame, if blame there be, for the last phase of Oliver's career cannot be put wholly upon his shoulders. Mr. Graham Reynolds has noted that Oliver's sitters in his early years, before he was appointed in 1604 as limner to Queen Anne and taken up by the court, are mainly unidentified and presumably minor figures.[2] Hilliard's reference presumably to Oliver as pleasing the 'common sort' has already been quoted. It may be suggested that it was the 'common sort', men not intimately connected with the court or with its conventions in miniature or oil-painting, who determined many of the qualities of Oliver's earlier work. In later years, as he came more to depend upon the functionaries of the State for his patronage he was increasingly being hammered and framed upon their anvil. At any rate he showed at the end of his life, in contrast with Hilliard, a desire to escape from the pressure of portrait-painting and to enter a wider and less time-bound field. Very early in his career he had painted a miniature of an aristocratic *fête galante* rather in the manner of such a contemporary Netherlandish miniaturist as Hans Bol. In his last years he spent much of his time on

[1] The *Frances Howard* is in the possession of the Earl of Derby; the *Lucy Harrington* is in the Fitzwilliam Museum.
[2] *Conn. Period Guides: Tudor*, p. 134.

miniatures with no apparent relation to contemporary society: on the enormous *Burial of Christ*, and the *Adoration of the Magi*, and on such studies as a *Prodigal Son*, a *Head of Christ* (Pl. 74 c), and a *Diana* (Pl. 72 e).[1] The first two exist now only in preliminary drawings in the British Museum. The others are significant for their revival of the qualities of depth and volume of the early Oliver. The presence of such qualities in these more personal productions suggests that his later portrait miniatures are more the results of his patrons' tastes than his own.

Hilliard and Oliver have in retrospect so dominated the miniature-painting of their era that their limner contemporaries are as shadowy figures as most of the painters in great. The names of several are known, but there are only two, Segar and Rowland Lockey, who can be even remotely connected with any existing miniatures. Dr. Auerbach has shown that the miniature of Colet on the statute-book of St. Paul's School is by one of the Segars, either Sir William, Garter King at Arms, or his brother Francis.[2] Mr. Graham Reynolds has tentatively attributed the *Unknown Lady* in the National Gallery at Melbourne to Rowland Lockey,[3] and Dr. Otto Kurz has attributed to him a miniature of the family of Sir Thomas More.[4] Lockey, according to Haydocke, was equally at home in 'Oyle and Lim'[5] and from the Lumley Inventory we know that 'Segar' painted in great. Although Hilliard is known to have painted one large-scale picture and Oliver may have painted several, such works were a minor part of their output, or at least played a minor part in establishing their contemporary reputation. Segar and Lockey, however, would appear to have been at least as busy on large-scale paintings as on miniatures[6] and one may well suppose that the dominance of Hilliard and Oliver prevented lesser

[1] The *Prodigal* is in the possession of the Duke of Portland. According to Norgate (*Miniatura*, p. 55), he also spent two years on a Madonna.

[2] *Tudor Artists*, p. 121.

[3] *Conn. Period Guides: Tudor*, p. 134.

[4] 'Rowland Lockey', *Burl. Mag.* xcix (1957), 13–16.

[5] *Tract concerning the Artes of Painting etc.* (Oxford, 1598), Introduction.

[6] D. Piper in *Conn. Period Guides: Tudor*, p. 54; R.A. *Catalogue of an Exhibition of British Portraits* (1956–7), pp. 29–30; E. Auerbach, *Nicholas Hilliard*, pp. 255–6, 271–80.

talents from obtaining any significant patronage in the restricted market open to miniaturists.

With the passing of the giants in 1619 and 1617 there was a more open field, and from then until 1625 there are known works by four limners, Lawrence Hilliard, Edward Norgate, Balthazar Gerbier, and Peter Oliver.[1] The younger Hilliard is perhaps the least of these, an uninspired practitioner of his father's method making some concessions in his colour-scale and attempts at elegance to the fashionable taste. He succeeded his father as Royal Limner and may have been responsible for many of the routine miniatures of the royal family turned out during the last years of Nicholas's life. Norgate and Gerbier, although of very dissimilar origins, are alike enough in their works, and may both be recognized as followers of the style of the later Oliver. Norgate in his treatise gave theoretical expression to his own practice in advocating the colour-scale of the oil-painters and a 'bold, stout and judicious manner' of expressing 'whatsoever you see in the Life'.[2] His picture of his first wife, painted in 1617 and now in the Victoria and Albert Museum, is a practical illustration of his theories (Pl. 72a). Gerbier's three known works are all dated between 1616 and 1619. The *Prince Maurice of Orange* in the possession of the Queen of the Netherlands is typical. It has a mauve background with a distant green landscape to the sitter's left, yellow-brown armour, an orange scarf, a white ruff, a blue ribbon, and grey and pink flesh tints. In its colouring and its use of shadow it is very similar to Norgate's work.

The career of Peter Oliver, the most talented of the *epigoni*, is an illustration of the miniature's loss of its unique and independent position. Nearly all of his original portraits were painted during or before the 1620's. From then onwards he was employed almost wholly on copies of great paintings, mainly of Charles I's Italian masterpieces. Quite apart from such elements of contemporary oil-painting in his work as the dramatic character and the use of

[1] The known biographical facts about Lawrence Hilliard, Peter Oliver, and Edward Norgate are to be found in Auerbach, *Tudor Artists*, pp. 168, 179, 180; *Nicholas Hilliard*, pp. 224–32, 282–4.

[2] *Miniatura*, p. 30.

Sir Nathaniel Bacon's pink, this deflexion of his talents reveals clearly that the miniature as an art-form quite independent of oil-painting was now defunct. His father had shown in the great set-pieces of his later years that he recognized the direction in which the miniature was developing. By Peter's time not only miniaturists but their public as well knew that the development that had begun with Isaac's early works had reached its climax. The miniature was becoming on the whole a small-scale version of the contemporary oil-painting, and not, as Oliver's had been, of Dutch and Flemish, but of contemporary English portraiture.

The jewelled setting played so important a part in the effect created by the Elizabethan miniature that a brief account of con-temporary jewellery will perhaps be useful here. It will be remem-bered that Hilliard attempted to establish a mystical link between the precious stones and the 'perfect colours' of limning, and such gems as the *Drake Pendant* and the *Armada Jewel* in enamelled gold, set with diamonds, pearls, and rubies, and containing miniatures of the Queen, are examples of the close connexion between limn-ing and jewellery, and help to explain why the two leading miniaturists of the age were the sons of goldsmiths. It was not only in Hilliard's mind that an aura of magic still clung to jewellery, and in association with the general liking for emblematic figures and esoteric allusions produced such examples as the *Lennox Jewel* of *c.* 1575. This is a pendant of gold in the shape of a heart, the cognizance of the Douglas family, worked with emblems and allusive inscriptions and intended by Margaret Douglas to com-memorate her husband, the Earl of Lennox. A commoner form of jewellery was the hat-badge, generally with a personal allusion in its design, worn by many men. Perhaps the finest of these is the gold-enamelled medallion acquired by the British Museum in 1955 (Pl. 75*a*). Its subject, Christ with the Woman of Samaria, is unusual and its workmanship is outstanding. That it is by an English craftsman and of late rather than of early Tudor origin seems fairly certain[1] and it is evidence of the standard that native workers in this field could sometimes attain.

[1] H. Tait in *B.M. Quarterly*, xx, No. 2 (Sept. 1955), 37.

# VI

# FUNERAL MONUMENTS AND SCULPTURE

THE history of English sculpture between 1553 and 1625 is inseparable from a history of fashions in funeral monuments, upon which most of the sculptural effort of the period was expended. Those fashions determined and very severely restricted both the subject-matter and the style of the sculptors and bound them nearly as tightly as the easel-painters. They were, however, somewhat freer than their fellow craftsmen because they enjoyed the patronage of many classes besides the courtiers, and in consequence were not limited to the expression of 'Statist' ways of thought and the adornment of massive architectural tombs. They were often called upon to express the less restricted feelings of minor men and this presented them with problems that forced them to develop their art to a point from which—when the virtuosi appeared—it could go farther, eliminate architecture from funeral monuments, and turn them into independent works of sculpture.

The social and religious changes of the early sixteenth century had a twofold effect upon native sculpture. They destroyed the wealth and influence of the medieval Church, and thereby the widest market and deepest inspiration of the medieval sculptor, at the same time as they created new classes of wealthy but individually powerless landed proprietors with a more or less Protestant ideology. The religious feeling of these new men could not be expressed in the old way, in erecting or adorning churches; within a church it could reveal itself upon little but their tombs, and since, while not equating wealth with worth, they tended to regard the former as an outward sign of the latter, they made these display their rank and station. To be impressive they needed to be large, for the trade-nature of tomb-making at the time, carried out by men all at much the same level of skill and with the same lack of inspiration, allowed wealth to reveal itself only in the size of the monument and the richness of its ornament and material. By about 1600 it was almost *de rigueur* for a landed family to have a series of magnificent tombs in the local church. The epitaph of Sir Thomas Caryll at Shipley, Sussex, remarks of its subject, not without a hint of resentment at the convention, that he was a man 'who but for fashion needs no stone'. At Margam in Glamorganshire Sir Edward Mansell raised a monument to his grandfather, not for any outstanding virtues he may have had but 'because he was the first purchaser of this seat'. As Weever remarked at the end of the period, although he was perhaps by then a little out-of-date, 'Sepulchres should be made according to the qualitie and degree of the person deceased, that by the Tombe every one might be discerned of what ranke hee was living.'[1]

The individualism that underlay this conception is clear enough when these tombs are compared with the most expensive form of late medieval monument—the chantry chapel. These were often imposing structures and none more so than the latest of them all, that of Bishop Gardiner, erected in Mary's reign in Winchester Cathedral. They were, however, buildings within a building, intended as enclosures wherein priests could say masses for the dead man's soul and not as backgrounds against which to display his rank, his family, and his connexions. Some of them were certainly magnificent, even perhaps ostentatious, but the magnificence was for the greater glory of God and not for that of a man. The secular nature of Renaissance monuments on the other hand was so marked that they gave offence to some members of a slightly later generation whose piety took a different form. Hatton's tomb in St. Paul's had been criticized in the late sixteenth century for its unmannerliness, for elbowing all others out;[2] in the early seventeenth century Richard Corbet had a different complaint: that its 'Pyramis, Above the Host and Alter reared is'.[3]

This new type of tomb developed within the framework of an old society in which 'descent through the blood' had been the

---

[1] John Weever, *Ancient Funeral Monuments* (1631), p. 10.
[2] E. St. John Brooks, *Sir Christopher Hatton* (1946), p. 354.
[3] 'Elegy on the Death of Dr. Ravis', written *c.* 1609. *Poems* (Oxford, 1955), pp. 3–4.

means of holding and consolidating feudal property and had made lineage and membership of a family of great importance. The great and lesser medieval families had been able to take their 'line' for granted; these later men could not, and so they emphasized it wherever they could. Their tombs, therefore, were not only monuments to a man but to the family which he was continuing or founding. This is seen clearly in the universal display of heraldry, often of doubtful authority, and the occasional erection of tombs to hitherto neglected ancestors. In 1606 Sir Gabriel Poyntz commemorated some of his in a series of monuments at North Ockendon, Essex (Pl. 78).[1] At Chester-le-Street Lord Lumley not only manufactured effigies for some of his forefathers but also appropriated the genuine effigies of other men's,[2] and so too did the Strangways at Melbury Sampford.[3] At Hughenden the Wellesbournes went farther and manufactured both the effigies and the ancestors.[4] More common, however, for the present was more important than the past, was the placing of accessory figures of his wife and children upon a man's monument. As a result the tombs of the age are characterized not only by their great size but also by their quality of family records.

The importance of this aspect was recognized and sanctioned by the State. In 1560 a Royal Proclamation was issued forbidding the destruction and defacing of tombs and monuments. It would be pleasant to think that this was done from an appreciation of their aesthetic value, or at least from a moral dislike of vandalism, but the royal unconcern at the artistically more disastrous destruction of innumerable statues and murals shows that such considerations had little part. What was felt to be at stake was the 'honorable and good memory of sundry vertuous and noble persons deceassed' and the preservation of the images of 'Kings, Princes, or noble estates of this Realme, or of any other that have been in times past set up, for the only memory of them to theyre posteritie in common

[1] R.C.H.M. *Essex*, iv. 100.

[2] J. G. Mann, 'Instances of Antiquarian Feeling in Medieval and Renaissance Art', *Arch. Journ.* lxxxix (1932), 254–74.

[3] L. Stone, *Sculpture in Britain in the Middle Ages* (1955), pp. 218, 268.

[4] E. J. Payne, 'The Montforts, the Wellesbournes and the Hughenden Effigies', *Records of Bucks.* vii (1897), 385–412.

Churches, and not for any religious honour'.[1] Tombs, in short, had a secular and family purpose and attacks on them were attacks on the 'virtuous and noble' ancestors of the present rulers and, in the long run, on the social fabric. It was a point on which Elizabeth felt strongly, so strongly that in 1573 she abandoned her natural parsimony and spent money on providing her Yorkist ancestors in Fotheringay Church with new tombs in place of their mutilated old ones.[2]

The concept of tombs as family properties was sufficiently strong by the mid-sixteenth century to over-ride government's desire for religious uniformity. There is a group of tombs in Sussex notable for their representation of religious scenes and subjects disliked by the reformers and extending in date over the whole period from the Dissolution to the accession of Elizabeth. At Old Selsey, on the tomb of John Lews (d. 1537) and his wife Agas, are scenes of St. George and the Dragon and of the martyrdom of St. Agatha. The monument (c. 1540) of Richard Sackville at West Hampnett has a representation of the Trinity with the naked Son reclining lifeless in the Father's arms; that of William Ernle (d. 1545) at West Wittering has an *Ecce Homo*, an Annunciation, and a Virgin and a Child. The brass of Richard Covert (d. 1547) at Slaugham has a Resurrection, and the very late monument of John Gounter (d. 1557) at Racton has the Risen Christ. Whatever government in London might want, and however much pressure there might be against open expression of the ways of thought of the old religion, these men did not intend to allow, and were sufficiently powerful locally to prevent, any interference with such personal or family effects as funeral monuments.[3]

This, however, was an attitude that in the long run worked far more against the artistic expression of the old religion than for it. The point has been made that Catholic as well as Protestant families played their part in the spoliation of the church. The fact calls for some explanation, and it is not sufficient to fall back on cynicism and assume that their cupidity got the better of their convictions.

[1] The Proclamation is printed by Weever, op. cit., pp. 52–54.
[2] P. M. G. Dickinson, *Historic Fotheringay* (Gloucester, 1946), p. 26.
[3] Cf. K. A. Esdaile, *English Monumental Sculpture since the Renaissance* (1927), p. 25.

Doubtless in some cases it did, but to suppose that all Catholics who enjoyed church lands did so with a bad conscience is to blink the facts and miss an important point. There were enough irreconcilables, and even martyrs, among land-grabbing Catholic families to demonstrate a sincere adherence to their beliefs. The Pagets of Beaudesert, Staffordshire, are a good example. William Paget, who served all of the last four Tudor sovereigns, obtained grants of church property from Edward VI and made extremely advantageous exchanges of it for lands belonging to the Bishop of Lichfield. His second son, Thomas, who inherited in 1569, later had to flee abroad because of his implication in a Catholic plot, and another son, Charles, was a professional Catholic agent. The devotion of these two to their religion was beyond dispute but Thomas, at least, was able to enjoy church lands without any qualms.[1]

Since their devotion allowed them to secularize church property, they were themselves imbued with many of the ideas of which the Protestants were the most extreme exponents. In other words, they were not medieval but Tudor Catholics. Whether they were good or bad ones is for Rome to decide; what matters to us is that, dogmas and observances apart, they shared much of the viewpoint of their Protestant contemporaries. In particular, they shared the view of funeral monuments as family records, and it is this that explains the curious failure of the Marian *revanche* to bring about any noticeable change—Gardiner's chantry at Winchester and the Fitzroy and Norfolk tombs at Framlingham are exceptions—in the character of these monuments. In fact, the practice of portraying a man's family upon his monument, prominent in later tombs, can be seen to begin even before the State's adoption of the Reformation and to develop uninterruptedly throughout the mid-century.

The tomb of William Rudhall (*c.* 1530) at Ross-on-Wye has kneeling parents and children together with angels and a scene of the Annunciation (Pl. 75*b*); that of Julian Nethermyll (d. 1539) in the destroyed Coventry Cathedral was similar, but with the Annunciation replaced by a crucifix. One of the latest of the Sussex

[1] S. Erdeswicke, *A Survey of Staffordshire* (1717), pp. 72–73; S. Shaw, *History and Antiquities of Staffordshire*, i (1798), 213–16.

tombs, that of John Gounter, has kneeling figures of his wife and children. It is not only the date of these that is significant but their combination of the family convention with at least some of the attitudes of the old religion. There was, of course, a religious sanction also to this praise of fruitfulness. It is well illustrated by the brass at Sherfield-on-Loddon, Hants, to Mary Palmes, who died in childbirth in 1595 at the age of 32 and after having borne ten children, with its revealing quotation from the first Epistle to Timothy—'Notwithstanding through bearinge of children she shalbe saved'.

As important as the presence of the family upon the tomb is the pose adopted by them. As early as the Rudhall tomb and almost universally in later years they are shown kneeling in prayer, a reminder that it was the prayers of the individual that moved Heaven and not the chanting of priests or lamentation of weepers. The contrast between the old and the new may be seen in the almost contemporary tombs of George Brooke, Lord Cobham, at Cobham (Pl. 77a) and of the second Duke of Norfolk at Framlingham. Brooke's tomb was erected in 1561[1] and Norfolk's perhaps a few years earlier; the former has kneeling children, the latter standing figures of the Apostles.

Thus by the accession of Elizabeth the function of monuments as family records was, at least among lesser men, well established. The vast architectural tomb, a more direct product of the secularization carried out by the Reformation, was only just appearing. Possibly one of the earliest and certainly one of the finest is that of Sir Robert Dormer (d. 1552) at Wing in Buckinghamshire; a very pure piece of classicism with columns carrying a tester and with finely carved details of bucrania and swags (Pls. 76a, 79a).[2]

[1] R. H. D'Elboux, 'The Brooke Tomb, Cobham', *Archaeologia Cantiana*, lxii (1949), 48–56.

[2] The Dormer tomb is generally said to have been erected in 1552 because that date is on a label on the sarcophagus. However, Dormer died in that year and it is possible that nothing more than an allusion to the date of his death is intended. On the wall at the back of the monument are two brass inscription plates, side by side and symmetrically arranged. One refers wholly to Dormer himself; the other refers to his wife and descendants and shows knowledge of an event that did not occur until 1567. It might be supposed that part of this second inscription was cut later, a common enough practice. It has, however, an odd feature that makes this impossible. It begins

It is, however, quite out of the ordinary run. There is in Buckinghamshire and Bedfordshire a series of tombs—of Lord Mordaunt (d. 1562) at Turvey, of Alexander Denton (d. 1576) at Hillesden, and of Anthony Cave (d. 1576) at Chicheley—of a quite advanced classicism. They have fluted Doric columns, or pilasters, and entablatures with triglyphs and guttae and with palmettes in the metopes. The architectural features generally frame a sarcophagus and effigy in a recess, and there is a sparing use of such Anglo-Flemish motifs as strapwork and jewel ornament. The caryatides on the Mordaunt tomb are well-proportioned, and even those on Cave's tomb, which are not, have an air of elegance. Similar in their restraint are the tombs of Richard Covert (d. 1579) at Slaugham in Sussex, of Sir Ambrose Cave (d. 1568) at Stanford-on-Avon and of Thomas Wylmer (d. 1580) at Staverton in Northamptonshire (Pl. 76b).

Wholly different in detail but yet similar again in form are the tombs of John and Richard Harford at Bosbury, by John Guldo, or Guldon,[1] a craftsman from the county town of Hereford. The sarcophagi of these have been compared with Italian examples,[2] but there is little other Italian quality in his work, with its medley of detail covering every free space, and varying from crude foliage and tendril decoration to mild attempts at acanthus leaf and egg-and-dart moulding. His sculpture is as poor as his ornament and the figures flanking the recess of Richard Harford's tomb are bad by any standards, ill-modelled and ill-proportioned (Pl. 79b).

with the genealogy of Lady Dormer, goes on to make a reference to the event of 1567, and ends with the death of Lady Dormer in 1541. It is clear that the inscription is a whole and that therefore all of it must have been cut after 1567. But if the tomb was erected in 1552 one of two equally difficult conclusions must follow: either the family waited fifteen years—for events of which they could have no foreknowledge to occur —before doing Lady Dormer, who was already dead in 1552, the courtesy of a mention upon her husband's tomb; or else, and this is something much more unusual than an addition to an inscription, they replaced the original plate with the present one. In style the monument stands alone and fits 1552 or 1567 equally ill; in conception it is closer to the later than the earlier date. (See W. J. Hemp, 'The Dormer Tombs at Wing', *Trans. Mon. Brass Soc.* vi (1910–14), 59–74.)

[1] The tomb of John Harford is signed by Guldon, and it would be misplaced charity to attempt to absolve him of Richard's.

[2] At Pisa, Modena, and Ferrara. See K. A. Esdaile, *English Church Monuments 1510–1840* (1946), p. 13, n. 1.

Again different in detail but yet similar in their character of architectural pieces are the monuments of Sir Richard Lister, erected in 1567, at St. Michael's, Southampton, of Sir John Newton (d. 1560) at East Harptree, Somerset, and of Sybil Penn (d. 1562) at Hampton, Middlesex. On these there is an effigy upon an altar-tomb set against the wall or in a recess and provided with classical columns carrying an entablature on three sides. The detail varies considerably; the side of the Lister tomb, for example, is orna-mented with quatrefoils in a late fifteenth-century manner. Similar in its form, although it has a sarcophagus and not an effigy, is that of John Caius at Gonville and Caius College, Cambridge, begun in 1573 and completed in 1575, and almost certainly carved by Theodore Haveus of Cleves.[1] In its detail it is notable for its very early lavish use of Flemish motifs, but this must not be allowed to obscure the quite 'native' nature of its form.

Another architectural show-piece, in this case with no details that imply a Continental as distinct from a general classicizing influence, is the 'tester' tomb of John Leweston (d. 1584) at Sher-borne Abbey. Six fluted Corinthian columns, rising from the ledger with its effigies, carry an arcade, with an entablature above, on which are stumpy allegorical figures. It is not free-standing but projects lengthwise from the wall face and is, in this, intermediate between the wall-monument and the later free-standing 'tester' tombs (Pl. 80).[2] Such tombs as those of Sir Gawin and Sir Peter Carew erected in 1589,[3] and of Sir John and Lady Gilbert, both in Exeter Cathedral, are local variants of the same general conception.

In their motifs and in their choice of a ledger or of a sarcophagus all of these differ widely from one another; they have, however, a common purpose: they are all intended to be imposing monu-mental constructions reflecting the worth of the man or the family

[1] R.C.H.M. *City of Cambridge*, pp. 74a, 76a.
[2] It should be mentioned that Mr. Girouard has attempted to link this tomb, and the Gardiner Chantry at Winchester, with Allen Maynard, a French carver who appears in the Longleat Accounts (*C.L.* cxx (Sept. 1956), 594-7).
[3] Rev. Preb. Granville, 'The Carew Monuments in Exeter Cathedral', *Exeter Diocesan Architectural Soc. Trans.* 3rd ser. iii (1915-20), 35-37.

that had them erected. Their style is of minor importance and indeed, as the wide variety of style shows, almost of chance determination. It is because of this that the search for foreign 'sources' of design is a sterile proceeding, and there is little point in debating from what obscure tomb in what far-away Italian town the Bosbury sarcophagi may derive. It is more pertinent to notice that the sarcophagus as a form almost completely vanished in the next few years and the altar became almost universal. This, however, was a traditional English form, and it is indeed possible to show that the wall-tomb and the 'tester' tomb are, in essence, adaptations to a new purpose of two very common tomb-types of the late Middle Ages.

The wall-tomb, with or without a recess, is in the direct descent from the late medieval Purbeck marble tomb in which an altar, with or without an effigy, is placed against a wall-recess, with a brass inscription plate or figured scene. The West Sussex examples referred to earlier have a brass or carving in low relief and are mostly of this type. It is not accidental that some of the later ones, e.g. the Dormer and Wylmer tombs, retain the brass inscription plate, and those of Sir Hugh and Sir Amyas Poulett at Hinton St. George, Somerset, which were probably erected about 1550, are more elaborate and imposing versions of this type (Pl. 84a). The Frowyck tombs at South Mimms, probably of c. 1540, and that of Sir John Horsey and his son (d. 1546, 1564–5) in Sherborne Abbey, are in the same vein but given a canopy and dressed up in early Renaissance detail. The huge structures of the 1560's and 1570's are merely larger versions of these, achieving their effect by the use of tall and stately classical columns or caryatides and using a more up-to-date set of motifs.

The 'tester' tomb, often favoured by the very great in later years, is in form an open chantry with the low walls that sheltered a priest but tended to hide the effigy cut away to show the dead man. There is at least one instance of an intermediate stage between the chantry and the 'tester', the monument of John, Lord Marney at Layer Marney, Essex. This is a 'tester' tomb contrived between two piers of an arcade but provided at one end with a curious slab-like projection. Marney's will of 1525 shows that this was intended as an altar at which a priest should say masses for his soul.[1] The Reformation, with its abhorrence of masses and altars, considerably hastened a development that this tomb foreshadows.

With this twofold development in mind it is clear that the presence of Pisan or other motifs in a Herefordshire village is not of much significance in itself. It is, however, a symptom of the chaos in applied ornament upon the tombs of the time, and the conjunction of this with the homogeneity in form and intention of monumental sculpture was later to give the Southwark School the opportunity to achieve a near monopoly with their standardized products.

The greater monuments of the third quarter of the century, with the exception of one or two of the later ones, do not include figures of the dead man's family. These are found at first upon the simple and unarchitectural altar-tombs, a form that became less and less common but never wholly disappeared throughout the period. It is best represented by the works of the Midland alabasterers, craftsmen who, although they had migrated from Nottingham to Burton-on-Trent, had a centuries-old tradition behind them. Until about the end of the 1560's they were often turning out competent effigies, well-proportioned and carved with considerable skill and realism, upon well-designed and often delicately ornamented altar-tombs. One of these craftsmen, Richard Parker, is known to have made the tomb of the first Earl of Rutland at Bottesford, Leicestershire, in 1543–4, and to have received £20 for it (Pl. 81b).[2] Its character is typical of the best of the school in the mid-century; simple in conception, competent in execution, with some, but not over-much, rather out-of-date *quattrocento* ornament and with an occasional charming touch, such as Sir Thomas Bromley's daughter holding a flower, at Wroxeter (Pl. 81a), and the animals upon the base of Sir John Vernon's tomb at Clifton Campville in Staffordshire.[3] Of the same type, although differing

[1] F. C. Eeles, 'The Black Effigies at Layer Marney Re-examined', *Essex Archaeological Soc. Trans.* N.S. xxii (1940), 272–5.    [2] H.M.C. *Rutland*, iv. 340–1.

[3] The best accounts of the Burton School in the sixteenth century are by Sir James Mann, 'English Church Monuments 1536–1625', *Wal. Soc.* xxi (1932–3), 1–22, and P. Chatwin, 'Monumental Effigies of the County of Warwick' Part III, *Birmingham Archaeological Soc. Trans.* xlviii (1922), 136–68.

in details and execution, are those of Sir Richard Cholmondeley (d. 1544) in St. Peter ad Vincula in the Tower, of Thomas, Lord Wharton (d. 1568) at Kirkby Stephen, and of Sir Robert Tyrwhitt (d. 1578) at Leighton Bromswold.

Not all of these altar-tombs have children upon them, but it is upon them that figures of children first appear. The very early Rudhall and Nethermyll tombs have already been mentioned; the Rutland tomb has standing figures around the side whose difference in dress suggests that the children of the dead man and not medieval 'weepers' are intended. The sons of the second Earl of Huntingdon (d. 1561) upon their father's monument are identified by labels with their christian names, a trick repeated very much later on the tombs of Sir Anthony Poulett at Hinton St. George and Francis Small-wood at Kinnersley in Herefordshire. On all of these, however, the figures are in relief and generally have the standing pose of weepers. One of the earliest monuments of men of higher social standing than Rudhall or Nethermyll on which at least one of the children is kneeling is the Cave tomb of 1568 at Stanford-on-Avon; on the Brooke tomb at Cobham all of them are kneeling, and are side-ways to the spectator, a pose that was to be common in later years. The pose itself was nothing new; what was new was its appearance on the monuments of men of a higher social standing and pre-sumably, if not in imitation of those of lowlier men, then as a result of ideas and feelings spreading from lower to higher social groups.

Such figures upon the sides of altar-tombs were well enough there, where the eye is kept at a low level, but could not be so effective upon massive architectural monuments towering up almost to the roof. Here the problem of effectively representing the dead man's descendants was less tractable. Some of the first attempts at solving the problem were essentially adaptations of the older methods. On Anthony Cave's tomb at Chicheley and on that of Richard Covert at Slaugham the children are shown in relief at eye-level on the wall at the back, in the manner of the recessed Sackville and Ernle monuments of the 1540's. On the Wylmer tomb, where they are represented on a brass inset, the attempt at adapting an older method to a new situation is even clearer. Other attempts at a solution of the problem can be seen in the very similar tombs of the second Earl of Rutland (d. 1563) at Bottesford and of Sir Thomas St. Pol. (d. 1582) at Snarford in Lincolnshire. These take the form of a buffet with the effigies of the parents upon a slab at ground level and figures of the children upon a table-top above them. The Burton craftsmen too, while still clinging to the altar-tomb, made some attempts at solving the problem by putting small figures of the children in relief upon a slab set into the wall above their parents' tomb. Examples of this are the monuments of Humphrey Peyto (d. 1585) at Chesterton, Warwicks., of William Clopton (d. 1592) at Stratford-upon-Avon, and of Thomas Blount and his wife in St. Mary's, Kidderminster.[1]

There had, however, been an early portent of the ultimate solution in the mid-century Poulett tombs. On these, diminutive kneeling figures, wholly free-standing, are placed upon the top of the ledger in a conspicuous position (Pl. 84a). The Poulett tombs, although imposing, were small affairs compared with later ones, and such small figures were not greatly out of place upon them. For larger monuments, however, they were too small to be effective, and only after some time and several experiments was it realized how well they had solved the problem of position, and that an increase in their size solved the problem of proportions. This double problem is solved on the tomb of Sir Anthony Cooke (d. 1576) at Romford, Essex, where the children are life-size kneeling figures, wholly free-standing, placed upon the top of the ledger. The principals too are kneeling, again in the manner of brasses, for the life-size of the children allowed the parents to be shown as life-size kneeling rather than recumbent figures without any ridiculous discrepancy arising between their proportions and those of their children (Pl. 84b).

That a solution to a common problem had been found is shown by its endless repetition in the next sixty years. It is shown too by the disappearance of the sarcophagus that had been frequently used

[1] The exact date of the Blount tomb is uncertain. Blount died in 1568 and his wife in 1595 (A. J. Perrett in *Worcs. Archaeological Soc. Trans.* n.s. xix (1942), 10–13). The children's figures are flanked by the degenerate Renaissance ornament of the late Burton school and are probably of the 1590's.

in the third quarter of the century. A sarcophagus is a whole in itself; to place children or anything else upon its sides or its top is to destroy the conception of it at once; but an altar-tomb is essentially nothing but a rectangular box, not an artistic whole, and can have many forms and figures placed upon it without any incongruity. Its very lack of character allows it to be used as the base for more important things. The disappearance of the sarcophagus illustrates something else as well. By about 1580 English craftsmen had developed a type of monument, derived from native sources, that met their patrons' needs by combining magnificence with a display of family pride. Imported motifs could vary from tomb to tomb and jostle native ones everywhere; imported forms from Pisa or anywhere else could obtain for a time a certain popularity, but in the end it was the English form, answering the needs of English patrons, that established itself to the exclusion of all others. Taste in decorative motifs might range and vary; forms, expressive of deeper currents in English society, were more intimately related to that society and in consequence more stable. Just how stable they were is shown by the kneeling figures so common upon monuments throughout the period. Until very late, and even then with only a few exceptions, they are sideways to the spectator. This convention developed from the mid-sixteenth century brasses whereon the popular composition of husband and wife kneeling at either side of a prayer-desk with the sons and daughters behind them was almost necessarily expressed by a sideways portrayal of the figures. But long after these compositions had been translated into stone and long after brasses ceased to be common, the kneeling figures in any composition remained the same. On the Countess of Derby's very late tomb at Harefield, Middlesex, where the figures are placed each in its own niche, in a late medieval manner, they are, unlike late-medieval weepers, still placed sideways.

By about 1580 the period of experiment was over, the main problem of the tomb-designers had been solved, and the moment was opportune for an exploitation of that solution which would satisfy the potential mass-market. It was this situation that provided the opportunity for the foreign carvers of the late Southwark

School. These men had been preceded by what may be called, although there is no documentary evidence for any of the works associated with it, the early Southwark School. It is possible that William Cure, the elder, who came over from Holland in 1541 to work at Nonsuch, was one of its leading figures, and he is almost certainly the 'Cure' who was paid £4 in 1573 for drawing 'the ground playtes and uprights' for a projected tomb for Henry VIII.[1] Works that may be assigned to this school are the altar-tomb of Lord Williams (d. 1559) and his wife at Thame, the altar-tombs, with identical decoration, of Sir Philip and Sir Thomas Hoby at Bisham (Pl. 83b), and of the Duchess of Suffolk, erected in 1563, in Westminster Abbey. The tomb of Sir Thomas Gresham (d. 1579) in St. Helen's, Bishopsgate, is either by the same school or by a sculptor closely related to it (Pl. 82). The effigies are not remarkable or noticeably better than those of Richard Parker and his fellows, but the carving of detail is more precise and delicate, and the motifs are extraordinarily restrained and dignified: a finely cut achievement-of-arms with under-cut mantling, delicately fluted columns, a frieze of fluting above acanthus leaf, enriched pilasters with trophies and armour, and an occasional piece of thin strapwork. In their style and workmanship and in their avoidance of the grandiose family monument these carvers were quite out of touch with contemporary native or provincially patronised work, and it is clear that they appealed only to a small circle.

At the beginning of the last quarter of the century a new trend appeared in their work, revealed at first by a use of coloured marbles and of coarser motifs. The tomb at Ingatestone of Sir William Petrie (d. 1572) and his wife is an early and timid example, an altar-tomb with the sides divided by Tuscan columns flanking shell-niches and with Flemish jewel ornament in the spandrels. A few years later, that of Margaret, Countess of Lennox, in Westminster Abbey was a bolder experiment; with its coloured marbles, obelisks, and bevelled and gadrooned edge to the table top it has many of the details of the later Southwark School (Pl. 77b).

The use of coloured marbles is a good example of the Southwark trick of elaborating and exaggerating native practices. The colouring

[1] H.S.L. Proc. vii (1901–4), 69; P.R.O. E. 351–3209.

of monuments was, of course, a very old habit, though in the mid-sixteenth century a group of monuments, including the Dormer tomb at Wing and the tombs of Lord Williams and Sir Thomas Gresham, show a very restrained use of colour, and rely for their effect upon the artistry of their design and the skill of their carving. In later years—and the later Southwark School played their part in this—large sums were spent upon the painting and gilding of monuments. James Mauncy received £265 for the work he did upon Mary Queen of Scots' tomb. Such a sum was as exceptional as the cost of the tomb itself,[1] but considerable amounts were often spent and in 1592 John Matthew of Nottingham was paid £20 for 'enriching' the two Rutland tombs at Bottesford.[2]

The Lennox tomb marks another step towards the native conception, for at its sides are kneeling figures of the Countess's sons. By 1591 the Southwark marblers had completely succumbed to or closed with the native demand for massive architectural tombs with family figures upon them. In that year Garret Johnson received the final instalment of a sum of £200 for making the tombs of the third and fourth Earls of Rutland in Bottesford Church.[3] That of the fourth Earl is typical of much that was produced in the next forty to fifty years: the alabaster effigies upon an altar-tomb with bevelled and gadrooned edge, the Corinthian columns carrying a rich entablature and surmounted by shields-of-arms, the arcading of the wall face supported on pilasters or coarse brackets, and the children kneeling at the sides of and upon the ledger (Pl. 83a). The bulk of later Southwark work is little more than a repetition and variation of the design, the motifs, and the tricks of the Rutland tombs.

By the end of the century the Southwark men had completely taken over the native form of tomb. They then proceeded to use their superior technical skill and greater acquaintance with Continental motifs to exploit the market they had moved into in a number of ways. They took the 'colossal' architectural character of

[1] The tomb was made by Cornelius Cure, son of William and father of another William, at a cost, excluding the painting, of £825. 10s. Mauncy's bill was for painting and gilding, *Pell Records, James I* (ed. F. Devon, 1836), pp. 168–9, 190.

[2] H.M.C. *Rutland*, iv. 404.                          [3] Ibid. iv. 397.

monuments to new heights, or depths. The vast tomb of Sir Christopher Hatton in Old St. Paul's was criticized even by contemporaries as megalomaniac;[1] that of the Earl of Hertford in Salisbury Cathedral, rising from floor to aisle roof, and those of Queen Elizabeth and Mary Queen of Scots in Westminster Abbey are gigantic edifices. They also applied to the native form of tomb a more knowledgeable range of motifs, a more modish use of architectural detail and a greater number of the fashionable emblematic figures. They were able to carve, in a manner that outclassed the native craftsmen, the figures of parents, children, and 'virtues' that the social and intellectual ideas of the time demanded. Further, they set out to capture a broad market by producing an architectural tomb complete with columns, arched recesses, kneeling figures, virtues and obelisks on a scale small enough to be set upon a wall-bracket. Since their work was deliberate shopwork with a competence but with no fineness of execution and design, the cost of it varied directly with the amount of labour and materials involved and prices could be scaled down, by a scaling-down in size, to suit almost any pocket with anything in it at all.

Because their work was shopwork it was not difficult to imitate and before long competent and not so competent copies of it were common. The tomb of Sir John Jefferey at Whitchurch Canonicorum in Dorset is a clear country craftsman's copy of a standard Southwark product (Pl. 85). The names of several such imitative sculptors have been preserved. The tomb of Francis Whitstones in Barnack Church, which is signed 'Tomas Greenway of Derby 1611', is an example of this copying; that of Thomas Seckford in Trinity College chapel, Cambridge, carved by a certain Edward Woodrofe,[2] is another. The West Country sculptor, Samuel Baldwin of Stroud, has his own characteristics but his work, for example the tomb of Joan Young (d. 1603) in Bristol Cathedral, is in the main an echo of the Southwark style.[3] The work of the 'East Anglian School', exemplified in such a monument as that of Grizel Barnardiston at Kedington, Suffolk, is merely a local version

[1] Brooks, *Sir Christopher Hatton*, p. 354.    [2] R.C.H.M. *City of Cambridge*, p. 220.
[3] For certain and possible works by Baldwin see I. M. Roper, *Monumental Effigies of Gloucestershire and Bristol* (Gloucester, 1931).

of this same style. So widespread was the taste for it that it was possible for a foreign sculptor, Joseph Hollemans, to settle at the end of the century in Burton-on-Trent itself and work for such important families as the Spencers.[1]

This was brought about not only by positive but by negative factors; the Southwark men were able to spread their style so rapidly partly because there was no competition from any native school. The fall in the demand for sculpture that followed the Reformation was intensified by the new taste for tombs that, as architectural compositions, were more the affair of the mason than of the sculptor. There is, indeed, some evidence to suggest that by the end of the third quarter of the century English sculptors were a dying race. At that time, at least, the Marblers of London were petitioning for absorption into the Masons' Company.[2] The West Sussex school, which had survived the Protestant triumph under Edward VI, finally disappeared during the Catholic revival under Mary. The only native tomb-maker of the early years of Elizabeth of whose work anything is at present known was John Guldon; and he appears to have been primarily a mason. In the Hereford City records he is referred to in 1577 as a 'freemason', in 1580 as 'freemason and joiner', in 1583 as 'joiner and freemason', and only once, in 1582, as 'freemason, joiner and carver'.[3] Anthony Tolly, who signed the tomb of Bishop Freake in Worcester Cathedral in 1591, was described in the inventory of his goods taken in 1593–4 as a 'joiner'.[4] Walter Hancock, best known as the builder of Condover, was also a tomb-maker. He was described at his death as 'a very skilful man in the art of masonry, in setting of plottes for buildinges and performing the same, ingraininge in alabaster in other stone or playster' and was said to have been responsible for 'most sumptuous buildings, most stately tombes, most curyous

---

[1] For certain and possible work by Hollemans see K. A. Esdaile, 'The Interaction of English and Low Country Sculpture in the 16th century', *Journ. W.C.I.* vi (1943), 80–88. Since Esdaile gives the reference wrongly it should be said that the documentary evidence for Hollemans is in H.M.C. *4th Report*, Appendix, p. 367.

[2] K. A. Esdaile in *Yorks. Archaeological Journ.* xxxv (1943), 365.

[3] *Woolhope Club Trans.* xxx (1939–41), 58–59.

[4] A. Macdonald, 'Anthony Tolly and the Tomb of Edmund Freake', *Worcs. Archaeological Soc. Trans.* N.S. xix (1942), 1–9.

pictures'.[1] Here again we seem to have a man who was primarily a mason turning his hand to monumental sculpture.

Only the Burton alabasterers survived, and they did nothing more than survive. The decline in their craftsmanship and artistic sensibility is seen in the contrast between the work of Richard Parker and his contemporaries and that of the family of Royley, alias Cartwright. Documented works by Richard Royley and his son Gabriel are the tombs of Thomas Fermor (d. 1580) at Somerton, Oxfordshire (Pl. 89a), and of John Shirley (erected in 1585) at Breedon-on-the-Hill, Leicestershire.[2] Not all of the earlier Burton work had been of a high standard; it is the hallmark of the later work that it is of a very low one. Sir James Mann has adequately described it: 'The effigies are distinguished by receding chins and globular eye-balls, sure signs of an in-bred stock' and 'the elbows are bent stiffly and the legs are long and weak-kneed'.[3] The attendant figures and the carvings upon the sides of the tombs are stiff, featureless and ill-proportioned, without any of the charm of the earlier Bromley and Cave monuments. The motifs are mainly an ignorant and progressively lamer miscopying of those of the early Renaissance, wherein the vases and candelabra turn eventually into what look like dice-boxes.[4]

Poverty of execution is not the only characteristic of the school; it is also remarkable for its long-continued concentration upon the old-fashioned altar-tomb. The combination of these two deficiencies reveals the causes of the decline of this school and the demise of the others. Men trained in the old traditions were unable—despite their employment of profuse and significantly misunderstood Renaissance motifs—to adapt themselves in a short space of time to the new demands for architectural composition and sculpture in the round. They found themselves, therefore, deserted by

[1] 'Extracts from the Parish Registers of Much Wenlock', *Shropshire Archaeological Soc. Trans.* xi (1888), 15.

[2] The contracts for these tombs have been published by E. P. Shirley: 'Extracts from the Fermor Accounts', *Arch. Journ.* viii (1851), 185–6; *Stemmata Shirleiana* (1841), pp. 76–77.

[3] 'English Church Monuments 1536–1625', *Wal. Soc.* xxi (1932–3), 9.

[4] The miscopying of Renaissance motifs by these later Burton men is well illustrated by P. Chatwin in *Birmingham Archaeological Soc. Trans.* xlviii (1932), 138–40.

all patrons, or patronized only by those content with the old style and ready to pay only the old prices. While Garret Johnson was paid £200 for two tombs at Bottesford in 1591 and Richard Stevens nearly £300 for the triple tomb of the Earls of Sussex in Boreham Church in 1587–8,[1] the Royleys received a mere £40 for the Fermor and £22 for the Shirley tomb. Such patrons were likely to be both undiscriminating and unable or unwilling to pay for good work. They therefore neither would nor could demand works of artistic merit, and in consequence not only did the style of the school stagnate, but the quality of its craftsmanship deteriorated. And so, in failing to compete with the new style, the Burton alabasterers became less and less able to compete at all.

The Southwark marblers, therefore, both in their own work and in the work which their competition was elsewhere forcing into being, were able to give to the tombs of the period, already uniform in conception, a corresponding uniformity of sculptural and decorative style. These imposing monuments were often adorned with a ribbon motif upon the wall face or in the spandrels of the arcades, with coffering to the soffits, with various emblems of more or less obscurity, with obelisks, and later, figures of the Virtues upon the cornice, and with as many brightly painted shields-of-arms as the pedigree-mongers could warrant and space would allow. Various coloured marbles, or painted freestone, and the painting in correct detail of costumes, added to their conspicuousness and magnificence. The sculpture was as mass-produced as the design and decoration. Except in rare cases, it attempts nothing but a competent realism of surface detail and a reasonable representation of the proportions of the human body. In general the figures, apart from the Virtues, are stiff and rigid and confined to one or two stock poses.

To insist, however, upon nothing but the uniformity of these productions is to miss much of that uniformity's significance. Social needs in combination with an individualist philosophy created the typical Elizabethan and Jacobean tomb. Society, however, had many levels and individualism many facets, and while

[1] Vertue Notebooks, *Wal. Soc.* xxiv (1935–6), 143.

the rule of a particular class ensured the dominance of particular traits in the ideology of the time, it did not prevent the existence of others. These too found expression upon tombs, and although such tombs were not common before 1625, they are important as the forerunners of those that were to supersede the older type.

Just as many of the landed classes expressed in their tombs their pride of position, so merchants and tradesmen, emphasizing another aspect of the ideology of the time, expressed their conviction that they had done what they could to obtain salvation by labouring in their calling. This attitude was prevalent among sections of the gentry as well and was indeed heavily stressed in Brathwait's *English Gentleman*, whose title and argument appear to be intended as a non-courtier counterblast against, or at least a corrective of, Peacham's *Compleat Gentleman*.[1] At first it reveals itself mostly in the inscriptions, where it had appeared occasionally in earlier years. The brass of Robert Beauver, a monk of St. Albans (*c.* 1460), meticulously records his 46-year-long service in the offices of third prior, kitchener, refectorer, infirmarer, sub-refectorer, and spicerar. Later inscriptions, however, tell of more secular activity. Not far from Beauver's brass at St. Albans is that of Ralph Rowlatt, erected some time before his death in 1543 and recording his membership of the Staple at Calais. The memorial tablet to Edward Wilkinson (d. 1567–8) at St. Luke's, Charlton, Kent, mentions nothing more about him than that he had been Master-Cook to Queen Elizabeth. The concept of immortalizing a calling could however be extended to the monumental recording of an exploit, and the inscription to Sir John Pelham (d. 1557) at St. Michael's, Lewes, records his defeat of a French raid on Seaford. By the reign of Charles I this function of a tomb had become sufficiently important for Weever to open his book, *Ancient Funeral Monuments*, with a definition of them as things 'erected, made, or written, for a memoriall of some remarkable action, fit to be transferred to future posterities'.[2]

It was not long, however, before the need to emphasize the deceased's occupation or achievements led to scenic representation. Where Edward Wilkinson had been content with an inscription,

---

[1] Richard Brathwait, *The English Gentleman* (1630), ch. 5.
[2] Weever, *Ancient Funeral Monuments* (1631), p. 1.

Blanche Parry, at Bacton in Herefordshire about forty years later, had herself portrayed kneeling before the Queen in the performance of her duties as a maid of honour. At about the same time Sir John Farnham, at Quorn, was shown standing in soldier's dress before a detailed scene of the siege of a city; and Sir Michael Dormer (d. 1616), at Great Milton, Oxfordshire, referred to his military career in a similar way. Civilians too could have their occupation or achievements scenically rendered. The tomb of Thomas Sutton, in the chapel of the Charterhouse that he re-founded, has a large bas-relief of the brethren attending chapel. At Merton College, Oxford, the monument to Sir Henry Savile, Warden of the College and Provost of Eton, has painted views of Merton and Eton Colleges and, in reference to his endowment of the Chairs of Geometry and Astronomy, figures of Euclid and Ptolemy and of two men taking the altitudes of the stars (Pl. 88). A former organist of Exeter Cathedral, Mathew Godwin (d. 1586–7), has a monument there showing him before his organ with music books and instruments beside him, and reference has already been made to the tomb at Ightham of Dorothy Selby, reproducing two of her proudest pieces of embroidery. So important, in fact, might a man's profession be to his memory that the man himself might seem to matter little, and at St. Mary's, Rotherhithe, the tomb of Captain Anthony Wood, who died in 1625, dispenses altogether with effigy or bust in order to show nothing but the Captain's ship.

Before long other matters were the subject of scenes: the burial of Sir James Hales (d. 1589) at sea, Jane Fitzalan's children at prayer in a private chapel, Jane Best (d. 1622) at prayer in a church,[1] and Sir Thomas Lucy (d. 1640) reclining in armour among his books and riding on horseback before a house and landscape probably meant for Charlecote Park. These last three are particular manifestations of a general desire to portray the dead as in life. Its commonest expression is the reclining effigy, half-turned to the side and leaning on one hand 'as though'—for who can resist requoting Webster?—'they died o' the toothache'. This pose was

---

[1] The Hales Monument is in Canterbury Cathedral; the Fitzalan at Cheam, Surrey; the Best at Lugwardine, Herefordshire.

probably borrowed, as Mr. Lees-Milne suggests,[1] from Etruscan and Roman sarcophagi, with their scenes of the dead reclining on a couch at a banquet in the Elysian Fields. In the earliest known example, on the Hoby tomb at Bisham (Pl. 83*b*), its origin and allusion may well have been understood; in later ones it probably was not, for more exalted persons than craftsmen could copy a motif without understanding it. The important consideration was to show the dead man in a way that, with its air of leisured ease, expressed, as Weever said, 'of what ranke hee was living'. The Mompesson monument (*c.* 1633) at Lydiard Tregoze, which has been aptly called a 'seated conversation-piece', is the clearest example of this aim.

In the history of sculpture too much must not be made of these scenes, for they are nearly all incised slabs or brasses or in low relief. They are of importance not so much in themselves as in their role of re-establishing scenic representation as acceptable on a tomb. More immediately important and equally significant of the individualism of the age was the attempt to represent the deceased not merely as a member of a social class but as a man with his own peculiar physical traits. It is possible, because of their individual features, that some of the effigies by the early Burton alabasterers are intended as true 'likenesses', and it is clear that those by the Royleys are not. Most of the later effigies seem to be personal portrayals, but it is difficult to find any very early documentary evidence of a sculptor's contracting to carve an individual portrait, and one must not infer back from what is known of the later period. On the tomb of Sir Robert Watter (d. 1612) and his wife that was erected in St. Crux Church at York the inscription reads 'Here lie the true portraiture of Robert Watter, . . . and of his wife Margaret'. The agreement for the monument of Sir Richard Scott, who died in 1638, called for the effigy to be 'as near as may be, according to the direction, to be like his favor, simily and likeness'.[2] It is clear that attempts at portraiture were common;[3] it is equally clear, as the qualification in this late contract shows, that there were many difficulties in the way.

---

[1] *Tudor Renaissance* (1951), p. 36.    [2] J. Hunter, *Hallamshire* (1869), p. 438.
[3] In a letter to Sir Dudley Carleton (19 Jan. 1622) John Chamberlain tells how

Efforts have been made to prove the demand or absence of demand for likenesses from the wording of contracts, but very few are as specific as that just cited. Mostly they use expressions which cannot be certainly translated into modern terms. The Shirley contract of 1585, for example, calls for 'the picture or portraiture of a gentleman representing the said John Shirley'. Although it has been argued that this proves that no likeness was intended I think that, if the monument were not still in existence, I could equally well argue it the other way. The contract of 1600 by Bartholomew Atye and Isaac James refers only to 'two lieng pictures',[1] but all the same, likenesses may have been intended. James's and Stone's contract of 1615 for the Earl of Northampton's tomb has been cited as definite evidence of the demand for a likeness because it calls for the 'picture or similitude' of Northampton.[2] But it also calls, in a context where there can be no question of an individual portrait, for the 'similitude of a little boy holding an escucheoun'. It is clear that the meaning of all these agreements depended not so much on semantics as on what was in the parties' minds; and in general the evidence for likenesses must be got from the monuments themselves and not from the contracts relating to them.

The clearest indication of a desire for individual portrayal is the increasing fondness for bust memorials—rare in the late sixteenth century and becoming commoner as the seventeenth advances—wherein all the interest is concentrated on the subject's personal features. They are, of course, a cheap form of monument and especially suitable to men of limited wealth and with no descendants, and it is this that explains their frequency in the chapels of the Oxford colleges, then peopled, apart from the head of the house, by unmarried fellows;[3] but cheapness is not the whole answer, for

Nicholas Hare's executor 'requested me two days since to intreat your Lordship for a copy of the picture you have of Master Hare, and that it may be drawn by Michaell Jansen or some other good hand, for that he means to make some monument wherein he shall have use of it', *Letters*, ed. N. E. McClure (Philadelphia, 1939), ii. 422.

[1] R. C. Fowler, 'The Denny Monument in Waltham Abbey Church', *Essex Archaeological Soc. Trans.* n.s. xvi (1923), 57–59.

[2] K. A. Esdaile, 'Three Monumental Drawings from Sir Edward Deering's Collection', *Archaeologia Cantiana*, xlvii (1935), 222–4.

[3] Mr. Howard Colvin has suggested to me, however, that in part this may be an

there are tombs of considerable size that dispense with an effigy and concentrate interest upon a bust. Those of the Duchess of Suffolk at Spilsby and of Provost Murray at Eton are examples, and in both cases the standard of carving of the bust, whether good or bad, is well above that of the rest of the monument. On Nicholas Stone's monument of Sir Robert Drury in Hawstead Church, made in 1617 at a cost of £140,[1] the effigy is replaced by a sarcophagus, but in an attic above the arcading is a free-standing bust of Drury. The tomb of John Bingham (d. 1625) in Southwark Cathedral is a comparatively large two-stage structure, with an inscription tablet in base and a half-length of Bingham in the upper stage (Pl. 86a). By 1633, when Stone executed the monument to Sir Thomas and Lady Merry at St. Mary, Walthamstow, not only were the effigies of the principals displaced by busts but the kneeling figures of the children as well.

In some cases where the conventional kneeling figures of the principals are retained they are turned full-face to the spectator, an attempt to keep the devotional posture and yet have the advantages of the bust. This may be seen on the double-tomb of the Walrond brothers (c. 1615) at Aldbourne in Wiltshire and on the far more sophisticated monument of Sir Francis Egioke (d. 1622), at St. Margaret's, Westminster. On the tomb of Thomas Goddard, also at Aldbourne, not only the deceased but his wife and four children are kneeling and turned full-face towards the spectator. This manner, however, failed to develop very far, for it had to fight the established tradition of the sideways pose.

Each in its own way, the practice of representing a man's occupation or achievements and that of emphasizing his individual features both played their part in bringing about the disappearance of the typical Elizabethan and Jacobean tomb: the one by imparting

ecclesiastical convention of which the late-medieval priest at Tong, preaching or reading from a prayer-book, is an example; and that in the late sixteenth and early seventeenth centuries the intention may sometimes have been to portray clergymen officiating as ministers, and laymen, with equal propriety, as members of the congregation at prayers.

[1] The dates and authorship of the works of Nicholas Stone referred to here and later will all be found in W. L. Spiers, 'The Note-Book and Account-Book of Nicholas Stone', *Wal. Soc.* vii (1918–19); see also *O.H.E.A.* viii (1957), 104–15.

to it a pictorial interest that was at odds with its character of an architectural structure, the other by placing an emphasis upon the individual, apart from his social status, that could be better realized in a simple bust or statue than in a grandiose construction. Mrs. Esdaile has pertinently noted that Evesham, one of the most pictorial of all the tomb-makers, showed, in contrast to most of his colleagues, a fine disregard for the Vitruvian proprieties and thereby for the architectural qualities of monuments.[1]

In the early seventeenth century these practices were powerfully reinforced by ideas and feelings that had been maturing in former years and were now able to express themselves, because the concept of a funeral monument as a proof of social worth alone had already been partially broken down. These new sentiments were threefold: a deepening freedom of emotion between individuals and within a family, a reaction of many among the upper class against the austere Puritanism of the earlier generations and the consequent adoption of a more emotional attitude towards religion, and the consciously held aesthetic views of the virtuosi. The last two have been discussed elsewhere;[2] the first is partly revealed by the monuments themselves and partly by contemporary comment. The growth in the status of women and of affection between husband and wife and between parents and children in the course of the sixteenth century has been remarked on by several writers.[3] By the early years of the next century love matches in defiance of authority were not infrequent even among the upper classes: Raleigh and Elizabeth Throckmorton, Southampton and Elizabeth Vernon, Lord Compton and Elizabeth Spencer, John Donne and Anne More. Even the divorce of Frances Howard from Essex and her subsequent alliance with Somerset, for all its sordid aspects, reveals at least a freer attitude towards marriage. This went hand-in-hand with a greater affection and respect for children. As early as 1591 Charles Gibbon was advancing all the now incontrovertible

[1] *Derbyshire Archaeological Soc. Journ.* N.S. xiii (1939), 97; *English Church Monuments 1510–1840*, p. 53.

[2] See above, pp. 8–10.

[3] See, for example, C. L. Powell, *English Domestic Relations 1487–1653* (New York, 1917); L. Einstein, *Tudor Ideals* (1921); D. Stenton, *The English Woman in History* (1957).

arguments for allowing marriages to be decided by the children's rather than the parents' wishes.[1] Sir Henry Wotton, about 1630, was recommending and practising a very careful observation of the ways of children as creatures with a nature of their own.[2] Letter-writers of the time begin to give their correspondents admiring accounts of their children's doings and sayings. Ben Jonson was writing poems on the deaths of his daughter Mary and of the young Salathiel Pavy, and Elizabeth Drury, who died in 1610 at the age of 15, was commemorated by a splendid monument, a full-length painting and two poems by John Donne.[3]

These liberated feelings reveal themselves in several ways, and perhaps most clearly on some of those tombs where the dead man's children appear. In place of the rows of expressionless kneeling figures, testimonies to success in founding or continuing a line rather than objects and subjects of affection, there now occurs occasional evidence of parental and filial sorrow. This is preceded, for a deepened affection coincides with a closer observation, by studies of the ways of children. On the modest monument of Thomas Andrews (d. 1590) at Charwelton, Northants., a monument conventional enough in most respects and furnished with a row of kneeling descendants, there is a trace of this new sentiment. The youngest daughter is not kneeling as the rest are, but standing solicitously over her yet younger brother and holding him to prevent a fall (Pl. 86b). Such a rendering of childish artlessness, of a child's innocence of the pomps and ceremonies of her elders, is new and significant. Although monuments to children remained rare, nevertheless Princess Sophia, who died as a baby in 1606, was commemorated with a tomb by Maximilian Colt, in the form of a cradle with a child asleep in it.[4]

These, however, are modest enough evidences of feeling compared with the display of emotion on two tombs by Epiphanius Evesham, those of Sir Thomas Hawkins (d. 1618) at Boughton-

---

[1] *A Work Worth Reading* (1591), ch. 1.

[2] *A Survey of Education*, ed. H. Kermode (1938).

[3] The painting of Elizabeth Drury is reproduced in an engraving in J. Cullum, *History and Antiquities of Hawsted* (1813), p. 172.

[4] Colt was also responsible for the tomb of Princess Mary, *Pell Records, James I*, ed. F. Devon (1836), pp. 60, 88.

under-Blean (Pl. 89b) and of Lord Teynham at Lynsted in Kent (Pl. 87a).[1] In general design these tombs are little different from the run of the mill and the effigies are nothing out of the ordinary; but in place of the formal rows of pious but unperturbed descendants there are sculptured scenes of the dead man's daughters, in various poses and giving way to a great deal of grief. Even the sons are shown in a less formal manner than usual. The two sons of Lord Teynham are both kneeling, one in conventional armour, but the other in ordinary dress and with his hound and hawking-perch, as though fresh come from his normal pursuits to mourn his father. Mrs. Esdaile has made the point that under Evesham's hand the formal row of descendants turns into a family group;[2] but a further point must be made, that they turn into a group conscious not of their common descent and ancestry but of their common personal loss. These tombs, carried out for Catholic families,[3] stand alone in the unrestraint of the emotion that they render. They are, however, different in degree and not in kind from some others. Protestantism and social convention prevented most men from going as far, but even those who had most affected the 'magnificent Monuments' that Fuller was still admiring in the 1650's were beginning to display personal feelings. On the late monuments of the Dukes of Lennox and of Buckingham in Westminster Abbey the emblematical figures of Faith, Hope, and Charity and of Neptune

[1] Evesham's other known works, all signed, are: a tablet to Margery Collyns (d. 1595) at Hythe, Kent, another to John Collyns (d. 1597) at Mersham, Kent, the brass on the monument to Edmund West (d. 1618) at Marsworth, Bucks., and a floor-slab to John Erdeswicke (d. 1622) at West Hanningfield, Essex.

[2] *Yorks. Archaeological Journ.* xxxv. 369.

[3] A. Vallance, 'The Ropers and their Monuments in Lynsted Church', *Archaeologia Cantiana*, xliv (1932), 147; E. Hasted, *History of Kent*, iii (Canterbury, 1790), 5 n. G. On the evidence of the Roper and Hawkins Monuments K. H. Jones long ago suggested that Evesham himself was either a Catholic or very near it (*Archaeologia Cantiana*, xlv (1933), 205). It is now known that Evesham worked as a sculptor in Paris from 1601, or earlier, until 1614, or later, and that his commissions included a monument to the Archbishop of Sens in Notre-Dame: M. Jurgens, 'Quelques Actes Inedits concernant Epiphanius Evesham', *Bulletin de la Société de l'histoire de l'art français* (1960), 175; I owe this reference to the kindness of Dr. Margaret Whinney. This appears to explain the curious gap, from *c.* 1597 to *c.* 1618, in the dates of his known works in this country. His stay and activities, in such a Catholic stronghold as Paris was at this time, lend some colour to the suggestion that he was a Catholic.

and Mars have lost their old elegant aloofness and are weeping copiously.

This emotion was not confined to relations between parent and child; it is shown also in the effigies of women on their death-beds, often after childbirth. An early forerunner is the tomb of Margaret Legh (d. 1605) in Fulham Church whereon a seated woman holds a child in swaddling clothes in her arms (Pl. 87b). Far more emotional are Stone's effigies of Lady Elizabeth Carey at Stow Nine Churches and of Mrs. Cooke, at Bramfield in Suffolk.[1] The tomb of Jane Crewe (d. 1639) in Westminster Abbey is another example, and most emotional of all is the Kymer monument, of uncertain date but probably about 1625, at West Chelborough, Dorset. On this a dead or dying woman lying exhausted beneath a coverlet is just touching with the tips of her fingers the head of a young baby at her side (Pl. 92a). This work is clearly by a country craftsman and in skill cannot compare with that by Stone, but both express in another medium the feelings that Henry King put into his poem to his dead wife.

These works were in a way out of their time but that their time was not far distant is shown by a slightly later comment. Fuller complained of Princess Sophia's monument that 'vulgar eyes, especially of the weaker sex, are more affected (as level to their cognizance, more capable of what is prety than what is pompous) than with all the magnificent Monuments in Westminster'.[2] Such a monument of the early seventeenth century could appeal to mid-century taste only because that taste already existed in germ in the earlier years.

As a parallel with this increasing representation of personal feeling, there is imported into some of the monuments of the time a display of religious symbolism and, later, emotion. In its most widespread form, it shows itself in the fashion for such an emblem of mortality as an hour-glass, and in later years turns into a considerable parade of the more unpleasant aspects of death. The cadaver, so popular with the late Middle Ages, reappears on Maximilian Colt's tomb of Robert Cecil at Hatfield (c.

---

[1] The Carey monument was set up in 1619, and the Cooke in 1634.
[2] T. Fuller, *Worthies of England*, ed. J. Nichols (1811), i. 490.

1612).[1] Formerly a skull and cross-bones had been a sufficient *memento mori* but on the tomb of Dean Fotherby (d. 1619) in Canterbury Cathedral nearly all the separate bones of the human body and the skeleton of a whole trunk are carved in hideous detail. Occasionally, as on the painted St. John monument at Lydiard Tregoze and on the tomb of Sir Thomas Barnardiston at Kedington, the coffins of the deceased are depicted, and John Donne when sitting to Nicholas Stone in 1631 chose to array himself in his shroud. All of these may be regarded as evidence of that morbid preoccupation with death that led Essex, when in command of Parliament's troops, to encumber the baggage train of his already sufficiently discouraged army with his own coffin.

At the same time some of the practices of the early sixteenth century began to reappear. The frieze of the tomb of William Byrde (d. 1590) in the Mayor's chapel at Bristol is carved with a series of scriptural scenes, unknown since the Fitzroy tomb at Framlingham. The escutcheon of the monument to Hester Salisbury (d. 1614) at Stansted Mountfichet bears not the boast of heraldry but emblems of the Passion, and has a Crown of Thorns for a crest. This had been common enough earlier, and the emblems of the Passion together with the Five Wounds appeared on the tomb of Elizabeth Swellington (*c.* 1546) in Coventry Cathedral. Mrs. Esdaile has noted that full-length angels reappear on tombs of the early seventeenth century,[2] and she finds it odd that 'no thought of Popery' was suggested by them. In fact, they and other motifs probably suggested it to a great many people but those in authority were no longer anxious to proceed against 'Popery'. For reasons suggested in the Introduction they were, both from intellectual sympathy and from political opportunism, relaxing the former persecution of Catholics and allowing the expression, at least in part, of Catholic and near-Catholic views and feelings, and it was this that made possible some of the sculpture, and a great deal of the outstanding sculpture, of the period.

[1] The tomb had been begun or at least projected in Cecil's lifetime; in 1614 it was still unfinished and Simon Basil estimated that a further £460 would be needed to complete it: *C.L.* lxi (June 1927), 462–3; J. J. Antrobus, *Bishop's Hatfield* (Bishop's Hatfield, 1912), p. 59.　　　　　[2] *English Church Monuments 1510–1840*, p. 90.

These feelings expressed themselves at first, and in an extreme form almost solely, upon the tombs of minor men and, as did the expression of personal emotion, appeared in scenic form first of all upon brasses and small monuments. An early example is the brass of James Grey (d. 1591) at Hunsdon (Herts.), which combines a reference to his occupation of park-keeper with a scene of his death from the charge of a stag. The brass of Dr. Erasmus Williams (d. 1608) at Tingewick (Bucks.) is mainly concerned with his occupation but includes a large figure, doubtless of some symbolic significance, of Lot's wife. The brasses of Thomas Sparke (d. 1616) at Bletchley and of Humphrey Willis (d. 1618) at Wells, and that, signed by Evesham, on the tomb of Edmund West[1] at Marsworth (Bucks.), are filled with religious symbols and scenes; and Evesham has included a Risen Christ.

On the more imposing stone monuments this expression at first and more usually takes the form of adapting the conventional kneeling figure by placing it under a curtained canopy drawn aside by angels. The tomb of Sir Robert Chamberlain (d. 1615) at St. Bartholomew the Great, and the Drury and Pope monuments of 1617 and 1624 at Riddlesworth and North Barningham in Norfolk are examples. On the monuments of less fashionable or more devout families the figured scenes of the brasses are occasionally translated into stone. Evesham's monument to Lord Teynham has already been cited for the personal emotion displayed upon it, but there is religious feeling there as well. Teynham's daughters are, in the midst of their weeping, looking ecstatically towards winged figures in the clouds, and a hand holding an escutcheon is issuing from the sky above Teynham's sons. On the scenes of the Hawkins monument are two inscriptions 'Nox Vita Lux Anima' and 'Vive ut post Vivas', sentiments in some contrast with such a common earlier inscription, for example, on Caius's tomb, as 'Vivit Post Funera Virtus'. This religious emotionalism reached a climax in the years immediately after 1625 upon the tomb of Constance Whitney (d. 1628) in St. Giles, Cripplegate, and that of Sara Colville (d. 1631) at Chelsea All Saints (Pl. 90a). On each of these the dead woman is in her shroud, rising from the tomb and

---

[1] The identification is made by Mill Stephenson in *Records of Bucks.* x (1916), 223.

lifting her hands in ecstasy to the heavens above; on the first draped cherubs are offering wreaths and chaplets, and on the second the scene is dramatized by a broken tomb.

The third new element in the sculpture of the early seventeenth century was a concern for the human form and a greater freedom of pose than before. The freer pose is largely a natural result of the demands made upon sculpture by the display of emotion, which in many cases, for example upon the Kymer tomb and the Colville and Whitney monuments, was expressed precisely through the abandonment of a rigid funeral pose. There were other causes as well. One was the fashionable practice of giving to effigies a reclining, or even sitting, position. More important was the fashion, typical of the later Southwark School, of placing free-standing emblematic figures upon tombs. These had been known earlier, upon the Leweston tomb in Sherborne Abbey for instance, but it was the Southwark men who exploited their possibilities, and with their superior skill transformed the stumpy figures of Sherborne into the elegant and freely-posed 'Virtues' of the later tombs.

When, therefore, the virtuosi appeared and took an interest in sculpture they had not to struggle alone against the dead weight of tradition, for other men and earlier advances had brought monumental sculpture to a point where there was considerable freedom of conception and many sculptors with skill enough to exploit it. But there was more than this. The mark of the virtuosi was not so much any particular aesthetic doctrine as a knowledge of European sculpture and its interest and delight in the human form. It was this interest that sculptors in England were beginning to adopt in order to solve the problems presented to them by the varied poses they were being called upon to represent. This was possible because the respective parts played by artists and by patrons were much less sharply defined in sculpture than in painting. Weever, in fact, attributed some of the new qualities of seventeenth-century sculpture to the sculptor's rather than the patron's initiative,[1] and there is some evidence to support his view. Apart from a remark by Coryate on the difference between English and Italian practice in representing the human form,[2] there is little literary evidence of

[1] *Ancient Funeral Monuments* (1631), p. 11.        [2] *Crudities* (1611), p. 131.

any interest in sculpture before 1625. It is true that Arundel was forming his collection of statuary from about 1615 onwards, but Peacham's neglect of sculpture in the 1622 edition of *The Compleat Gentleman* suggests that Arundel was, up to then at least, a very lone figure. Yet in the first two decades of the century not only were many elegant and sometimes half-naked figures produced but some, such as those by Stone of William Curle and Lady Elizabeth Carey and by Colt of Robert Cecil, had shown far greater qualities than a mere attempt at elegance. Weever was clearly right to this extent, that the sculptors were occasionally practising new methods on their own initiative throughout James I's reign. And this was made possible because of the broad range of patronage that they enjoyed among sections of the population who desired monuments, for example those with figured scenes, that allowed the sculptor a wide variety of choices.

Nevertheless, most of the examples occur after Charles's accession and at a time when some of the members of a leisured class were taking as much interest in sculpture as they had earlier taken in painting. The 1634 edition of *The Compleat Gentleman*, in contrast to that of 1622, devotes considerable space to sculpture and to the activities of Arundel, Charles I, and their protégés. Furthermore, there are some impressive parallels between the sculptors and the patron-dominated painters. The work of any one sculptor is, in general, indistinguishable from that of his colleagues. They collaborated with another to an extent that shows there was little artistic independence amongst them. The only well-documented sculptor—Nicholas Stone—produced monuments so variable that two recent writers have given their opinion that but for the preservation of his note-books his work would never be assigned to one man,[1] a remark that echoes what has been said of the only well-documented painter of the period, Hans Eworth.

From all this two things seem clear. On the one hand the sculptors could only fashion a new style when a new type of patron had appeared. On the other, those patrons could get that new style from native craftsmen only because those craftsmen had, in the presence of earlier different opportunities, developed to a stage

[1] C. L. S. Linnell and S. J. Wearing, *Norfolk Church Monuments* (Ipswich, 1952), p. 11.

from which the transition was not difficult. The virtuosi, in fact, were able to see their viewpoint expressed in stone because a broader class of patrons had earlier succeeded in expressing one that the virtuosi despised.

In its most obvious form this new quality shows itself in such emblematic figures as the half-naked Neptune on Buckingham's monument, the undraped 'Fame' on that of Lord Rich at Felsted,[1] and the bare-breasted women posing as 'Virtues' on many other tombs. Occasionally something more is attempted; on two monuments by Nicholas Stone, of William Curle (1617) at Hatfield and of the Lyttelton brothers (1635) at Magdalen College, Oxford, not merely a subsidiary figure but the person commemorated is naked to the waist, and in a very natural pose that emphasizes the form of the human body. This is particularly noticeable at Hatfield, where the figure gives the impression of having been washed-up on the shore (Pl. 90b). By 1631 this trend was pronounced enough to run into opposition and Weever complained of those who 'garnish their Tombes, nowadayes with the pictures of naked men and women'.[2] It is from a consideration of these examples that the attitude behind Sir Henry Wotton's scorn for painted monuments as an 'English Barbarisme'[3] can best be appreciated. In place of the surface-realism of the painted monuments of the conventional tomb-makers, men like Wotton wanted the deeper realism of the best European sculpture, which had little use for the irrelevancies and distractions of colour. In consequence, the greater attention to form in English sculpture is accompanied by a new or, rather, a revived fashion for 'black and white' monuments.

A corollary to this representation of the body in many attitudes was the portrayal of movement. One example is the monument to Sir Henry Bellasis of 1615 in York Minster, on which one of the attendant figures is released from the stiff kneeling pose and allowed to rise on one knee. The conception is taken farther in the

[1] Since the R.C.H.M. (*Essex*, ii. 75a) gives the impression that the Rich monument is of the late sixteenth century, it must be said that Mrs. Esdaile has put forward convincing reasons for believing it to be of c. 1620; 'The Monument of the First Lord Rich at Felsted', *Essex Archaeological Soc. Trans.* N.S. xxii (1940), 59–67.

[2] *Ancient Funeral Monuments*, p. 11.

[3] *The Elements of Architecture*, ed. S. Prideaux (1903), p. 71.

half-kneeling bearers of the Salisbury tomb at Hatfield, and farthest on that of Sir Francis Vere (d. 1609) in Westminster Abbey (Pl. 92*b*). Here the bearers of the heavy slab, half-risen, are given an air of tension and strain that creates an illusion of life. It was of this tomb, and that of Sir John Norris by Isaac James,[1] with its finely sculptured figures and its lively battle scene in relief, that an anonymous writer remarked nearly a century and a half ago, 'Sculpture is detached from Architecture and not encumbered by it. . . . The artist is at liberty to describe all that he intended.'[2]

This liberty from architectural dominance had been earlier but only partially achieved in bust monuments and was finally accomplished in the self-sufficient statue. The opportunity for this had been created in part by the architectural monuments themselves with their subsidiary standing figures, for example those in relief on the Sutton tomb and those in the round on the Bertie tomb at Spilsby and the Jefferay tomb of 1612 at Chiddingly, Sussex. When Stone executed the monument in Westminster Abbey to Sir George Holles, probably about 1626, he introduced a standing statue, not of a subsidiary figure, but of Holles himself, and made it the main subject (Pl. 91*a*). At about the same time he commemorated Francis Holles with a seated figure upon a pedestal, and in 1633 Le Sueur's monument to Sir Richard Leveson in Wolverhampton Church was merely a standing statue of the man.[3] Holles and Leveson, or Stone and Le Sueur, were not alone in their conceptions of funeral monuments. In his will Arundel, the beau ideal of the virtuosi, directed 'That my Tombe bee my owne Figure . . . sitting and looking upwards, leaning upon a Lyon holding an Escochion';[4] and a man of a very different background, Robert Graye, a wealthy and charitable clothier, is shown life-size and standing on his monument in St. Mary Magdalene at Taunton.

Although some of these examples fall just outside our period they are part of it, for they are a product of the same ideology that

---

[1] For James's authorship of the Norris Monument see K. A. Esdaile in *C.L.* cvii (Feb. 1950), 464.

[2] *Gent. Mag.* 1818, i. 490.

[3] S. Shaw, *History and Antiquities of Staffordshire*, ii (1801), 158.

[4] Mary Hervey, *Life, Correspondence and Collections of Thomas Howard, Earl of Arundel* (Cambridge, 1926), p. 460.

had created the great architectural tombs. In the early seventeenth century that ideology could take divergent forms, and some of those forms were hostile to the aesthetics of earlier years. There is no doubt that the tombs just described were very much in a minority and that some of their features are partly due to a copying of foreign models. Despite this they are as native as the others. They reflect not so much the artistic development of another country as the intellectual trends that conditions in early Stuart England were developing. And they were only able to come into being because English monumental sculpture had already developed to a point from which a transition could be made. The work of Nicholas Stone, or some of it, marks an artistic revolution when compared with that of Garret Johnson, but this revolution, like most others, was not merely imported from abroad but prepared by a long evolution at home.

The homogeneous nature of the arts of the time is clearly shown in the often close parallels between sculpture and portrait-painting. Throughout the period many portraits were 'effigies domesticated' and show the same concern with rank and occupation as the monuments. New elements in painting often coincide with similar ones in monumental sculpture. The portrait by Geldorp of the second Earl of Salisbury against a background of Hatfield House is paralleled by the monument of Sir Thomas Lucy with its scene of Lucy riding in Charlecote Park. The death-bed scenes of the Cooke, Kymer, and Carey monuments may be compared with the painting of Sir Thomas Aston at his wife's death-bed and that of the Saltinstall family. The draped curtains above a kneeling effigy that are common on early seventeenth-century monuments are in the same vein as the background curtains of the 'Gheeraerts' school of painting. The real space of the background in the portraits of the time coincides with similar backgrounds, for example upon the tombs of Jane Fitzalan and Jane Best, in sculpture.

It is true that there is one case—the monument of Sir Henry Savile—where it is possible to explain certain features in one medium as a copy of those of another. As far as I know, this monument is unique in its two small panelled scenes of Eton and Merton Colleges, of which Savile was Provost and Warden. It cannot be accidental that this occurs on a monument at Oxford where, in earlier years, Sampson Strong had produced a number of 'College-Founder' portraits with inset scenes of the college buildings. In general, however, it is idle to speculate whether painting was 'influencing' sculpture or vice-versa, for it is clear enough that both arts were developing in parallel under the common influence of the prevailing intellectual and emotional temper.

Domestic sculpture was very much less common than monumental and yet commoner than survivals would suggest. It has two quite clearly distinguishable forms: ornament upon architecture, and ornament within a garden. Apart from these there was a great amount of decorative carving sometimes, especially upon fireplaces and in later years, amounting to sculpture.

The character of the first form is illustrated well enough by its position within niches or roundels upon the exterior of a building. At Montacute a series of niches along the top story is filled with standing figures; at Wollaton and Longleat the façades are liberally supplied with roundels, some containing busts and all presumably meant to do so. Gresham's Royal Exchange had a great number of niches along the courtyard elevations originally intended for statues. All of these examples are of the late sixteenth century, but the practice continued into the next. At Trinity College, Cambridge, statues of Henry VIII, James I, Queen Anne, and Prince Charles (Pl. 91b) were added in the early years of James's reign to the Great Gate that had been completed about 1535.[1] In 1610 a proposal was made to the Court of Aldermen that the vacant niches at the Royal Exchange should be filled,[2] and in 1625 Nicholas Stone was making four royal statues for them;[3] Cecil's New Exchange too was meant to have statues, and Maximilian Colt was working on one of them in 1608.[4] Even where sculpture was set up within a building it was nearly always given an architectural setting. The statue of James I in the King James Room at Hatfield was placed centrally in a niche in the overmantel. At

[1] R.C.H.M. *City of Cambridge*, p. 216a.
[2] W. H. and H. C. Overall, *Analytical Index to Remembrancia* (1878), p. 261 n. 1.
[3] W. L. Spiers in *Wal. Soc.* vii (1918–19), 57–58.
[4] L. Stone, 'Inigo Jones and the New Exchange', *Arch. Journ.* cxiv (1959), 112–13.

Lumley Castle the wooden equestrian statue of Edward III and the busts of his six sons were placed beneath an arch.[1] Another equestrian statue, that of James I, was erected at Aldersgate in 1618.[2]

The iconography of this sculpture was extraordinarily limited. Easel-painting was restricted to family portraits and portraits of famous men, and domestic sculpture, for similar reasons and also because of its niche-background, was confined to statues and busts. But figures on the exterior of a building, often at a great distance from the eye, were valueless as likenesses and in consequence they were nearly always of persons, such as the Nine Worthies at Montacute, whose features were quite unknown and in any case unimportant. Indoor sculpture had the same subject-matter: Plato, Aristotle, and the Tudor sovereigns at Lumley, the roman emperors in the summer-house at Theobalds.[3] Private and family portraits that were so common in easel-painting hardly appeared at all; the only notable ones are those of Sir Nicholas Bacon, of his second wife, and of his son, Francis, at Gorhambury.

The statues are of a uniform mediocrity, lifeless, and generally squat, very much in the manner of the accessory figures upon the rather better country-craftsmen's tombs. In part this may be attributed to their makers' lack of skill, but their character of applied ornament also had an effect. In many cases, as at Trinity Great Gate, the sculptor had to fit both niche and figure to an already determined space: but even where the sculpture was contemporary with the building it had to accommodate itself as best it could to niches whose low and broad proportions show that they were determined not by the sculptor's but by the architect's needs. The sculpture was not necessarily an afterthought, but it was ruthlessly cut to a pattern imposed by the general design. The effect this had is shown by the younger William Cure's statues at Trinity, which are a very long way below his usual level of attainment.

[1] See L. Cust, 'The Lumley Inventories', *Wal. Soc.* vi (1917–18).

[2] Vertue is sometimes quoted as the authority for attributing this statue to Gerard Christmas, but it is clear that he had, in fact, some doubts about it; 'Vertue Notebooks', *Wal. Soc.* i. 84, 136; ii. 86; v. 36.

[3] P. Hentzner, *A Journey into England 1598*, ed. H. Walpole (1757), p. 54.

The poor quality of Cure's work at Cambridge, which is in stone, is attributed by Mrs. Esdaile to his lack of familiarity with that material.[1] There may be something in this, but it is not the whole story, for it is as much the proportions of the figures as their execution that are at fault. One cannot help wondering what sort of figures Cure would have produced if he had been asked to fill the niches on the West Front at Wells. They are long and narrow and the figures in them are tall and graceful. It may be that the proportions of the niches determined those of the figures, or it may be the other way round, or the qualities of both may be a compromise between the claims of each. One thing, however, is clear; at Wells the sculpture was from the beginning an important element in the design, and the builders sacrificed some of the strength of their buttresses in order to accommodate the decorative scheme.[2] Sculptural ornament was never an integral part of an Elizabethan design, and if niches were included they had to accommodate their proportions to those of the building and not of the human figure and, in consequence, were low and broad.

In contrast, busts were generally of a very much higher standard. Those at Lumley of the four Tudor sovereigns have been described as 'of the highest interest, the sculptor of which should rank with the greatest artists of his time'.[3] The busts at Gorhambury are equally good, well modelled and with great actuality and expression (Pl. 94). It is very doubtful whether these are by an English sculptor and they are not at all typical; on the contrary they probably represent the very highest achievement of the period. That achievement was far superior to the very best of non-monumental figure sculpture because busts were, from their nature, less restricted by an architectural setting than statues.

Probably as important as architectural sculpture was that in the pleasure gardens that were attached to most great houses, and it is unfortunate that our knowledge of it comes almost wholly from contemporary descriptions and from drawings. These reveal that there was a great amount of garden sculpture. At Whitehall the

[1] 'William Cure II and his Work at Trinity College, Cambridge', *Burl. Mag.* lxxx (1942), 21–22.    [2] P. Brieger, *O.H.E.A.* iv (1957), 33–34.
[3] L. Cust in *Wal. Soc.* vi (1917–18), 15–16.

Queen's garden had thirty-four columns with heraldic beasts upon them;[1] at Hampton Court, apart from innumerable heraldic figures, there were thirty-eight stone statues of Kings and Queens;[2] the 'long walks' at Sir Arthur Ingram's house in York were 'adorn'd with many kinds of beasts to the Life, with most lively Statues in many shapes and formes'.[3] From 1614 onwards Arundel was making his collection of antique and foreign statues, with some of which in Peacham's words he 'began to honour the Gardens and Galleries of Arundel House'.[4] Not every garden was as profusely planted as these but nearly all of which we have descriptions had some statuary; and it is clear that the character of this work was very different from that already discussed. It had a very much wider range of themes. At Nonsuch in the 'Grove of Diana' was a fountain with Actaeon turned into a stag;[5] a fountain at Kenilworth was covered with 'storie work';[6] at Wilton were fountains with figures of Venus and Cupid, Diana bathing, Suzanna, and Cleopatra and the Serpent, and statues of Flora and Bacchus.[7] The fountain erected at Hampton Court in 1591-2 was surmounted by a figure of Justice[8] and one of the fountains at Lumley by another emblematic figure.[9] At Holdenby there were two giant figures, compared by a contemporary with Gog and Magog in the Guildhall,[10] and apparently intended as symbolic guardians of the gate.

This difference in iconography between the two main classes of domestic sculpture is paralleled by that in easel-painting between pictures in the ordinary rooms and galleries of a house and those that were, for example, in Somerset's bowling alley.[11] Gardens and

[1] 'A Journey through England and Scotland by Leopold van Wedel 1584-5', *Trans. R. Hist. Soc.* ix (1895), 234-5.

[2] R. Dutton, *The English Garden* (1937), p. 35.

[3] 'A Short Survey of 26 Counties 1634', ed. L. G. W. Legg, *Stuart Series*, vii (1904), 21.

[4] *Compleat Gentleman* (2nd ed. 1634), pp. 107-8.

[5] P. Hentzner, *A Journey into England 1598*, ed. H. Walpole (1757), p. 84.

[6] J. Nichols, *Progresses of Queen Elizabeth* (1823), i. 475 n.

[7] 'A Relation of a Short Survey of the Western Counties made in 1635', ed. L. G. W. Legg, *Camden Miscellany*, xvi (1936), 66-67.

[8] P.R.O. E. 351-3226.                 [9] *Wal. Soc.* vi (1917-18).

[10] R. Corbet, *Poems* (Oxford, 1955), pp. 36-37.

[11] See above, pp. 151-2.

bowling alleys were places of disport and the tyranny of formal State iconography could be thrown off there. Once they stepped out of the open air, however, even garden sculptures, it seems, were disciplined and in the summer-house of which something is known —Theobalds—there were, as far as is recorded, nothing but busts of the roman emperors.

It is extremely difficult to assess the qualities of these works. The figure on the fountain at Lumley was illustrated by a contemporary when the inventory was drawn up and there is a drawing of a similar fountain and figure among the Hatfield Mss.[1] At Hawstead the figure of a Wild Man or Woodhouse was erected in 1578, probably to mark the visit of Queen Elizabeth in that year, and was illustrated by Cullum and again by Nichols.[2] As far as can be judged the Lumley and Hatfield figures are very similar in style to the 'Virtues' and others that the later Southwark School placed upon the pediments and cornices of their monuments. It seems likely that the Southwark sculptors were not infrequently employed upon work of this sort; in 1591–2 Garret Johnson was paid £30 for making and carving two new fountains for the Privy Garden at Hampton Court,[3] and £70 for a figure of Neptune at Hatfield in 1611.[4] Not every fountain had a piece of sculpture upon it, but most of these recorded garden statues were in fact placed upon fountains. In contrast with these the Hawstead Wild Man is the usual ill-proportioned and squat figure of most country work of the time. The evidence is clearly slight but as far as it goes it suggests that garden sculpture, freed from architectural restriction, had at least the opportunity of reaching a comparatively high level. Whether it did so depended upon the skill of the carver and the taste of his patron.

By the beginning of James I's reign monumental sculpture had broken at least some of its bonds. Sculpture in and upon buildings began to follow this lead and to resist the tyranny of its imprisoning niches. It did so in two ways. At Blickling, following the example

---

[1] Most easily accessible in B.M. Mss. Dept. Facs. 372, i. 13.
[2] J. Cullum, *History and Antiquities of Hawsted* (2nd. ed. 1813), p. 156; J. Nichols, *Progresses of Queen Elizabeth* (1823), ii. 121.    [3] P.R.O. E. 351–3226.
[4] H. A. Tipping, *English Homes*, Period III, ii. 332.

of the Southwark tomb-makers, sculptured figures were placed unrestrainedly upon the porch and upon the apices of the gables. They are well-proportioned and occasionally lively. In interiors similar changes are apparent. The figures flanking the fireplace in the Saloon at Charlton and those in the Morning Room at Hatfield have been almost wholly freed from architectural restraint. At Apethorpe, on the pediment of the overmantel in the Prince's Room, are the elegant reclining figures of the fashionable contemporary tombs. Tomb-makers, we know, were employed on such works; e.g. Maximilian Colt and the younger William Cure in the years between 1609 and 1614 at Whitehall, St. James's and Somerset House,[1] and Colt at Hatfield.[2]

When the present screen was added (*c.* 1626) to the east side of the courtyard at Rushton something quite new occurred: the niches flanking the entrance were made as tall and as narrow as those at Wells in order to accommodate well-proportioned statues (Pl. 93*b*). Sculpture here had escaped from the dominance of architecture and was even beginning to determine some of the architectural details. Thus although domestic and monumental sculpture differed in many ways they sailed in convoy in the years between 1553 and 1625 and made the same landfall, an independence of architecture that amounted at times to a control over it.

Many of the trends apparent in painting and sculpture are also to be found in the new and popular medium of engraved prints.[3] These differed from oil-paintings and miniatures in two important ways. In the first place they had their origins, in England at any rate, in book-illustration. The first line-engravings carried out in this country by a known engraver were those of Thomas Geminus that accompanied an edition of Vesalius issued in 1545; and such later and diverse works as Shute's book on architecture, the Bishops' Bible of 1568, the large number of geographies, travels, histories, and emblem books were embellished with engravings. As a result the craft early acquired a tradition of diversification of interest.

---

[1] P.R.O. E. 351–3244–8.          [2] Tipping, *English Homes*, Period III, ii. 322.
[3] The outstanding works on English engraving, on which I lean heavily, are S. Colvin, *Early Engraving and Engravers in England* (1905), and A. M. Hind, *Engraving in England in the Sixteenth and Seventeenth Centuries*, 2 vols. (Cambridge, 1952–5).

Secondly, it had a potential mass-market. The relationship between engraving and the other graphic arts was, in this respect, similar to that between the printed book and the manuscript. Thus when the engraved print appeared in some numbers as a self-sufficient entity it had both a wide public to appeal to and a wide range of subject-matter to appeal with. By the end of the sixteenth century the importance within the craft of book-illustration was proportion-ately less, and the existence of the self-sufficient print as a major form is testified to by the appearance of such print-sellers as Sud-bury and Humble, and Compton Holland. The tendency had been apparent for many years before in the production of a series of engravings—the large prints of Gresham's Royal Exchange of 1569, Marcus Gheeraert's *Knights of the Garter in Procession* of 1576, Theodore de Bry's *Funeral of Sir Philip Sidney* of 1588—published separately and never intended as book-illustrations.

Because engravings were a product of the same society, their subject matter had much in common with that of the other graphic arts, and in consequence portraits were commoner than anything else. Yet the proportion of these to others was very much less. Portraiture did not have a complete monopoly of oil-paintings and miniatures but other subjects were extremely rare; in engravings they were common. Apart from the prints mentioned above there are those by Augustin Ryther, from Robert Adam's drawings, that were intended to accompany the text of the translation of Ubaldini's account of the defeat of the Armada; there are maps and panoramas of London, Oxford, and Cambridge, for example, popular satirical pieces like *All doe ride the Asse* (c. 1600–10) (Pl. 93a), Renold Elstrack's *Satire on Women* of 1620, and Martin Droeshout's *Dr. Panurgus* of about the same date. There are also overt propaganda-pieces, Cockson's anti-papal *Revells of Christendome* of 1609 and several representations of the Gunpowder Plot. These last, of course, can be paralleled in oil-painting, for example in the picture commemorating the frustration of that plot, now at New College, Oxford; but that picture was itself closely connected with con-temporary engraving,[1] and propaganda paintings that are not primarily portraits are extremely uncommon.

[1] See above, p. 146.

By contrast, there is a lack, among engravings, of the scenes of classical mythology and the *galanteries* that are found in some of the great picture collections of the time. Doubtless a taste for semi-pornography was not an exclusively upper-class vice, and Peacham's reference to 'lewd prints' suggests that there were such engravings in circulation, but it seems clear that they were, or at least that Peacham liked to think that they were, of foreign import and not of native manufacture.[1]

The difference of audience affected engraving not merely by giving it many subjects besides portraiture, but also by giving a different character to its portraiture. Although there are many engraved portraits that differ little from the rigid and lifeless oil-paintings, nevertheless there are many that have other qualities. In the first place they have a far more obvious and direct propaganda content than the oil-paintings. Indeed it is noticeable that while the latter are rarely reproduced in engravings, one of the few overt propaganda pieces in oils—the *Henry VIII and Elizabeth with figures of 'Peace' and 'Plenty'* at Sudeley—was engraved as a self-sufficient print by William Rogers.[2] An exception to the indifference amongst engravers to the general run of oil-portraits is Francis Delaram's engraving in *Basiliωlogia* of Queen Mary, a copy of an oil-portrait known in two versions,[3] but the engraving was one of a series of Royal portraits, mostly imaginary, and the artist was probably only too glad to have an authentic likeness to copy. Rogers's earliest known portrait of Elizabeth—the *Eliza Triumphans* of 1589—is, compared with almost any oil-painting, a piece of obvious propaganda (Pl. 96). Elstrack's engraving of 1604 with twenty-four miniature portraits to celebrate the 'Happy Union' of England and Scotland, his probably contemporary print of James I sitting in state in the Lords, and Delaram's *Betrothal of Charles and*

---

[1] *The Gentleman's Exercise* (1612), pp. 9–10.

[2] There is an engraving (Hind, ii. 394–5, pl. 248), of which the only known print is dated 1679, which is either a copy or the original of the New College 'Gunpowder Plot' painting. Mr. Hind considers the print is a reissue, in connexion with Titus Oates' 'Popish Plot', of an engraving of 1612 or earlier. I am inclined to believe that it is a copy of the painting, a later example of the translation of a propaganda painting into a popular medium.

[3] L. Cust, 'The Painter HE', *Wal. Soc.* ii (1912–13), p. 22, pl. viic.

*Henrietta Maria* are similar in content. This content tends to alter their character, for in place of the hieratic or elegant figures of the usual royal portrait in oils these either invest their subjects with an awesome and commanding aspect or show them actively engaged in their kingly duties.

Their propaganda nature reveals itself in another way too. As in painting so in engraving there was a fondness for collections of portraits; the Lumley Collection on the one hand and the series of portraits of the *Basiliωlogia* of 1618 and the *Herωologia* of 1620 on the other. While the Lumley and Leicester collections contained portraits of friends and foes, of co-religionists and of unbelievers, the *Herωologia* limits itself strictly to English worthies[1] or to defenders of the Protestant faith. Propaganda, however, was not a weapon that only one party could or would wield. The supporters of the Spanish match, whose feelings towards Rome had at least mellowed, saw their views reflected in, if they did not directly instigate, the engraving, probably by Willem van de Passe, of Philip IV of Spain and Prince Charles in amity and concord. They were pertinacious and provident as well as pacific, for as the negotiations dawdled and the years passed the print was re-issued with the features of the prospective father-in-law and bridegroom suitably aged to preserve an air of topicality.

Just as kings are shown in a more lively manner than in oil-paintings, so too are ordinary mortals. While equestrian portraits are very rare in oils before 1625, they are comparatively common in engravings; and while there are many engravings in which, as in oils, the subject sits stiffly or elegantly upon a docile nag, there are some—for example, Cockson's prints of Charles Blount, of the Earl of Cumberland and of Essex and a portrait of Howard of Effingham—in which he is actively riding a fiercely rearing charger and doing other things as well. What he is doing is little enough—waving a vague baton against a background of a distant battlefield that is clearly beyond his immediate control—but the attempt to portray a man in action is plain (Pl. 95*b*). The same attempt is

[1] And even so the only Roman Catholics that gain admittance are More, Wolsey, and Pole, all of whom could be plausibly represented as something more, or something less, than good Catholics.

apparent in the print of 1612 of Prince Henry exercising with a lance (Pl. 95*a*) and in Elstrack's portrait, published in 1615, of Sir Thomas Overbury writing at his desk.

All these are quite out of sympathy with contemporary oil-painting but are well in step with that aspect of monumental sculpture which was beginning at this same time to portray men, and women, in action. By its contrast with the one and similarity with the other, the iconography of engraving illustrates and partly explains both the unrelaxing 'Statist' domination over oil-painting, and the greater freedom from that domination that its wider audience allowed to monumental sculpture.

# BIBLIOGRAPHY

As the following bibliography is not comprehensive, it will perhaps be thought to need some explanation of its principles of selection. These have not been the same for all aspects of the art-history of the period. There is a considerable bulk of literature on architecture; much of it, in the form of monographs on individual buildings or topographical surveys such as the volumes of the Royal Commission on Historical Monuments, has been excluded. The latter are too well known to need mention, while nearly all the monographs can be found by referring to the topographical card-index in the library of the Society of Antiquaries. The articles on particular houses in *Country Life* are often extremely valuable but they too can be found easily enough, in the index that appears twice a year in that journal at the end of June and of December; like the monographs they have been excluded unless they are of wide interest. To find one's way through the literature on painting and on miniatures is not so easy, but as there is a great amount, some sifting is obligatory, and I can only hope that the selection made here, again excluding items of narrow interest, will be found useful. Sculpture on the other hand has had so little written about it that nearly everything of any value at all has been included. I have not presumed to attempt a selection of the literary works of the time, or of later works on political, social, or economic history, but I have included those books and articles that I have found most useful on the relationships between the historical, intellectual and artistic developments; amongst these I owe an especial debt to R. R. Bolgar's *The Classical Heritage and its Beneficiaries*. Further references will be found in the footnotes.

The place of publication when none is given is London.

## CONTEMPORARY SOURCES: MANUSCRIPT

Caesar, Sir Julius. Papers of. B.M. Harl. Mss. 12,498.

D'Ewes, Sir Paul. Bargain with Jan Jansen for a Tomb. B.M. Harl. Mss. 98, No. 15.

Digby, Sir Kenelm. Papers of. B.M. Add. Mss. 41,846.

Leicester, Earl of. Inventory of his carpets and hangings. B.M. Lans. Mss. 57, No. 55.

Paymasters of the Royal Works. Accounts of. 1547–1625. P.R.O. E. 351/-3200–3258; A.O.I. 2422, 2449.

Powle, Stephen. Account of his Travels. B.M. Lans. Mss. 100, No. 20.

Salisbury, Marquess of. Plans and Drawings belonging to. Photostat Copies B.M. Mss. Dept. Facs. 372.

Smithson, John. Plans and Drawings. R.I.B.A. Library.

Stickelles, Robert. Observations on the Proportions of Buildings, 1595, 1597. B.M. Lans. Mss. 84, No. 10.

Strode, John, of Chantmarle. Account Book. Dorset County Record Office MW/M4.

Thorpe, John. Plans and Drawings. Soane Museum.

Treatise on Perspective. B.M. Sloane Mss. 536.

Tresham, Sir Thomas. Papers of. B.M. Add. Mss. 39828–36.

Whiteway, William. Diary of, 1618–34. B.M. Eg. Mss. 784.


## CONTEMPORARY SOURCES: PRINTED

ASCHAM, R. *The Scholemaster*, ed. D.C. Whimster (1934).

*Arte of Limming* (1573).

BACON, FRANCIS. *Essayes* (1625).

—— *Instauratio Magna* (1620).

BALDWIN, W. *A treatise of Morall Phylosophie* (1547).

*Bolsover Castle Building Account*, ed. D. Knoop and G. P. Jones (1936).

BOORDE, ANDREW. *Dyetary of Helth*, ed. F. J. Furnivall, Early English Text Society Extra Series x (1870).

BRATHWAIT, R. *The English Gentleman* (1630).

CAMDEN, W. *Britannia*, ed. R. Gough, 3 vols. (1789).

CHAMBERLAIN, J. *Letters*, ed. N. E. McClure, 2 vols. (Philadelphia, 1939).

CLIFFORD, LADY ANNE. *Diary*, ed. V. Sackville-West (1923).

CORNWALLIS, LADY JANE. *Private Correspondence 1613–44*, ed. Lord Braybrooke (1842).

CORYATE, T. *Crudities* (1611).

DAVIES, R. 'An Inventory of the Duke of Buckingham's Pictures at York House in 1635', *Burl. Mag.* x (1906–7), 376.

DEE, J. 'A Supplication . . . for the recovery and preservation of ancient Writers and Monuments'; 'Account of his Life and Studies', ed. T. Hearne, *Chronicle of John of Glastonbury* (Oxford, 1726).

—— *Private Diary*, ed. J. O. Halliwell, Camden Soc. xix (1842).

DIETTERLIN, W. *Architectura* (Nuremberg, 1598).

*Documents relating to the Office of Revels to Queen Elizabeth*, ed. A. Feuillerat (Louvain, 1908).

DU CERCEAU, J. A. *Les plus excellents bastiments de France. . .* (Paris, 1576–9).

DÜRER, A. *Schriftlicher Nachlaß*, ed. E. Heidrich (Berlin, 1910).

FILMER, SIR ROBERT. *Patriarcha*, ed. P. Laslett (Oxford, 1949).

FULLER, T. *The Holy State* (1642).

GEDDE, W. *A booke of sundry draughts . . .* (1615–16).

GOODMAN, G. *The Court of James I*, ed. J. S. Brewer, 2 vols. (1839).

HALLIWELL, J. O. *Ancient Inventories* (1854).

HARRISON, S. *The Arches of Triumph Erected in honor of . . . James the First . . .* (1604).

HARRISON, W. 'An historical description of the Islande of Britayne' in Holinshed, R. *Chronicles* (1577).

HAYDOCKE, R. *A Tract containing the Artes of Curious Painting Carving Building* (Oxford, 1598).

HENTZNER, P. *A Journey into England 1598*, ed. H. Walpole (1757).

HILLIARD, NICHOLAS. 'The Art of Limning', ed. P. Norman, *Wal. Soc.* i (1912).

HOBBES, T. *Leviathan* (1651).

HOBY, SIR THOMAS. 'Travels and Life', ed. E. Powell, *Camden Miscellany*, x (1902).

—— *The Courtyer* (1588).

HOLLES, G. 'Memorials of the Holles Family', ed. A. C. Wood, *Camden Soc.* 3rd ser. lv (1937).

'Inventory of Thomas, Lord Wharton 1568', ed. J. Evans, *Arch. Journ.* cii (1945), 134.

'Inventory of the goods of the Earl of Lennox at Temple Newsam 1565', ed. E. W. Crossley, *Yorks. Arch. Journ.* xxv (1920), 91.

'Inventory of the Pictures belonging to the Earl of Leicester 1588', *Notes and Queries*, 3rd. ser ii, 201, 224.

KYNASTON, SIR FRANCIS. *The Constitutions of the Museum Minervae* (1636).

'Kyre Park Building Account', ed. Baldwyn-Childe, *The Antiquary*, xxi, 202, 261; xxii, 24, 50 (1890).

LOMAZZO, G. P. *Trattato dell'arte della pittura, scultura ed architettura* (Milan, 1584).

L'ORME, PHILIBERT DE. *Nouvelles inventions pour bien bastir . . .* (Paris, 1561).

—— *Le premier tome de l'architecture* (Paris, 1568).

*Loseley Manuscripts*, ed. A. J. Kempe (1835).

'Lumley Inventories', ed. L. Cust, *Wal. Soc.* vi (1918), 15.

'Lumley Inventory of 1609', ed. M. F. S. Hervey, *Wal. Soc.* vi (1918), 36.

MANNINGHAM, J. 'Diary', ed. J. Bruce, *Camden Soc.* xcix (1868).

MERES, F. *Palladis Tamia* (1598).

MORE, SIR WILLIAM. 'Extracts from his Private Account Book', ed. J. Evans, *Archaeologia*, xxxvi (1855), 284.

NICHOLS, J. *The Progresses of Queen Elizabeth*, 3 vols. (1823).

—— *The Progresses . . . of King James the First*, 4 vols. (1828).

NORDEN, J. *Historical Description of Middlesex* (1593).

—— *The Description of Hartfordshire* (1598).

—— *Delineation of Northamptonshire 1610* (1720).

—— *Description of Cornwall* (1728).

—— *Description of Essex 1594*, ed. H. Ellis (1840).

—— *Description of Norfolk*, ed. C. M. Hood (Norwich, 1938).

NORGATE, E. *Miniatura or the Art of Limning*, ed. M. Hardie (Oxford, 1919).

OSBORNE, F. *Traditional Memoyres of the Raigne of King James* (Oxford, 1658).

PALLADIO, A. *I quattro Libri dell'Architettura* (Venice, 1570).

PARADIN, C., and SIMEONI, G. *Heroicall Devises* (1591).

PEACHAM, H. *Art of Drawing* (1606).

—— *Gentleman's Exercise* or *Graphice* (1612).

—— *Minerva Britanna* (1612).

—— *Compleat Gentleman* (1622, enlarged edition 1634).

PLATTER, T. *Travels in England*, 1599, ed. C. Williams (1937).

PRATT, SIR ROGER. 'Certain Short Notes concerning Architecture', 1660, ed. R. T. Gunther, *The Architecture of Sir Roger Pratt* (Oxford, 1928).

*Queen Elizabeth's Entertainment at Mitcham 1598*, ed. L. Hotsen (Yale, 1953).

'Relation of the Island of England', ed. C. A. Sneyd, *Camden Soc.* xxxvii (1847).

RYE, W. B. *England as seen by Foreigners* (1865).

SERLIO, S. *Il Libro primo (-quinto) d'Architettura* (Venice, 1551).

—— *Tutte l'Opere d'Architettura* (Venice, 1584, English edition 1611).

SHAW, W. A. *Three Inventories of Pictures in the Collections of Henry VIII and Edward VI* (1937).

'Short Survey of 26 Counties', ed. L. G. W. Legg, *Stuart Series*, vii (1904).

'Short Survey of the Western Counties made in 1635', ed. L. G. W. Legg, *Camden Miscellany*, xvi (1936).

SHUTE, J. *The First and Chief Grounds of Architecture*, ed. L. Weaver (1912).

STETTIN-POMERANIA, DUKE OF. 'Diary of a Journey through England . . . 1602', *Trans. R. Hist. Soc.* N.S. vi (1892), I.

STONE, N. 'Note-Book and Account Book', ed. W. L. Spiers, *Wal. Soc.* vii (1919).

STOW, J. *Survey of London*, ed. C. L. Kingsford, 3 vols. (Oxford, 1908).

TRESWELL, R. *A Relation of . . . the Journey of . . . Charles Earle of Nottingham . . . to the King of Spaine* (1605).

*Two Italian Accounts of Tudor England*, ed. C. V. Malfatti (Barcelona, 1953).

VAN WEDEL, L. 'A Journey through England and Scotland in . . . 1584-5', *Trans. R. Hist. Soc.* N.S. ix (1895), 223.

VASARI G. *The Lives of the Painters, Sculptors & Architects*, translated A. B. Hinds, 4 vols. (1927).

—— *On Technique*, translated L. C. Maclehose, introduction by G. Baldwin Brown (1907).

VITRUVIUS. *De Architectura libri decem* (innumerable editions throughout the sixteenth century).

VRIES, J. VRIEDEMAN DE. *Architectura ou Bastiment prins de Vitruve &c.* (Antwerp, 1577).

WEEVER, J. *Ancient Funeral Monuments* (1631).

WELDON, SIR A. *Court and Character of King James* (1651).

WHITNEY, G. *A Choice of Emblems* (Leyden, 1586).

WILLIAMS, THOMAS. *The historie of Italie* (1549).

WOTTON, SIR HENRY. *The Elements of Architecture* 1624, ed. S. Prideaux (1903).

—— *A Survey of Education*, ed. H. Kermode (1938).


### LATER WORKS

ADDLESHAW, G. W. O., and ETCHELLS, F. *The Architectural Setting of Anglican Worship* (1948).

ADHÉMAR, J. 'French 16th Century Genre Paintings', *Journ. W.C.I.* viii (1945), 191.

ADLER, I. 'Die Clouet. Versuch einer Stilkritik', *J.K.S.W.* N.F. iii (1929), 201.

AUERBACH, E. 'More Light on Nicholas Hilliard', *Burl. Mag.* xci (1949), 166.

—— *The English Portrait and Patronage of Art from c. 1520–90*. Unpublished Ph.D. Thesis London Univ. (1950).

—— 'Holbein's Followers in England', *Burl. Mag.* xciii (1951), 44.

—— 'Portraits of Elizabeth I', ibid. xcv (1953), 197.

—— *Tudor Artists* (1954).

—— 'Some Tudor Portraits at the Royal Academy', *Burl. Mag.* xcix (1957), 9.

—— *Nicholas Hilliard* (1961).

BAKER, C. H. COLLINS. *Catalogue of British Paintings in Huntington Library and Art Gallery* (San Marino, California, 1936).

—— and CONSTABLE, W. G. *English Painting of the Sixteenth and Seventeenth Centuries* (Florence and Paris, 1930).

—— and JAMES, M. R. *British Painting* (1933).

BANKART, G. P. *The Art of the Plasterer* (1908).

BARKER, W. R. 'On the later Monuments in the Mayor's Chapel, Bristol', *Bristol and Gloucester Arch. Soc. Trans.* xv (1890–1), 76.

BARNARD, E. A. B., and WACE, A. J. B. 'The Sheldon Tapestry Weavers and their Work', *Archaeologia*, lxxviii (1928), 255.

BARON, H. *The Crisis of the Early Italian Renaissance* (Princeton, 1955).

BARRY, E. M. 'A View of Elizabethan and Jacobean Architecture', *Builder*, xxxvi (1878), 179, 205.

BENESCH, O. *The Renaissance in Northern Europe* (Harvard, 1945).

BERNHEIMER, R. 'Gothic Survival and Revival in Bologna', *Art Bulletin*, xxxvi (1954), 263.

BIRCH-HIRSCHFELD, K. *Die Lehre von der Malerei im Cinquecento* (Rome, 1912).

BLAKISTON, N. 'Nicholas Hilliard: Some Unpublished Documents', *Burl. Mag.* lxxxix (1947), 187.

—— 'Nicholas Hilliard and Queen Elizabeth's Third Great Seal', ibid. xc (1948), 101.

—— 'Nicholas Hilliard as a Traveller', ibid. xci (1949), 169.

BLAKISTON, N. 'Nicholas Hilliard at Court', ibid. xcvi (1954), 17.

BLOMFIELD, SIR. R. *History of Renaissance Architecture in England 1500–1800.* 2 vols. (1897).

BLUNT, A. F. 'The Hypnerotomachia Polyphili in 17th Century France', *Journ. W.C.I.* i (1937), 117.

—— *Artistic Theories in Italy 1450–1600* (Oxford, 1940).

—— *Art and Architecture in France 1500–1700* (1953).

BOLGAR, R. R. *The Classical Heritage and its Beneficiaries* (Cambridge, 1954).

BULLOCK, A. E. *Some Sculptural Works by Nicholas Stone* (1908).

BUXTON, E. J. M. *Sir Philip Sidney and the English Renaissance* (1954).

CARDEN, R. W. 'Italian Artists in England during the 16th Century', *Proc. Soc. Ants.* 2nd ser. xxiv (1911–12), 171.

CASPARI, F. *Humanism and the Social Order in Tudor England* (Chicago, 1954).

CASTLE, S. E. *Domestic Gothic of the Tudor Period* (New York, 1927).

CESCINSKY, H., and GRIBBLE, E. R. *Early English Furniture and Woodwork* (1922).

CHATWIN, P. 'Monumental Effigies of the County of Warwick Part III', *Birmingham Arch. Soc. Trans.* xlviii (1922), 136.

CLAPHAM, A. W. 'The Survival of Gothic in 17th Century England', *Arch. Journ.* cvi Supplement (1952), 4.

—— and GODFREY, W. H. *Some Famous Buildings* (1913).

CLARK-MAXWELL, W. G. 'Sir William Sharington's Work at Lacock, Sudeley and Dudley', *Arch. Journ.* lxx (1913), 175.

COLDING, T. H. *Aspects of Miniature Painting, its Origins and Development* (Copenhagen, 1953).

CROSSLEY, F. H. 'Post-Reformation Effigies of Cheshire', *Trans. Hist. Soc. Lancs. and Cheshire*, xci (1939), 1.

CUNNINGHAM, P. 'New Materials for the Life of Paul van Somer', *Builder*, xxii (June 1864), 417.

CUST, L. 'Foreign Artists of the Reformed Religion working in London from about 1560 to 1660', *Proc. H.S.L.* vii (1903), 45.

—— *Illustrated Catalogue of . . . Portraits of English Historical Personages who died prior to the year 1625* (Oxford, 1904).

—— *The Royal Collection of Paintings at Buckingham Palace and Windsor Castle* (1905–6).

—— *Eton College Portraits* (1910).

—— 'Notes on the Collections formed by Thomas Howard, Earl of Arundel', *Burl. Mag.* xxi (1912), 256.

—— 'The Painter HE (Hans Eworth)', *Wal. Soc.* ii (1913), 1.

—— 'Marcus Gheeraerts', ibid. iii (1914), 9.

DAVIES, M. *The British School* (National Gallery Catalogue, 1946).

D'ELBOUX, R. H. 'The Brooke Tomb, Cobham', *Archaeologia Cantiana*, lxii (1949), 48.

DENVIR, B. 'Sir Nathaniel Bacon ... a Significant Artist', *Conn.* cxxxvii (1956), 116.

DIMIER, L. *French Painting in the 16th Century* (1904).

—— *Le Portrait en France au XVI<sup>e</sup> siècle* (Paris and Brussels, 1924).

DOUGLAS, R. L. 'Some Portraits of Ceremony of the Jacobean School', *Conn.* cxxvi (1950), 162.

DRESDNER, A. *Die Kunstkritik, ihre Geschichte und Theorie* (Munich, 1915).

DULEEP SINGH, PRINCE. *Portraits in Norfolk Houses*, 2 vols. (Norwich, 1928).

DUNLOP, I. 'Nonsuch Palace', *Conn.* cxxviii (1951), 113.

DUTTON, R. *The English Garden* (1937).

—— *The English Interior 1500–1900* (1948).

DVORAK, M. *Kunstgeschichte als Geistesgeschichte* (Munich, 1924).

EELES, F. C. 'The Black Effigies at Layer Marney Re-examined', *Essex Arch. Soc. Trans.* N.S. xxii (1940), 272.

EHRMANN, J. 'Massacre and Persecution Pictures in 16th Century France', *Journ. W.C.I.* viii (1945), 195.

EICHLER, A. 'Shakespeares Begriff des Gentleman', *Germanisch-Romanische Monatsschrift* ix (1921), 358.

EINSTEIN, L. *The Italian Renaissance in England* (New York, 1902).

—— *Tudor Ideals* (1921).

EMDEN, C. S. 'Sir Henry Unton, An Elizabethan Story-Picture', *Oriel Papers* (Oxford, 1948).

ENGLEFIELD, W. A. D. *History of the Painter-Stainers' Company of London* (1923).

ESDAILE, K. A. *English Monumental Sculpture since the Renaissance* (1927).

—— 'English Sculpture at Cambridge from the Sixteenth to the Eighteenth Century', *Proc. Cambridge Antiquarian Soc.* xxxiv (1934), 1.

—— 'Three Monumental Drawings from Sir Edward Deering's Collection', *Archaeologia Cantiana*, xlvii (1935), 219.

—— 'Post-Reformation Monuments, mainly in Derbyshire', *Derbyshire Arch. Soc. Journ.* lx (1939), 84.

—— 'The Monument of the First Lord Rich at Felsted', *Essex Arch. Soc. Trans.* N.S. xxii (1940), 59.

—— 'Sculpture and Sculptors in Yorkshire', *Yorkshire Arch. Journ.* xxxv (1940–3), 362; xxxvi (1944–7), 78, 137.

—— 'William Cure II and his work at Trinity College, Cambridge', *Burl. Mag.* lxxx (1942), 21.

—— 'The Inter-action of English and Low Country Sculpture in the Sixteenth Century', *Journ. W.C.I.* vi (1943), 80.

—— 'English Sculpture in some Berkshire Churches', *Berks. Arch. Journ.* xlv (1941), 45, 86; xlvi (1942), 22, 69.

—— *English Church Monuments 1510–1840* (1946).

—— 'Renaissance Monuments of Buckinghamshire', *Records of Bucks.* xv (1947), 32.

ESDAILE, K. A. 'The Part played by Refugee Sculptors 1600–1750', *H.S.L. Proc.* xviii (1948–9), 254.

ETTLINGER, L. 'Pollaiuolo's Tomb of Sixtus IV', *Journ. W.C.I.* xvi (1953), 239.

Exhibition Catalogues. *National Portraits*, South Kensington (1866–8).

—— *Portrait Miniatures*, Burlington Fine Arts Club (1889).

—— *Early English Portraiture*, ibid. (1909).

—— *Pictures of Mr. Robert Holford*, ibid. (1921).

—— *Late Elizabethan Art*, ibid. (1926).

—— *British Art*, R.A. (1935).

—— *Nicholas Hilliard and Isaac Oliver*, V. & A. (1947).

—— *Works by Holbein and other Masters of the 16th and 17th Centuries*, R.A. (1950).

—— *British Portraits*, R.A. (1956).

—— *Italian Art and Britain*, R.A. (1960).

FARRER, E. *Portraits in Suffolk Houses* (1908).

FARRINGTON, B. *Francis Bacon, Philosopher of Industrial Science* (1951).

FINBERG, A. J. 'An Authentic Portrait by Robert Peake', *Wal. Soc.* ix (1920–1), 89.

FOKKER, T. 'Origin of Baroque Painting', *Art Bulletin* xv (1933), 299.

FOWLER, R. C. 'The Denny Monument in Waltham Abbey Church', *Essex Arch. Soc. Trans.* N.S. xvi. (1923), 57.

FOX, L. (Editor). *English Historical Scholarship in the 16th and 17th Centuries* (Oxford, 1956).

FREEMAN, R. *English Emblem Books* (1948).

FREY, D. *Englisches Wesen in der bildenden Kunst* (Stuttgart, Berlin, 1942).

—— *Kunstwissenschaftliche Grundfragen* (Vienna, 1946).

FRIEDLÄNDER, W. 'Die Entstehung des antiklassischen Stiles in der italienischen Malerei um 1520', *R.K.S.* xlvi (1925), 49.

FRY, F. M. *Historical Catalogue of the Pictures . . . at Merchant Taylors' Hall* (1907).

FRYER, A. C. 'Wooden Monumental Effigies in England and Wales', *Archaeologia*, lxi (1909), 487.

—— 'Monumental Effigies by Bristol Craftsmen', ibid. lxxiv (1925), 1.

—— 'Monumental Effigies in Somerset, 16th century' *Somerset Arch. Soc. Proc.* lxxii (1926), 23; lxxiv (1928), 10; lxxvi (1930), 28.

GANZ, P. *The Paintings of Hans Holbein* (1950).

GARNER, T., and STRATTON, A. *The Domestic Architecture of England during the Tudor Period*, 2 vols. (2nd ed. 1929).

GIROUARD, M. 'New Light on Longleat: Allen Maynard, a French Sculptor in England in the 16th Century', *C.L.* cxx (Sept.-Oct. 1956), 594, 785, 954.

GODFREY, W. H. *The English Staircase* (1911).

—— *The English Almshouse* (1955).

GOLDSCHMIDT, E. P. 'Nicholas Hilliard as a Wood Engraver', *Times Lit. Supp.* 9 Aug. 1947, p. 403.

GOMBRICH, E. 'Zum Werke Giulio Romanos' Versuch einer Deutung', *J.K.S.W.* N.F. viii (1934), 79; ix (1935), 121.

GOODISON, J. W. 'George Gower, Sergeant Painter to Queen Elizabeth', *Burl. Mag.* xc (1948), 261.

—— *Catalogue of Cambridge Portraits*, vol. 1 (Cambridge, 1955).

GORDON, D. J. 'Poet and Architect: the Intellectual Setting of the Quarrel between Ben Jonson and Inigo Jones', *Journ. W.C.I.* xii (1949), 152.

GOTCH, J. A. *The Buildings erected by Sir Thomas Tresham* (Northampton, 1883).

—— *Architecture of the Renaissance in England*, 2 vols. (1894).

—— 'Development of House Design in the Reigns of Elizabeth and James I', *Journ. R.I.B.A.* xvi (1908–9), 41.

—— *Early Renaissance Architecture in England* (2nd ed. 1914).

—— *Inigo Jones* (1928).

—— *Growth of the English House* (2nd ed. 1928).

—— *Old Halls and Manor Houses of Northamptonshire* (1936).

—— *Squires' Homes and Old Buildings in Northamptonshire* (1939).

GOULDING, R. W. 'Notes on Additional HE Portraits', *Wal. Soc.* iii (1914), 118.

—— 'The Welbeck Abbey Miniatures', *Wal. Soc.* iv (1916).

—— *The Wriothesley Portraits* (Oxford, 1920).

—— *Bolsover Castle* (5th ed. Oxford, 1928).

—— and ADAMS, C. K. *Catalogue of the Pictures belonging to the Duke of Portland* (Cambridge, 1936).

GRUNDY, C. R. 'Gerlach Flicke's Lost Diptych Portrait', *Conn.* xlv (1916), 163.

HAKE, H. M. *The English Historic Portrait Document and Myth* (1944).

—— and O'DONOGHUE, F. *Catalogue of Engraved British Portraits . . . in the British Museum*, 6 vols. (1908–28).

HASKINS, C. *Salisbury Corporation Pictures and Plate* (Salisbury, 1910).

HAUSER, A. *The Social History of Art* (1951).

HAUTECŒUR, L. de. *Histoire de l'architecture classique en France*, 2 vols. (Paris, 1943, 1948).

HERVEY, M. F. S. 'Some Portraits of Tudor Times', *Burl. Mag.* xv (1909), 151.

—— 'Notes on a Tudor Painter—Gerlach Flicke', ibid. xvii (1910), 71, 147.

—— 'Two Portraits by Haunce Eworth', *Wal. Soc.* iii (1914), 114.

—— *Life, Correspondence and Collections of Thomas Howard, Earl of Arundel* (Cambridge, 1921).

HIND, A. M. *Engraving in England in the 16th and 17th Centuries*, i (1952); ii (1955).

HISCOCK, W. G. 'Notes on some Christ Church Portraits', *Oxoniensia* xi (1946–7), 147.

HOSKINS, W. G. 'The Rebuilding of Rural England 1570–1640', *P. and P.* iv (1953), 44.

HOUGHTON, W. E. 'The English Virtuoso in the 17th Century', *J.H.I.* iii (1942) 51, 190.

HOWARD, C. *English Travellers of the Renaissance* (1914).

HUMPHREYS, J. 'Elizabethan Sheldon Tapestries', *Archaeologia*, lxxiv (1925), 184.

HUSSEY, C. 'Longleat, Wiltshire', *C.L.* cv (Apr. 1949), 798, 862, 926, 990.

HYMANS, H. *Antonio Moro, son œuvre et son temps* (Brussels, 1910).

ILCHESTER, Earl of. 'Queen Elizabeth's Visit to Blackfriars June 16 1600', *Wal. Soc.* ix (1921), 1.

JEAVONS, S. A. 'The Monumental Effigies of Staffordshire', *Birmingham Arch. Soc. Trans.* lxix (1951), 1; lxx (1952), 1; lxxi (1953), 1.

JENKINS, M. *The State Portrait, its Origin and Evolution* (U.S.A. College Art Association, New York, 1947).

JOHNSON, F. R. 'Gresham College: Precursor of the Royal Society', *J.H.I.* i (1940), 413.

JOHNSTON, P. W. 'Mural Paintings in Houses', *Journ. Brit. Arch. Ass.* N.S. xxxvii (1932), 75.

JONES, K. H. 'The Hawkins Monument by Epiphanius Evesham at Boughton-under-Blean', *Archaeologia Cantiana*, xlv (1933), 205.

JOURDAIN, M. *English Decoration and Furniture of the Early Renaissance* (1924).
—— *English Decorative Plasterwork of the Renaissance* (1926).
—— *English Interior Decoration 1500–1830* (1950).

JURGENS, M. 'Quelques Actes Inédits concernant Epiphanius Evesham', *Bulletin de la Société de l'histoire de l'art français* (1960), 175.

KELSO, R. *The Doctrine of the English Gentleman in the 16th Century* (Urbana, U.S.A., 1949).

KENDRICK, A. F. 'The Hatfield Tapestries of the Seasons', *Wal. Soc.* ii (1913), 89.
—— *English Decorative Fabrics of the 16th to 18th Centuries* (Benfleet, 1934).
—— and TATTERSALL, C. E. C. *Guide to the Collection of Carpets.* Victoria and Albert Museum (1931).

KENDRICK, T. D. *British Antiquity* (1950).

KENNEDY, H. A. 'Early English Portrait Miniatures in the Collection of the Duke of Buccleuch', *Studio, Special Number* (1917).

KNIGHTS, L. C. *Drama and Society in the Age of Jonson* (1937).

KNOOP, D., and JONES, G. P. *The 16th Century Mason* (1937).

KOCHER, P. H. 'The Idea of God in Elizabethan Medicine', *J.H.I.* xi (1950), 3.

KURZ, O. 'Holbein and Others in a 17th Century Collection', *Burl. Mag.* lxxxiii (1943), 279.
—— 'Rowland Lockey', ibid. xcix (1957), 13.

LATHROP, H. B. *Translations from the Classics into English from Caxton to Chapman 1477–1620* (Madison, U.S.A., 1933).

LEES-MILNE, J. *Tudor Renaissance* (1951).

LEES-MILNE, J. 'Two Portraits at Charlecote Park by William Larkin', *Burl. Mag.* xciv (1952), 352.

—— *The Age of Inigo Jones* (1953).

LEGG, L. G. W. 'On a Picture commemorative of the Gunpowder Plot', *Archaeologia*, lxxxiv (1935), 27.

LINNELL, C. L. S. 'Suffolk Church Monuments', *Proc. Suffolk Institute of Archaeology*, xxvii (1958), 1.

—— and WEARING, S. J. *Norfolk Church Monuments* (Ipswich, 1952).

LLOYD, N. *A History of English Brickwork* (1925).

—— *A History of the English House* (2nd ed. 1949).

LONG, B. *British Miniaturists* (1929).

LUGT, F. *Le Portrait-miniature illustré par la collection de S.M. la Reine des Pays-Bas* (Amsterdam, 1917).

MACDONALD, A. 'Anthony Tolly, and the Tomb of Edmund Freake', *Worcs. Arch. Soc. Trans.* N.S. xix (1942), 1.

MACQUOID, P., and EDWARDS, R. *Dictionary of English Furniture*, 3 vols. (1954).

MANN, J. G. 'Instances of Antiquarian Feeling in Mediaeval and Renaissance Art', *Arch. Journ.* lxxxix (1932), 254.

—— 'English Church Monuments 1536–1625', *Wal. Soc.* xxi (1933), 1.

MASON, S. F. 'The Scientific Revolution and the Protestant Reformation', *Annals of Science*, ix (1953), 64, 154.

MATTINGLEY, G. *Renaissance Diplomacy* (1955).

MERCER, E. 'The Decoration of the Royal Palaces from 1553–1625', *Arch. Journ.* cx (1953), 150.

—— 'The Houses of the Gentry', *P. and P.* v (1954), 11.

MERTON, R. K. 'Science, Technology and Society in 17th Century England', *Osiris*, iv (1938), 360.

MILLAR, O. 'Abraham van der Doort's catalogue of the collections of Charles 1', *Wal. Soc.* xxxvii (1958–60).

—— *see* WHINNEY, M.

MORGAN, F. C. 'Two Hereford 16th Century Sculptors, John Gildon and Epiphanius Evesham', *Woolhope Club Trans.* (1933–5), p. 111.

MOSSE, H. R. *The Monumental Effigies of Sussex (1250–1650)* (Hove, 1933).

MUTHESIUS, H. *Das englische Haus*, 3 vols. (Berlin, 1908–11).

MYRES, J. N. L., and ROUSE, E. C. 'The Painted Frieze in the Picture Gallery', *Bodleian Library Record*, iii, No. 30 (Oct. 1950), 82; No. 32 (Aug. 1951), 201; iv, No. 1 (Apr. 1952), 30.

NASH, J. *Mansions of England in the Olden Time*, 4 vols. (1839–49).

NEVINSON, J. L. *Catalogue of English Domestic Embroidery*. Victoria and Albert Museum (1950).

—— 'Portraits of Gentlemen Pensioners before 1625', *Wal. Soc.* xxxiv (1952–4), 1.

—— 'Captains of the Trainbands', *Conn.* cxli (1958), 159.

NIVEN, W. *Illustrations of Old Worcestershire Houses* (1873).

—— *Old Warwickshire Houses* (1878).

—— *Old Staffordshire Houses* (1882).

OBERNITZ, W. von, *Vasaris allgemeine Kunstanschauungen* (Strassburg, 1897).

O'DONOGHUE, F. M. *A Descriptive and Classified Catalogue of the Portraits of Queen Elizabeth* (1894).

—— *Catalogue of Engraved British Portraits in the British Museum* (1908).

OGDEN, H. V. S., and OGDEN, M. S. *English Taste in Landscape in the 17th Century* (Ann Arbor, U.S.A., 1955).

OSWALD, A. *Country Houses of Kent* (1933).

—— *Country Houses of Dorset* (1935).

—— 'Montacute Re-visited', *C.L.* cxviii (Nov. 1955), 1020.

PALME, PER. *Triumph of Peace. A Study of the Whitehall Banqueting House* (Stockholm, 1956).

PANOFSKY, E. *Idea* (Leipzig, 1924).

PAPWORTH, W. ' "Architecture" . . . in England in the 15th and 16th Centuries', *Builder*, xvii (1859), 756.

—— '*John Shute*', ibid. xxxvi (1878), 826.

—— *The Renaissance and Italian Styles of Architecture in Great Britain* (1883).

PAYNE, E. J. 'The Montforts, the Wellesbournes and the Hughenden Effigies', *Records of Bucks.* vii (1897), 385.

PEVSNER, N. 'Gegenreformation und Manierismus', *R.K.S.* xlvi (1925), 243.

—— *Academies of Art Past and Present* (Cambridge, 1940).

—— 'The Architecture of Mannerism', *The Mint*, ed. G. Grigson (1946), 116.

—— 'Double Profile', *Arch. Rev.* cvii (1950), 147.

—— *The Planning of the Elizabethan Country House* (1960).

PHILIP, I. G. 'Balthazar Gerbier and the Duke of Buckingham's Pictures', *Burl. Mag.* xcix (1957), 155.

PINDER, W. *Das Problem der Generation in der Kunstgeschichte Europas* (Berlin, 1926).

—— 'Zur Physiognomik des Manierismus', *Festschrift Ludwig Klages* (Leipzig, 1932).

PIPER, D. 'Contemporary Portraits of Oliver Cromwell', *Wal. Soc.* xxxiv (1952–4), 27.

—— 'The 1590 Lumley Inventory: Hilliard, Segar and the Earl of Essex', *Burl. Mag.* xcix (1957), 224, 299.

—— *The English Face* (1957).

PIRR, M. *Die Architectura des Wendel Dietterlin* (Gräfenhainichen, 1940).

POOLE, Mrs. R. L. *Catalogue of Oxford Portraits*, 3 vols. (Oxford, 1912–26).

—— 'The De Critz Family of Painters', *Wal. Soc.* ii (1913), 45.

—— 'Marcus Gheeraerts, Father and Son, Painters', ibid. iii (1914), 1.

POPE-HENNESSY, JOHN. 'Nicholas Hilliard and Mannerist Art Theory', *Journ. W.C.I.* vi (1943), 89.

—— *A Lecture on Nicholas Hilliard* (1949).

—— 'Elizabethan Style', *Art News,* lii (Summer 1953), 40.

POWELL, C. L. *English Domestic Relations 1487–1653* (New York, 1917).

PROPERT, J. L. *History of Miniature Art* (1887).

READER, F. W. 'Tudor Mural Paintings in the Lesser Houses in Bucks.', *Arch. Journ.* lxxxix (1932), 116.

—— 'Tudor Domestic Wall-paintings', Part I, ibid. xcii (1935), 243; Part II, ibid. xciii (1936), 220.

—— 'A Classification of Tudor Domestic Wall-painting'; Part I, ibid. xcviii (1941), 181.

REISZMANN, K. 'Die Entwicklung der Liegefiguren in der Architekturplastik von Michelangelo bis zum Klassizismus', in *Festschrift Wilhelm Pinder* (Leipzig, 1938).

REYNOLDS, G. *Nicholas Hilliard and Isaac Oliver.* V. & A. Handbook (1947).

—— *English Portrait Miniatures* (1952).

—— 'Portraits by Nicholas Hilliard and his Assistants of King James I and his Family', *Wal. Soc.* xxxiv (1952–4), 14.

RICHARDSON, C. J. *Observations on the Architecture . . . of Queen Elizabeth and James I* (1837).

—— *Studies from Old English Mansions,* 2 vols. (1841–5).

—— *Architectural Remains* (1840).

ROBERTS, J. F. A. 'English Wall-Paintings after Italian Engravings', *Burl. Mag.* lxxviii (1941), 86.

ROPER, I. M. *Monumental Effigies of Gloucester and Bristol* (Gloucester, 1931).

ROSENBERG, E. *Leicester, Patron of Letters* (New York, 1955).

ROUSE, E. C. 'The Kederminster Library', *Records of Bucks.* xiv (1941–6), 50.

—— 'Domestic Wall-Painting at Chalfont St. Peter and elsewhere', ibid. xv (1948), 87.

—— 'Post-Reformation Mural Paintings in Parish Churches', *Lincolnshire Historian* i (1957), 8.

—— See MYRES, J. N. L.

ROUSSEAU, T. 'The Triumph of Mannerism?', *Art News,* liv (Sept. 1955), 18.

SALERNO, L. 'Seventeenth Century English Literature on Painting', *Journ. W.C.I.* xiv (1951), 234.

SAXL, F., and WITTKOWER, R. *British Art and the Mediterranean* (1948).

SCHARF, H. *Account of the Russell Monuments . . . at Chenies . . .* (1892).

SCHIRMER, W. F. 'Chaucer, Shakespeare und die Antike', *Bibliothek Warburg Vorträge* (1930–1), 83.

SEKLER, E. F. 'The English Staircase', *Arch. Rev.* cix (May 1951), 301.

SHAW, H. *Details of Elizabethan Architecture* (1839).

SIEGEL, P. N. 'English Humanism and the New Tudor Aristocracy', *J.H.I.* xiii (1952), 450.

SIMMONS, JACK. 'Brooke Church, Rutland: with notes on Elizabethan Church-Building', *Trans. Leics. Arch. and Hist. Soc.* xxxv (1959), 36.

SIMPSON, D. 'Dudley Castle. The Renaissance Buildings', *Arch. Journ.* ci (1944), 199.

SMALL, T., and WOODBRIDGE, C. *Mouldings of the Tudor Period* (1930).

—— *English Brickwork Details 1450–1700* (1931).

SMITH, L. P. *Life and letters of Sir Henry Wotton*, 2 vols. (Oxford, 1907).

STALLEYBRASS, B. 'Bess of Hardwick's Buildings and Building Accounts', *Archaeologia*, lxiv (1913), 347.

STEEGMAN, J. 'Two Signed Portraits by Paul Van Somer', *Burl. Mag.* xci (1949), 52.

STONE, L. 'The Building of Hatfield House', *Arch. Journ.* cxii (1955), 100.

—— 'Inigo Jones and the New Exchange', ibid. cxiv (1959), 106.

STONE, P. G. *Architectural Antiquities of the Isle of Wight* (1891).

STOPES, C. C. 'Daniel Mytens in England', *Burl. Mag.* (1910), 160.

—— 'Gleanings from the Records of James I and Charles I', ibid. xxii (1912–13), 276.

STRATTON, A. *The English Interior* (1920).

SUMMERSON, J. 'John Thorpe and the Thorpes of Kingscliffe', *Arch. Rev.* cvi (1949), 291.

—— *Architecture in Britain 1530–1830* (1953).

—— 'Three Elizabethan Architects', *Bulletin of the John Rylands Library*, xl (1957), 202.

—— 'The Building of Theobalds', *Archaeologia*, xcvii (1959), 107.

SUMNER-SMITH, JOAN. 'The Italian Sources of Inigo Jones' Style', *Burl. Mag.* xciv (1952), 200.

TATTERSALL, C. E. C. *A History of British Carpets* (Benfleet, 1934).

TAYLOR, E. G. R. *Late Tudor and Stuart Geography* (1934).

—— *The Mathematical Practitioners of Tudor and Stuart England* (Cambridge, 1954).

TAYLOR, H. *Old Halls in Lancashire and Cheshire* (Manchester, 1884).

TENISON, E. M. *Elizabethan England*, 12 vols. (Leamington, 1932–61).

THOMPSON, W. G. *Tapestry Weaving in England* (1914).

TILLYARD, E. M. W. *The Elizabethan World Picture* (1943).

TIPPING, H. A. *English Homes*, Period III (Late Tudor and Early Stuart), 2 vols. (1927, 1929).

VALLANCE, A. *Art in England during the Elizabethan and Stuart Periods* (1908).

—— 'The Ropers and their Monuments in Lynsted Church', *Archaeologia Cantiana*, lxiv (1932), 147.

VENTURI, L. *History of Art Criticism* (New York, 1936).

VERTUE, G. Notebooks, *Wal. Soc.* xviii, xx, xxii, xxiv, xxvi, xxix (Index), xxx (1930–52).

WATERHOUSE, E. K. *Painting in Britain 1530–1790* (1954).

—— 'The Decline of the Miniature', *Penguin Parade*, 2nd ser., No. 1, p. 42.

WEISBACH, W. *Der Barock als Kunst der Gegenreformation* (Berlin, 1921).

WHIFFEN, M. *Stuart and Georgian Churches outside London* (1947).

—— *Elizabethan and Jacobean Architecture* (1952).

WHINNEY, M., and MILLAR, O. *English Art, 1625–1714* (Oxford, 1958).

WILLIAMSON, G. C. *History of Portrait Miniatures*, 2 vols. (1904).

WILLIS, R. J., and CLARK, J. W. *Architectural History of the University of Cambridge*, 4 vols. (Cambridge, 1886).

WILSON, E. C. *England's Eliza* (Harvard, 1939).

WINTER, C. *Elizabethan Miniatures* (1943).

—— 'Holbein's Miniatures', *Burl. Mag.* lxxxiii (1943), 266.

—— 'Hilliard and Elizabethan Miniatures', *ibid.* lxxxix (1947).

—— 'The British School of Miniature Portrait Painters', *Proc. Brit. Acad.* xxxiv (1948), 119.

WITTKOWER, R. 'Michelangelo's Biblioteca Laurenziana', *Art Bulletin*, xvi (1934), 123.

—— 'Principles of Palladio's Architecture', *Journ. W.C.I.* vii (1944), 102.

—— *Architectural Principles in the Age of Humanism* (1949).

—— 'Inigo Jones Puritanissimo Fiero', *Burl. Mag.* xc (1948), 50.

—— 'Inigo Jones Architect and Man of Letters', *Journ. R.I.B.A.* lx (1953), 83.

—— *Art and Architecture in Italy 1600–1750* (1958).

WÖLFFLIN, H. *Kunstgeschichtliche Grundbegriffe* (Munich, 1915).

—— *Die klassische Kunst* (8th ed. Basle, 1948).

WOOD, T. 'The Buccleuch Miniatures', *Studio*, lxix (1917), 163.

—— 'The Beauchamp Miniatures', *ibid.* lxxi (1917), 85.

WOODWARD, J. *Tudor and Stuart Drawings* (1951).

WRIGHT, L. B. *Middle Class Culture in Elizabethan England* (Huntington Library Publications, 1935).

WÜSTEN, E. *Die Architektur des Manierismus in England* (Leipzig, 1951).

YATES, F. A. 'Paolo Sarpi's History of the Council of Trent', *Journ. W.C.I.* vii (1944), 123.

—— 'Queen Elizabeth as Astraea', *ibid.* x (1947), 27.

—— *French Academies of the 16th Century* (1947).

ZUPNIK, I. L. 'Aesthetics of Early Mannerism', *Art Bulletin*, xxxv (1953), 302.

# INDEX

*References in black type are to plates*

I. *a*. LONGLEAT, WILTSHIRE: FROM THE SOUTH-WEST. Completed after 1567
*b*. BARRINGTON COURT, SOMERSET

2. *a*. WIMBLEDON HOUSE, SURREY. BEGUN *c*. 1588. Engraving by H. Winstanley
*b*. LONGFORD CASTLE, WILTSHIRE. BEGUN *c*. 1588

3. *a*. CASTLE ASHBY, NORTHAMPTONSHIRE: SOUTH FRONT, *c*. 1580: THE SCREEN, *c*. 1630
*b*. HARDWICK NEW HALL, DERBYSHIRE: WEST FRONT, 1590–7

4. HATFIELD, HERTFORDSHIRE: SOUTH FRONT, 1607–12

5. HATFIELD, HERTFORDSHIRE: NORTH FRONT, 1607–12

6. *a.* BRERETON HALL, CHESHIRE: THE ENTRANCE GATEWAY, *c.* 1586
*b.* KIRBY HALL, NORTHAMPTONSHIRE: PORCH IN COURTYARD, 1572

7. *a.* HARTWELL HOUSE, BUCKINGHAMSHIRE: ORIEL
*b.* BRAMSHILL, HAMPSHIRE: FRONTISPIECE, 1605–12

8. WOLLATON, NOTTINGHAMSHIRE: SOUTH-EAST TOWER, 1580-8

9. *a.* NORTH CADBURY COURT, SOMERSET, *c.* 1581
*b.* NEWTON SURMAVILLE HOUSE, SOMERSET, 1608–12

10. *a*. KINGSTON MAURWARD HOUSE, DORSET, 1591
*b*. ANDERSON MANOR HOUSE, DORSET, *c*. 1622

11. *a.* LOSELEY, SURREY, 1562–8
*b.* LILFORD HALL, NORTHAMPTONSHIRE, *c.* 1635

12. *a.* WHITEHALL, SHREWSBURY, 1578-82
*b.* BOYTON HOUSE, WILTSHIRE, *c.* 1618

13. *a*. LULWORTH CASTLE, DORSET: FROM THE SOUTH-WEST, *c.* 1588–1609
*b*. TIXALL, STAFFORDSHIRE: GATEHOUSE, 1580

14. *a*. WOOLMORE FARM, MELKSHAM, WILTSHIRE, 1631
*b*. TOSELAND, HUNTINGDONSHIRE, *c*. 1600

15. *a*. LACOCK, WILTSHIRE: WINDOW
*b*. STOCKTON HOUSE, WILTSHIRE: WEST FRONT

16. *a*. BOLSOVER CASTLE, DERBYSHIRE: BEGUN 1612
*b*. LINCOLN COLLEGE, OXFORD: CHAPEL, 1629–31

17. *a*. CHANTMARLE, DORSET: BEGUN 1612
*b*. QUENBY HALL, LEICESTERSHIRE

18. *a.* LONGLEAT, WILTSHIRE: BAY OF SOUTH FRONT, AFTER 1567

*b.* DEENE PARK, NORTHAMPTONSHIRE: WINDOW, 1549–72

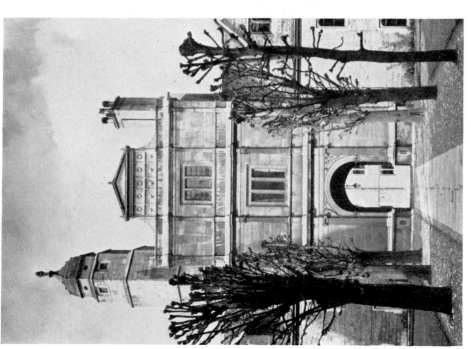

19. *a.* GONVILLE AND CAIUS COLLEGE, CAMBRIDGE: GATE OF VIRTUE, *c.* 1565
*b.* GONVILLE AND CAIUS COLLEGE, CAMBRIDGE: GATE OF HONOUR, *c.* 1573

20. GAYHURST, BUCKINGHAMSHIRE: SOUTH-EAST ELEVATION AND FRONTISPIECE

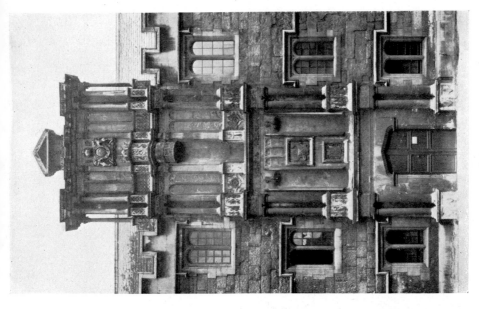

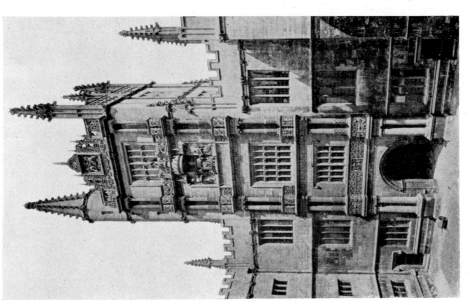

21. _a_. SCHOOLS QUADRANGLE, OXFORD: FRONTISPIECE, 1613–24

_b_. MERTON COLLEGE, OXFORD: FRONTISPIECE IN FELLOWS' QUADRANGLE, 1608–10

22. BURTON AGNES, YORKSHIRE: GATEHOUSE, c. 1610

23. CRANBORNE MANOR, DORSET: LOGGIA, 1607–12

24. BLICKLING HALL, NORFOLK: EAST FRONT, C. 1625

25. *a.* ELMSTEAD HALL, ESSEX: WALL PAINTING OF 'ANTIQUE WORK'

*b.* GROOMBRIDGE, KENT: CHURCH PORCH, 1623

26. CHARLTON, KENT, 1607–12

27. LAKE HOUSE, WILTSHIRE, C. 1600

28. NO. 3 CORNMARKET, OXFORD: WALL PAINTING

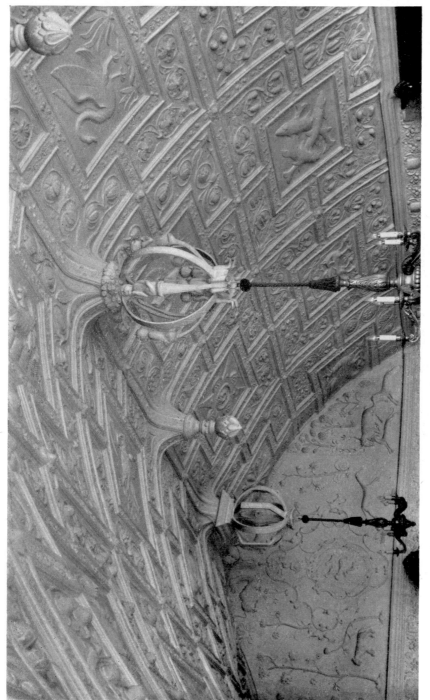

29. HERRINGSTON, DORSET: CEILING PENDANTS

30. *a*. LITTLE STRICKLAND HALL, WESTMORLAND: CEILING
*b*. MELBURY SAMPFORD, DORSET: CEILING IN MELBURY HOUSE

31. AUDLEY END, ESSEX: HALL SCREEN

32. *a*. WADHAM COLLEGE, OXFORD: CHAPEL SCREEN
*b*. MONTACUTE, SOMERSET: HALL SCREEN

33. *a*. BLICKLING HALL, NORFOLK: DETAIL OF CEILING. CENTRAL PANEL
TAKEN FROM PEACHAM'S 'MINERVA BRITANNA'
*b*. MAPPERTON, DORSET: OVERMANTEL

34. KNIGHTSLAND FARM, SOUTH MIMMS, MIDDLESEX: 'THE PRODIGAL SON' WALL PAINTING

35. *a.* BURTON AGNES, YORKSHIRE: CEILING OF LONG GALLERY. Now destroyed

*b.* LOSELEY, SURREY: CHIMNEY-PIECE

36. *a.* PARK HALL, OSWESTRY: CEILING WITH FIGURE OF NEPTUNE. Now destroyed
*b.* HARDWICK NEW HALL, DERBYSHIRE: FRIEZE IN BEDROOM

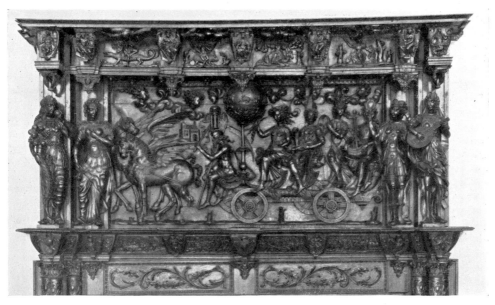

37. *a.* ASTLEY HALL, LANCASHIRE: PAINTED PANELS, *c.* 1625
    *b.* CHIPCHASE CASTLE, NORTHUMBERLAND: CHIMNEY-PIECE

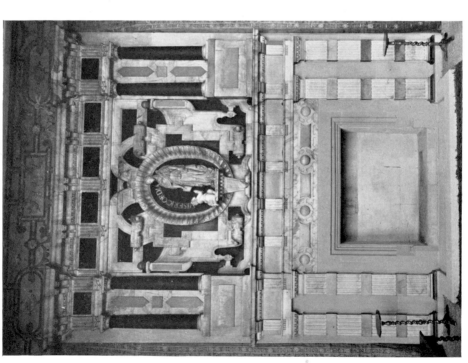

38. *a*. HARDWICK NEW HALL, DERBYSHIRE: CHIMNEY-PIECE IN GALLERY
*b*. HARDWICK OLD HALL, DERBYSHIRE: CHIMNEY-PIECE

39. *a.* HATFIELD HOUSE, HERTFORDSHIRE: CHIMNEY-PIECE WITH MOSAIC PORTRAIT OF ROBERT CECIL, 1610

*b.* KNOLE, KENT: STAIRCASE

40. *a*. ASTON HALL, WARWICKSHIRE: STAIRCASE
*b*. HILL HALL, ESSEX: WALL PAINTING: KING HEZEKIAH BEFORE THE TEMPLE

41. HATFIELD HOUSE, HERTFORDSHIRE: FIGURE UPON STAIRCASE. CARVED BY
JOHN BUCKE, c. 1612

42. BED FROM MORETON CORBET CASTLE, SHROPSHIRE, 1593
Victoria and Albert Museum

43. PILE CARPET OF ENGLISH MANUFACTURE, 1614. Sir Westrow Hulse, Bt., Breamore, Hampshire

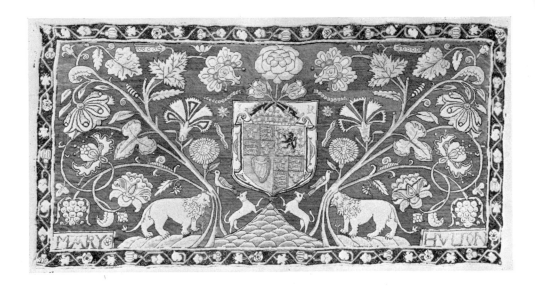

44. *a*. CUSHION COVER WORKED BY MARY HULTON. Victoria and Albert Museum

*b*. INLAID CHEST. Victoria and Albert Museum

45. A MORALITY. Derek Sherborn, Esq.

46. LIFE AND DEATH OF SIR HENRY UNTON.    National Portrait Gallery

47. LEVINUS VOGELARIUS: THE DARNLEY CENOTAPH, 1567. Holyrood Palace

48. MEETING OF THE ENGLISH AND SPANISH PLENIPOTENTIARIES IN 1604.   National Portrait Gallery

49. *a*. HANS EWORTH: THOMAS WYNDHAM, 1550. Earl of Radnor, Longford Castle
*b*. HANS EWORTH: DUCHESS OF NORFOLK, 1563. Hon. Robin Neville, Audley End

SAT
SVPER
EST

50. GUILLIM SCROTES: HENRY HOWARD, EARL OF SURREY
Hon. Clive Pearson, Parham Park

MY CHYLDHODDE PAST THAT BEWTIFIID MY FLESE
AND GONNE MY YOVTH THAT GAVE ME COLOR FRESHE
YAM NOWE CVM TO THOS RYPE YERIS AT LAST
THAT TELLES ME HOWE MY WANTON DAYS BE PAST
AND THERFORE FRINDE SO TVRNES THE TYME ME
Y ONS WAS YOVNG AND NOWE AM AS YOV SES

AETATIS XXXVI
M·D·LXVI·

51. HANS EWORTH: JOAN THORNBURY, 1566. Oliver Watney, Esq., Cornbury Park

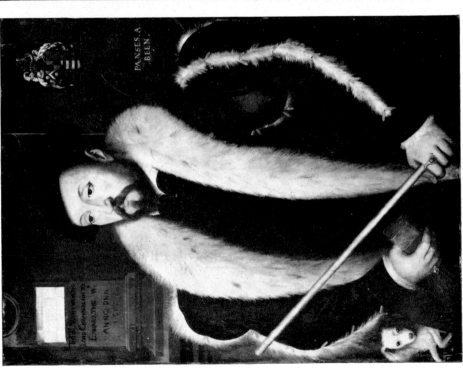

52. *a.* 1ST LORD WENTWORTH, 1547.  National Portrait Gallery
    *b.* 2ND LORD WENTWORTH, 1568.  National Portrait Gallery

53. *a.* CORNELIS KETEL: WILLIAM GRESHAM (DETAIL), 1579. R. H. G. Leveson-Gower, Esq., Titsey Park

*b.* SIR EDWARD HOBY, 1578. Miss E. Paget

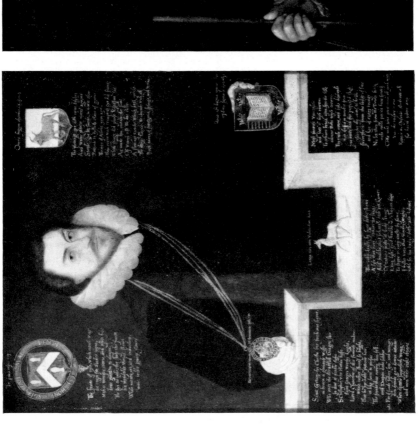

54. *a.* SIR CHRISTOPHER HATTON AS CHANCELLOR OF THE UNIVERSITY OF OXFORD.　National Portrait Gallery

*b.* HENRY CARY, LORD HUNSDON, 1591.　Col. V. N. Stopford Sackville, T.D., O.B.E., Drayton House, Kettering

55. *a.* GEORGE GOWER: LADY KITSON. Tate Gallery

*b.* GEORGE GOWER: SELF-PORTRAIT, 1579. Earl Fitzwilliam, Milton, Peterborough

56. *a.* THE 'COBHAM' QUEEN ELIZABETH. National Portrait Gallery

*b.* THE 'RAINBOW' QUEEN ELIZABETH. The Marquess of Salisbury, Hatfield House

57. *a*. LADY TANFIELD. Loel Guinness, Esq.
*b*. LADY AND CHILD. Trustees of the late A. J. C. Wall, Esq.

58. SIR HENRY NEVILL, 1582. Lt.-Col. Sir Edmund Bacon, Bt., Raveningham

59. PAUL VAN SOMER: ANNE OF DENMARK BEFORE OATLANDS, 1617
Windsor Castle. Reproduced by gracious permission of Her Majesty the Queen

60. THE EARL OF ESSEX. The Duke of Bedford, Woburn Abbey
By kind permission of the Duke of Bedford

61. THE 'DITCHLEY' QUEEN ELIZABETH. National Portrait Gallery

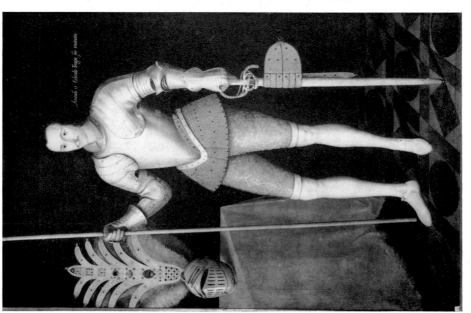

62. *a.* THE EARL OF SUSSEX, *c.* 1595. Tower of London

*b.* PRINCE HENRY HUNTING. Hampton Court. Reproduced by gracious permission of Her Majesty the Queen

63. *a.* NICHOLAS HILLIARD: UNKNOWN MAN AGAINST A BACKGROUND OF FLAMES. Victoria and Albert Museum
*b.* NICHOLAS HILLIARD: UNKNOWN YOUTH AMIDST BRIARS. Victoria and Albert Museum

64. *a.* GEORGE GELDORP: 2ND EARL OF SALISBURY BEFORE HATFIELD HOUSE. The Marquess of Salisbury, Hatfield House

*b.* SIR NATHANIEL BACON: SELF–PORTRAIT. Earl of Verulam, Gorhambury

65. *a.* LADY ANNE RICH. British Embassy, Madrid
*b.* UNKNOWN LADY, 1614. National Portrait Gallery

66. LUDOVIC STUART, DUKE OF RICHMOND AND LENNOX, 1608
Lord Tollemache, Helmingham Hall

67. MARCUS GHEERAERTS: LADY RUSSELL, 1625

The Duke of Bedford, Woburn Abbey. By kind permission of the Duke of Bedford

68. SIR NATHANIEL BACON: JANE BACON. Earl of Verulam, Gorhambury

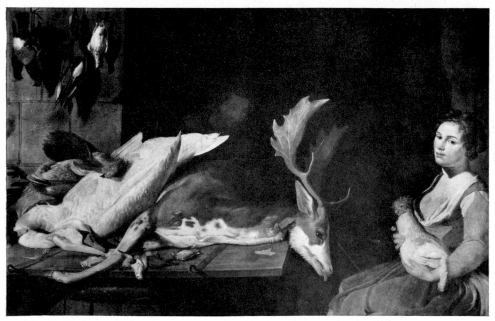

69. *a*. SIR NATHANIEL BACON: THE COOKMAID. Earl of Verulam, Gorhambury
*b*. SIR NATHANIEL BACON: COMPANION TO THE COOKMAID. Earl of Verulam, Gorhambury

70. NICHOLAS HILLIARD: SIR ANTHONY MILDMAY, *c.* 1605. Cleveland Museum of Art, Ohio

71. ISAAC OLIVER: RICHARD SACKVILLE, EARL OF DORSET, 1616
Victoria and Albert Museum

72. *a*. EDWARD NORGATE: JUDITH NORGATE, 1617. Victoria and Albert Museum

*b*. NICHOLAS HILLIARD: 'ELIZABETH OF BOHEMIA'. Coll. the Earl of Derby

*c*. ISAAC OLIVER: UNFINISHED PORTRAIT OF QUEEN ELIZABETH. Victoria and Albert Museum

*d*. NICHOLAS HILLIARD: MRS. HOLLAND, 1593. Victoria and Albert Museum

*e*. ISAAC OLIVER: DIANA. Victoria and Albert Museum

*f*. ISAAC OLIVER: LADY IN MASQUE COSTUME. Victoria and Albert Museum

73. NICHOLAS HILLIARD: *a*. QUEEN ELIZABETH, 1572. National Portrait Gallery
*b*. NICHOLAS HILLIARD: QUEEN ELIZABETH. Victoria and Albert Museum
*c*. NICHOLAS HILLIARD: SELF–PORTRAIT, 1577. Victoria and Albert Museum
*d*. ANON: UNKNOWN LADY, 1549. Victoria and Albert Museum
*e*. NICHOLAS HILLIARD: UNKNOWN MAN AGED 24, 1572. Victoria and Albert Museum
*f*. NICHOLAS HILLIARD: LEONARD DARR, 1591. Coll. of the Duke of Portland

74. *a*. ISAAC OLIVER: SELF–PORTRAIT. Coll. the Earl of Derby
*b*. NICHOLAS HILLIARD: SIR CHRISTOPHER HATTON. Victoria and Albert Museum
*c*. ISAAC OLIVER: HEAD OF CHRIST. Victoria and Albert Museum
*d*. ISAAC OLIVER: 'SIR ARUNDEL TALBOT', 1596. Victoria and Albert Museum
*e*. ISAAC OLIVER: UNKNOWN YOUTH, 1588. Coll. Brinsley Ford, Esq.

75. *a.* GOLD ENAMELLED HAT BADGE: CHRIST AND THE WOMAN OF SAMARIA, *c.* 1560
British Museum

*b.* TOMB OF WILLIAM RUDHALL (DETAIL). Ross-on-Wye, Herefordshire

76. *a.* CANOPY OF THE DORMER MONUMENT. Wing, Buckinghamshire
*b.* MONUMENT OF THOMAS WYLMER (d. 1580). Staverton, Northamptonshire

77. *a*. TOMB OF GEORGE BROOKE, LORD COBHAM, 1561. Cobham, Kent
*b*. MONUMENT OF MARGARET, COUNTESS OF LENNOX (DETAIL). Westminster Abbey

78. MONUMENTS TO HIS ANCESTORS ERECTED BY SIR GABRIEL POYNTZ, 1606. North Ockendon, Essex

79. *a.* MONUMENT OF SIR ROBERT DORMER (d. 1552). Wing, Buckinghamshire
*b.* TOMB OF RICHARD HARFORD, 1573. Bosbury, Herefordshire

80. MONUMENT OF JOHN LEWESTON (d. 1584)
Sherborne Abbey, Dorset

81. *a.* TOMB OF SIR THOMAS BROMLEY: FIGURE OF HIS DAUGHTER MARGARET
Wroxeter, Shropshire
*b.* RICHARD PARKER: TOMB OF THE 1ST EARL OF RUTLAND, 1543–4
Bottesford, Leicestershire

82. TOMB OF SIR THOMAS GRESHAM (d. 1579). Great St. Helen's, Bishopsgate

83. *a*. GARRET JOHNSON: MONUMENT OF THE 4TH EARL OF RUTLAND, 1591. Bottesford, Leicestershire

*b*. TOMB OF SIR PHILIP AND SIR THOMAS HOBY. Bisham, Berkshire

84. *a.* TOMB OF SIR HUGH POULETT. Hinton St. George, Somerset. By courtesy of Earl Poulett
*b.* MONUMENT OF SIR ANTHONY COOKE (d. 1576). St. Edward the Confessor,
Romford, Essex

85. MONUMENT OF SIR JOHN JEFFEREY (d. 1611)

Whitchurch Canonicorum, Dorset

86. *a.* MONUMENT OF JOHN BINGHAM (d. 1625). Southwark Cathedral

*b.* MONUMENT OF THOMAS ANDREWS (d. 1590). Charwelton, Northamptonshire

87. *a.* EPIPHANIUS EVESHAM: THE DAUGHTERS OF LORD TEYNHAM. On his monument at Lynsted, Kent

*b.* MONUMENT OF MARGARET LEGH (d. 1605). All Saints, Fulham

88. MONUMENT OF SIR HENRY SAVILE. Merton College, Oxford

89. *a*. RICHARD AND GABRIEL ROYLEY: DETAIL OF TOMB OF THOMAS FERMOR
(d. 1580). Somerton, Oxfordshire
*b*. EPIPHANIUS EVESHAM: THE DAUGHTERS OF SIR THOMAS HAWKINS
On his monument at Boughton-under-Blean, Kent

90. *a.* MONUMENT OF SARA COLVILLE (d. 1631). All Saints, Chelsea

*b.* NICHOLAS STONE: MONUMENT OF WILLIAM CURLE, 1617. Hatfield, Hertfordshire

91. *a.* NICHOLAS STONE: MONUMENT OF SIR GEORGE HOLLES (DETAIL). Westminster Abbey

*b.* WILLIAM CURE THE YOUNGER: PRINCE CHARLES, *c.* 1614–15. Great Gate, Trinity College, Cambridge

92. *a.* MONUMENT OF A WOMAN OF THE KYMER FAMILY. West Chelborough, Dorset
*b.* MONUMENT OF SIR FRANCIS VERE (d. 1609). Westminster Abbey

93. *a.* ANONYMOUS: ALL DOE RIDE THE ASSE
*b.* RUSHTON, NORTHAMPTONSHIRE: THE SCREEN

94. BUST OF SIR NICHOLAS BACON. Gorhambury, Hertfordshire